D1234725

LEISURE: *THEORY and POLICY*

Wiley Consulting Editors

LEISURE:

THEORY and POLICY

Max Kaplan

Director, Leisure Studies Program
University of South Florida, Tampa

JOHN WILEY & SONS, INC.
New York London Sydney Toronto

Library of Congress Cataloging in Publication Data:

Kaplan, Max, 1911–
  Leisure : theory and policy.

Includes bibliographical references and indexes.
1. Leisure. 2. Recreation. I. Title.
GV14.K34   790'.0135   75–1380
ISBN 0–471–45710–8

Printed in the United States of America

10 9 8 7 6 5 4 3 2 1

To
Joffre Dumazedier

my esteemed friend and colleague who has
served the scholarship of leisure with
leadership, creativity, dedication, organizational skill, scientific contribution, and
his own *joie de vivre*.

Foreword

Several sociologists and social philosophers have analyzed the new problem of leisure in American society. However, their analyses often have been incomplete and temporary and have not survived the fashion of the 1950s. Max Kaplan belongs to the small group of researchers who quickly guessed the permanent and profound interest (although hidden) in social and cultural questions raised today. He was one of the first to discover long before the search for the quality of life became a major concern, that through leisure the problems of the style of life and of the art of living ought to be tackled. The question is, "Should we always have more or should we learn how to be more?" For more than twenty years Max Kaplan has attracted the public's attention to the cultural changes brought by leisure and has pointed out the necessity of inventing ethics and politics to make these changes beneficial to man. He has made of leisure the main focus of his research despite the indifference or opposition that he encountered. He emerged as the most active and creative member of the Research Committee on Leisure and Culture of the International Association of Sociology, of which he was the vice-president for a long time. This book is a summary of his questions, experiences, knowledge, thinking, and expectations. It explains how his humanistic questions guide his sociological observations and how the latter provoke the former.

The problems that he deals with reveal the extent and finesse of a personal culture that is also scientific and artistic. Max Kaplan is a distinguished musician and a faithful student of the sociologist, Zaniecki. His thinking is inspired by the work of Aristotle and the "calculs" of the Club of Rome. A great globe-trotter, he knows what is happening in the United States, Japan, and Europe. American sociologists are usually blamed (rightly or wrongly) for visualizing the world only through their own country. This is not true of Max Kaplan. There is not a single sociologist in the field of leisure whose international awareness is superior to his.

Kaplan puts order in the inumerable fragmentary and scattered results of sociological observations. His proposals are not theories that, in the existing state of knowledge, are arbitrary.

They are models, founded on incontestable knowledge and intriguing questions. In a grouping of 60 slightly arbitrary, practical propositions, Kaplan lists and classifies the established relationship between leisure and the different aspects of the economy, culture, and society. He completes these propositions with hypothetical relationships that are stimulating. Without being "bookish," he uses rich, qualitative, quantitative documentation. He not only observes what is, but he wonders what will be, and the future is more important to him than the present. He resorts to evolution to minimize the uncertainty of the future. He likes the prospective approach and uses the utopia of a Bellamy as well as the calculations of a Wiener to free our imagination from today's or yesterday's stereotypes.

His book will be of interest to readers who have not perceived the hidden relationship among the evolution of work in the family, of education, and what can be called the cultural revolution of leisure. The book will be useful to *animateurs,* educators, and social workers, who often underestimate the negative conditions or do not know the prerequisites for a cultural and recreative action for the transformation of school and communal collectivities. Only sociological meditation can preserve some of us from the illusion that everything is possible and some of us from the illusion that nothing is possible.

Joffre Dumazedier
Professor of Social Sciences,
University of Paris, René Descartes;
founder and first chairman,
International Sociological Association
Research Committee on Leisure and Culture.

Preface

This book includes a broad mixture of data, charts, tables, propositions, and hypotheses. Many statements are based on research; others, undoubtedly, are my own opinions, which may seem to be unsupported by data or evidence. What, then, is the purpose of this volume? Is it a scientific work in which humanistic materials are secondary, or is it the reverse?

I am not concerned with form but with issues on leisure. Since an abundance of material has appeared in recent years, I believe that the broad issues, especially those related to values, need to be identified. Economists and sociologists are seriously studying the field; de Grazia brought history and philosophy to bear on the subject; other disciplines and many applied fields (including recreation, the arts, and adult education) are carefully examining theoretical formulations.

I am becoming more and more convinced that the *ultimate issue in studies of leisure is the renewed study of human values as they are affected by the new leisure, especially industrially oriented leisure.* Therefore, this book is not intended to be a "scientific" document in which every conclusion or observation must rely on "data." A pretense that vital issues of social value *must,* or *can* be, subject to "science" is, in my view, destined to failure; it also misinterprets the limits of social science and "boxes" in leisure studies in such a way that it ruins their potential influence on a changing society. The very heart of our transition to a "postindustrial society"—I prefer the term "cultivated social order" to emphasize the importance of goals—is the revolutionary integration of scientific and humanistic methods and perspectives.

Thus this volume deals with leisure, not with disciplines such as sociology or even with social science as a whole. It raises issues that relate leisure to other kinds of phenomena and human experiences through a "model" or "design," so that a particular system is emphasized and the student knows where the discussion is headed. Here, the issues have been raised with sufficient illustrations and suggestions to serve diverse interests, both theoretical and applied. Furthermore, a system has been brought to bear on the subject with rigor but also, hopefully, with imagination and intuition.

My objectives are as follows.

1. To establish that there is, indeed, a set of issues which has roots in the past, relevance to important social changes of the present, and consequences for the future.
2. To systematize the study of these issues for students, scholars, laymen, and policymakers in occupations or disciplines that are concerned about them.
3. To report and interpret the attempts of persons, families, businesses, labor unions, industry, communities, or others in meeting the issues of leisure.
4. To establish a philosophy for persons, groups, and society, which is applicable to significant changes in leisure.
5. To provide a foundation for private behavior and public policy based on relevant data, philosophy, decision making, implementation, and evaluation.

This volume departs from its predecessor of more than a decade ago* in these characteristics:

1. Much has happened in this field since 1960, and the present volume brings the data and issues up to date; for instance, it includes a great many current European studies.
2. Society itself has changed in the 1960s: wars, student protests, more urbanization and urban problems, a dawning of the space age, and computerization—among many others. These changes are assessed in relation to leisure.
3. I hope I have grown in my views and values. I have been more explicit, here, in my use of history. In the past decade I visited eastern and western Europe and made some observations. It is more important now, for me and others, to arrive at a philosophy as a basis for action. As I grow older, description and analysis become more of a tool than an end. As a teacher in a large university, I find it imperative that the Leisure Studies Program become more than a matter of descriptive studies, no matter how important these studies may be.
4. This volume is attuned to the future for evident reasons. Interdisciplinary emphases are vital to escape the parochialisms and blinders of a single discipline, which is frequently defined by its historical location in the university instead of its reality in the living

*Max Kaplan, *Leisure in America: A Social Inquiry,* Wiley, 1960.

world. Leisure provides a unique opportunity toward these ends: the crossing of cultures, of disciplines, of occupations, and of historical periods. Its ultimate purpose is to assist man in mastering time —that is, himself.

MAX KAPLAN

ACKNOWLEDGMENTS

I am indebted to many people, especially to the ones who are mentioned below.

Cor Westlund of Ottawa, for conversations in Rotterdam, Tampa, and Montmorency, for his critical letters in the course of preparing Chapter 1, and his request for a comparison with Dumazedier's conceptions.

Miro Mihovilovich of Zagreb, who extended many personal courtesies to my wife and me in his country, and who brought together sociologists of Yugoslavia to respond to the theoretical model of this volume.

My team colleagues, **Herald Swedner of Lund** and **Miklavz Prosenc of Hamburg,** for opportunities to discuss with their graduate students in Sweden and West Germany the ideas presented here.

Vladimir Stein of Brno for permitting several visits to his home for an exchange for views and for visits to the beautiful park system that he directs in Bohemia.

Premysl Maydl (*and the European Centre for Leisure and Education*), for personal courtesies to us in Prague, several nights of close conversation as a guest in our home, and for including in his publication, *Society and Leisure,* portions of Chapter 1 and all of Chapter 2.

Three scholars of leisure, for their close reading of the full manuscript, resulting in changes that have undoubtedly improved the work:

Al Clarke, Professor of Sociology, Ohio State University.

Professor Doug Sessums, Director, Recreation, School of Education, University of North Carolina.

Professor Tony Mobley, Chairman, Recreation and Parks, College of Health, Physical Education, and Recreation, The Pennsylvania State University.

My Tampa colleagues and friends, **Nelson Butler** and **Phillip Bosserman** for ongoing encouragement; and **Professor Mark Orr,** the university officer to whom the Leisure Studies Program has been responsible for his support.

My wife, **Barbara,** whose alert mind entered into many family discussions, and whose understanding came from her own creativity as a musician and author.

                                                                    M.K.

Contents

TABLES

CHARTS

PART 1
Introduction:
Theories of Leisure

Chapter 1
Issues–Old and New

Almost all Western and Eastern countries, including the USSR, Bulgaria, Romania, Yugoslavia, Hungary, and Czechoslovakia, maintain research centers on leisure. These not only feed data to their governments or private sectors on such matters as tourism, mass media, or adult education, but they also provide broad interpretations of what industrialization, more time, rising affluence, urbanization, television, automobiles, higher aspirations, and literacy mean to the future of their societies.

In the United States we have intensive studies of who watches movies and television, how often, and with what effect. Early in the 1960s the 27 reports of the Outdoor Recreation Resources Review Commission led to the creation of the Department of Outdoor Recreation under President Kennedy.

In 1968 two economists of Princeton prepared a major volume, sponsored by the Twentieth Century Fund, on *The Performing Arts: an Economic Dilemma.* [1] Studies of library usage, gambling, and drugs are available. We know in considerable detail about the life patterns of the elderly. Joe Papp's theater for the parks of New York has been observed by social scientists, as have been the cocktail parties on Park Avenue. In short, there are many studies of diverse leisure.

However, what is lacking everywhere is the serious attempt to develop a total theory so that we can interrelate fruitfully issues that are sociological, psychological, economic, legal, philosophical, and even theological. A biological element came to the forefront in meetings held a few years ago at the Center for the Study of Democratic Institutions, when leading biologists promised to extend our life span another 20 years; the rest of us wondered aloud about the potential augmentation in boredom and loneliness unless we gave bold thought to new social roles or to the charge suggested by Dennis Gabor in his provocative volume, *Inventing the Future.* [2]

Economic theory alone cannot approach the new leisure. It is impossible to split the economic from the social, political, and technical; we deal with whole systems to see these relationships. A study of leisure cannot be geared to an economics of scarcity, but must give way to the "socioeconomics" illustrated by Robert Theobald in his volume *The Economics of Abundance.*[3] A major reason for this necessary shift in theory is that the concept of work as we have known it is changing, and we are no longer sure that work beyond maintenance is a basic need of man. Indeed, there is sufficient historical evidence to argue that the so-called Puritan ethic is not divine in origin, that as the Industrial Revolution began men had to be pushed almost literally into factories.

The mythology of work as the source of manhood and salvation took hold strongly, but its fragility was evident when, led by Ford, the five-day week became common. In 1926, Ford said, "It is the influence of leisure on consumption which makes the short day and the short week so necessary." A week later, E. H. Gary of U.S. Steel declared that the five-day week was "impractical," it would imperil competition with Europe, and it violates the commandment, "Six days shalt thou labor;" only 40 years after, U.S. Steel negotiated a contract providing 13 weeks of paid vacation every fifth year, in addition to the now accepted level of a 37-hour week and three weeks annual vacations. Now, labor in many parts of the world has locked in with the demand for time, quite free of guilt. France, by law, provides a one-month paid vacation for every worker. Russia has decreed the 41-hour week for office and factory workers.

This change in values by the work force will continue. For one, the new time is more and more in bulk; a full week off accommodates a trip that seven individual days do not. Furthermore, the public gains experience and confidence in the use of time; adult education, for example, keeps expanding, as do winter and summer vacations. At the same time, in an exchange of time for income, we begin to recognize that the dollar is constantly decreasing in value, while the hour—in its potential for alternative uses—is increasing. Finally, in the United States the normal extension of automation has reduced weekly work hours roughly from 70 to 37 in the past century, almost four hours per week less each decade; thus an additional reduction of 12 hours by the year 2000—an oversimplified projection, to be sure—is so intensified that with the help of computerization, the additional time off could be five hours in the 1970s, six in the 1980s, and seven in the 1990s. The result could be a workweek of 20 hours at the century's end. Amidst the debate on social impact of automation, studies lead some to believe that there are levels of consumer satiation. Computerization, furthermore, becomes absolutely cheaper in cost by increasing standardization of machines and relatively cheaper as labor costs go up.

Therefore the projection of free time for many uses, including leisure, is not bound up only with pure economic and technological forces such as cybernation, but with our values, our personal and national philosophy, our moods, fashions, and the difficult question of carry-over from today's youthful questionings to their life-styles in later years. We can, says Duke economist Juanita Kreps, choose to retire at 38 by 1985 and still maintain our GNP per capita constant of $3181.[4]

The fundamental choice, both for employer and employee, is whether we want to carry on in the traditional pattern of the present industrial order—education, work from 20 to 60, then retirement, for about 60 percent of us—or in flexible patterns whereby we can, from 20 or 25 to 75 or 85 alternate freely and in economic security among work, travel, education, painting one's house for a month, extended sabbaticals, and so forth. In simple terms, a four-hour day also implies a built-in choice of working a half day, half week, half month, half year, or half a lifetime. One of American industry's significant decisions on the leisure dimension, including leisure industries and locations of equipment, could come from a recognition that industry can get maximum participation in the distribution of work and nonwork time. It is, for instance, only a holdover from agrarian times that we work during the best hours of sunshine. In Yugoslavia, Bulgaria, and Turkey some workers start at 6:30 a.m. and are free in the early afternoon. American banks, in concert with industry, could loan "free hours" to those in their thirties as they now loan money, to be repaid in both cases equally by work later, when men want to work in their later years.

Evidence begins to come in of American industry catching on. *The Wall Street Journal* (October 15, 1970) noted that Mutual of New York already has one unit of 35 employees that works three days a week, 12 hours a day. The four-day week, beginning to spread, "increases productivity, decreases absenteeism, boosts worker morale, and cuts work turnover."

But time is only one dimension of our problem. In regard to total expenditure, the Department of Commerce reports that recreation takes around $28 billion, or 6.2 percent, of the consuming expenditure. The Merrill Lynch document on leisure in 1968 was titled "Investment Opportunities in a $150 Billion Market"; it predicted that the market would go up another $100 billion by 1975.[5] Peter J. Enderlin sees a 7 percent growth annually this decade for "leisure-related goods and services." A more cautious view is to add some items to the Department of Commerce list under "leisure," such as 60 percent of passenger car costs and maintenance that can be attributed to pleasure trips, and come to a total of $110 billion, or perhaps triple the Commerce estimate.

Yet the new issues and interpretations require some historical perspective as a framework. Several periods from American history have been selected for general summary below, bringing us again to the current scene.[6]

1850

In the middle of the last century, just before the Civil War, sharp regional differences existed: slavery in the South: the intellectualism of the New England area; expanding industrialism of the North and Midwest. Only six cities had populations of over 100,000 among the total population of less than 25 million. Agriculture, of course, dominated the world of work; even city workers put in over 65 hours per week. The horse and buggy were still the major source of transportation. Railroads were in their infancy.

On social levels, the sexes kept apart; rural people suspected the life of the cities. Rural "leisure," especially fishing and hunting, was in part necessary to sustenance. Horse racing was popular at county fairs.

College rowing began in 1852 as a spectator sport (Harvard versus Yale); the New York Knickerbockers began as a professional baseball team in 1846. Along came professional prizefights and widespread participation in billiards and pool. Museums and traveling showmen (P. T. Barnum in 1850) developed. Stage shows came to the large cities with burlesque, minstrel, and variety offerings as well as drama. The lyceum lecture movement developed, sanctioned by the church.

Familiar activities everywhere were horseshoes, socializing, dancing, and cards. Rural areas, notes Orthner, saw much in the way of "log-rolling, house and barn-raisings, candle dippings, sheep-shearing . . . quilting bees. Any excuse to get together was boisterous—funerals, weddings or housewarmings."

Churches were often the center of social activity; music was played widely; purchasing of sculpture was a fad.

Yet 1850 was not a static point in time. A long record of the frontier had led up to this time in American history. What becomes apparent even from the short summary above is that a transition had set it toward the urbanized complexity of the late nineteenth century. There were still times—as in the case of rural sports and purposes for visitation—when work and play were closely allied: women used the occasion of canning as a social gathering. An even closer union of social purposes and work could have been seen a generation or two before this—the fusion of religious-emotional experiences with psychological escape from the hard routine of frontier life. James Leyburn spoke of this synthesis in *Frontier Folkways*. The pioneers of this country, he reminds us, engaged in constantly strenuous physical work, and any outlet of an emotional nature was welcomed.[7]

"The itinerant 'show' or circus, was the talk of the countryside for months after its visit. Sessions of country court were attended for the human contacts they made possible. Church services provided an opportunity as much for companionship and gossip as for spiritual benefit. Whiskey, it is true, offered the men a chance for emotional debauch. . . . Women had not even that outlet. The strain upon them of incessant hard work and childbearing left them with a crying need for some release."

Leyburn then describes an example of such "release," the camp meeting that went on for five days and attracted persons from many miles around.

"The greatest of all such meetings was at Cane Ridge, Kentucky in the summer of 1801. It had been advertised for weeks before. Between twenty and thirty thousand people attended, coming from as far as a hundred miles. Services began on Friday and lasted until Thursday, with almost continuous preaching and exhorting by seventeen preachers, drawn from all three important denominations, aided by numerous lay volunteers. The congregation was thrown into a frenzy by the lurid sermons and the denunciations of sin. Their shouting, singing and howling were audible five miles away; the ground shook as the thousands stamped and leaped in their frantic efforts to escape hell. People dropped unconscious to the ground. Some jerked as though with violent hiccoughs; others barked like dogs. Throughout the forest, preachers mounted stumps and screamed threats of hell and promises of heaven. Little children ran barking and jerking through the throng, or were carried triumphantly on the shoulders of the ministers. Young and pure girls dropped fainting under their consciousness of sin. It is estimated that at one time three thousand lay unconscious before the preaching stand; five thousand barked and jerked in unison; one fifteen-minute prayer caused several hundred to faint."

Questions arise when such an occasion becomes an amalgam of commitment to a belief and the need for drama or release: how do these elements feed into each other, transforming the other; how does each element succeed, it it does, in remaining what it was? These questions become pertinent if we jump from 1801 to the present, 17 decades later since, in the civil rights "campground," we find parallels. Again—in the slums now—we find a combination of the blacks, with equal belief in their cause, engaged in extended demonstrations. From miles around, they, too, have come. In the rioting in Detroit on July 22, 1967, numerous witnesses told of

"the carefree mood with which people ran in and out of stores, looting and laughing, and joking with the police officers ... looters paid no attention to residents who shouted at them and called their actions senseless. *An epidemic of excitement had swept over the persons on the street.*

A spirit of carefree nihilism was taking hold. To riot and to destroy appeared more and more to become ends in themselves ... it appeared to one observer that the young people were dancing amidst the flames."

During the first nine months of 1967, 164 disorders occurred in American cities, according to the Committee headed by Governor Otto Kerner of Illinois. No one can doubt that there was a significant aspect of religious sentiment in the last century and that at present there is a similar commitment among significant numbers for action on behalf of freedom. Yet somewhere, mixed in with both phenomena, there is the additional factor of drama, "play" in Huizinga's large sense, or "dramaturgy" in the symbolic sense as discussed by Hugh Duncan.

Not only do wars, religious and race riots, or lootings provide for "play" elements to enter into the fundamental purposes, but each provides an even more explicit "theater" for observers whose leisure becomes a parasite, feeding off the blood of rioters, the prayers of congregants, or the tragedy of armies. I have myself "participated"— as one of the several thousand curiosity seekers at the Sorbonne during the study riots in the summer of 1968, or as a passive observer when the Pope blessed "us" in St. Peter's Square in 1955.

Yet as we view the "leisure" of 1850 of America, how quiet and unconcerned it seems to have been–horseraces, spelling bees, fishing, the beginnings of organized baseball, circuses. A quiet time, quiet just before the storm that was to split the nation for a long time and lay the seed for the disorders of our day.

Half a century goes by. What issues are raised by the leisure of the new century?

1900

By now our population had grown to 75 million. With the large migration from Europe came long hours of work, low pay, crowded housing, and poor working conditions. Labor unions had emerged as a force with the growth of cities and factories. Orville Wright flew in 1903; a total of 4000 cars were owned by the rich; the horse was still the major form of transportation for the masses. Packaged foods were now on the market, electric lights were in homes, and telephones became common. The middle class developed, with an average weekly pay of $10 not uncommon among large numbers for a 6-day workweek of 10 hours per day.

The Puritan ethic remained strong, with a corresponding suspicion of play. But commerical entertainment made inroads into that attitude; vaudeville, "taxi-dance" halls, and amusement parks became popular. The two leagues we know in baseball today were in full swing. College football was already two decades old. Boxing flourished. Basketball had come in 1882 and was adopted by colleges by the turn of the century. Croquet was one of the few games that brought men and women together; gold was still for upper-class men; Kodak saw to it that photography became a democratic pastime. By 1904, 15,000 pleasure boats were sailing.

The church, notes Orthner, "had mixed attitudes toward all this. Some of the Puritan tradition held tenaciously to the old ways of conduct and comdemned the urban entertainments. . . . The church began to listen to the people, realizing that it had lost the power to impose 'arbitrary prohibitions.' " Indeed, the church began to use entertainment for its own purposes, both to keep its flock and to raise money by socials, fairs, suppers, and festivals.

The turn of the century marked the beginnings of outdoor public recreation. By 1910, almost 200,000 persons had visited the five national parks; playgrounds were by then to be found in 180 cities; summer camps began to appear. Men and women now swam together. Familiar rual recreational patterns, while still there, found less support among the young.

Since the 1850 leisure picture was soon to be interrupted by a great war among the states and had evolved into a quiet period after the frontier era, so 1900 was a transition. In a decade and a half we would be involved in a world war and the major contributors to the character of the American life by 1900 were the growth of cities and the waves of immigrants.

There were good reasons why the presence of so many immigrants —from 1880 to 1900—reinforced instead of changed the course of leisure. First, most immigrants came to our cities, but had lived in rural areas in their native lands. As strangers, they were not "change agents," but were sensitive to learning the ways around them; this was especially true of their children, who often felt that their acceptance among others depended on the reflectionism of their own parents. It would seem that the expansion of leisure described above (professional baseball and bicycling) could have been predicted from movements unaffected by immigration. Yet underneath these ongoing developments were deep changes that must be spelled out.

First, the immigrant homes and neighborhoods were often breeding grounds for artistic and intellectual abrasiveness. Our immigrant parents, whatever else they were, had been capable of at least one major decision—to leave familiar surroundings and move to a new country; behind this there must have been years of discontent, indecision, self-examination, economic or political disaffection, and—as in the case of our peoples in the Czarist and Polish zones—outright *pogroms.* These people had not come to America lightly; their commitment was not just to a change but to a search, and we, their sons, were their instrumentalities as well as their fulfillment. My earliest memories, in the immigrant colony of Milwaukee during the formative years of childhood (about 1916–1925), were of weekly gatherings in our home and in others; often they started after 8 or 9 p.m. when the small businessmen among the circle of *landsmen* had closed their shops. Until the small hours, while the children (before the baby-sitting era) were piled on beds supposedly to sleep, our parents argued world politics or Zionism, sang songs, or listened to one of us fiddle a tune. The colony (or ghetto community) had its theater, its politically oriented social dances to raise money for various good causes. I am sure it is the same with Hungarians, Italians, Irish, and all the others. As we grew into early manhood, some of us left our parents and grew away from their traditions as we become professional people and suburbanites. We had been encouraged to develop our skills; if we were artistically oriented, father might not have quite understood, but he did not often put his foot down in objection—symbolically or financially, he had no "foot" to put down. Our generation went into entertainment fields—the Eddie Cantors, the Frank Sinatras, the Paul Munis.

These were some of the currents of life early in this century. To the American of later generations it may seem that these were minor in numbers as well as in minorities in their cultural patterns; yet it was from among these subcultural groups—in ways unrevealed by the surface of ordinary leisure history or statistics—that the base was being laid for the intellectual and aesthetic growth of later decades. Outlines of the democratic "mass culture" were being formed. They were to take on more substance as well as more risk after World War II.

But first there was an intervening period that raised other issues for the movements of leisure in the United States.

1930

The Great Depression left nothing untouched—our attitudes, our politics, our behavior, or our pocketbooks. Many large industries were paying 20 to 30 cents per hour for the work they still maintained. Roosevelt's New Deal began to pour millions into work programs that were devised by local bodies. Some of these were in the arts, thus keeping alive men who now, four decades later, dominate the literary and artistic scene; audiences were developed; local institutions, such as museums and theaters, were funded.

On the surface, there were expansions of leisure developments from the decades before and a few new innovations. Cars continued to catch on, depression or not; outdoor recreation kept growing, and the trailer made its appearance. By 1939, about 23,000 movie houses were in business. The one radio station of 1920 by now had multiplied to over 600. College football and professional basketball matured. People still hunted and fished, but more and more used local parks and playgrounds; public play space grew in acreage four times the size of the population. Depression economics encouraged the simplicity of family activities in the backyard. Again, the issues go far deeper.

What happened in the Depression was an answer to the question, how do we support masses of the population when work is removed by the interplay of economic forces so that there is a breakdown of the whole system? The answer was an unprecedented expansion of federal help.

Franklin D. Roosevelt was no radical by nature yet, by the emergence of the times, he had to apply radical techniques to keep the capitalistic system alive. He made enemies from his own social class who had neither his compassion, his flexible view of the system, nor his responsibility of office.

In the early days of the Depression—and for many Americans until the war period closed this tragic era—many Americans were given "public relief": they obtained a check according to their "needs" and local legal regulations, or they received a card with their needs checked off (so much sugar, so much milk), which they presented in person to a designated station. It was "public" indeed; the recipients stood in line with others, in full view of not only the others in line but anyone else who passed by, not to speak of the welfare staffs. I spent 18 months as a "visitor" in the system of "outdoor relief"—outdoor in that we went to them, thereby minimizing somewhat the inherent indignity of the whole process. Then, with the succession of federal programs—C.C.C., P.W.A., W.P.A.—millions of the American men and women were given the chance to work, often for no more in amount than they formerly might have been given outright in goods or a relief check. If the question was asked, in view of the agencies, did they *really want* to work and why? the answer again is clear; they would rout us out of bed in the early hours with phone calls, insisting they be put to work projects. The "work," if it was assigned, was often far from their familiar skills. At one point, I carried on "research" for a federal community that was built near Milwaukee (Greendale); my "research staff" consisted of a former United States ambassador, a grocery store proprietor, a schoolteacher, and a plumber. Then why did they insist—far more than the unknowing critics of public welfare ever believed—in *working?* The answer is embedded in that old phrase "self-dignity," whatever scientific or humanistic phraseology one cares to add. One detected the overpowering need among men *to be needed, but not necessarily to produce according to the previous work content they had mastered.* Americans in that period displayed *an eclecticism in work* that the later scientific studies at Western Electric only verified—the importance of the work *situation* instead of the specific task or product. This point has enormous implications for the future of American society in the "postindustrial" era: the nature, the flexibility, the fluidity that are possible as the society will again face the issue of *inventing* or *enlarging* the opportunities for involvement. Only this time the situation will arise not from scarcity but abundance, not from breakdown of the economic system, but from a radical transformation of life in which economic-political-social-educational move toward fusions and interdependence. The depression had shown that, in the 1930s, time itself, *enforced* free time created simply by the lack of work, was not desired. It was, in fact, distasteful and psychologically damaging. "Free" time was a prison unless it came out of, or is related to, the release that work provides for relatedness to the "real" world. The clue to the future is the nature of that "relatedness," and work or its counterparts as *instrumentality.*

There was something else about leisure of the 1930s that runs underneath the mere report of activities. And that, starkly put, is the power of leisure as an *antirevolutionary force.* We have all grown up with stories of the Roman circuses as devices by which the masses were distracted from their misery by the emperors or, in recent times, the Nazi use of great pageants and rehearsed pomp. Motion pictures which, in the 1930s, gave many Americans the precious hours of preoccupation with a fantasy world, were not staged by rulers. They were commercial in origin and motivation, and they were desired by the young and old alike. In addition to becoming fantasies of the present, motion pictures depicted the homes, the beautiful people, and the symbolic or romantic prospects of the future.

It is basic to our subject to note that some forms of leisure in their use as symbols more than others have separated or unified the social classes. A century ago, the fine arts served as a barrier; now they serve as a bridge on which all may cross. The motion picture in the 1930s, as much as TV in the 1960s, also served as a common denominator for all classes and all backgrounds.

Even a listing of major events after 1930 is sufficient to suggest the enormous changes from that dark period to the present.

The 1930s were dominated by the Depression in this country and the beginning of the Hitlerian nightmare. The Dionne quintuplets were born in 1934 and Will Rogers died in 1935. The Spanish Civil War started in 1936, and Hitler invaded Austria in 1937. The New York World's Fair came at the end of the decade.

The most destructive war of all history came in the next decade and, by the time Hitler committed suicide in 1945, 6 million Jews had been destroyed in a "final solution." All other events fade before those phenomena, yet it was a decade filled with drama from other directions: the end of Mussolini in April 1945; the founding of United Nations only a few months later; the beginnings of the Marshall Plan, which contributed $12 billion to revive Western Europe; the tragic shooting of Gandhi in New Delhi; the establishment of Israel as a free state.

POST-WORLD WAR II

"Quality of life" topics find a paradoxical content in times of crisis and war. On the one hand, the subjects associated with the personal or collective "good" seem out of place as a more "basic" issue—survival—takes over. Yet, on the other hand, a time of crisis is precisely when goals—survival for what?—are most essential. On the personal level, for instance, Viktor Frankl's *logotherapy* is based on the importance and method of assessing one's suffering in terms of "man's search for meaning."

If leisure is taken narrowly—as "free time," "pleasure," or "play"—then World War II had such implications as morale building. Indeed, the recreation movement was for this reason an important concern of the United States military and always remains so on both land and sea as a tool to counteract boredom and to develop good relationships between military personnel and the nearby community of civilians.

If, on the other hand, leisure is taken broadly (as implied in the first part of this chapter) it is an integral issue within any discussion of national directions and values. In this sense, the postwar discussion helped to formulate the issues that were fundamental to mature concerns with our way of life.

No great single event colored all of the 1950s. Drama then was the conviction for treason of Dr. Klaus Fuchs and the Rosenbergs in the early years, or of Fidel Castro's assumption of power in 1958. Stalin died and Kruschev entered office in 1953, a few months before the first climbings of Mt. Everest. Senator Joseph McCarthy played God a little too much and was condemned by the Senate. Racial segregation in schools was banned by the Supreme Court in a decision of May 17, 1954. The AFL and CIO merged to become 15 million strong. The Soviets invaded Hungary and Egypt seized the Suez Canal in 1956. The first domestic jet connected New York and Miami in 1958. The space age advanced with the USSR Luniks I-III, orbiting the moon and returning photographs.

But the events following World War II brought important technical and social changes. Electronics alone, as in computerization and television, was sufficient to mark this era unique in all human history. As suggested earlier, a foundation of change was laid in all industrial societies that brought leisure into the front line of broad issues. The destiny of the common man was one element; a general abundance was another; additional influences, which led into the 1950s and then the uneasy 1960s—climaxed by Vietnam—were the questions of youth on an existential level, profound changes in the church, and the simultaneous and perhaps interfacing movements among blacks, women, and youth. Hunger was officially acknowledged in the richest of all nations.

As I write, almost half way through the 1970s, there is little doubt that an important new influence on leisure may be the "energy crisis." The dramatic aspects of this long-range problem developed in the first few months of 1974, when one result of the Yom Kippur war in the Middle East was the oil embargo aimed at the United States and other nations by the oil-producing Arab nations. A "czar" of energy was named by President Nixon. Quotas of oil and gasoline were clamped on each state in proportion to alleged availability and formulas of past consumption. Long lines of cars were to be seen everywhere, with such controls as "odd" and "even" licenses eligible for supply on alternate days; prices zoomed; rationing was advocated by many, but opposed by the administration. Car lines ceased in late February 1974 as the embargo was lifted.

The question remains: did the short-lived scare have any long-range implications for changes in life-styles? It can be demonstrated roughly (by average miles per gallon, average city speeds, and average time spent at various destinations), that a gallon of unused or unattainable gasoline represents about an hour of time. That is, whether because of price levels or scarcity, 10 gallons less use per week is comparable to 10 hours of "free time." Those may be qualitatively different hours than free-willed time, as on vacations. A study, still unreported, was made in England of the uses of time during its enforced three-day workweek; the qualitative distinctions may be borne out there as well.

Obviously, the types of leisure directly affected by an energy shortage are those based on mobility, as through cars, camp vehicles, or boats. Less clear are the types of leisure "compensation"; will there be more TV watching, more social visiting, or more use of such neighborhood and community facilities as libraries, museums, parks, playgrounds, or sports arenas? If there are observable changes in life-styles, it is possible that local agencies—adult education sponsors, libraries, and so forth—have encouraged the changes by opening for longer hours, improving communications with the citizenry, or otherwise enlarging their services. In short, 1974 to 1980, when a planned attempt will be made by public and private bodies to develop new resources for energy, will be an important period to observe changes in leisure patterns as well, based on reallocation of material provisions and on behavioral responses.

All these, however, are variations of an old issue in leisure: who gets it, what do they do with it, and how is its quality for the person affected by social change?

If American history can be looked at as a whole, its several transformations may be identified as those from simple to complex life, from heterogeneous origins to homogeneous national values, from outdoor to indoor recreation patterns, and from the private-public blend of leisure to more and more commercial influence.

There was a new issue, larger than these and incorporating them, that emerged from the flow of change in the past half century, not only in the United States, but in all industrializing nations. We may see it as the fluctuation, interaction, or potential conflict between the impersonal and person, the technological and humanistic, or the continuum of modernization—traditionalism. It is the place of leisure within these respective poles that identifies it as a major policy issue as the industrial societies approach a new century.

A NEW ISSUE: MODERNISM VERSUS TRADITIONALISM

Academician F. Sorm, President of the Czechoslovak Academy of Sciences, sets the tone of an inquiry that was undertaken in 1965 by a unit of the Academy, The Institute of Philosophy.[8]

"The dynamic advance of scientific discovery in recent decades, together with the rapid development of the material base of human life, are assuming the magnitude of revolutionary changes that promise in the long run to transform the nature of civilization and open up boundless prospects for a new form of society. These considerations underscore the urgency of probing the substance of the scientific and technological revolution of our day—its social and human roots and implications."

This potential conflict of technology and humanism has been put in many forms by many authors, and has even been put in the context of the underdeveloped societies. If the socialist societies claim to have a superior grasp of the issues—a thesis of the Czech document—the Western societies have discussed the issues with equal concern. There is a sizable library as evidence, including official government documents in the United States, collaborative inquiries by such *ad hoc* committees in The Triple Revolution, reports by foundations such as the Twentieth Century Fund, innumerable commentaries by individual scholars, and entire conference proceedings. The main arguments are recalled by the mention of writers such as Jacques Ellul, Lewis Mumford, Hannah Arendt, Robert Heilbronner, Eric Fromm, David Riesman, or Alan Touraine. Snow's *Two Cultures* touches on the issue, arguing two mentalities, the cultural and the scientific, as they impinge on insights of the world. A whole field, the "sociology of knowledge," originating in Germany, traces the social and ideological context within which forms of knowledge, including technology, are perceived. In between these poles—the originating mentalities and the recipient cultural conditions—this new issue has emerged: do the facts show that *technology has a momentum of its own that carries with it, modifies, destroys, or subordinates the so-called humanistic impulses?*

Philosophical movements have grown up around this controversy. Existentialism, as Paul Tillich noted,[9] rebels in the name of personality against the depersonalizing forces of technical society.

Psychotherapy provides another example, putting the liberation of the person against the forces of anxiety that emanate from technology, bringing Fromm to question even the "sanity" of such society. One of the major proponents of the "nonrepressive civilization" that would free "one-dimensional man" is Herbert Marcuse, who, in the first page of his *Eros and Civilization: A Philosophical Inquiry into Freud,* puts the issue into a framework of work and nonwork.[10]

"—the capabilities of this society, and the need for an ever increasing productivity, engender forces which seem to undermine the foundations of the system. These explosive forces find their most telling manifestation in automation. Automation threatens to render possible the reversal of the relation between free time and working time on which the established civilization rests: the possibility of working time becoming marginal, and free time becoming full time. The result would be a radical transvaluation of values, and a mode of existence incompatible with the traditional culture. . . ."

Alvin Toffler's popular *Future Shock* approaches the confrontation of technics and human values in a perspective of time: so rapid is the "acceleration" in the pace of life that the failure "to grasp this principle lies behind the dangerous incapacity of education and psychology to prepare people for fruitful roles in a super-industrial society."[11]

Throughout the contemporary literature on leisure, allusions or relevances to the issue of modernism-traditionalism will be found. The transformation to industrial work and its dependence on urbanization and technology is at the heart of the history of leisure (as in De Grazia's work). Indeed, the heart of Dumazedier's writings on leisure is the dominance of the work situation and its tendency to diminish. Within the substantive areas of research, research on outdoor recreation probably comes most directly to the issue, as in portions of the reports of the Outdoor Recreation Resources Review Committee.

Yet there has been no direct study of leisure as a major issue within the modernism-traditionalism issue.[12] This might have been a central issue if the field had become a focus of political science or of cultural anthropology. Even within the present dominance of sociology as a theoretical home and recreation as an applied base, there is a surprising lack of communication or cooperation with the environmental movement. The area of tourism is, of course, an applied area for leisure research, and here the vested interest in the national or regional value of traditionalism is obvious; but again, general theories of leisure are just emerging from their beginnings.

In Chapter 2 we examine several traditions of leisure study and the model of construction for the rest of the textbook.

Chapter 2
Conceptions of Leisure

WHAT IS LEISURE: SOME TYPES OF CONCEPTUALIZATIONS

There are several conceptual traditions of leisure that are basic to an understanding of the subject. Each is useful for a given purpose and is within a definable universe of content or context. Related to each are implied aspects of motivation, purposes, time use, and potential equipment and costs.

1. The *humanistic* model of leisure sees it as an end in itself, illustrated by the contemporary Chinese and the ancient Greeks. Sebastian de Grazia and Joseph Pieper revive the Hellenic concept of *paidia* in their volumes— leisure as contemplation, a celebration of life, the basis of culture, and the arts.[1] It stems from elitism, in good part, and serves the post-de Tocqueville critique for lambasting mass culture.
2. The *therapeutic* model of leisure sees it as a means, an instrument, a control. Illustrations are seen in the cliché "the family that plays together stays together," or that Boys Clubs keep the kids off the streets, or the Roman and Nazi circuses as diversions, or recreation as morale in confirming situations.
3. The *quantitative* model of leisure views it as the time left over when the work necessary for maintaining life is finished. This is the most familiar conception. If, however, not all "free time" is "leisure," we are still in conceptual difficulty as work patterns become fuzzier in a period when the American manpower picture is turning to services.
4. •The *institutional* conception of leisure seeks to distinguish it from such behavior and value patterns as the religious, marital, educational, or political. Only to suggest the possibilities here, one could deal with dialectic processes: leisure that provides movement or rest, freedom or discipline, isolation or sociability, recreation or self-growth.
5. The *epistomological* conception of leisure relates activities and meanings to the assumptive, analytic, and aesthetic views of the world: that is, those that repeat and confirm the world, like playing a familiar game; those that examine the world, like a political book; and those that transform the world, like painting a picture or marching in protest.
6. Finally, the *sociological* conception, following the lead of Max Weber,[2] sees leisure as a construct with such elements as an antithesis to the work of the

participant, a perception of the activity as voluntary or free, a pleasant expectation and recollection, a full range of possibilities from withdrawal in sleep or drink to highly creative tasks. This kind of construct is not to be taken as a random collection of elements; it invites the theorist to look at all major human activities as constructs and to exchange elements from one to the other. For example, the major preoccupation of a political system is the creation and distribution of power, but it includes other elements, such as myth making. Myth making, however, is a more fundamental responsibility of religion; yet religion, too, has elements of power hierarchy. Thus, as we all know, elements of leisure are to be found in work, family, and education; conversely, elements from those constructs are often to be found in leisure. From this view, nothing is definable as leisure per se, and almost anything is definable as leisure, given a synthesis of elements as suggested.

FURTHER COMMENTS ON CONCEPTIONS OF LEISURE

Conceptualization is so important that the remainder of this chapter is devoted to three topics: some extended comments on the several conceptual traditions noted above: a comparison of the conception of this book with that of Dumazedier; and suggestions to the student as he considers his own position among these several conceptual approaches.

Leisure as End: The Humanistic Model

Bennett M. Berger noted in 1962 that there are two traditional approaches to leisure that have little in common.[3]

"One tradition, probably dating from the relatively early stages of industrialization in the West, conceives of leisure as 'free time' or time not devoted to paid vacations; leisure activities are viewed primarily as re-creative and restorative; historically, the problems involved are associated with the poor, the dependent, or the laboring classes. The much older, classical tradition conceives of leisure in the Greek sense as 'schooling' or cultivation of the self, as a preoccupation with the values of high culture. Historically this tradition has been associated with the functions of aristocratic, patrician, or leisure classes, since other classes were not culturally important."

Of course, the historical concept of leisure that deals with goals comes from the Greeks, the concept of *paidia.* In Aristotle's *Politics VII* this passage is to be found.

"The whole of life is further divided into two parts, business and leisure, war and peace, and of actions; some aim at what is necessary and useful and some at what is honorable. And the preference given to one or other part of the soul and its actions over the other; there must be war for the sake of peace, business for the sake of leisure, things useful and necessary for the sake of things honourable. . . . For men must be able to engage in business and go to war, but leisure and peace are better; they must do what is necessary and indeed what is useful, but what is honourable is better."

To Aristotle, happiness and leisure are active terms, not the negative of work or business. One advocate of this position is Sebastian de Grazia in his important volume, *Of Time, Work and Leisure:* "Leisure refers to a state of being, a condition of men." It is a freedom from necessity. In a neo-Hellenic commitment to contemplation (comparable to the Greek word Theorein, or "theory for us"), de Grazia notes: [4]

"The life of leisure leads to a greater sensitivity not to truth alone, but also to beauty, to the wonder of man and nature, to its contemplation and its recreation in word or song, clay, colors or stone. . . . To clear the way to truth, to be serenely objective. The life of leisure may accomplish many things; it can promise nothing. Freedom, truth and beauty, is its religion. . . . Leisure is an ideal. One can only try to get as close to it as possible . . . The life for thinkers, artists and musicians."

We find in de Grazia, then, a restatement of *paidia,* applied almost word for word to the desirable goals for the postindustrial society. However, one of de Grazia's basic beliefs is that "Democratic society could not and cannot offer the kind of freedom that one has in Leisure." This de Tocqueville-like judgment will be encountered again later in the discussion on leisure and mass culture as the ideological godfather of intellectuals who "are inclined to be pessimistic about the possibilities of raising popular taste."

The utility of approaching leisure from the Hellenic origins as an end is self-evident: the formulation itself provides its built-in criterion if the *nature* of the end is specified. But what if the ends are strange, and indigenous to a culture quite different than the Hellenic? Consider the Chinese conception of the ideal leisure as idleness but rooted in the highly personal integration that flows from Confucianism. Lin Yutang indicates that according to the values of his society, the man who is wisely idle is the most cultured man. There seems to be a philosophic contradiction between being busy and being wise. The wisest man is therefore he who loafs most gracefully. [5]

"Here I shall try to explain, not the technique and varieties of loafing as practiced in China, but rather the philosophy which nourishes this divine desire for loafing in China gives rise to that carefree, idle, happy-go-lucky—and often poetic—temperament in the Chinese scholars. How did that Chinese temperament—that distrust of achievement and success and that intense love of living as such—arise? . . .the Chinese theory of leisure, as expressed by a comparatively unknown author of the eighteenth century, Shu Paihsiang, who happily achieved oblivion, is as follows: time is useful because it is not being used. 'Leisure in time is like unoccupied floor space in a room.' Every working girl who rents a small room where every inch of space is fully utilized feels highly uncomfortable because she has no room to move about, and the moment she gets a raise in salary, she moves into a bigger room where there is a little more unused floor space, besides those strictly useful spaces occupied by her single bed, her dressing table and her two-burner gas range. It is that unoccupied space which makes a room habitable, as it is our leisure hours which make life endurable."

F. S. C. Northrop, in his classic discussion of the East, again and again speaks of the "aesthetically intimate" and "intuitive," which has no counterpart in the Western "theoretic-component." But, as distinct from the Greek reliance on community values, the Confucian emphasis, as seen in his *Analecta,* was on personal experience. Again, in comparison to the Hellenic traditions of *paidia,* ingrained by private tutors on the young aristocrats of Athens, the ordering principle of *li* is difficult to discern; again the burden is on the individual. The emptiness of leisure that Lin Yutang describes above is not in a vacuum, but exists with a well-ordered set of principles in which great emphasis is placed on *jen*—a quality that Northrop describes as "compassion" or "man-to-man-ness." Thus, according to Tzu Ssu, *jen* and knowledge (*chih*) "are spiritual powers (*te*) inherent in man, and they are the bridge bringing together the outer and the inner." This "bridge" becomes *tao*—the "way," and relates Confucianism to the aims of Taoism and Buddhism.

The conceptualization of leisure as an end has merit as well as venerable historical roots in both East and West, but the word *end* is enormous in scope, impervious to ethnocentricity. Yet the opposite danger is more to be cautious about, that is, that *end* is synonymous with *anything.* That would reduce the concept to a mere shamble. For this reason I referred to this approach as *humanistic.*

Leisure as Means: The Therapeutic-Change Model

This category refers to the uses of leisure for such purposes as social status, therapy, or social control. Leisure is then a medicine, a symbol, or a tool. More than an activity is implied, as in the category above, because now leisure is looked on as a part of a dynamic pattern.

The most pertinent aspect of this concept of leisure deals with social class. Leisure as "conspicuous consumption" became a familiar concept with Thorstein Veblen's *Theory of the Leisure Class:* the need by the rich to assert their freedom from work in symbolic acts. Remember, however, that the definition of leisure as "social climbing" or as a symbol of class is not to be associated with the upper classes alone. For example, David Riesman treats leisure in contemporary terms by distinguishing its uses by "inner" and "other" persons. Certain types of activities *within* leisure, such as the arts and foreign travel, have been seen as peculiarly suited by the affirmation or acquisition of social status.

Leisure as a therapeutic aid is familiar to the mental hospital world, where "recreation" and "occupational therapy" more and more have become tools for rehabilitation. We may anticipate more systematic attention to the conceptualization of leisure in relation to mental health in the open community. A psychiatry of leisure is presently undeveloped but has been recognized by such leaders in the field as Dr. Karl Menninger and Dr. Stanley Lesse, editor of the *American Journal of Psychotherapy,* who in a November 1969 letter to me, expresses a concern with trends in the study of leisure, and notes:

"While it is to the credit of the social scientist that he has recognized the overall problems dealing with leisure both with regard to the present and future, I foresee nothing but trouble if this is to be considered purely as a social problem. Leisure will be a reflection of the general trends that are likely to determine our future society. It should help man optimally to adapt to his future and to prepare him to live in a more humanistic fashion. As such, leisure should be seen not only as a social phenomenon, but in terms of how it directly affects the psychic structure of the individual."

Along similar lines, Dr. Alexander Reid Martin, former chairman of a committee on leisure for the American Psychiatric Association, refers to leisure as a state of grace. "It is a particular state or condition of the whole personality . . . the occasion and the capacity of the whole personality to open up to all stimuli. The mood is one of affirmation in contrast to idleness, which has a negative mood." [6] He refers to Emerson's advice that man had best surrender to the universe, and to Thoreau's enrichment of the spirit through leisure, and to Walt Whitman's line in *Leaves of Grass,* "I loaf and invite my soul."

Turning to leisure as a symbol of the rich, Cleveland Amory provides descriptions of the American rich in their resort areas; Ferdinand Lundberg details life in their urban clubs, where major business and political decisions are made.

If the rich of various societies have used the leisure milieu (club, horse race, social gathering, etc.) to effect political rapport, history has many instances of political causes using leisure as a tool. The Roman circuses come to mind and, over the centuries, a parade (almost literally) of pageants, festivals, sports, and ceremonies. For years, Henry Ford in Detroit sponsored symphony concerts over the radio that served as a pretext for conservative propaganda. The carefully planned public events under Hitler are in the memory of living millions.

With the current high activity of the Communist nations in studies of leisure, some preliminary observations are useful in this early portion of the volume.

Among the Marxists of our time, the raising of popular taste is a fundamental article of faith. Little effort is needed to uncover such instrumental views of leisure as in the following paragraph.[7]

"The Rumanian socialist state is profoundly interested in the continuous raising of cultural level of the population, as it conditions, to a great extent, the many-sided development of the working people, the growth of their conscience and activity in production and in socio-political life. The cultural revolution taking place in the R.P.R. in the years of socialist construction was materialized in the liquidation of illiteracy, in developing education of all degrees, developing ideological activity, the network of theatres and cinemas, the radio-relay network among the masses, increasing the number of houses of culture, libraries, museums, of printed books and the circulation of newspapers, magazines, etc."

A recent statement by the President of East Germany is even more pointed in this regard.[8]

"In the future, the mutual relation between working-time and work-free time will increase more and more. The meaningful utilization of spare time through education, qualification, creative artistic and sporting self-performance will become an ever more important source of strength for the development of the creative capabilities of individuals in socialistic production. We must pay much more attention to these questions in the conscious planning and management of our social development."

On the other hand, one of the foremost contemporary scholars of leisure in the USSR, Dr. Boris Grushin, leaves no doubt of the unexpected parallelism between the current Russia and ancient Hellenic view. In his 1966 study, Grushin notes the "Marxist principle of comprehensive development of the human individual . . . to strengthen and develop various beneficial (that is, not antisocial) inherent qualities and

abilities of the individual and the physical, spiritual, emotional, intellectual, social and other aspects of his being." [9]

Yet this incongruity among current followers of Marxism were predicated on the breadth of Marx himself. As Albert Salomon noted,[10] "It
is indispensable to mention the system of Marx among the religions of
progress. His scientific socialism is romantic . . . whatever might be the
scientific quality of the works for economics and sociology. . . . Marx's
work shows most distinctly that under modern conditions, religions of
progress and revolutions must merge." On the "romantic" side, he was
able to relate leisure with economic freedom. Capitalism would create
leisure, and the shorter workday is the basis for freedom. "The interesting thing," writes de Grazia, "is that Marx seems to be groping for a
fresh expression of the classical concept. (This should not surprise us too
much: Marx's doctoral thesis was on Epicurus.)" [11] But for Marx the
transformation of the person through leisure as economic freedom must
be based on the democratic ideal, so that "for all practical respects the
ideals of democracy and socialism in regard to free time are twins,
similar if not identical." Indeed, Marx himself had written, "Time is the
space for human development. . . . A man, who has no free time at his
disposal, whose total life-time apart from purely physical interruptions
in the way of sleep, meals, etc.—is devoured by his labors for capital,
is less than a beast of burden."

The situation, theoretically, seems to be that the Marxist society can
approach leisure within the Hellenic tradition with emphasis on the
individual's growth, or it can see personal development as a fundamental tool for social purposes. This is theory and, to the degree that the
choice works its way into everyday life of any of the Eastern nations,
we have one significant clue to its freedom. In Romania itself, the
national favorite among TV shows—fully 80 percent of the half million
person audience—is a science program with little or no political connotations. In Yugoslavia, farthest removed from USSR control, the research studies—which bear a close relationship to policy, as in all these
countries—of retired sports stars, family life, town life, youth clubs, and
the Dalmatian coast for tourist development are all as objective and
businesslike as scientific studies in the West.

Another difference in these countries is that between members of the
Socialist or Communist parties and (as in the case of youth) activities
organized by them. We would expect that the free time of such members is taken by the party to further its ideological ends. The building
of bodies, through sports, games, displays, and festivals, is an end first,
but a means in the broader sense. This pattern, perhaps, indicates the
historical position of these nations: with the coming of urbanization and

industrialization they are applying research and public policy toward *obtaining* more time. In the Russian case, this is sought by such techniques as reducing time for travel to work, automating work processes, and electrifying the home. This step—developing the means—then may be used by the population for "bourgeoisie" purposes, such as listening to "decadent" jazz and rock by young people, or for more social purposes to help the society. The general directions that the masses will follow, given their new time resource, are not yet clear. If the masses (and intellectuals, to a lesser degree) turn to leisure as consumers on the American model, we will see a verification of Ellul's model of technological societies as autonomous in their values, materialistic, and impervious to humanistic attitudes.[12] In this sense the Eastern European countries will serve as a giant laboratory of the next decades for the impact that leisure may have in reinforcing or in supplementing the nonhuman values of the approaching cybernetic culture.

Leisure as Time: The Quantitative Model

This pragmatic approach is needed by those who seek to measure, experiment, or in other ways deal with the term for "objective" purposes. For example, in 1944, Henry Pratt Fairchild defined leisure in his *Dictionary of Sociology*[13] as:

"Free time after the practical necessities of life have been attended to. The adjective leisure means being unoccupied by the practical necessities, as leisure hours. . . . Conceptions of leisure vary from the arithmetical one of time devoted to work, sleep, and other necessities, subtracted from 24 hours. . .to the general notion of leisure hour as the time which one uses as he pleases."

The definition raises the further question of who judges the nature of "practical necessities of life"; aside from work, especially if it is work defined in its time structure by an employer, the scientist must bow to the judgment of the person being studied. We get one example of this in an instruction to employees engaged by a major American research agency engaged in a time-budget study.

"We ask the respondent to imagine where he would find varying amounts of time (1 hour, 3 hours, and 6 hours) during Diary Day if something extremely important and unexpected came up that could not be postponed. Most respondents. . .will begin to make room during their off-work hours. This is just what we want to know: this for most respondents represents their freest time."

May and Petgen spoke for many others as far back as 1928 in referring to leisure as the "time surplus remaining after the practical necessities of life have been attended to." [14] Paul Weiss, a full generation later, used about the same language: "—that portion of the day not used for the exigencies of existence." [15] Brightbill, in 1965, spoke of leisure as "essentially a block of time."

Time-budget studies, to which "Diary Day" above refers, have raised this issue of objective versus subjective definitions of leisure—as well as of other types of activities—in a pressing practical manner. Such studies long have been useful to discover, in a highly detailed manner, what people do with time that is relatively committed or that is "free." As workers fought for shorter hours, beginning in a dramatic way with the Parliamentary inquiries in England after the middle of the nineteenth century, labor unions fought for the "3 x 8" policy, with eight hours for leisure, eight for work, and eight for sleep. Everyone knew that "leisure" was not the whole of the "free time" segment; what, then, is "wasteful," and what is "essential" during those hours? Before World War II, the USSR, United States, England, France, and Germany were predominant in such studies. Szalai points out that the first sophisticated use of time budgets were carried out by S. G. Strumilin for planning purposes of the Soviet Union in 1924.[16] Professor George Lundberg and his associates pioneered the diary technique in their classic study of Westchester County, specifically devoted to leisure. The definition of leisure in those studies was relatively simple and imposed on the situation that leisure is "the time we are free from the more obvious and formal duties which a paid job or other obligatory occupation imposes upon us." [17]

OF TIME, WORK AND LEISURE

Each of the foregoing methods in approaching leisure has its important place. The construct we seek as an ideal research tool should grow out of those presented above, yet move us closer to the institutional concept discussed earlier. The construct is to be used in the "ideal type" tradition established by Max Weber in his analysis of Protestantism, capitalism, or the Chinese literati. The construct is a *typical,* not an average, picture against which a real situation may be assessed. *Leisure,* we might say, *consists of relatively self-determined activity-experience that falls into one's economically free-time roles, that is seen as leisure by participants, that is psychologically pleasant in anticipation and recollection, that potentially covers the whole range of commitment and intensity, that contains characteristic norms and constraints, and that provides opportunities for recreation, personal growth, and service to others.*

The first element of this conception is relative self-determination or voluntariness. There are degrees of freedom and varieties of self-deception: do I really want to cut the grass? am I attending the theatre because I want to go, or was the decision made by my wife? But even a psychological perception of freedom is valuable to the person.

Use of the term "activity-experience" implies an attempt to divorce leisure from the purely behavior element and to permit the possibility of inner, unobservable, or emotional results. Leisure as mere activity has, of course, long been a traditional assumption. The recreation profession, for instance, has often used the terms leisure and recreation interchangeably and, as in one of its authoritative manuals, deals completely from the activities approach, with a classification of arts and crafts, dance, drama, games-sports-athletics, hobbies, music, outdoor recreation, reading-writing-speaking, social recreation, special events, and voluntary services.

"Economically free time" immediately suggests that leisure is not necessarily the same as nonwork time, since one's "free time" is far more than his time for leisure. No one works 24 hours in the day. He sleeps, eats, washes, and engages in other biological or domestic functions related to keeping alive and functioning. It has been estimated, for example, that in a lifetime of 72 years, all of the hours spent in sleep generally total 22 years, those in work come to 10 years, and those of eating come to 6 years. Almost one half of the lifetime is still unaccounted for, and not even all of this would be called "leisure." De Grazia puts the difference clearly in the course of an introduction that sets the tone of his volume.[18]

"Work (he notes) is the antonym of free time. But not of leisure. Leisure and free time live in two different worlds. We have got in the habit of thinking them the same. Anybody can have free time. Not everybody can have leisure. Free time is a realizable idea of democracy. Leisure is not fully realizable, and hence an ideal, not alone an idea. Free time refers to a special way of calculating a special kind of time. Leisure refers to a state of being, a condition of man, which few desire and fewer achieve."

"Disabusing leisure of free time," says de Grazia, is one of the principal purposes of his book, *Of Time, Work, and Leisure.* He goes even further, as we will see later, and argues that the amount of "free time" is less than we often assume. On that point, I will take issue, but on the separation of the terms we are in full agreement.

The next phrase of the definition, "pleasant expectation and recollection," raises a serious question as to whether the experience should be considered as leisure if these elements are not present. As a partial answer, a further distinction must be made between the general act and its substance and between form and content. One may, for example, read a book in his leisure; this is favorably anticipated by him, because *to read* is a "good thing." However, the book might be Hersey's *The Wall;* within the reading experience, therefore, one may find tragedy.

The psychological element of pleasure that precedes, pervades, and follows leisure refers, accordingly, to the choice of reading *as reading.* This becomes a crucial distinction when we turn later to a discussion of possibilities for deepening or obtaining values through leisure, because then the issue is precisely the same: can we attract the person to some experience for the formal aspect and then, by affecting the content of the experience, contribute to new personal growth?

By saying that leisure can cover "the whole range of commitment and intensity," we seek to destroy the myth and image of leisure as only relaxation, fun, amusement, or idleness. This is one of the pervasive myths that has colored the literature for decades. So that there can be no mistake of the intentions of the construct, three large groupings of content are included, "recreation, personal growth, and service to others."

The phrase on "characteristic norms and restraints" needs to be emphasized. It asserts that leisure—like religious, educational, familial, or other activity-experience—exists within a cultural context. "Cultural," of course, is used here in the social science sense. Indeed, a major specification of the conceptualization in the next section is that the components of leisure must be removable, and components of religion or other institutions must be put into their place. If this can be done, then the study of leisure has entered a mature stage, and a *theory* of leisure, not just a study of leisure minutiae, can proceed.

Furthermore, as I will note in a later chapter, the phrase "recreation, personal growth, and service to others" is related to an epistemological scheme to be outlined in relation to the meanings of leisure. The first will be paired roughly with the *assumptive* key to one's perception of the world, the second to the *aesthetic,* and the last to the *analytic.*

Another position in the formulation is the relationship to other disciplines that becomes explicit, and presents another reason for suggesting the broadest approach to the issues. If the statement is taken apart, some of its ties to special fields can be seen.

FORMULATION	DISCIPLINES AND ISSUES
1. "—relatively self-determined activity-experience"	Psychology-psychiatry-sociology-political science a. How judgments and decisions are made b. Power structure in families c. Bases of obligations to friends and peers d. External conditions that affect autonomy or freedom, and so on
2. "—economically free-time roles"	Economics-sociology-history-law political science-industrial psychology a. Nature of "social roles" b. Nature of "work" c. Perceptions of time d. Psychology of wants and needs, and so on
3. "—seen as leisure by participants"	Psychology, sociology, linguistics, information theory, and business-related disciplines, literature, aesthetics a. Cognitive and affective stumuli b. Behaviorist theories c. Differential perceptions, and so on
4. "—pleasant anticipation and recollection"	Psychiatry, psychology, economics, human ecology, business, history a. Budget planning b. Dynamics of conversation c. Projected behavior, and so on
5. "—whole range of commitment and intensity"	All social sciences, philosophy, theology, gerontology, arts a. Quest for self-identity b. Search for meanings c. Nature of responsibility d. Roles in retirement, and so on

Such an interdisciplinary approach can be applied to leisure as a social institution.

In substance, leisure differs from other institutions. In the method of its study, leisure is approachable in the same way as other institutions. In research terms, this provides handles or major classifications that are useful for reference, for anchoring our hypotheses, for classifications of data for bibliographical listings, or for coding data preparatory to computerization. Since scientific solutions when simply achieved have been called "beautiful," even by scientists, I have adopted the model of the string quartet—one of man's classical solutions to the blend of individual and group—in a series of fourfold systems called institutions, clusters, cultures, and constructs. Into this mold, the "inner" square (I), the phenomenon being studied could be *any* institution, while II, III, and IV would remain as constants, applying to the central dynamic, whatever it might be.

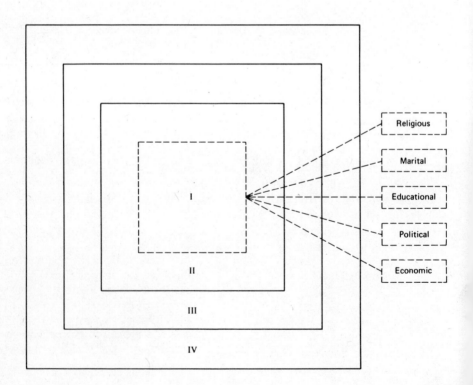

The inner square, the institution, changes not only its basic identity but also its constituent parts.

There might be some difficulty among scholars in reaching a consensus of components for institution. I offer these as mere illustrations:

Religious: Deities, ethics, hierarchies, symbolisms.
Marital: Sex regulations, legal relationships, roles, life-styles.
Educational: Teaching, research, service, counselling.
Political: Legislation, administration, enforcement, symbol.
Economics: Production, distribution, consumption, ideology.
Leisure: Condition, selection, function, meaning.

Altogether, what we have above is the beginning of a visual model. Models are used often in the behavioral sciences, whether as constructions in words, mathematical symbols, physical objects, or pictures. Their main purpose is sufficient comprehensiveness and flexibility to suggest specific units, elements, or parts—but within a larger "system" that invites the drawing of *relationships.* A successful model is not a pretty, static thing but a dynamic construction that generates data, ideas, and even hypotheses. Bernard Phillips reminds us of its potentials and limitations.[19]

"Like any device used in the context of discovery, models have their possibilities and their dangers. It is believed that the human mind learns best about the unknown by proceeding from the known, and the utility of scientific analogies or models lies in the fact that they dramatize the implications of the known. The use of models is standard practice in pedagogy: addition and subtraction, for example are often taught with the aid of concrete entities. . . . It is always possible to develop a model of a given phenomenon, for there is always some similarity between the system which constitutes the model and the system which constitutes the reality. The question the researcher must answer, however, is whether or not there is something further to be gained by setting up a model that goes beyond the apparent similarities with reality. Might such a model serve to suggest new ideas as to the nature or function of reality, ideas that might not otherwise be apparent?"

Phillips' question is met head on in Chapter 3, where 60 observations or propositions are extracted from the model as an exercise and as a basis for many pages of discussion throughout the volume. The model is intended as a tool, a sense of direction, a map of issues. In itself the model provides no answers. Its usefulness increases as it meets several specifications. It must (1) permit specific analysis of leisure activity-experience as well as of the total, institutional phenomena; (2) progress from simple (most measurable) to complex analysis; (3) include both time and space elements; (4) stimulate and simulate relationships between the model's component parts; (5) encourage both qualitative and quantitative investigations; (6) encompass as many disciplines as needed; and (7) move the theoretical inquiry toward bridges for policy formulation. Before proceeding to the model, two other questions can be raised.

1. What is the relationship of the *model* to the *conceptions* of leisure already given above?
2. Where does the model to be used as the core of this volume fall within the major methodological positions of the social sciences?

As to the first question, any definition or characterization is a mental construct that attempts to identify the subject being investigated; the model, however, seeks to explore possibilities for one or more theories. The model is a tool for potential exploration, to explain why and how certain things happen. Thus it makes little difference which conception of leisure is used as a basis for the study at a given moment; conditions such as health, income, or education must still be related to the community, to symbols of the culture, and so on. The nature of the propositions that emerge from the model will differ, depending on the conception of leisure that is the foundation of the entire study, and thus the differences between a humanistic or therapeutic concept of leisure enter prominently into the relationships established with factors such as social class. If the model is taken to be a "formal style" (distinct, for example, from a literary exposition), the nature of leisure as perceived by the participant, the scientist, or the society is the subjective "content." Obviously, propositions about content can be created without any model, but the model provides the overall system by which data exists within a totality instead of (as is often the case in social science) as isolated material.

The model finally provides a certain rhythm, order, and priority among the propositions—a rhythm that, as in the case of a musical theme, is not only found by the creator but, indeed, carries him along almost in a life of its own. Where the scientist ends and the artist takes over is not always easy to determine. In the present case, some of the propositions of Chapter 3 had been in my mind, perhaps somewhat hidden from consciousness; however, in what Abraham Kaplan calls its value for "deductive fertility," the model serves to "squeeze out of our data a great deal of content not otherwise available to us, or at least not easily available." [20]

The relation of the model to traditions (therefore, to controversies) within social science brings us to the terms *empirical* and *rational-logical.* The first is a way of working with data that puts complete faith "in the senses, firm belief in the power of observation, willingness to be ruled by observable evidence, and belief that scientific conclusions should never get beyond the realm of extrapolation. . . ." [21] In contrast, the rationalistic method holds that truth is derived by the mind, conceptualizations, constructs, and the use of logic.

The recent history of American sociology has been dominated by empiricism. The results were mixed, bringing both self-deception on the crucial matter of "objectivity" and more accuracy as a science. The long and often bitter debates between proponents of these positions need not detain us here.

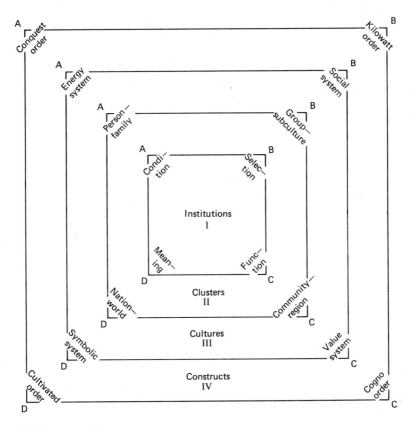

Chart 1

Conceptualization of leisure in society

This textbook and the way in which the model is constructed and used stands between these extreme positions. It falls among those who are critical of neo-positivism (a position that the social sciences should be oriented to methods of the physical sciences). Among the leaders of the middle position have been Hughes, MacIver, Merton, Parsons, Sorokin, and Znaniecki. Florian Znaniecki, an eminent Polish scholar and coauthor with W. I. Thomas, of *The Polish Peasant*, has influenced this textbook, especially through his use of *analytic induction.*[22] The full scheme is presented in Chart 1 on page 33.

The discussion below will identify each of the 20 components of Chart 1; the next chapter presents 60 propositions that illustrate at least one relationship between each of the components of leisure to those of systems II, III, and IV.

I. Leisure as a Dynamic System

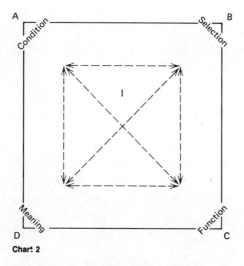

Chart 2

Leisure as a system of components

The dynamics of a "system" is the relationship between its components (see Chart 2). If in Level 1 in the diagram, a change occurs in A, will B, C, and D be affected? In what way, how much, and why? Place of residence, as we will see, falls within 1A. If a person moves from New York City to Tuscaloosa, what changes occur in his habit of playing chess for relaxation? The answer may be that he gives up chess altogether because he cannot find a partner; it may be that he has found a chess club, and he continues as before. That "condition"—change of residence—has not been important; but, if the condition of his health changes, even if he stays in New York, he may quit chess altogether. Each component therefore has to be looked at in some detail.

In the actual course of observation, we might start anywhere on the diagram. One day I observed a social dance in which the men of various ages were all dancing with elderly women; several men were lying on the dance floor. We can start with the direct question—why?—and find the meaning of D in A, B, and C.

A. *Condition.* These men were schizophrenics in a VA hospital; the women were members of Ladies Aid; those on the floor were other patients.

B. *Selection.* The men did not have much else to do; how often do they have a chance to dance with a woman, young or old?

C. *Meaning.* A change from the ward life; a source of continuity with the past.

We can, for research or observation, start anywhere on the diagram, jump to any point, and move freely from a given activity-experience to a universe of leisure. Answers by the hospital administration—medical priorities, VA policies, and availability of the volunteers—could be applied to more than one type of event. The following is a brief discussion of each element in the total scheme.

A. *Condition.* The "condition" of leisure means a factor outside of the leisure pattern itself that can or may determine the selection, function, and meaning of the leisure. A bare listing of some factors is enough to open an immense area for commonsense observations or for more subtle studies: age, sex, place of residence, income, health, education, the nature of one's work, the amount and structure of one's time. Several of these will be discussed in some detail in Chapter 4.

B. *Selection.* The "selection" of leisure means the process of choice that may lead one to a game of cards instead of to a book, a walk, a television show, a conversation, or other possibilities. A lack of money may seem to suggest the card games for a month instead of an ocean cruise but the same factor does not explain the choice of a game instead of a book.

C. *Function.* The "function" of leisure means the intention of the participant as well as the effects that are brought about. The one lies primarily in the psychological and philosophical realm; sociology is more likely to view the behavioral consequences or processes.

D. *Meaning.* The "meaning" of leisure means the significance, sense, import, force, essence, interpretation, and tenor of the leisure to the participant, to an onlooker, or to the general society. Here, too, as with the problem of function, the real and the symbolic become entwined.

As Chart 2 suggests by its arrows, each component is related to all the others. They are not necessarily of equal importance in the analysis of a specific action. In some situations they reinforce each other; in others, they interfere or are in direct conflict with each other; and in other situations, one component ignores or is indifferent to another. Illustrations will be provided later, as each in turn is treated in a full chapter.

II. The Dynamics of Clusters in Leisure

Perhaps the single most significant change in the relationships of human beings has been in the speed and range of communications. In the second level of the conceptual scheme, the assumption is made that in studies of leisure this range must extend potentially from one person to every other person in the world, necessitated by the direct contacts across national lines, the processes of tourism, militarism, trade, study abroad, and—most important—films and television. The scheme below assumes four pairs of relations or interdependencies that create an ecological as well as a communications order. They are called "clusters," referring to the prospect that each cluster (such as person-family) will show a set of characteristics sufficiently important to distinguish it from other clusters (see Chart 3).

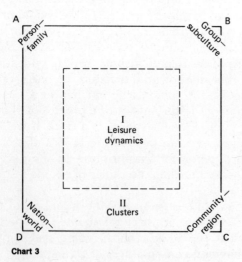

Chart 3

Relation of leisure to the level of clusters

A. *Person-Family.* For leisure studies, person and family units cannot be understood separately, in spite of many polling studies that concentrate on the individual person. There can be no division of functions here between psychology and sociology. All leisure students will gain from the immediate recognition that leisure as a whole is by its nature interdisciplinary. The person's leisure is inextricably affected by, and it in turn affects, the family.

B. *Group-Subculture.* Each person communicates with groups outside of his family, friends, club members, neighbors, church congregations, political parties, and colleagues in work. Some of these groups are more influential than others in their impact on leisure; a person might find most of his fellow players among his work colleagues instead of among his neighbors. The "groups" are therefore composed of persons he knows or with whom he has direct contact. The "subculture," on the other hand, is a term applied to "youth," or "retirees," or "suburbanites." There may be positive values within the group itself that have an influence on leisure, or the group may carry an image in the minds of outsiders, with the net result of influencing the psychological environment in which these people live.

C. *Community-Region.* No longer can a *Middletown* be written to describe the life and values of one community. The trend in social science now is to relate the community to larger forces because of the steady flow of images in and out. The region is the next natural area beyond the city, sometimes recognized now as the "megalopolis" when large communities, such as Boston-New York-Washington, are interrelated by common values and facilities. But all cities, even small ones removed from the dozen or more megalopolitan regions, are identified with and lend a general atmosphere to opportunities for leisure uses.

D. *National-World.* Finally, with mass media and easier transportation, much of the national picture is now available for the development of leisure aspirations and tastes. This includes immediate access to styles of entertainment, dress, fashions, motion pictures, TV shows, and advertisements. If anyone remains autonomous in his use of free time, it is not for the lack of effort of commercial taste makers who hope to affect his decisions and expenditures. And what is now true on the national level grows wider and wider in its outreach. Reading, tourism, TV, reports from friends, news dispatches, and other forms of images or impressions from many parts of the world constantly enter into the mind-life of almost every person. Whether in respect to usefulness for leisure purposes or for anything else, these world "snapshots" are seen differently by each of us, hardly escapable by anyone.

III. The Dynamics of Culture in Leisure

Leisure as a system of action together with other institutional systems, provides access to culture (see Chart 4). Perhaps the definition of culture that has best stood the test of time is that prepared in 1871 by E. B. Tylor.

> ... that complex whole which includes knowledge, belief, art, law, morals, custom, and any other capabilities and habits acquired by men as a member of society.

There are many ways in which the totality has been divided and subdivided. For our purposes a quartet of terms on the diagram deals with each as a "system": *energy, social life, values,* and *symbols.*

A. *Energy System.* An "energy system" is the total production and control of resources used or available to the society, together with attendant attitudes, motivations, rewards, and deprivations. The leisure phenomenon springs from many wells, but the technological system is undoubtedly a dominant factor.

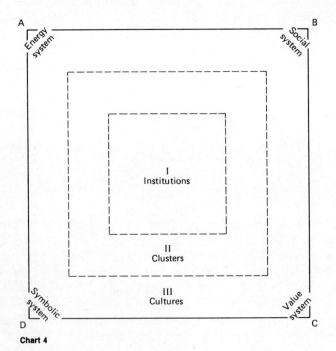

Chart 4

Relation of leisure to the cultural level

B. *Social System.* A "social system" is the structure and organization of persons into formal and informal groups. The purposes in each case give rise to such categories as social class, education, subculture, religion, family, club, audience, and public. Although the energy system may create the possibility of free time, it is the social system that may have decisive impact on the uses and meaning of that time or experience.

C. *Value System.* A "value system" is the nature of priorities and the process of judgment by which the person, the group, or the society chooses its interests and according to which it creates patterns of belief, faith, and behavior. Leisure is involved directly in images and judgments of good or evil, beautiful or ugly. The problem is circular: the value has influence on the choice and use of leisure, but conversely, the exercise of leisure may reinforce, modify, or contradict values. It is the second of these—leisure as a source for values—that lends new prospects to the subject.

D. *Symbolic System.* A "symbolic system" is the involvement of leisure in a particular form or as a total phenomenon in representing ideas outside of leisure. History has much to tell us about leisure as symbolic behavior for the rich, familiar in Veblen's adjective "conspicuous." However, the usefulness and exploitation of symbolic leisure goes beyond class and is seen on Sunday as a holy day of rest for Christianity, or on the Sabbath as Judaic "architecture of time." Thus time is a crucial ingredient of leisure but functions in close relation to symbolic aspects of space, content, and other persons.

IV. The Dynamic of Constructs in Leisure

The communications and influence of ideas goes on vertically in depth of time, as well as horizontally, in depth of penetration. A theory of leisure is essentially a theory of history. Thus it is no accident that *Homo Ludens* is one of the classic documents for our study and that J. Huizinga was an established historian.[23] Sociology in America is partially handicapped in approaching leisure because of its nonhistorical view; as E. H. Carr notes, understanding the present requires a concern with the future as well as with the past. But, for our purpose, we do not use history as it is used by traditional historians—to provide a one-directional narrative of events. Our use of history is to find in its pages some broad *types* of social orders, types that may appear and reappear, or types that may serve us toward a visualization of desirable futures. For example, in the constructs that follow, the Greek societies of Plato and Aristotle are placed under "cultivated" order, which is an explicit construction of the future! This is an overt commission for which an author takes full responsibility. Similarly, certain characteristics of our present will be found to be merely updated versions of "primitive" orders.

The components for the constructs to be used here are: *conquest, kilowatt, cogno,* and *cultivated* (see Chart 5). These terms are not in common use, and are therefore free of the kinds of connotations attached to more familiar schemes such as preindustrial, industrial, and postindustrial.

A. *Conquest Society.* This society, like the others to be described on Level IV, is a construct, not a specific historical period. It consists of (1) conquest over nature, which is a primary concern of primitive social orders, and (2) conquest by men over men in the milieu of the preindustrial pattern.

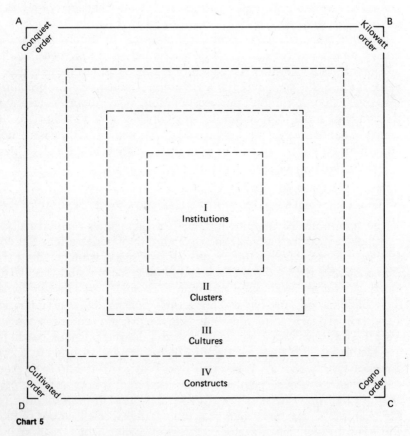

Chart 5

Relation of leisure to the level of constructs

Leisure among the primitives illustrates the nonutilitarian as well as the utilitarian function. The emphasis, rightly, has been to show the fusion of institutions; dancing, for example, is generally an integral part of the religious ceremony. But more recent anthropology stresses the enormous range of social systems; among the complexities that are now understood are drawings, designs on pots, basket patterns, symbols, sculpture, iron works, and other artistic forms that stand purely as art. Similarly, games and folklore are among the vocabulary of primitive groups of former centuries or of today. Nevertheless, the thread of pure game or play among relatively less stratified groups is of unique importance, in contrast to pure leisure in sophisticated society with its clear institutional structures.

As to the Conquest society that is closer to our present patterns, one thinks of Africa before its independence movement in the 1950s; or of China, India, and most of South America today; or of Central and Western Europe of the Middle Ages. Even with their vast differences, several broad similarities stand out. Here there are feudal structures, with rigid social and economic lines between the segments of rich and poor within each one. Here there are no middle classes. Power stems from land ownership or from sheer force exercised by outside colonialists. These are prescientific, conservative, religious, absolutistic, and muscle-dominated societies. Their economies are static; their politics are non-democratic. Kinship, neighborhood, kingdom, plantation, and fief are the contexts for human relationships within the *community or Gemeinschaft.* Within the community, too, as Durkheim points out, there is an "organic" instead of a "contractual" solidarity. A very rough delineation of life within each segment or social class can be represented by terms such as communal, simple, homogeneous, oral, rural, and religious.

Yet between the classes exists a rigid line that is not crossed, although there is surface familiarity between slave and master or landlord and serf. Relations across strata are functional, not personal. The total way of life of the rich is beyond any possible attainment by the poor, and no middle grouping exists to provide the social escalator. Servants are plentiful, and they serve to bridge across the high and the low before the day of the society page in the industrial-age newspaper.

Finally, the conquest over the poor masses is only one economic reality; another is the conquest of entire political areas by "foreign" rulers, although what is foreign and what is not is sometimes a subtle point in any historical or summary treatment of the sixteenth to eighteenth centuries. The presence of small, national, cultural, and political units created not only an international complexity—as in Italy before Mazzini—but also developed an international-mindedness that was particularly useful for development of the arts. These broad elements of Conquest Society exist in many parts of the world today.

B. *Kilowatt Society.* Kilowatt Society is machine powered, not muscular. It is driven by batteries, generators, control boxes, and ultimately by computers. Two types of displacement take place; first, machines replace muscle and second, machines supplement and almost supplant the mind. Ultimately, automation will cause man the worker (*homo faber*) to become man the postworker or player (*homo ludens*). *Kilowatt Society* is brought on by the growth of science and, in turn, encourages a furthering of science. As sheep become more profitable on the farms, men and women are pushed into the large cities. Urban centers become the magnet for other people, attracted by excitement, regular work hours, freedom, and the variety of occupations.

This society starts in Western Europe and the United States about the middle of the nineteenth centrury. It comes to an end during World War II with the dropping of the atomic bomb. During the nineteenth and twentieth centuries many changes occur: the dramatic migrations of millions; inventions for the economy and for personal use; the expansion of education for the masses; a communications and transportation revolution consisting of the car, the airplane, the radio, and television, and a mass consumption of news; a rising literacy; a decline of religion; changes of family life; the revolutions of thought influenced by Marx, Freud, and Darwin; and political revolutions.

Social class in the sense of consuming styles becomes an imponderable. In the United States, by the middle of the present century, the average middle-class family possessed the equivalent of 90 male servants in kilowatt power, using the muscular-energy standards of Conquest Society. Now, with energy, comes the need for blueprint readers, mass education, mass or market culture, secularism, transnational as well as internal mobility, growth of vast megalopolitan or supercommunities; a youth-centered, highly literate, restless, alienated, affluent, often lonely, television-glued, deep-frozen, and "other-directed" mass of humanity.

The suggested list of characteristics of feudal society can be matched roughly in converse by such terms as the following.

CONQUEST (GEMEINSCHAFT)	KILOWATT (GESELLSCHAFT)
Community	Society
Rural	Urban
Organic	Contractual
Simple	Complex
Preindustrial	Industrial

Homogeneous	Heterogeneous
Local oriented	Mass oriented
Religious	Secular
Superstitious	Scientific
Old-age centered	Youth centered
Stable	Changing

C. *Cogno Society.* The new human condition and the aesthetic condition inherent in Kilowatt Society are by no means seen or welcomed as a clear blessing. The issues they raise have come to the forefront since the close of World War II, a period here called the Cogno Society. Although the root of our term is *to know,* this is a paradox. It is a period of acquiring great knowledge and also of great doubting or reassessing. Discoveries in science reach to outer space, but moral foundations become weaker. Specialization in work and education requires synthesis. The strongest national powers find their safety through the United Nations. Many small, new nations seek their social and political directions. Men everywhere search for roots, seeking even why they should be seeking. . . . Thus the Cogno mentality is embarrassed with its material riches and moral debates. It has come to an earthly paradise and seeks the psychiatrist's couch to contemplate its incapacity. Thus it is a time for reconstruction and reordering.

It is a period comparable to the Renaissance, which lasted roughly from 1450 to 1600, and was a transition, from a period of medieval supernaturalism to one of modern science and thought. It was also a high point in the cultivation of the arts. Interpretations of the Renaissance differ, according to the historian Groethuysen,[24] "depending upon whether this epoch is more closely associated with the world of faith of the Middle Ages or with the scientifically grounded approach of modern times."

Our difficulty is that we are living in a time to which we are not privileged to apply hindsight. The difficulty is aggravated because, as Riesman notes, "serious discussion of the future is just what is missing in the United States: as our actual lifespans have lengthened, our timetables of the imagination have shrunk; we live now, think later."[25]

D. *Cultivated Society.* Cultivated Society will not begin at a given time. It will be an emergence of social and mental patterns as the questions raised above give way to systematic principles and policy in such fields as adult education, urban redevelopment, and political activity.

Kenneth E. Boulding attempts to describe what he calls "postcivilization" (following his categories of "precivilization," and our present "civilization"). He notes that until recently, only about 20 percent of all people could be spared "from food producing to build parthenons and cathedrals, to write literature and poetry, and to fight wars." [26] In the United States, we are almost at the point where 10 percent of the population can feed us all and produce surpluses, and fully 90 percent can be spared to produce "bathtubs, automobiles, hydrogen bombs, and all the other luxuries and conveniences of life." He foresees several varieties of postcivilization. Overall, it will be a worldwide society, having world styles in art, architecture, music, and other fields. It will be affluent, the proletariat will disappear, long life will be the rule, and other biological advances will be revolutionary. "Postcivilization," notes Boulding, "is a realization of man's potential; its credit balance is large. It gives us at least a chance of a modest utopia, in which slavery, poverty, exploitation, gross inequality, war, disease—prime costs of civilization—will fall to the vanishing point."

The presence of a vision as an integral component in the historical dimension is not merely to serve as a hope, nor even as a raw attempt at projection. Later discussions of this volume will have something to say about the "futurist" movement led by men such as Buckminster Fuller, Bertrand Jouvenel, Robert Jungkt, and Herman Kahn. The fact is that the visions that men have of tomorrow have some impact on the shape of the future. In leisure we may have a unique instrument toward furthering this end.

COMPARISON WITH DUMAZEDIER

I turn now to a comparison of the construct above with the definition of leisure used by Joffre Dumazedier. His pre-eminence in this field is undisputed. All of us presently in leisure studies look on him as the pioneer who has brought the field to a respectable status, inviting the active participation of UNESCO and the International Sociological Society. I can only pay my personal respects to a close friend and colleague by a frank comparison of his views and my own on the delineation of our common concern, "leisure."

Dumazedier's definition of leisure reads as follows.[27]

> Leisure is an activity—apart from the obligations of work, family, and society—to which the individual turns at will, for either relaxation, diversion, or broadening his experiences and his spontaneous social participation, the free exercise of his creative capacities.

Immediate parallels will be seen and some differences from my statement on page 26. Both statements emphasize the voluntary element
in leisure, one using the words "at will," the other, "self-determined."
While he separates leisure from obligations to "work, family and society," my view is that the relationships to family and society are not as
clear-cut as to be encompassed here. My preference for "activity-
experience" instead of "activity," although more awkward, is more
than (as I note earlier) to permit the possibility of "inner, unobservable,
or emotional results." The non-American reader rightly will interpret
my hope of moving the concept away from an "activist-" oriented
concept in my society, so much given to this emphasis. In addition, he
may not know that at present one of the new styles in educational
circles is to look for "behavioral objectives" in measuring learning; as
one who comes in part from the world of the arts, I have a visceral
feeling against judging the listener to Beethoven by more than his
unstated unacted inner response.

There is general agreement between the French scholar and myself
on the importance of designating substantive areas of leisure instead of
being content with processes or dynamics alone. Some differences exist
in this. He designates three "functions" of leisure. As Chapter 6 will
indicate, I use that word differently and prefer to refer to my listing as
areas or forms of leisure.

DUMAZEDIER: "FUNCTIONS"	KAPLAN: "FORMS"
Relaxation	—Recreation
Diversion	—Personal growth
Broadening his knowledge and spontaneous social participation	—Service for others

The French scholar writes of his first "function" that, "Relaxation
provides recovery from fatigue; leisure repairs the physical and nervous
damage wrought by the tensions of daily pressures, and particularly
pressures of the job." He refers to studies by P. R. Bize of Paris in which
85 percent of executives said they are overworked.

Entertainment is given as the second "function" of leisure, as "deliv-
erance from boredom." In a 1957 French study, this was by far the
largest reason given for leisure. Henri Lefebvre is cited for his analysis
of modern man's alienation and the need to break away from one's daily
atmosphere. "Escape" may serve as a compensation and, if realistic,
may lead not only to a change of place or style of life, but produce
an imaginary self, following the analysis of E.T.A. Hoffman and
Feador Dostoevski.

I agree with these functions and include both under the leisure form of recreation; the term was treated earlier in the chapter under the therapeutic approach.

When Dumazedier speaks of leisure as serving the function of "spontaneous social participation," he is speaking of full participation in "the family, the company, the union, the community, and all groups and classes." His book does not otherwise touch on what we refer to in the United States as voluntary action in the community, and the impression one gets—from many sources—is that such activity is far more developed here than abroad.

The major differences, then, between the conceptualization in the two volumes are the additional elements of leisure suggested here: "—as seen by participants," "—pleasant anticipation and recollection," "—the whole range of commitment and intensity," and "—characteristic norms and restraints."

In addition, there is some difference in our approach to work-leisure relationships. The question is appropriate with the changing nature of the economy and the growth of computerization: does "leisure" exist in the minds of persons (or in the collective judgment of the society) when there is or has been no tradition of work? This is more than a question of historical interest or of academic moment. Two highly relevant applications are, first, to the cybernated future, when many persons may be "free" from work for larger periods of their lifetime and, second, to the present position of the Negro in the United States, who (against his wish) is in that unhappy situation now.

In his article on leisure in the *International Encyclopedia of the Social Sciences*,[28] Dumazedier takes the position that leisure has certain traits that are characteristic only of the civilization born from the industrial revolution. In neither the primitive nor the agrarian society, he argues, was there leisure "in the modern sense." He notes that in both cases, work and rest, work and relaxation moved back and forth in a "natural rhythm." The sabbath belonged to religion, notes Dumazedier, but the ceremonial aspects and the energy invested in feast days were the "opposite" of normal life. Early eighteenth-century France, for instance, had 84 such holidays. Later, as among the elite of Greece, the gentry of many centuries later came to their idleness through their slaves, peasants, or servants. Although their nonwork activities contributed to the arts and other values of the mind, they had no true leisure, since "leisure" in the contemporary sense presupposed work.

The problem I would pose is whether the "work" had to be actually carried out by the men of "true" leisure or whether they could see and internalize the contrast by existing in a social context in which work is ever present, observable, and psychologically very much a part of their view of the order of things. Lorded gentlemen of the sixteenth century did not go from morning to night completely isolated from chores in and around the manors and castles—laundering, repairing, land cultivation, and food preparation—and they generally served as overseers of the peasants. Even accepting these status distinctions as a most natural state, they sought to justify their preferred position—usually with the arguments of God's will. In the reverse, the peasants were well aware of the kinds of leisure—such as sports, excursions to resorts, and arts— that were *not* a part of their lives, and of the folk arts and folk festivals that *were*. Indeed, the point of the *Fasching* in Germany was that the negation of social roles was the psychological negation of social classes, and hence, this annual festival served as a counterrevolutionary force for the society as well as a therapeutic factor for the person.

"In the modern sense," there is, to be sure, a new development and conceptualization of leisure; and Dumazedier's phrase is useful to denote that there is constant need to see that throughout history there have been *changes* in work, in education, in marriage, in religion, in statehood, in freedom, and in the arts. That all of these did exist *in the context of many social orders* can hardly be denied.

The *Encyclopedia* article imposes two "preconditions" for the society. First, argues the French scholar, leisure—to be "leisure"—must be the "unfettered responsibility of the individual," resulting from the ending of activities that are governed "by means of common ritual obligations." The whole matter of contemporary "mass culture" is here laid on the board. Much of what we do in our nonwork periods is hardly our "unfettered" responsibility; as consumers of mass media images we are as much nurtured and conditioned as Galbraith notes we are conditioned by buy cars, pills, or other industrial products. We can agree with Dumazedier that there is an ideal to be articulated in leisure—the ideal of true individuality—but the definition of the reality sets this ideal apart; the need now is for analysis that sets up strategies as well as goals, enabling us to move from recognition of the past and present, to the utilization of the strengths as focal points toward transformations.

The second condition for leisure to become possible, writes Dumazedier, is that work takes on arbitrary limits, "organized in so definite a fashion that it can easily be separated, both in theory and in practice, from his free time."

This may, I suggest, set up an impossible situation. The case of the professional person is a case in point. The leisure of the professor is often given to travel, to reading, and to good conversation. Yet, not unlike Plato himself, his conversation with friends may be on as high a level as with colleagues and students; he is always at "work," his work always contains "play" or "leisure" elements. The age of computerization is not an age when social institutions become more neatly definable, but more confused and undefinable in function and form.

There will be larger bulks of time, as in extended vacations and earlier retirement but, as this develops, the values formerly associated with work—commitment, identity, and usefulness—will hopefully become transplanted. We may therefore be headed, in our theorizing about leisure of the future, to minimize the term "work" and concentrate instead on "commitment."

This has further relevance to the American Negro. Many have *never* been employed, and many have never lived in a neighborhood or a home in which going to and returning from a job by fathers and friends was self-evident and built into the everyday reality of the growing child. Work values have little or no place in such ghettoized, unemployed centers of doing nothing. If, in fact, leisure has no meaning except as contrast to work values, then these young Negroes have neither.

With these qualifications in mind, which perhaps reflect the different cultures from which we come, Dumazedier and I are in complete agreement on what most counts—the desire to sensitize our social science colleagues and the society to the major issues that lie here under the seemingly undramatic term, leisure. As he writes on the first page of his major work:[29]

"Seen in the complex of its multiple relations to other aspects of our mechanized and democratic civilization, leisure is no longer a minor item, postscript to the major ones, to be studied or not, depending on whether there is time or money left. . . . Leisure is, on the contrary, the very central element in the *life*-culture of millions upon millions of workers. It has a deep-going, intricate relatedness to the largest questions of work, family, and politics, and these, therefore, must now be re-examined and reformulated. No theorizing about our basic social realities can be valid, in the mid-twentieth century, without consideration of the relevancy of leisure to them."

It is almost a decade since those words were written in France. They become truer with every new labor negotiation, every computer installation, every new retiree, every new examination of our industrial life in a call for *The Greening of America.*

PREFERENCE AMONG CONCEPTIONS OF LEISURE

The natural question comes to the mind of the reader: but where do I go from here? Now I know that there are various approaches, and you call them humanistic, therapeutic, quantitative, institutional, epistomological, and psycho-sociological. Which is the *best?* When someone asks you the simple question, what is leisure, what do you say?

One can ask a question in return: can you give me a simple, single definition of God, religion, education, life . . .? Any honest response will note, first, that in every case there are assumptions or *starting points* from which various traditions have developed for each of these terms. And the "definition" then becomes a technique or tool in the service of the purpose that is implicit in the assumption. Let us try a few examples.

1. Assume that my starting point is a belief that when man is free of the necessities of providing his maintenance needs, he should read, ponder, and hear Beethoven. It follows that leisure, to me, is the Hellenic quality that in the discussion of this chapter is called humanistic.
2. My starting point is that in one's free time one should exercise; from strengthening his body, he improves his mind and his attitudes toward everything else. Hence the conception that is most useful is the therapeutic; again, the definition *follows* the assumption.
3. Now my starting point is a need to know how many hours of TV time I have to get at you in selling my pills. Leisure, to me, is a quantity, an available segment free of work or other commitments that takes my customer from home.
4. I start with a belief that leisure is a beacon light that can be turned on the past, the present, or the future. Perhaps I am a historian, and I look at games as ongoing links with the past; or I am a science-fiction writer, and I see my books as a means to have you live in the future. The classification of "epistomology" is not a divine postulate to describe such a conception of leisure; but useful as our tool. The reader is completely free, and in the tradition of science, if he uses his own terminology as his tool.
5. Finally, the psycho-sociological construct is "best" if none of the preceding is inclusive enough. In this state of mind, I do not want a *simple* or *unitary* view of leisure. I want something that can move in several directions at once. This may spring from my position as a journalist, a teacher, a cultural philosopher, or a social scientist who needs a humanistic approach to all concepts.

There can be no doubt that life is not made simpler with this general reply. One may envy de Grazia's commitment to the Hellenic view. He

has his starting point and a long tradition behind it, and therefore a set
of criteria by which he can, and does, tell us that America has *no* leisure.
One envies our statistical colleagues, impatient of such discourse, who
require accuracy and measurability as the basis of their "knowledge,"
who can therefore tabulate time slots, and tell us that $x.y$ percent of
every 1440 minutes is spent by the villagers of country P in leisure
categories 1, 2, and 3.

Each approach is right—for its purpose. A definition is applicable
vis-a-vis something outside of the matter being defined. As to the individual who says, finally, *this* is my leisure, and I do not care what you
academics call it—he is right. The observer must draw clear lines: academic enterprise may, indeed (based on generalizations from many
observations), help the public, as in contributing to public policy by a
better planning of land use. But the fundamental point is never to be
lost: leisure to the participant, like his religion and his love, is what he
thinks it is, because on that kind of assumption he acts out his life.
Indeed, lest the point be lost, a part of Chapter 19 is devoted to The
Person, largely as a caution to counselors, friends, preachers, parents,
and teachers. Theory may prove to be useful to the Person, who is the
ultimate end of our purposes; it is designed as well to influence the
milieu and the designers of public policy whose decisions will provide
the alternative within which the person exercises his "free choice."

AN EPILOGUE ON DEFINITIONS

We think that definitions are difficult in social sciences, philosophy,
aesthetics, theology, and education. But they can be as difficult in the
hard sciences. Take biology, and the report by one of its leaders, Paul
Weiss.[30] He tells of the World Security Board's investigation of some
tapes that were discovered on Mars in the year 2064. When the language was decoded, a precise description came of the visits to the Earth
made a century earlier. The Martians did, indeed, find life on Earth.

"There were streaks of light like knotted ribbons. They seemed to move
in waves like knotted ribbons, mostly in one direction. From a still
closer view, the knots proved to be separate bodies; they moved indeed,
in spasms of alternating spurts and stalls. If life is motion, here was life.
Each luminous knot was obviously an individual organism. . . . Why they
should move in file and unison did not become clear to us until we came
in still closer and saw the cause. They were all positively phototactic,
attracted by a flickering light source."

These knots, continues the report, by their separate existence and
independence, revealed themselves as the "true elemental carriers of

life on Earth." The careful scientists from Mars did note "a pair of structures" in each unit of life; they were squirming, some sort of "wiggly endoparasites." The Earthians, like themselves, were shown to metabolize, eat, drink, groom, generate heat and light and sound, proliferate, and die: "and they, like us, vary in size and mood; in short, have individualities."

The "obligatory parasites"—the squirming, unimpressive bodies inside the Earthians—did at times, stray outside, but never far off or for long; even then, they showed "only extremely limited capacity for independent motion"; furthermore, since they made only an unstable two-point contact with the ground, they undoubtedly belong to a "degenerative class."

The report gives a name to the squirming degenerates, "Miruses," and goes into considerable length on the Earthians themselves: their intake of food through tubes; their forward brain, protected by a "huge operculum"; grooming by a swiping motion, but astonishingly, only in the front and, on occasion, two Earthians are "fiercely attracted to each other, embrace in a crushing hug, losing their shape, vitality—indeed, identity—in the encounter. They evidently gave up their individual existence for a higher union. . . ."

The reader may read further details in Weiss' complete report, which he ends with this commentary on the deluded Martians who could confuse cars with men. "Would we ever let ourselves be deluged by such glib contentions?" Would we not "exercise our native faculty for sober, balanced, critical, restrained, and undogmatic judgment? Would we?"

Chapter 3
Sixty Illustrative Propositions

RELATIONSHIPS BETWEEN COMPONENTS

The content and relationships of the 20 components in the model presented in Chapter 2 will constitute the remainder of this volume. However, a condensed methodological and substantive exercise will comprise the present chapter. Only one proposition—a broad assertion, not a formal hypothesis—will be posited between each component of Level I to each of the other three points of the same level before relating each of these to every other point. More concretely still, only one element within IA—*time*—will be our consistent illustration. *The volume will roam far beyond these 60 propositions, and even these are only cursorily discussed here.* These propositions are general observations, quite different in their intent from hypotheses. The latter would need to be presented in more rigorous, testable form.

RELATIONSHIPS WITHIN COMPONENTS OF LEISURE

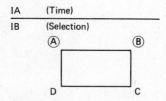

1. The amount of free time useful for some leisure choices is dependent on the arrangement of this time, especially in the difference between fragmentary and bulk time.

"Fragmentary" here refers to time that is of relatively short duration; "bulk" refers to extended time periods such as the end of the day, the week, the work year, or the lifetime. Any hour during retirement is surely different from a Sunday evening hour before one returns to work on Monday. The odd moments that are used to glance at a newspaper or to catch a newscast on the radio are fragmentary periods that constitute small leisure activities. A three-week vacation, on the other hand, demands different decisions and leads to different issues in analysis. The proposition simply asserts that a fishing trip requires a more consecutively extended time period than a glance at the newspaper.

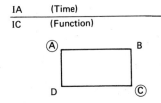

2. Specific time periods—such as seasons, days of the week, or hours of the day are often associated with characteristic leisure activities.

There is the old adage: he who drinks at 8 p.m. is a gentleman, he who drinks at 8 a.m. is an alcoholic; similarly, there are acceptable times for going to the theater or making love. An interesting change is now taking place in the desire for winter vacations by workers on salary; this may be partly a natural psychological urge, or it may for some be a breakthrough into an upper-class pattern.

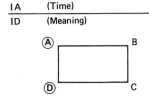

3. Time carries different images, meanings and associations at various stages in the life of a person as well as in various types of activities.

The first part of this proposition is illustrated in the following poem by Franz Werfel.[1]

> The nursling sleeps the night and day right through
> Time is to him as meadow-grass it were.
> Youth's sleep tips up the scales by adding to
> The waking hours which endlessly recur.
> The man, who futile problems must pursue
> Consumes eight hours in sleep, though he demur
> The aged rise betimes, refreshed anew
> By curtailed slumber rendered livelier.
> The westward slope of life has this relief:
> God lengthens time, as time becomes more brief.

In a felicitous comment on statistical techniques where comparable units of time are attributed to incomparable meanings of activity, Sebastian de Grazia notes:[2]

"Thus, by using a strictly quantitative assembly-line conception of time —time as a moving belt of equal units—one ignores the significance of much activity. A moment of awe in religion or ectasy in love or orgasm in intercourse, a decisive blow to an enemy, relief in a sneeze, or death in a fall is treated as equal to a moment of riding on a bus or shoveling coal or eating beans."

This presents one inescapable shortcoming of all statistical studies of the time studies of leisure, but the difficulty is shared in other statistical applications as well: no two robberies mean the same, the second divorce in the family is not "equal" to the first, and so on. And yet, such studies must be done, just as in the census count no two lives are the same, but it is useful to know the gross fact of how many people there are. The caution to be observed is that for purposes that should be concerned with attitudes and total contents, we are not content with mere numbers.

The matter of the meaning of leisure, aside from offering problems to the quantitative approach, leads to an issue as important as accuracy, and that is the problem of grasping the whole picture instead of the momentary phenomenon. The American television industry is guilty of shortcomings in this realization. While careful studies do go on of its listeners, the major decisions in programming every 13-week segment of offerings are made on highly abstracted snapshots of the single fact of how many persons watch a particular show.

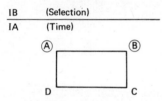

4. New aspirations in living and leisure have a significant impact on the amount of free time one wants.

Increased time is a result as well as a causal condition. It results partly from a need to have more time for the trip, the vacation, or the full day for a particular purpose. More and more the novelty of more time *qua* time will be replaced by the time that is allocated for conscious purposes.

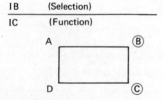

5. Selection in leisure is generally determined by a complex of purposes, and it is the configuration of such purposes that determines the use of a specific experience.

One may read a book for several reasons: for filling blank time; for information; for close study; for keeping up with others; or for enjoying a story. The manner in which the reading is done—speed, degree of concentration, in a room with others—varies from one occasion to another, depending on the priority or combination of purposes. Furthermore, as in the case of any group activity—a community orchestra, an athletic team—the primary function of the conductor or leader is to emphasize the levels, standards, and unity in terms of the art or sport, minimizing the individual motivations. A major principle of leadership emerges, as in the field of the performing arts: that the individual submotivations that led to this choice will usually be best fulfilled when the leader raises the primary collective purpose, such as creating music well.

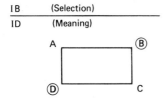

6. The original anticipation of meaning brought to a leisure experience may, under capable leadership, be modified toward more depth and personal growth.

Hence arises a major philosophical and educational issue among leaders and planners in recreational fields: the degree to which and the method by which a group is moved ahead. Much depends on conceptions brought to an activity by the participant. Four people in a bridge game may go beyond sociability or scores and absorb techniques during the evening; the same four players in a string quartet might consciously put their time toward musical growth.

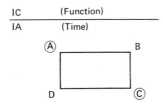

7 A general rule-of-thumb criterion for uses made of a leisure activity-experience is that success is correlated with paucity of time, failure with overabundance of time or boredom.

Time is not experienced in a social or psychological vacuum, but always in relation to a subjective association with attitudes or with objective awareness of action. The "long" wait for one's beloved illustrates the first; his rational knowledge that it will take her 30 minutes for the trip is the second. We know very little about either the sociology or psychology of time: much that we do know may be subject to change as expanding leisure becomes both a large objective and subjective reality. Wilensky's studies, noted under number 51 below, deals with "low leisure competence" of men without work or with short work weeks; they then "spend their time compulsively absorbing much of our least inspiring television as a time filler."

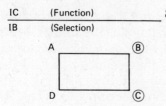

8. Like the child who learns to enjoy the water after he knows how to swim, many of us—in whatever the original situation that led us to it —use a leisure experience first and then assess the experience for subsequent decisions.

Howard S. Becker has concluded the truth of this in relation to marijuana.[3] We are reminded of Spencer's theory about one's emotion of happiness following his laughter. This verifies another notion, held by some, that the educator's criterion of success is the *exposure* he facilitates instead of the converts he counts.

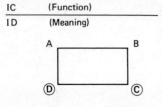

9. The nature of one's use of leisure experiences includes a variety of elements, such as use-length, time of day (week, month, year), exposure, companionship, sequence in relation to past and future experiences, required skills, and challenges; therefore the meanings that are associated with, or that derive from, a given experience also exist on many levels of analysis.

Implicit in this proposition is the difficulty, even the danger, of overly simple measurement of leisure meanings on behalf of accuracy. Above all, we must avoid the security of ascribing a single meaning to a leisure experience. Each category of experiences carries its own characteristic subtleties; witness the difficulty even in studying the meanings of a single activity—watching television—for persons belonging to different class or age levels.

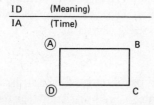

10. The overall meaning of time as a desirable value is increasing to the point where it overrides potential increase in income, goods, and comforts.

This conflict in relative affluence—time or income—is a new one for the common man in history. The growth of cybernation may—regardless of political philosophies—bring the industrial-capitalist order to a redistribution of energy and its resultant goods in some form of welfare state. The alternatives among types of goods will not be new: the balancing of time (especially the bulk time of weeks, months, or years) versus money, goods, or services has already arisen. Every worker who moonlights makes one choice, as opposed to the worker who extends his vacation at a financial loss, or who retires before he has to.

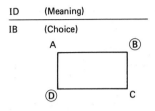

11. The meaning of a leisure activity is often assigned to the activity as such instead of to the consequence of the activity chosen.

Thus, in regard to television watching, the tendency is often to turn the set on, then to fish for a program that might be palatable. A grab-bag process takes place. Something of the sort takes place in going to a movie yet, since the commitment is far greater for the consumer, some care is taken in the choice, even as little as examining the photographs of the theater lobby. A similar process takes place when one decides (1) that he will go to evening school and (2) what courses he will take; or, when planning his vacation, he chooses in the order (1) that he will travel and (2) where he will go. The reverse would be to decide that he wants to study French and, therefore, he will attend evening school, or that he desires to visit the Vatican and will therefore have to travel on his vacation. It is like the bachelor who decides to marry and then finds the girl, as distinct from meeting the irresistible girl and deciding that to keep her he must marry. Each of us is affected by this difference; it would seem that part of the problem of education for discrimination in taste is to free ourselves of the activity-for-its-own-sake complex (opera, reading, etc.) and to select the activity more carefully (Don Giovanni, Gunther's *Twelve Cities*).

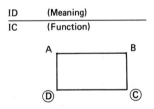

12. The major function of a leader in leisure activity is to insure that the participant uses the experience to obtain a maximum benefit that may go beyond the limited expectation or meaning he brought to it.

A major motivation in much leisure activity, especially when it is equated with "play," is "to have fun," to "enjoy" it, to find a "change." This is what is sometimes meant by those, like Louis Kronenberger, who insist that leisure must remain an end in itself. The question is whether this implies that enjoyment and fun are bars to experience of some depth. The string quartets with which I have played have increased their "pleasure" with a higher expenditure of effort directed toward levels of excellence. There can hardly be any question of this for amateur artistic activity. Again, the issue has special bearing on the matter of who affects the masses in "mass culture"; does the television industry fulfill its commitment to the use of public airways by mere entertainment, or can it be induced to entertain through programs of merit?

RELATIONSHIPS: LEISURE COMPONENTS TO LEVEL OF CLUSTERS

Again we experiment with relationships, in this case between the "time" element and the components of the clusters diagram.

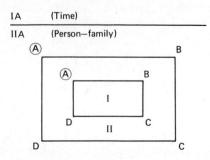

13. The increase of time for the worker has contributed to a less formal relationship among roles in the family, with leisure a more and more fundamental element of family style.

Work and functional roles, as they existed in the farm family, have given way to a colleagueship in consumption. Yet relationships built around functions recognizable to each other are comparatively simple; family life based on freedom, play, or leisure, requiring new attitudes and areas of personal growth, provides greater potentials for both common growth or for failure in communications.

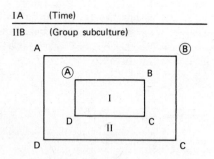

14. Time divisions of the week and the year have been essential characteristics of religious, generational, and other subcultural divisions, and therefore are related to leisure patterns of each.

Most important are the religious time structural distinctions of the Judiac, Christian, Mohammedan, and other Eastern religions. The Christmas season in Western culture is the peak of social activity for the year. School vacations of youth set them into special yearly cycles. One clue to the standarization that accompanies complexity is the erasure of such time lines.

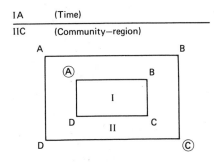

15. The new resource of time enlarges the concept of community and transposes it from a geographical to a psychological and cultural entity.

Almost no concept is undergoing such change as "community." The megalopolis subsumes what we have known as urban and rural into a pluralistic unit. The community as a producing unit under industrialism will become a *behavioral* unit under postindustrialism, in which nonwork activities—social, intellectual, artistic, and craft—will operate alongside the service and knowledge industries, with new functions and new space and time relationships.

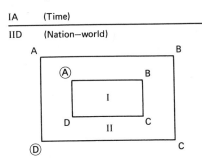

16. The unity of time and space are ultimately realized in the nation and the world as the increasingly normal scenes of action and knowledge.

The nation and the world come to us via the various media, and we go to once far-off places with new comfort and freedom from inhibitions formerly placed on us by limitations of time or affluence. Tourism will widen in its appeal, but the invention of significant tasks to provide for human dignity in the shadow of computerization will have to conceive of needs on a national and world scope.

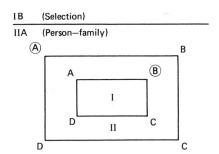

17. The choice of leisure activities inside or outside of the home provides a major clue to relationships between family members and is useful as one modality for affecting the roles and character of family life.

There is no single formula for successful family life, but leisure is so wide in its range of tastes, skills, costs, and fashions that one measureable standard is the balance or distribution between individual and group activity. The two most popular activities, travel and TV, lend themselves to either choice and use pattern. The change in family life based on greater freedom for children often centers on their new role in the determination of vacation and TV choices.

IB   (Selection)

IIB   (Group—subculture)

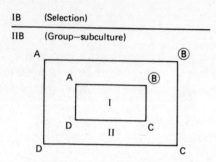

18. The choices of leisure that are heavily influenced by the sub-culture (religious, recial, teen-agers, retirees, etc.) are more deep-seated and permanent than those affected by social or friendship groups.

The unity of subcultures often derives from attitudes of outsiders as well as from internal values and are therefore grounded in historical as well as in social or psychological factors. The Negro is a case in point. His patterns, to the degree that they are identifiable, spring from his social positions. We may expect that as general discrimination lessens, there will be correspondingly less distinctions in his leisure life as well. Middle-class blacks are not substantially different from whites in this sphere, so that individual differences take over.

IB   (Selection)

IIC   (Community—region)

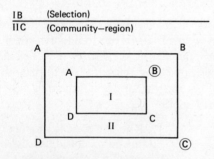

19. Since the first objective limitation on choice of leisure is the absence of alternatives, the major policy criterion of community and regional planning concerns the physical provision of opportunities for many tastes, skills, and interests.

This has become the central philosophy of progressive thinking in urban reconstruction—the pursuit of human renewal, thus implementing the concept of community as a way of life advocated in such writings as the Goodmans, Mumford, Jacobs, and Geddes, or illustrated in the greenbelt suburbs near London.

IB   (Selection)

IID   (Nation—world)

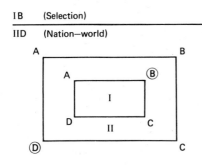

20. The extension of communications and transportation has moved the geography of leisure by mass media image and literal experience toward McCluhan's "world village."

What TV and travel fully mean is far from being understood. One is not sure that even the right questions are being asked. It is no mere coincidence that TV and computers both came into use in 1946, extending both our productive and consumptive worlds in revolutionary instead of evolutionary ways.

IC   (Function)

IIA   (Person—family)

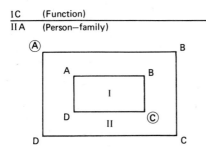

21. In societies such as the United States where work (even farming) is decreasingly passed along in family lines, leisure patterns become the primary heritage from one generation to the next.

It is too early now to tell whether the current "generation gap" will seriously change this situation. Youth of the seventh decade in this century are questioning all of our values but have not yet created any nonwork patterns unknown long ago. Withdrawal or group isolation has been the mark of the hippies, symbolized by their *Fasching-like* garb. The 1980s will reveal whether there are constructive elements in the situation.

IC   (Function)

IIB   (Group—subculture)

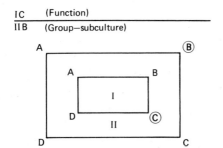

22. Leisure can be used as a social device to maintain and to nurture social and ideological pluralism as well as to provide an integrative or assimilative vehicle among subcultural groups.

The presence of large cities, literacy, quick communications and transportation, affluence, national crises such as wars—these tend to remove the pluralism that followed the dramatic migrations into the United States; the present black-white confrontations, youth protests, and the ethnic security of the third generation all accentuate, even idealize, a variety of values and traditions. The attractions of LSD and marijuana may be as much a symbolic attack on the Establishment as a realistic "trip."

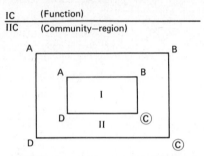

23. We may expect to see more use of leisure devoted to volunteer activity for significant tasks in the study of community and regional issues, accompanied by programs of transformation by various methods, in many cases as a full commitment of time.

With our conception of leisure as "covering the whole range of commitment and time," the civil rights movement, student protests, and other phenomena of the 1960s can be classified as leisure activities; this does not minimize the seriousness, dedication, or importance of such efforts. This country has always seen its professional educators, welfare workers, politicians, and arts promoters assisted materially by volunteers. It is a mistake to assume that these were largely upper-class women; such women were only more visible in surroundings strange to them, and their activities in "charity" roles still provide attractive society-page items. Volunteerism was built into the communities of immigrants from the late nineteenth century on, with services to families, community centers or settlement houses, considerable lodge activity, study groups, *turnvereins,* social affairs, and the like. Today's volunteerism is community or region based; its participants are more educated and want to be closer to decision making; all age groups are involved, including high school youth and retirees; and often they are playing for higher stakes in social change and power.

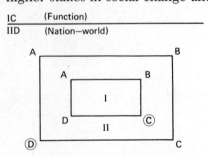

24. The standarization of goods, which has gone far in this country and abroad, tends to create similar standardizations in the use of time that is freed by the new industrial processes.

One writer speaks of the "standard menus, standard kitchens, standard furnture, standard decor, and so on, which springs not from Americanism but from the "method of production." "And so," he observes further, "the highly organized worker by day finds that even outside working hours he with thousands of others live and play in similarly designed dwelling houses and apartments, similarly arranged catering establishments, drinking houses, supermarkets and low-cost launderies; there is a sameness about his furnishings and theirs, his entertainment and theirs, his clothes and theirs, his holiday and theirs."[4]

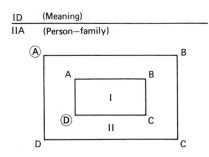

25. The concept of "togetherness" in leisure participation by all members of a family is often a gestural cliché that is challenged by the disparity in meanings that they bring to the same activity.

The disparity may extend to the interpretation that children attach to the actions of parents, such as the desire of the latter to "remain young," to "hang on" to their children, and to "compensate" for their own frustration in youth. Serious critism of Little League baseball by many laymen and professional leaders in recreation is precisely along these lines. There are, on the other hand, advantages of togetherness in leisure, such as acquaintanceship on a basis of companionship, the transmission of skills, or growth of honesty in relationships. Both sides of the coin can be observed on any family vacation trip.

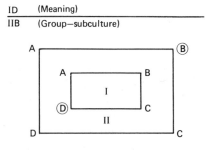

26. One large differentiation of leisure meanings among all cultures is related to social roles of men and women.

International studies, as we will see, agree that women continue with ongoing tasks in the home whether or not the women work and whether or not the husband retires. The change in the home by the introduction of vacuum cleaners and other devices has not reduced, but modified the commitments of the wife and mother.

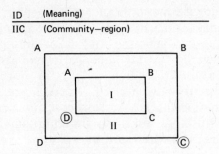

27. Those communities or regions in which leisure is a dominant tradition or characteristic are in the peculiarly unique position of having to broaden their concepts of leisure of prepare for the conditions of tomorrow.

California and Florida provide classic illustrations. Beaches, marinas, golf, sports, horse races, entertainment, and sun all have their place. These will continue to be their drawing powers, yet there is sufficient evidence that other elements will be necessary in the decades ahead: good schools, arts, libraries, adult education, volunteer opportunities, civic pride, and so on. Among the reasons for this is that businesses seeking new locations now must consider a balanced area for their employees; retirees, too, become more and more educated and demanding of their environment. As universities in hedonistic areas contribute a new dimension, aspirations for a rounded life become mature.

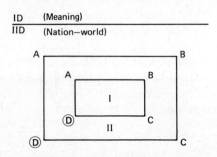

28. Contrary to the hopes of humanists, the meaning of the worldwide search for leisure seems to be the desire for "happiness" in materialistic terms.

This is not a happiness in the Aristotelian sense of *eudaemonia*, as a life of activity governed by reason. Instead, it is a desire, in both the developed and the developing countries, for a life of things, pleasures, opportunities for enjoying life. In a larger sense this is a universal search for freedom from toil, economic and political serfdom, poverty, disease, illiteracy, and war. Each type of society goes about this quest in its own way. One authority for the interpretation of *Proposition 28* is Georges Friedmann of Paris; similar readings of recent cultural trends will be seen in Erich Fromm, Lewis Mumford, Pitirim Sorokin, Jacques Ellul, and others.

RELATIONSHIPS: LEISURE COMPONENTS TO CULTURE LEVEL

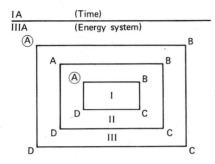

29. Leisure potential in relation to time distribution—as well as in amount—is markedly different within an energy system based on electronic than one based on former types of energy.

Electronic energy differs from energy derived from the use of muscle or machines geared to gasoline, coal, water, or other elements; computers, for example, can be located independently of such resources as water or sun and therefore open the way for a total reorganization of manpower that is needed for their operation. The door is wide open for experimentation in the reorganization of labor as a resource.

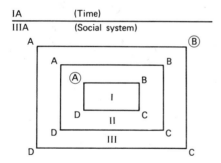

30. Time as a psychological element in leisure is geared closely to age roles, and its increase or redistribution could have tangible impact on the conception of such roles and their associated expectations of behavior.

If the reduction or redistribution of time in a cybernated culture makes the flexible life-style already mentioned more and more possible, then education will lose its association with youth, or retirement with old age; education and retirement will tend to become temporary choices instead of inflexible, ascribed behavior dictated by external forces.

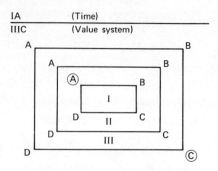

| IA | (Time) |
| IIIC | (Value system) |

31. The increase and redistribution of free time is, in itself, a sufficient factor to modify or bring into question familiar assumptions about the purposes of life, its aspirations and goals, and the stratification of the population into social classes as a manifestation of these patterns.

There are many complex factors that form and influence value systems in family, religion, or social class. Time as a factor in each is complicated by the causal relationship: a change in attitude toward work, for example, may lead to sufficient change in family life or a release from traditional theology, leading to freer appropriation of time for personal use.

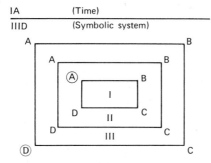

32. Since the amount and characteristic use of free time was long a symbol of class position, and these elements have taken a foothold among the masses, we may expect change, perhaps confusion, in such leisure dimensions as the arts and education.

This proposition takes us to the heart of "mass culture." The new accessibility to the arts and learning becomes a fact, but is challenged by those who question the ability of the masses to utilize their opportunities.

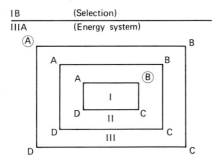

33. A significant race has developed between the speed at which the productive, industrial elements of our time have enlarged our leisure choices and the pervasiveness of parallel energy to capture those choices for profit making.

The home is one scene for this race, with mass media and time-saving gadgets as partisans. The argument can be made that the profit-making system was responsible for developing the wide distribution of both time-giving and time-consuming gadgets. Others hold that the same values—"scientism"—apply to a reliance or reverence for all gadgets; the inference is that a new kind of problem has developed for all of us in a self-balance of gadget absorption.

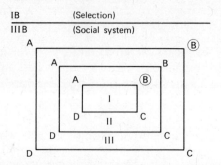

34. While, in past generations, the choice of leisure activities was largely affected by one's roles and position in the social system—as in class, family, religion, and so on—now the leisure pattern itself defines one's place in the social system.

Here is one of the most significant changes of the present century: instead of the activity serving as a symbol of position, it is now usually available on its own merits to the masses. The trip to Europe by a middle-class family is decided on for natural reasons, such as curiosity or education; or one plays golf because he enjoys it, whether or not other consequences follow. This freedom and naturalism in choice may well be judged in terms of honesty; historically, one might, with some justification, say that leisure choices are a sensitive clue to honesty of motivation and of person.

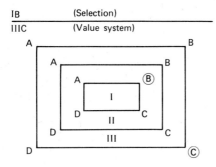

IB	(Selection)
IIIC	(Value system)

35. There is no objective or scientific judgment of values in leisure choices, so that all priorities by the participant or by the observer must reflect some external assumptions, whether consciously or not.

This statement reflects almost a century of scholarship in which social science freed itself from philosophy. There are, however, assumptions that, as Gunnar Myrdal tells us, the social scientist holds but cannot or does not admit.

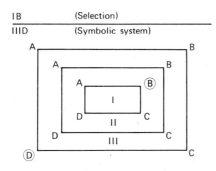

IB	(Selection)
IIID	(Symbolic system)

36. The selection of leisure within a symbolic system provides various dimensions or forms of reality, thus enlarging the modes or responding to or entering man's environment.

Play in all of its forms, as distinct from the work of most of us, offers a separate system of order, as Huizinga noted. The variety of symbolic systems is large, even among such activities as the physical, manual or practical, intellectual, artistic, and social. For example, the symbolism of return to nature that is contained in gardening provides a direct contrast to participation in a chamber music group with its symbols of urbanism; the first is related to religious beliefs and symbols of growth and good, the second, to aesthetic traditions and legends related to man's own creativity. The gradual release from work challenges man to the development of his imaginative qualities in a secular, urban, scientific milieu; his need for symbolic levels is greater, not less, as an antidote to the pragmatic philosophy that was essential in the building of a technical society.

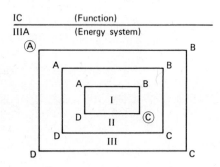

37. One major significance of the transformation from man power to machine power to cybernation is the availability to the common man of bulk time, resulting in significant differences of use.

This bulk-time—a long weekend, a vacation, a "sabbatical" from work, partial or full retirement—permits uses of activities that are substantially different from the momentary or limited to one evening. The different use is also psychological and emotional. Many persons need a week or more of relaxation to shed the tensions of normal life and work. More important, bulk time for the head of the household may be a contributing factor to reorganization of the school year for children as well as a new direction among adult educators in planning for *less* than the current term or semester, and for the recreation leader in planning for *more* than his current terminal activities.

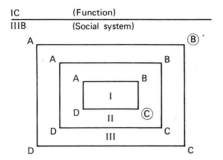

38. There is no doubt that the social system has direct effect on every component of the leisure process; a growing issue will be the impact of leisure, as a vehicle for value maintenance and change, on such aspects of the social system as family life, social class, and education.

Sociology has much to say on processes of social change. Leisure patterns as carriers of values have been studied on the whole in relation to the upper classes, especially by Veblen and the commentary thereupon. Where the masses are discussed, as in the rubrics "mass culture," "popular arts," and so forth, the analysis has been severely critical. A few—Max Lerner, Edward Shils, and Leo Lowenthal among them—have attempted a more balanced view. A far more difficult and neglected area is the attempt to interrelate all forms of leisure into a coherent theory.

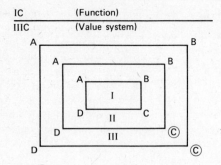

39. The uses of leisure are manifestations of special kinds of values inherent in the possibilities of leisure, not of all values.

Just as education has perhaps been ascribed more responsibility for shaping personal and collective values than it should have, so we must be cautious about setting too high an expectation for value-formation from the field of leisure. Activities such as observing nature, hearing music, or reading good literature may be more effective in *confirming* attitudes and values instead of in *changing* or *providing* them. The functions of leisure spelled out in Chapter 6 do, perhaps, point to the kinds of values that are most accessible through leisure.

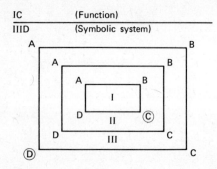

40. Each of the functions for leisure (movement-rest, freedom - discipline, play - entertainment, sociability - isolation, construction - distraction, self-growth-recreation) is the center of symbolic expression —metaphors, legends, maxims, proverbs, theater art, visualizations, and the like; these symbolic representations are sometimes the reality for participants, raising subtle issues about the selection as well as the meanings of leisure.

Among familiar examples are the injection of social class symbols (resorts, country clubs, fox hunting, etc.), church teachings (on dancing, gambling), and educational cliches ("the old cannot learn," etc.). There is no doubt that some go to opera to attain "respectability," others go to football games to attain "youth," and still others go to Florida to acquire "suntan."

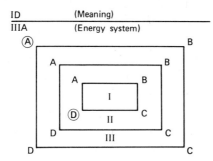

41. The major types of leisure meanings related to energy systems are those emanating from agricultural-industrial or rural contrasts.

In reference to the functions of leisure to be discussed in Chapter 6, four of the five pairs seen generally clear in their division:

PRIMARILY URBAN	PRIMARILY RURAL
Movement	Rest
Freedom	Discipline
Play	Entertainment
Sociability	Isolation

This must be viewed cautiously, and only in the broadest sense. If isolation is taken as somewhat synonymous with anonymity, the term could be applied as well or more accurately to the urban order.

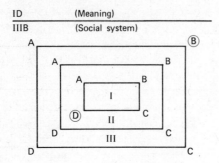

42. The crucial element within the social system for the development of a philosophy of meaning for the new leisure is education at all levels.

Education has the difficult assignment of passing on a cultural heritage at the same time that its curriculum is inherently a statement of the future; its students, at every level, are expected to look back and forward at the same time. The difference between traditional and progressive school systems lies less in the first than in the second, and there the issue is activism: to what degree should the school itself become an agent of transformation?

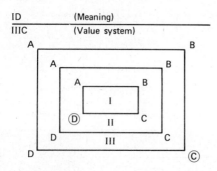

43. The meaning of leisure in a milieu of work values is that it has to have been earned or it is accompanied by feelings of guilt; there is reason to believe that a guilt-free leisure will require commitments parallel to those of work.

Such commitments will have to be enlarged far beyond the current level of community activity, even with the recent level of participation in civil rights, Vietnam protest, student activity, and the rest. Some experience with different rationales exists in federal work programs of the depression days. VISTA is a pale image of that experience in quantity, but with the more appropriate motivation. With church membership in the United States down to about 42 percent of the population, the work ethic finds its present roots in a secularist tradition of activism and building instead of in a theological position of salvation or manhood.

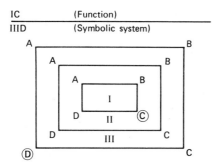

44. The obvious meaning of leisure experience, which is grounded in symbolism, is the fullest participation in those values; there is reason to believe that the rise of individualism is equal to or superceding those of conformism to symbols.

The general theory of mass society is that a visible conformity to symbolism of status or success, expressed in objects and possessions, is paralleled by conformity to ideas. This theory does not explain how the youth of today, raised on symbols of affluence, could have rejected those roots so radically. There are apparently the seeds of deviancy that, as in the case of other changes, proceed "one-hair-at-a-time" until the bare face of a new order has appeared. Furthermore, the technology of the future will feed any tendencies of individuals to go anywhere, study anything, and alternate work more freely with nonwork.

RELATIONSHIPS: LEISURE COMPONENTS TO SOCIAL ORDERS

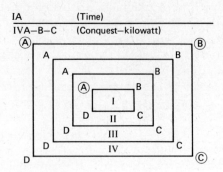

45-46-47.
Time in conquest-primitive societies is general, geared more to seasons than to seconds; conquest-feudal time is fundamentally geared to occasions and rituals; kilowatt time is specialized, narrow in its dimensions and structured by work.

These respective societies—in terms of time—are regulated by the stars, the priesthood, and the clock. The first lends itself to poetry, the second to authority, the last to time-slavery for the worker. The computer is neither tribesman, congregant, nor muscular slave; it is neutral, and always a machine, no matter how sophisticated or what its "generation." Thus we come to the final proposition on time at its most crucial as we look ahead.

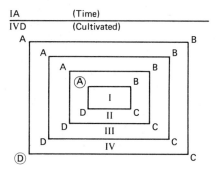

48. Since the emerging society will be characterized by computerization of many basic production processes, and the clock is less important for service and knowledge industries, time for the emerging society may revert to the primitive-poetic in its essential nature and purpose.

One factor is the continued elongation of life—as some predict—to an average age at death of over 90 before the end of the century. Another factor is the transformation of time away from the precision of the clock as the general loosening of time-bonds in work become less and as leisure grows. Third, and most striking, is that the postindustrial social structure literally takes on some major characteristics of life in the conquest eras, both primitive and preindustrial. These I will characterize as "fusions of institutions" in a later chapter. The essential point is not that the clock tells us time, but that the use of our time dictates our attitudes toward the clock. Leisure-time is 180 degrees different from work-time.

IB   (Selection)
IVA   (Conquest)

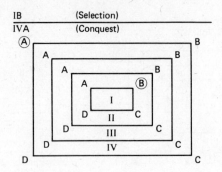

49. The choices of leisure in the conquest-primitive social order are limited in absolute terms by the absence of a material base, but they are relatively abundant by the fusion of institutions.

Our choices are seen within the perceptual frameworks of our own culture. For instance, Oscar Lewis demonstrated that economically poor Mexican groups develop their own patterns of social exchange, leading to a "culture of poverty" that is subtle and satisfying.[5]

IB   (Selection)
IVB   (Feudal)

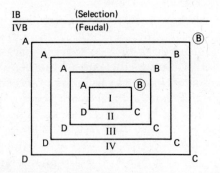

50. The choices of leisure interests and activities in a conquest-feudal order are dictated by the rigid class structure, with the leisure area serving to reaffirm social divisions; the broad accessibility of a middle class to such choices and symbols is as threatening to elites as the possession of property or political rights.

Leisure can be a major revolutionary force, a social control of great importance; among the earliest decrees by the Communists and Nazis were those over the arts. Desegregation rulings by the United States Supreme Court, which related to public parks, beaches, and lands, were very important, if less publicized than school rulings. As pointed out in Chapter 11, one of the basic characteristics of the United States in its leisure history is the absence of a feudal tradition.

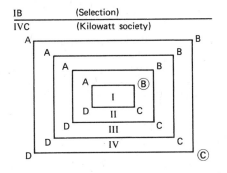

IB   (Selection)

IVC   (Kilowatt society)

51. Character types and alienation —as discussed by Riesman and Fromm in relation to industrial society—are made manifest in the selection of leisure activities.

Two problems seem to preoccupy many social critics of the contemporary scene: the way in which our society encourages various types of character and, conversely, how we respond to our technological era. Examples of the first are David Riesman's Inner, Other, and Autonomous persons; and W. I. Thomas' and Florian Znaniecki's Bohemian, Creative, and Philistine. The second is spelled out or implicit in Erich Fromm's approach to alienation or in generally comparable terms (such as anomie and rootlessness), or Pitirim Sorokin's sensate, as distinct from ideational. Wilensky relates alienation and use of leisure to the person's commitment to his work: those whose work is more demanding and interesting enjoy more diversified leisure, and are able to enjoy TV without being compulsive about it.

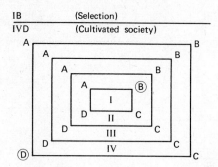

IB   (Selection)
IVD   (Cultivated society)

52. The direction of leisure choices in the future will vary from those of today more in the direction of depth and challenge instead of in variety.

Margaret Mead foresees greater pinpointing of commercial and public facilities toward special tastes and abilities. Her projection is suggested currently in the 60 percent or more of American homes with a color TV and a black and white TV; in the growth of the audience to the 217 educational TV stations; in more challenging family games that now can be purchased; in tours abroad aimed at such special interests as the arts, education, and religion.[6] Looking ahead, some observers see a renaissance of interest in handicraft goods.

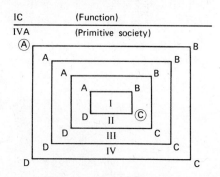

IC   (Function)
IVA   (Primitive society)

53. The useful lesson to be learned from conquest-primitive societies is that play—particularly in the arts—is an integral part of ongoing processes and institutional functions.

The analysis of integration among all processes of the society has been carried further by the late Pitirim Sorokin, eminent Harvard sociologist. His student, Kavolis, has extended the analysis of art. Graduate students looking for significant topics could profitably apply Sorokin's thesis to the largest of leisure issues.

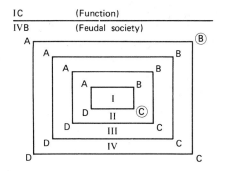

54. The lesson to be learned from the classbound leisure of the conquest-feudal society is the value of the creative minority in maintaining levels of excellence.

The value judgment that is expressed here has no reference to the economic and political servitude that gave time and wealth to the rich, nor to the power of the church. A major problem of democratic society is whether creativity becomes lost and levels of tastes are ignored without the patron class. Another current, related problem is the process of change by which influential "change-agents" affect the others. In feudal society the influential leisure-rulers were the rich and the noble, who also represented stability; at present, the centers of leadership are often in the middle-class pockets of the public, with less vested interests in the status quo, functioning in the midst of enormous social change.

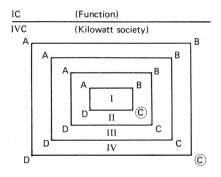

55. The lesson to be learned from kilowatt society is that the social and technical process that produces accessibility for the masses to all levels of taste also raises barriers to the maximum use of these opportunities.

Can the best of both worlds be attained: democratization and quality? De Tocqueville and many others hardly believe so, including de Grazia; Shils, Toffler, and others see the mass potential more favorably. Lerner is in the center, calling himself a "possibilist."

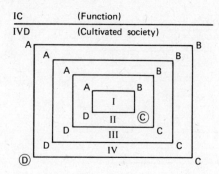

56. The uses of the future leisure can be applied to our present public policies.

One purpose of studying the future is to transform the present from a wider perspective. Examples come to mind: the need for more control by federal agencies over TV on matters such as public service; more planning for adult and family activity by the recreation profession; more commitment to economic support of the arts by private business and by government. In each example above, the opposite is actually developing. What business means by planning for the future is invariably about how to anticipate trends for profit purposes.

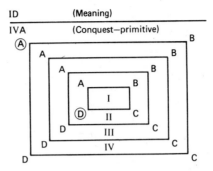

57. The general meaning of leisure to the conquest-primitive societies is a oneness with nature.

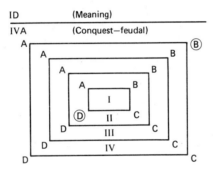

58. The general meaning of leisure to conquest-feudal societies is a symbol of hierarchy, with God at the epitome of power.

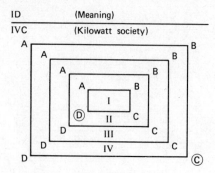

59. The general meaning of leisure in kilowatt societies is a transitional process of changing accessibility by the masses to opportunities and to power.

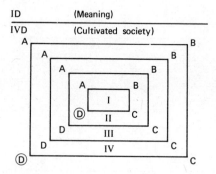

60. The meaning of leisure to cultivated society is the ideal of time that is freed by technology for its value as a source of knowledge.

The common theme that runs through numbers 57 to 60 is the relation of leisure to freedom. In feudal, religious periods, it was a freedom to serve God and church; conformity was at its highest in human history, and little was made of man's struggle to be an individual, to think for himself. The seeds were there, but the weights of custom, church, and community were against it. Industrial society turns man from both church and nature into building things and communities with a pragmatic, materialistic system of values, but literacy becomes vital to this process and leads not only to a middle class of teachers as well as small businessmen, but to a new stress on the individual. The desirable futuristic society, to the degree that it lies within our control, is ideally a construct that borrows on the contributions of the past: it seeks to recapture the oneness with nature, the discipline and sense of purpose, and the dynamic of constructive revolution; these it shapes into a synthesis to serve the new condition of man in the last decades of his present century and into the next.

I will have occasion to return to some of these propositions as the discussion now turns to each of these components. As we view them—conditions, selections, functions, and meanings—the intention is simply to sharpen the tools to enable us to look more deeply into the "society as a patient" and discern the degree to which this symptom—leisure—is a cause for concern.

PART 2
Components of the Model

Chapter 4

Conditions: Objective Aspects of the Individual Situation

The very first proposition of Chapter 3 touches on the amount of time which one has for leisure. This illustrates a conditioning factor, that is, something that is identifiable as generally external and that is distinguishable from internal factors such as "will," "judgment," "personality," "conscience," or "taste." The division is not always clear-cut; for instance, the choice of residence is an "external" factor that in itself may have direct bearing on the alternatives of activity from which one will choose. However, the external conditions are more generally beyond the person's control, and are therefore more objectively measurable. Mrs. Brown, who now lives in New York City, has Central Park available to her, which she did not have in Nashua; she *may* not walk in that park, but as long as she stayed in New Hampshire, she *could* not. We have a clearer statistical item in the second situation, and this is where we begin. The question of why she prefers to have coffee with her neighbor instead of strolling in the park is a more difficult problem and will be considered in the next chapter.

We will in this chapter consider seven external factors or conditions that may, in a given situation, affect the choice, use, and meaning of leisure: *age, sex, income, work, place of residence, education,* and *time.* Research relevant to each will be suggested only briefly. Other "conditions" are relevant to leisure, such as available space, nature of housing, health, and family situation.

AGE

Among all cultures, there is differentiation in what various groups are supposed to do, and specific rituals, confirmations, or *rites de passage* are employed to lend symbolic support to the transitions. In leisure, as well as in other institutions, age distinctions are drawn in our society.

89

These are based on three considerations: (1) accepted social roles, (2) skills and physical energy, and (3) customs or traditions.

Clear examples of social role are the association of childhood with "play" and of older persons with "retirement." The relationships of play and aging are confused in the theory of gerontology and not less so in education; in teacher training, for instance, there is very little attempt to tie youth and adulthood into an overall philosophy or theory. As a result, we know, from studies such as Piaget's, a great deal about the play of the child and its relation to his development; in gerontology, blocked by old clichés about a decline in the ability to learn, we have no comparable theory of play, growth, education, or leisure. Another illustration of social role and age is sex as a form of leisure. The norms of acceptable ages in this are undergoing change; we now know, for instance, that the sexual life of persons in their 60s and 70s can be active and satisfying.

As to skills, it is apparent that some leisure activities-experience require some kinds of skills that come with the years, such as music making or tournament chess. The element of talent, "bent," or genius applies to leisure and nonleisure situations alike; that is, the same skills are pertinent to play hockey whether the game is for professional or amateurs. The more important point is that custom or tradition still dictate the proper age for certain forms of leisure, so that young people are barred by law from some motion pictures and by social "habit" from playing serious bridge.

However, change is taking place among the generations here as in other areas of life. Now the student is seen to enter into more serious political and education concerns, and the elderly become freer to engage in many activities ranging from frivolous play to serious commitment. Mixtures of all generations are to be seen in VISTA and the Peace Corps. In a recent week-long auction to help maintain a community television station in Florida, the 3500 volunteers ranged from 13 to 72 years in age. Nevertheless, physical differences join custom in the association of age roles with activities; the main emphasis is on the modification of traditions that exaggerate the physical and minimize such factors as accumulated experience.

SEX

The male or female element is easily observed as a factor that influences, or explains, a considerable range of leisure behavior. In some cases—wrestling, football—the difference in biology may be the clue; entrance to lounges and clubs, or participation with the other sex in golf take us into custom and attitudes. The current Women's Liberation Front may open doors to equality in all leisure, as well as in work; already over the centuries there has been a considerable diminishing of sex divisions in the behavior patterns of sociability, games and sports, the arts, education, or volunteerism in the community. Many more men are raising funds for welfare purposes in their free hours, many more women go fishing with their husbands, and many more home gatherings see a mingling of men and women even after the meal is over.

The arts provide an interesting case in the history of the division of the sexes. There has always been the overwhelming proportion of men in the professional sphere of the performing arts because of such factors as the assigned roles of women in the home and the former difficulties of travel. Was it the contrast of arts from business and other "work"— a symbolic allegiance to the *yin* and *yang* of the Chinese? Was it the heritage of femininity and upper-class mannerisms with such arenas and symbols as the salon or the opera box? That such associations still exist is seen in the attitude of many male youths toward studying the ballet, in spite of the obvious athleticism which is required.

There is a considerable body of research on sex differentiation in leisure. One example is a correlation between numerous social factors, including sex, with theater attendance in the United States, England, France, Norway, Finland, Denmark, and Sweden over a 10-year period. Professor Herald Swedner, of the University of Lund in Sweden, concluded that

"women are more interested in the theatre . . . than men, but that the difference . . . for the frequency of theatre visits of men and women is rather small; men tend to go more often to the theatre in order to 'represent' in their capacity of being active in business life or because they are theatre professionals, theatre critics, theatre writers, etc. . . ."[1]

Swedner also concludes that women begin going to the theater regularly before the age of 20, somewhat earlier than men.

INCOME

Leisure activities range in cost from nothing to many thousands for the purchase and maintenance of a yacht, for heavy gambling, or for the Grand Tour. Yet, the trip around the word in "80 days" by a Jules Verne has been replaced by "80 payments" or less by almost anyone via the credit card. The American Express Card is harder to come by, but everyone, even against his desire, is tempted by Mastercharge or Bank-Americard. Thus the leisure phenomenon is no more the simple matter of what costs what, or who can afford what, but the matter of credit and one's style of life.

The definition of leisure, in part, as an agent for social status is closely related to the matter of income. The major symbols of wealth in past societies were, naturally, expensive. That was the major reason for their use, whether a fox hunt or a house in the mountains. But, one by one, these and other symbols of wealth became accessible to the new middle classes: cars, sports, special dress, travel, summer homes, vacations, the arts.

One upshot of these changes is that a contemporary discussion of leisure cannot follow Veblen's lead of "conspicuous leisure." Income is still needed to buy or to do certain things in one's leisure, but more and more the choice of free-to-expensive leisure is open to larger segments of the population; the judgment of motivations in such terms as class imitation is less and less useful. The style of life that any person chooses to pursue is far more within his control than it was half a century or more ago. Income thus becomes a highly subjective as well as an objective factor in these studies; as affluence grows, it becomes a manifestation of values instead of opportunity.

One critical segment of the American population in all of this is the Negro. To what degree do his patterns of life change toward the majority culture as his proportion of the nation's income goes up? He serves, unfortunately, as a constant reminder of the undeniable disparity of income in the United States. In his recent volume, *Rich Man, Poor Man,* Herman P. Miller, an economic statistician who heads the population division of the Bureau of the Census, notes this disparity:[2] the highest fifth of families, with incomes of over $13,500 per year, have over $4 of every $10 in national income; those who earn $23,000 or more per year, although only 5 of every 100 families, earn $14 of every $100 of the total. In contrast the lowest fifth of our families (under $4000) get only 5 percent of the total income.

One example of the correlation of income to leisure is found in total days per year that Americans of 12 years or older spend each year in outdoor camping. (Table 1)

There is a strict correlation here—the higher the income, the more camping days. Usually the matter does not come out in such a neat package.

WORK

Five major work factors immediately establish conditions for leisure: (1) the nature of the work itself; (2) the relation of this work to raw materi-

TABLE 1   **Work   93**

Days per year spent by Americans 12 years or older in outdoor activities, 1960

Income	Total Days per Person
Less than $3,000	18.5
$ 3,000– 4,999	33.5
$ 5,000– 5,999	33.3
$ 6,000– 7,999	40.5
$ 8,000– 9,999	42.4
$10,000– 14,999	44.2
$15,000 and over	49.7

Source Adapted from Table 7, ORRRC Report, *Outdoor Recreation for America,* U.S. Government Printing Office, 1962.

als and thus to possibilities of location; (3) the meaning of this work to others in the community; (4) the continuity or discontinuity of skills, habits, and values from work to nonwork life, and (5) the attitude toward work itself, as expressed in such terms as the "Puritan ethic."

1. There are over 600 official occupational groups with such obvious categories as farming, teaching, business, manufacturing, selling, preaching, printing, and tailoring. Each of these general types of work, as well as the unique circumstances *within* each plant, office, or school, provides an atmosphere from which the worker goes home with attitudes about himself and the world, with varying amounts of energy, with frustrations, hopes, disappointments, and relationships to his colleagues, car pools, janitors, formen, secretaries, bosses, customers, or policemen he passes on the way home. All this sets patterns of attitudes and moods. There are both direct and subtle influences from all of this that bear on whether the worker comes home to read, watch TV, argue with his mate, go out to the nearest bar, or just vegetate.

2. The location of the work—as on a farm, village, medium-sized community or metropolitan area—limits or opens various leisure possibilities such as museums, professional sports, or evening classes.

An example is provided by a newspaper story from Sudbury, Ontario, carried in the *New York Times* of October 23, 1966. The report notes the practical extinction of the storytelling that was common in sailing ships and in logging camps until the coming of radio. Reverend German Lemieux, director of an Institute of Folklore at the University of Sudbury catalogued 600 folktales, and he has on file over 3000 folk songs, in an attempt to preserve the past. He relates that in former days professional storytellers were often engaged to avoid boredom in the long and cold winters. The lumbermen, he reports, were largely illiterate: "They sat around in groups as large as 200 to listen to songs and stories and years later pass them on to their children and grandchildren without even writing them down."

A somewhat similar pattern of storytelling and reading took place earlier in this century in cigar factories before they became automatized, except that the readings, unlike the lumber camps, took place during work periods and included the reading of newspapers and novels.

3. The work—as physician, as professor, as drug store clerk—carries meanings to the community and the society, first, in the approximate income level that can be expected, second, in the social status that leads to types of friendships, access to various organizations, or invitations for civic participation.

4. Some occupations, such as teaching, have some built-in characteristics and values—in this case, reading or following world events—that provide an easy continuity to weekend, vacation, or retirement. Many businessmen have real problems in retirement, as do career military officers, largely because of the discontinuity or general uselessness of their professional skills and related values outside of the camp and store.

5. Perhaps most crucial is the prevalent attitude toward *work* itself. I noted this persistent attitude in a former discussion:[3]

"In work man has gone much further than mere sustenance: in it he has found the core of his life. Work in its largest perspective is closely tied in with his relation to family, to other persons, to nature, to objects, to movement, to concepts of God, and to the meaning of life itself. Its impact is on the state of his freedom and responsibility, his position in the esteem of others, his particular relation in the production of goods, his attitude toward government and authority, his mental capacities and achievements, his material level, his circle of acquaintanceships and friends, his concept of himself as a person, and his 'chances in life' or the chances of his mate and children. Hence it is folk wisdom at its best and not idle curiosity that asks of the stranger, 'And what do you do?' As one writer suggests, 'Work is not part of life, it is literally life itself.' "

Leaving the sphere of commonsense relationships between work and leisure, I turn to several examples of research on more subtle aspects of the matter. Professor Harold L. Wilensky of the University of California-Berkeley has taken the concept of "life-styles" and applied the term to lawyers, professors, and engineers, in special search of elements commonly ascribed to the "organization man."[4] These are men, Wilensky notes, who normally "play it safe, seek security, cultivate smooth human relations." Their roots in the community are shallow; friendships are transient, values are unstable, behavior is conformist. Various measures were taken of 490 men, comparing them on a scale of "other" or "inner" directedness. Differences were, indeed, found between engineers who are on higher echelons ("diversico") than those who are lower placed ("unico"), lawyers who work alone or who are members of firms, and professors from church-related schools as opposed to those connected with urban universities. Among "diversico" engineers, for example, there is a significant higher proportion who engage in community organization activities, have fluid friendships, and (like lawyers who work for firms) are more likely to be married to wives who are also active in the community. Wilensky refined his data to obtain a view of four hierarchial levels or social strata among his total of 1156 men and found a noticeable difference of "expedient conformists" among them.

Top level:	30%
Upper middle:	39%
Lower middle:	31%
Bottom:	20%

Wilensky found that the "organization men" among his professors, lawyers, and engineers were characterized by "ambition (persistent drive for income), cultural discontinuity (up or down in religion compared to mothers and in ethnicity through marriage), some work alienation, a medium social-economic status, and strong life-cycle squeeze." Blocks to conformity are found among Jews, secularists, and "professionals." Political conservatism is illustrated in "organization" engineers by a general sympathy among one in six for Senator Joseph McCarthy (even years after that period in American history), or by the fact that three of four engineers and over half of *lawyers* in firms "show little or no appreciation" of the Fifth Amendment in safe-guarding civil liberties.

As one might expect, the more organization-orientation, the more free time is used for programs of self-improvement related to the career. A strong religious component—as well as hyperpatriotism—is to be found; one is not surprised to find that of Wilensky's sample half of the church-university professors show intense commitment to religion; but *24 percent* of the diversico engineers (half of whom are strong to moderate Protestants) pray several times a day. Later in this volume Riesman's theory on the relation of leisure to other-directed persons is summarized; his observations seem to be generally applicable to Wilensky's results; Wilensky's own failure to extend his findings further into the implications for leisure is only a matter of detail. His contribution in the paper above is to help characterize several occupational groups and to become sensitive to variations of allegiance to the values of the higher echelons within each. Further material relevant to this issue of recognizing segments of the population will be found under the later discussion of groups and subcultures.

The research of Sally Hacker is based on the hypothesis that greater similarities of work and leisure exist when workers are "most satisfied with, committed to, active within, and skilled at the nature of their work. . . ." Her study covers 4000 young women teachers in 1964. Her data proved a more positive correlation to career commitment, with emphasis on expectations of the future instead of on immediate satisfactions.[5]

RESIDENCE

Place of residence may be a major condition in affecting types, uses, and meanings of leisure. The reasons for this are so elementary that only a brief mention is needed, in preparation for the fuller discussion of Chapter 10. Ten reasons quickly come to mind, among others.

1. The resources of nature, such as beaches, forests, mountains, and flatland.
2. The presence of man-made resources that compose an array of resources such as sports arenas, parks, riding paths, or playgrounds.
3. The nature of local public policy that might provide various opportunities (or, equally important, deny them): band concerts, community television, parades, community centers, adult education, or camps for children.
4. The presence (or absence) of such commercial opportunities as television, motion picture houses, horse races, or jai alai.
5. The unique social structure of a community—or its lack of structure—in terms of religious patterns, social class, or the quality of race relations.
6. Special historical traditions such as Fasching in communities along the Rhine or the tulip festival in Holland, Michigan.
7. The density of population with its resulting traffic conditions as one factor in whether to go to a picnic or visit friends.
8. The kinds of people in the area, community, neighborhood, or apartment complex: factors of safety, similar tastes, potential "playmates" for a game of bridge or a conversation.
9. General climate conditions.
10. Occupational and ecological structure of the area, such as farm situation, a slum, a suburb, and the like.

When all of these variables are extended, with all of their ramifications, we have left unanswered—granting the potential validity of each item above—the reasons for enormous *differences* in leisure practices *within* the area of residence. That is another question: a full description of the collective presence of such factors as listed above helps explain what the person *may be able to do,* and that is the rationale for isolating the external "conditions" of leisure. These lay a foundation for the presence of alternatives, but not necessarily their utilization.

EDUCATION

The importance of education as one of the influences on leisure is due to (1) the influence that education has on one's occupation, income, and status, and (2) its impact on style of life, taste, curiosity, sense of discrimination, and values.

Consider the first. It is necessary to break down the educational factor as it applies to various types of work. The differences in leisure patterns among lawyers, teachers, and doctors, for example, comes partly from the nature of the work and partly from the kinds of persons attracted to each. A crucial test is the phase in between—the students who are being trained on the college level. For instance, Ted K. Bradshaw of Berkeley correlated various subgroups of almost 8500 students in 189 colleges and universities and found decided differences in "where cultural life flourishes and where it starved."[6] The total proportion of students who rated "high" on the index of six items—attendance at concerts, plays, art gallery attendance, reading nonassigned books, and the like—was 12 percent. Yet putting students into a rank order by subject fields revealed the following scale in "cultural life": humanities studies, 25 percent; social science, 14 percent; physical science, 8 percent; education, 8 percent; engineering, 5 percent; business, 2 percent.

Apparently, not only are occupations characterized by their values, so also are students who are edging toward participation in these occupations. I have found in three decades of college teaching that occasionally the student, say in business, who somehow gets involved in humanistic values through his leisure (e.g., through the girl he dates) may leave his occupational field. Bradshaw finds that "students are often more cultural if they feel it is essential for their future to be original and creative, to live and work in the world of ideas, and to have freedom from supervision in their work."

We must therefore guard against gross comparisons in leisure practices between those with more and those with less education. Even limiting ourselves to formal college education, there are sharp differences.

However, leisure is a broader term than culture (as used by Bradshaw). The businessman and engineer, culture minded or not, will do far better economically than many others, and they will therefore have

TABLE 2
The amount of free time for men, 13-nation study (primary activities in hours)

	Educational Status			
	1	2	3	4
Poland (Torun)	4.6	4.6	5.1	4.9
U.S. (Jackson)	4.2	4.8	5.3	4.7
East Germany (Hoyerswerda)	4.2	4.5	5.0	5.1
Hungary (Gyor)	2.9	3.7	4.0	1.8[a]
Yugoslavia (Maribor)	3.0	3.6	4.5	5.3
USSR (Pskon)	4.0	4.5	5.2	5.0
Czechoslovakia (Olomonc)	3.3	4.5	4.9	5.2
West Germany (National)	3.7	4.5	4.6	5.4
Average	4.8	5.4	5.0	4.4

Code   1 — Illiterates or primary studies not completed.
      2 — Primary studies completed or secondary studies not completed.
      3 — Secondary studies completed or higher studies not completed.
      4 — Higher studies completed.
   [a] The result is not representative enough, since only three of those questioned had higher education.

a wide *potential* access to such leisure opportunities, which—because of their values—they may not choose to seize.

For a broad comparison of amounts of time that are open to leisure according to educational background, the 12-nation comparative research notes this result (Table 2).[7]

It is interesting that in the United States we find the largest time among high school graduates and also the most decline among college graduates.

A comparable study of women by the same international project indicates the following comparison of time among women (Table 3).

Here we see a decided reduction in the daily time spent on housework and a corresponding increase in free time among these women with higher education.

When specific activities are compared between women in groups 1 and 4, the preparation of food is reduced by 30 percent, and laundry and shopping time goes down by 50 percent.

There are several reasons for these results: more educated women, living under a higher standard of living, have more mechanical equipment; they have smaller families; men in educated families help their wives more than less-educated men; educated couples dine more often away from home; they are more aware of possible activities outside of the home.

TABLE 3
Domestic chores and educational status of working women in various countries

	Educational Status			
	1	2	3	4
Poland (Torun)	4.8	4.0	3.1	2.7
USSR (Pskon)	4.4	4.1	3.1	2.7
East Germany (Hoyerswerda)	4.7	4.8	4.2	3.8
West Germany (Osnabruck)	2.7[a]	4.2	3.0	2.0
U.S. (Jackson)	3.4	3.5	3.0	2.6
U.S. (National)	3.3	2.5	2.4	1.9
France (five cities)	3.8	3.3	2.9	2.5
Hungary (Gyor)	5.1	4.1	3.0	—[b]
Belgium (National)	3.6	3.8	2.5	2.2
Yugoslavia (Maribor)	4.8	4.9	4.0	3.5
Average	40.0	37.2	31.2	23.7

[a] This result was probably distorted by insufficient case numbers.
[b] Only one woman here has a higher education.

If an attempt is made to peel off these complex relationships and look at education *per se* as an influence, the task is more difficult. It would appear that the more educated person would be more aware of the alternatives, that is, he is not as likely to choose TV because there is nothing else to do in his home or community. It would appear that in relation to the activity itself, once chosen, he displays more "taste," and "sensitivity"—in his conversations, his response to pictures in the museum, to music in the concert hall, to his selection and understanding of reading materials. Finally, it would appear that the impact on the more educated person of leisure, whatever its nature, would produce a greater degree of growth, unfolding creativity, and "self-actualization."

"It would appear" has been my guarded qualifying phrase in all three regards. Clear evidence does not exist to support any of these hypotheses; social science has not yet demonstrated its ability to disentangle education from its related web of jobs, higher income, higher status, and urban life.

TIME

Time—physical, objective, chronological time, as well as subjective and psychological time—is the core issue of leisure as it pertains to projections for the future. A recent example is Kahn-Wiener's "scenario" of

1100 working hours per year (147 working days and 208 days free) for the postindustrial society. We are told by others that in the United States we have worked about 3 to 4 hours weekly less in each decade from the turn of the century. Thus, if we employ elementary techniques, we could project that by the end of the century we will average 12 hours less than that of the present 40-hour week, or 28 hours of work. Or if we add some flourishes for automation, a simple augmentation of additional free time could suggest the figures of 5, 6, and 7 per decade, taking us to a 22-hour week.

Yet these are overly simple procedures. We are told in recent studies that automation, while increasing our national product, need not result in either forced or voluntary disengagement from work. There may be, in fact, less displacement from work because of technological processes than some of us have assumed and, more important, such new time that results from new energy may be allocated by our own preference, in other ways than in leisure. I am inclined to agree with Dr. Emanuel Mesthene, of Harvard's program on technology and science, when he points out that the "first-order effect of technology is thus to multiply and diversify material possibilities and thereby offer new and altered opportunities to man."[8] Three types of "possibilities" that relate to time and projections will be suggested below: amount, content, and structure. Each will be discussed as an element of "time" that should engage the futurist, and possibilities within several will be noted.

Amount of Time

One approach to the future could be to take the figure of 1220 hours as the additional hours of nonworking time in the United States since 1890 and ask: if we kept the per capita income ($3181 in 1965) as a constant as our productive capacity goes up, what are the alternatives? Testifying before a Senate committee, Dr. Juanita Kreps, economist from Duke University, noted that we could then choose to drop the work week to 22 hours by 1985; or we could choose to work full time, but 27 weeks of the year; or, working a full day and week, we could retire at the age of 38. Another alternative would be to absorb about half the labor force in retraining programs; and another would be to pay the worker for full-time formal education. Still speaking of possible alternatives, Kreps writes:[9]

"Alternative allocations of leisure in the period 1980–85 might be as follows: given a $4,413 per capita GNP in 1980, achieved with a 37 ½ hour work week, a 48 week workyear, and providing retraining for 1 percent of the labor force, society could choose to retrain much more heavily (4.25 percent of the labor force per year) or, alternatively, could add 1½ weeks per year in vacation. In 1985, when per capita GNP should reach about $5,000, the choice could be between retraining almost 7 percent of the labor force annually or taking an additional 3 weeks of vacation. Obviously, other choices could be made, involving a further reduction in the workweek, a lowering of retirement age, or an increased educational span for those entering the labor force."

Whatever the choices we make of our enlarged technology, these observations seem fairly clear.

1. The alternatives suggested by Kreps will not be "across the board" but will be approached differently by various segments of the labor force, or even by major union groups.
2. We may expect, whatever the effect of automation on employment, that the total amount of nonwork time will move steadily upward; there may be a saturation point for the factor of boredom, but neither the Calvinist ethic nor fear of time could stop the American worker from moving easily into the four-day week, more legal holidays, longer vacations, and fewer hours. As more facilities are provided and as more experience is gained by individuals and families in using time—for whatever the level of "significance"—more time will be accepted and negotiated. One recent study to bolster this irrevocable trend (barring war or some other major interruption) was issued by the Southern California Research Council, a nonprofit group sponsored by business and educational agencies. Their stress was on the current absence of facilities such as libraries and artistic institutions; the well-known federal studies by the Outdoor Recreation Resources Review Commission a few years back came to about the same conclusion in its call for more parks and similar facilities as a means of meeting growing needs.

Content of Time

Projections of objective or physical measurements of time in the future available for nonwork are bound to be inaccurate—no matter how carefully drawn—without an understanding of the expansion of the hourly potential. The question is not how many minutes less we work now than we did a century ago, or tomorrow; instead, what are the constraints or possibilities of a given time unit? If we can travel further, communicate farther, be assured of better health, have the wide world brought to us by television, or have more literacy to read more journals, then in each case the "value" of the hour has gone up, just as, and for many of the same social or technological reasons, the value of the dollar has gone down. Indeed, almost a social law emerges of one increment at the expense of the other!

Now two sets of alternatives are apparent. When the dollar or the hour contracts, we must choose to rearrange what is left. That is the basis of Szalai's question of leisure in Hungary: as workers move to the cities and take more time to get to work, what do they eliminate? We all know the familiar question in reverse. If you had an unexpected month (or a large sum of money) to do with as you pleased, what would you do? What we confront in the next few decades, in all industrialized areas, is the possibility of the dual expansion: more nonwork hours and the expansion in possibilities for the use of each hour. de Grazia argues well that "free time" is not the same as "leisure," just as the recent Russian studies accept "leisure" as only one form of activity within the larger umbrella, "nonwork."

These distinctions are important to the futurist since, by the last two decades of the century, distinctions between work and nonwork may be quite diminished. Even if, in the United States, a maximum freeing from work by automation were to be envisioned, there is no end of jobs to be done, as in our current VISTA and Peace Corp programs, or in the reconstruction of our schools.

And even if—as may be predicted—the United States comes to some form of guaranteed annual income in place of the current hodgepodge of relief and welfare programs, there will always be jobs waiting to be done, even if not with the economic work structure we have long known. Being paid as an adult for a university education is one such illustration. Dennis Gabor has called for more inventing of new commitments. Freda Goldman, an American authority in adult education, has conceptualized new meaningful roles for workfree women.

Structure of Time

At the moment, studies seem to indicate that most workers, still at a loss in accommodating themselves or their families to long bulks of time—such as a conceivable half year at a time—would rather break up work and nonwork into short, consecutive periods such as the half week. In that event we may anticipate no major transformations in the social structure. It is when, and if, larger bulks become available and natural that the futurist must be aware of radical possibilities. We have the first alternative illustrated at present among the electrical workers of New York, whose contract calls for a 25-hour week with guarantee of 5 hours overtime; the second plan was chosen by the steel workers who, aside from other annual vacations, have negotiated a 13-week paid vacation ("sabbatical") every five years. Studies are now going on in the latter situation to see how the time is being used. There are factors that could bring more segments of the unionized work force to something like the steel plan, or even more daring, that is, a wider popularity for foreign travel, more flexible educational schedules for children, and the popularity of installment payments for extended vacations. If enough workers, say from a cold area, decide to live in a warm climate for months at a time, public policy would enter such matters as the taxing of the family for welfare services and education. Already we had a precedent in this country when federal funds were used during World War II to pay directly to local communities as industrial needs required sizable movements of workers. The present mobility and lack of land traditions in this country make such prospects easier to anticipate than in other countries.

In addition to the sound structuring in *time*—as in man's work patterns—there is the reverse: the time structure in man is radically altered by the mass media. The movies were pioneers in this regard, blending the past, present, and future, and television has both miniaturized and amplified this psychic impact in each of our homes. The futurist will find that both levels of time structure are crucial to his projections. The first runs into traditions of what is the rational social and economic order; the second will reopen a world of parapsychology and paracommunications which science fiction writers, so often, have already opened to the scholars of futurology.

Conditional Variables and Social Controls

The remaining task of this chapter is to illustrate some interrelationships of leisure conditions within a larger system of social controls. In a previous volume, I spelled out the outlines of the elements of social control as they pertain to our subject under the classification.[10]

Consensus and conformity:	("everyone is doing it")
Tradition:	("I've been doing this for a long time, and feel secure about it")
Representation:	("this moves me toward what I want to be as a person, and known as")
Hierarchy:	("my idols and heroes are doing this")
Knowledge:	("this will improve me as a person and in my job as librarian")
Exclusiveness:	("not everyone can buy this Airstream and travel")
Imposition:	("I don't have much choice, my wife got me into this")

In the former volume these were illustrated by activities in leisure. Here the problem is quite different: to relate these seven types of *controls* to the seven types of *conditions*. For instance, what conditions already spelled out earlier (age, time, income,) are most likely to be affected by the theme of consensus ("everyone is doing it")? The following observations are impressionistic but may lead others into concrete research. A charting of the interconnections sets our course.

	Age	Sex	Income	Work	Residence	Education	Time
Consensus	X^a	C^b					
Tradition	C	C	C	C	C		C
Representation			X	X		C	
Hierarchy	X	C					
Knowledge	C					X	
Exclusiveness			C		X		
Imposition	X	C					C

[a] X – Clear relation.
[b] C – Changing relation.

The chart should not imply that there is no relationship in the squares that have been left blank, such as Consensus-Income, or Knowledge—Sex. However, the squares marked X denote a decided relationship that is worth noting; those marked C note a changing relationship of importance.

CONSENSUS. There seems to exist an ongoing relationship with age, such as an association of the elderly with shuffleboard or of hopscotch with children. No matter what changes occur to eliminate some distinctions between generations, a total elimination is forever impossible, given the long dependence of the child among *homo sapiens.* It is on the convergence with sex that dramatic changes are taking place.

TRADITION. In no other area are social controls changing as rapidly. Education is the area of least change, as suggested in the chart; that is, the institution of education has created less difference in how its graduates respond to leisure changes.

REPRESENTATION. This subject will be considered in Chapter 15, under symbols. Generally, the amount of income and kind of work are probably most changed in their association with leisure choices since World War II. This is reflected in the changing nature of social class in the United States. Although the schools have not, as a whole, confronted leisure as a new social theme, the public has lessened the importance of educational background as a criterion or input into leisure choices.

HIERARCHY. Again, the control over children in their formative play years is the most crucial fact in the hierarchical structure of leisure. The subordination of women, expressed in various forms of informal segregation, is on the way out.

KNOWLEDGE. To the extent that formal knowledge remains critical to leisure selection, such as one's choice of reading, educational background is pertinent and will generally remain so. That this is less relevant to age differences is witnessed in the growing sophistication of children through images they pick up from television; familiarity with space science is one example.

EXCLUSIVENESS. The ongoing importance of place of residence on leisure exclusiveness is evident in the contrast of upper-middle suburban life with the inner city. Exclusiveness is more than the matter of attitudes, illustrated in the country club syndrome; the slum resident is excluded from various opportunities open to the rest of the community simply by the lack of transportation, or his financial access to it. This is one major reason that leisure—its absence *vis a vis* opportunity—is a problem among the poor.

IMPOSITION. Here the interesting change is in relation to time structure, as we have seen earlier in this chapter. No more do traditional time patterns serve to control the selection of leisure as completely as in the past. An even further dramatic change will follow the home recording of television programs, so that the public will not be confined by time schedules worked out in New York City. Again, on the matter of age, we see the relative imposition of adults on children; and certainly the change away from domination of one sex over the other in leisure is fading in family life, which is more and more based on companionship instead of authority or differences in function.

We have already, especially in the last section, begun to discern the dynamics of leisure selection. Now I turn explicitly to this topic. Its importance lies in the complementary issue of changing, or at least, affecting leisure choices—if, indeed, that is an issue at stake.

Chapter 5
Selections: External, Internal, and Mediating Factors

EXTERNAL FACTORS

In Chapter 4 we examined a set of "external" conditions that enter into choices of leisure: age, sex, income, education, work, residence, and time. Several broad observations will help to demonstrate how they function in the selection of leisure.

1. *None of these external factors, in themselves, can explain a specific leisure choice.* Each provides only one indicator of a larger situation. Take another obvious factor, which might be called the "cultural and historical content." When we know that 98 percent of all Americans have a television set, no great insight is needed to say that they live in a period of electronic development not available to their grandparents; we have then noted the accessibility to TV, especially if we add such factors as the income to purchase a set, the time to watch it, and the eyesight to enjoy it. Conditions help explain the availability of the potential choice, but standing alone, they fail to explain why other alternatives were not chosen: the same eyes can also watch sunsets and paintings, the income could be applied to an encyclopedia set, and the time could go to conversation.

Thus we cannot say, in any scientific sense, that Mr. Jones goes to concerts because he "likes music," to the horse races because he goes to "gamble," or the library to "get a book." These are all partial, because there are other ways of hearing music, getting books, or gambling.

2. *External conditions always operate in configurations relative to leisure choices, and the dominance or relationship of these interacting elements are best seen only in the specific situation.* Getting the book, in the case above, may have been affected by (a) the closeness of the library, (b) the fact that Mr. Jones can't afford to purchase books, (c) that he likes to chat with the pretty librarian, (d) that he meets his friends

in the library; and dozens of more subtle reasons, such as passing the pet shop along the way. Some years ago, I served as research director of the Milwaukee Public Forum, a large federal adult education program. We attempted all manner of statistical correlations to explain why audiences came: their education, the newspaper coverage of various topics, the reputation of our speakers, and so on. All were indicators, but the single most predictable factor turned out to be the weather, since this took place during the Depression and many of our "audience" were warmer at the meeting than at home!

3. *The external conditions of leisure without exception must be studied on the actual and the perceptual basis—as we see the reality and as the participant sees it.* Is one too "old" to study the piano? Is the library "too far"? Is she "too tired" to attend the party? Does television show an "excess" of violence? Age, distance, tiredness, and degree of violence are perceptions as well as facts.

4. *One external factor may be a condition for several types* of leisure activities-experiences, thus providing to them a coherence.

RELATED EXPERIENCES	COMMON EXTERNAL FACTOR
X Play with baby Y Drive family for a ride Z Attend P.T.A. meeting	Be a father
X Watch Yankees play Y Visit Statue of Liberty Z Hear Chinese music	Live In New York City

5. *A leisure activity-experience, although affected by external conditions, may itself serve as the external conditioning factor that develops a collective impact on nonleisure levels.* One example of this is the way in which the German *verein*, a prevalent grouping exclusively for leisure activity, has served in recent years to help foreign workers adjust. A second example is the way in which tourism may serve to "bring people together" in respect to international understanding on people-to-people levels.

INTERNAL FACTORS

Internal factors for leisure choices refers to "personality," "taste," "judgment," "will," "desire," or "need." The term "internal" is, of course, an oversimplification, as was "external." These are used only for relative emphasis. There is no need here to review the major psychological thrusts into this vast subject, familiar to the reader of these lines.

A good example of a limited but valuable psychological study was done of outdoor campers by Professor Burch of the Yale School of Forestry.[1] The two concepts he tests are the "compensatory" and "familiarity" hypotheses.

The first echoes the surplus energy theories of Freidrich Schiller and the catharsis play theory of Herbert Spencer. If the compensatory thesis applies to campers, we should expect to find that many of them come from the cities. The ORRRC studies had, indeed, found this to be the case, noting that rural residents are also more likely to seek the city for vacations. Burch's studies were carried on in the Three Sisters Wilderness Area of Oregon in 1966 and covered 740 family groups of campers who stayed in the area one or more nights. Not only was Burch interested in the home location (farm, rural, nonfarm, small town, large city, and suburb) but also in the camping "styles," that is, those who stayed in areas of easy access or auto camping (254 families), those who stayed only in remote areas (62) and those who used some combination (424). The results seem to be varied. Over 70 percent of the total campers were, at the time of the study, living in cities of 5000 or more but, when all the campers were divided as to where their childhood had been spent and how this correlates with "easy access," "remote," or "combination" style of camping, no clear distinctions could be made. On the other hand, Burch feels that his studies "would seem to add further support to the compensatory hypothesis"; but later, looking more closely at his data, he writes, "It would appear that regardless of how one considers it—present residence, childhood residence, and experience, or spatial mobility patterns—the compensatory hypothesis seems less relevant than the attraction of familiar activities and locations. Perhaps the familiarity hypothesis is the more plausible explanation."

Familiarity, or force of habit, as a propelling force in behavior, suggests that manual workers would be attracted to camping more than professional persons; professional workers would also prefer easy access camping. Quite the opposite seemed to come out of the study. The remote areas attracted 27.6 percent of professional and technical workers compared to 10.3 percent from among lower-manual workers and 17.2 percent from middle-manual workers. An example of the unexpected results, to Burch, was the finding that medical men are as much attracted to remote camp areas as foresters!

Personality Types

One relevant social-psychological tradition has been the development of profiles, types, or constructs of personality as a summary of past behavior and a projection of what may be expected.

An illustration of the use of the social role concept is a study of leisure and "life-style" by Havighurst and Feigenbaum, who sought to relate the leisure activity of 234 persons (aged 40 to 70) in Kansas City to their roles as parent, spouse, homemaker, worker, citizen, friends, and club or association member.[2] Life-style was defined as the characteristic way in which these roles are combined. One rating scale was devised to measure the person's competence in fulfilling each of his roles and another to represent general expectations for the role of "user of leisure time." The "significance" of his favorite activities was evaluated on the basis of many factors: autonomy, creativity, enjoyment, instrumentation or expressiveness, ego integration or role diffusion, vitality or apathy, expansion or constriction of interests, development of talent, relation or leisure to work, service or pleasure, status and prestige, new experience or repetition, relaxation, and gregariousness or solitude.

Life-styles were grouped into four categories.

1. "Community centered" (high performance in all roles).
2. "Home-centered high" (fall below group 1 in roles of friend, citizen, and club member).
3. "Home-centered medium" (family centered but lower than 2).
4. "Low level" (low scores on complexity, with more important family and work role performance).

The community-centered style of leisure, generally carried on in theaters, concerts, and clubs, was usually practiced by autonomous persons seeking novelty and looking for a goal beyond the activity itself. They fell into the upper-middle class.

The authors conclude that in the selection of activities "the personality, more than the situation, determines the life-style." One evidence for this is derived by taking a number of community and home-centered people, equating them for age and socioeconomic status, and discovering that location in the suburbs was not the determining factor.

A famous study relating personality types to leisure choice and use is David Riesman's *The Lonely Crowd*.[3] His major argument is well known.

"inner-direction and other-direction are abbreviated ways—to describe two not incompatible tendencies of which people are capable: one tendency is to find the source of direction in aims which one has held affectively before one from an early age; and another tendency is to find the source of direction in those among whom one is thrown at any given moment in one's career."[4]

Within this large view Riesman correlates his character types to leisure. The other-directed home expects little work from its children,
who need not brush and clean—"they are less efficient than a vacuum
cleaner." There are few younger siblings to watch over. The mother,
furthermore, uses her household "job," enabling her to escape the problem of leisure. Yet, in the actual use of leisure, the means sometimes
becomes the end, as in the case of suntanning. Turning to a favorite
theme of his, consumer orientation, Riesman notes that entertainment
provides this training; "the audience tends to become a group working
at its role as consumer." Leisure is thus an "adult education of consumers." This education, however, is not to escape from himself, since he
has a "clear core of self to escape from." Contradicting himself somewhat, Riesman then tells us that his person finds "no clear line between
production and consumption . . . between work and play."[5]

To the inner-directed person, the sphere of pleasure and consumption "is only a side show," more so for the man. Such a person need not
choose whether to work or play: matters are decided for him by tradition. However, this person does have a "core of sufficient self-reliance"
to afford a "certain kind of escape." Escape "upward" is accomplished
by becoming "cultivated," as in the arts; escape "downward" is accomplished as in cheap novels, races, and barbershop songs.

Throughout the volume, Riesman alludes to many aspects of leisure.
For example, in the search for autonomy, the other-directed man finds
leisure more useful than work to break some of the "institutional and
characterological barriers. . . ." as it becomes the sphere for developing
skills and values. Also, leisure has various functions in relations between
the races; it is under more "race control" than is work, as in the matter
of sociability. Middle-class Negroes are forbidden to like jazz "because
there are whites who patronize Negroes as the creators of jazz"; other
blacks are "compelled" to take pride in jazz, just as Jews are "required"
to take pride in Israel. "Play and sociability are then consumed in guilty
or anxious efforts to act in accordance with definitions of one's location
on the American scene, a location which, like a surviving superstition,
the individual cannot fully accept or dare fully to reject."

The Puritan wing of inner direction destroyed or subverted a "whole
historic spectrum of play, in short, art, idleness, and other ceremonial
escapes. . . ." Among the last—play, rituals—he points to enforced holidays such as Mother's Day, and the plethora of commercially invented
"Weeks." Both the private and the sociable aspects of play are needed
for the autonomous spirit, but both become difficult because of the
"privatizations we have inherited and the personalizations we have
newly elaborated."[6]

Play is of "basic human importance" in the achievement of autonomy. To the other-directed person, play may provide a "postgraduate
course" in *consumership,* not in the object consumed, but in the "inter-
nalized image" of the consumer, especially in the field of entertainment. *Craftsmanship* is a second acquisition from play, as in gardening,
music, and other hobbies. A third benefit is *taste exchanging,* with roots
in the "connoiseurship of the era dependent on inner-direction," but
has now become a social by-product of affluence and luxury; judgments
must be made very quickly, whether on movies, literature, or anything
else in which one is called on to be a critic.[7]

Riesman finally discusses "avocational counselors," including "travel
agents, hotel men, resort directors, sports teachers and coaches, teachers of the arts, including dancing teachers, and so on."[8] Others provide
leisure counseling indirectly, as in the case of interior decorator or
architects. Other counsellors have weakened their hold, such as magazines; few are as useful now as *The New Yorker.* He advocates a new
kind of institutional analysis of various occupational groups from this
point of view. Some of his suggestions for criteria are intriguing.

"While the automobile salesman might sometime disappear (Americans
know enough about cars not to need salesmen) the sporting-goods salesmen of fish flies and golf clubs might stay. No more is it a question of
whether to have avocational counselors; they are already here, we need
to produce better ones who might, in relation to the other-directed
man, stimulate, even provoke, such a person to more imaginative play
by helping him realize how very important for his own development
toward autonomy play is."[9]

Consensus and Tradition as Focus of Personality

A powerful factor in selection among alternatives of leisure is the force
of whatever is being done by others. Before this force—"everyone is
doing it"—women give way to fashions in dress and men to styles in
cars. All of us, as at Christmas and Easter, are subject to an overwhelming spirit or atmosphere; the consensus may be within a limited group,
such as a gang or a collection of youth, or a national event that embraces
us all. An example is drawn from Fasching in Germany, which embraces all ages and has deep historical roots.

The "karneval," *Fasching,* came from pre-Lenten festivities in which
the Catholic church absorbed the pagan ceremonies of masked dancers
driving out the devils of winter. During the Seven Years War there
developed an antimilitary, anti-Prussian movement among soldiers
who returned from King Frederick's army. Even today, as groups of

young and old in such cities as Mainz can be seen wandering the streets until about 3 A.M.—singing, shouting, drinking, kissing, joining hands— many are dressed in "uniforms" of the eighteenth century. But the *Fasching*—unlike the Mardi Gras in New Orleans or the Rose Parade in Pasadena—is more than a revival of a religious or seasonal affair. The Rhine karneval, in addition, served historically as a highly effective vehicle for social control and for nonrevolutionary expressiveness—all under the guise of hilarity.

For example, the Feast of Fools—a forerunner of *Fasching*—had provided more than a distraction; it served, in an artificial way, to permit choirboys to act out the role of priests, or for serfs to become lords.

But everyone knew that the normal relationship of roles would quietly be resumed after the festivals. Meanwhile the collective catharis had succeeded as a puritive and no doubt as a counterrevolutionary force. The contrast to our own ineffectiveness next to the applied mass psychology of the medieval church and rules is shown in the way that many universities and governmental agencies have attempted to prevent current demonstrations against the going order of things. I recall a statement made by the former U.S. Attorney General Ramsey Clark that the dissenters among youth need to be given the freedom to shout and protest or they will do so in the courtroom (he was referring to the "Chicago Seven" trial under Judge Hoffman). Freedom of speech in London's Hyde Park is another example in contrast to our own traditions. In the *Fasching,* even of our day, the tradition of Rhineland democracy (except for the Nazi period) has been kept alive with the use of floats and pantomimes about German politics and other current issues.

The revelry these days is as well organized behind the scenes by businessmen and civic leaders as our own Mardi Gras and, in a similar way, there is a distractive presence of social class with special balls for the invited elite with their own elaborate ceremonials. Even comparatively young societies imitate this phenomenon. Tampa, for instance, annually celebrates the "capture" of the city by a "pirate" who comes down the river with a decorated ship. It is a chance for high social circles to be children again, costume and all.

In all of these occasions—fairs, pagaents, historical celebrations, holidays—we have an episode in collective leisure for which a meaning exists in history, or is created. The population as a mass is involved. There is a blend of planned order and of spontaneity. The element of "pleasant expectation and recollection" is played on by the press in our own day for such occasions.

MEDIATING FACTORS

Only in the roughest sense can we speak of age, sex, income, type of work as "external" or of personality as "internal." It is a reasonable division if we see the person in respect to a physical area, say a beach. Then there was something that happened so that last Sunday this person, P, went to the beach, B, when he might have stayed home and read, R, gone to a dog race, DR, visited a sick friend, SF, or sorted his colored slides, CS.

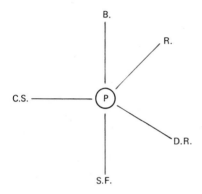

What "happened?" Perhaps one of several things, or a combination thereof.

1. He may have consciously thought about it; "I haven't gone swimming for a long time," or "I need the rest."
2. He may have "felt like it," for no rational reason but in a seemingly spontaneous mood.
3. He may have seen a television ad selling bathing suits, and the sight of the models was a factor.
4. He may have gone to the beach every Sunday of the summer; this visit was no exception.
5. The weather suddenly turned warm.
6. Just as he started to lie down at home, a friend called to suggest the beach.

These, and other "little" factors, when seen in the large perspective of national behavior, take on significant dimensions. For example, billions were spent in 1969 for advertising; a good portion of this was directed toward the leisure "market," the extent of which will be seen later.

Furthermore, the socio-psychological effort at explaining human behavior must turn to this mediating level to explain the endless differentiations within general categories of patterns: the place of friendship in the choice of a specific church or of a wife—among all the churches and all available women.

Dynamic I: External, Internal and Mediating Factors

The dynamics of these relationships between external, internal, and mediating factors is ideally seen in their relationship to real choices. We might take any single or aggregate of activities and question which of these three conditioning factors was foremost? It is immediately evident that some factors cut across *all* participants. Two such are time and space.

Time, as Kant noted in his *Critique of Pure Reason,* is the formal *a priori* condition of all phenomena.[10] Time has only one dimension; different times do not coexist but follow one another, just as different spaces do not follow one another but coexist. This insight applies with peculiar force to leisure activity-experience. The "space" may be in one's head, as he reads a book; for a football game the spatial "field" is several hundred yards, and for a trip abroad, several thousand miles. But reading, playing the game, or touring all necessitate *time.* The long book may actually consume more time than the journey abroad. However, *time is the only factor among those discussed earlier that permeates all considerations of leisure.* The nature of this universal permeation is twofold: (1) the time extension of the given activity-experience and, (2) the context within which *this* time finds itself *vis a vis* other activities of the person who is being studied. "Time-budget" studies, as we will see, are concerned with both aspects. The traditional manner in which official records of time expenditures are kept only succeed in giving us rough globs of comparisons. In Table 4, for example, the item "number of days per participant" gives us misleading clues. We see that the average person who took walks did so 15.2 days in 1965, compared with 5.5 for picnicking or 26.6 for riding his bicycle. The number of minutes for the average walk, picnic, or ride would have been more useful to the observer and made it more possible to develop hypotheses or meaningful observations on how the amount of time needed was tied in with the person's desires, or with such mediating factors as good weather, little auto traffic, or a Sunday for all the family to use together.

Thus the reader of the table above must be cautioned from assuming that the ranks, 1–25, mean anything as to preference. He should note that the choices 1, 2, and 3 (picnicking, driving for pleasure, and sight-

TABLE 4

Participation in selected outdoor activities—persons 12 years old and over: 1965

(Data pertain to the 1965 summer season only, with the exception of hunting and the three winter activities. The data for these activities are for the period September 1964 through May 1965. Based on a nationwide survey of outdoor recreation interests and participation of persons 12 years old and over, conducted by the Bureau of the Census, consisting of one sample involving approximately 7200 interviews)[11]

Outdoor Activity	Participants		Average Number of Days per Participant[a]	Number of Days of Participation, Total (Millions)
	Number (Millions)	Rank		
Picnicking	80.5	1	5.6	451
Driving for pleasure	77.7	2	12.1	940
Sightseeing	69.2	3	6.6	457
Swimming	67.8	4	14.3	970
Walking for pleasure	67.8	5	15.2	1031
Playing outdoor games and sports	53.7	6	17.3	929
Fishing	42.4	7	7.0	322
Attending outdoor sports events	42.4	8	5.8	246
Boating[b]	33.9	9	6.5	220
Bicycling	22.6	10	20.6	465
Nature walks	19.8	11	5.9	117
Sledding	18.4	12	(c)	(c)
Hunting	17.0	13	(c)	(c)
Attending outdoor concerts and plays	15.5	14	3.0	47
Camping	14.1	15	6.9	97
Ice skating	12.7	16	(c)	(c)
Horseback riding	11.3	17	6.8	77
Hiking	9.9	18	5.1	50
Water skiing	8.5	19	6.6	56
Bird watching	7.1	20	15.9	13
Snow skiing	5.7	21	(c)	(c)
Canoeing	4.2	22	4.5	19
Sailing	4.2	23	6.2	26
Wildlife and bird photography	2.8	24	5.9	17
Mountain climbing	1.4	25	3.1	4

Source   Department of the Interior, Bureau of Outdoor Recreation; *The 1965 Survey of Outdoor Recreation Activities, October 1967.*

[a] Data refer to number of days that individuals participated regardless of amount of time spent in participation.

[b] Other than canoeing and sailing.

[c] The 1965 survey did not measure activity days for ice skating, snow skiing, sledding, and hunting.

seeing) can all be done within the one day and almost at the same time. Even the activities listed as 4, 5, 6, and 7 are closely related in *both time and space;* only with number 8 do we come on something quite different. This means that the same mediating factors, such as a bulk of available time and land, a car, presence of water, and so forth, have to be present. To the boat manufacturer or maker of swimming suits this self-packaging of selections is useful in lowering his risk; and to the Department of Outdoor Recreation it is vital to know the rough relative demand within the vocabulary of outdoor possibilities.

However, we know that on the same clear Sundays on which some families picnic, sightsee, or take walks, others are moved by "internal" (Riesman: inner) factors to engage in other forms of leisure, as Table 5 tells us.

Note that the total expenditures in 1940 were $71 millions for theater, opera, music, and indoor entertainment, compared to $98 millions for spectator sports. The first were 42 percent of the second, but by 1970, these were reversed: spectator sports were 70 percent of the concerts, theaters, and entertainment. One could hardly infer that over the 30-year interval the conditions had been much affected. Age has had little to do with the reversal; as to sex, as women are more addicted to sports than they were in the past, men are more at home in the theater and in the concert hall, with no pronounced shift in the total; the cost of theater versus the football game is not a decisive matter; shorter workweeks or workdays have little bearing on the choice; and the Sunday afternoon concert, theater performance, or football game take about the same time. As to the mediating factor of advertising and public relations, sports would seem to have gained more in the past quarter century.

The major factor that remains, therefore, is the internal one of taste, attitude, changing milieu, or other elements that are equally difficult to isolate or weigh in their impact.

Another serious difficulty as we seek to apply the trio of selection factors arises when expenditures are related to actual use or to projected use; note, in Table 5, that the expenditures for flowers, seeds, and potted plants went up from $201 to $1436 millions from 1940 to 1970, or in a proportion of 1 to 7; books and maps went up from $234 to $3441 millions, for an increase of almost 15 times. There is no way of knowing that every seed was planted, but there is a fair certainty that not every book purchased was finished or even started. As de Grazia has well noted, "Expenditures may reflect an intention to spend free time but not its actual spending."[13] In the case of leisure intended but unfulfilled, we may have cases of visible objects (such as tennis racquet, boats, or

TABLE 5 Personal consumption expenditures for recreation: 1940–1971.

(In millions of dollars. Prior to 1960, excludes Alaska and Hawaii. Represents market value of purchases of goods and services by individuals and non-profit institutions. See also *Historical Statistics, Colonial Times to 1957*, series (500–515)[12]

Type of Product or Service	1940	1945	1950	1955	1960	1965	1966	1967	1968	1969	1970	1971
Total recreation expenditures	3,761	6,139	11,147	14,078	18,195	26,298	28,859	30,903	33,552	36,901	40,197	42,511
Books and maps	234	520	674	867	1,304	2,061	2,365	2,670	2,669	3,130	3,400	3,710
Magazines, newspapers, and sheet music	589	965	1,495	1,869	2,193	2,868	3,059	3,217	3,413	3,846	4,159	4,520
Nondurable toys and sport supplies	306	553	1,394	1,803	2,417	3,436	3,743	3,993	4,700	5,311	5,828	6,121
Wheel goods, durable toys, sports equipment, boats, and pleasure aircraft	254	400	809	1,386	2,106	2,933	3,248	3,481	4,012	4,517	4,846	5,105
Radio and television receivers, records, and musical instruments	494	344	2,421	2,869	3,412	6,013	6,905	7,409	7,852	8,274	9,292	9,743
Radio and television repair	32	88	283	516	801	1,032	1,072	1,143	1,227	1,266	1,312	1,392
Flowers, seeds, and potted plants	201	378	457	546	641	933	1,078	1,113	1,234	1,407	1,510	1,598
Admissions to specified spectator amusements	904	1,714	1,781	1,801	1,006	1,811	1,923	2,027	2,130	2,262	2,419	2,484
Motion picture theaters	735	1,450	1,376	1,326	951	927	964	989	1,045	1,099	1,162	1,214
Legitimate theaters and opera, and entertainments of nonprofit institutions (except athletics)	71	148	183	245	365	495	545	605	632	676	735	733
Spectator sports	98	116	222	230	290	389	414	433	453	487	516	537
Clubs and fraternal organizations[a]	203	281	462	569	733	879	934	988	1,049	1,112	1,158	1,179
Commercial participant amusements[b]	197	284	448	584	1,161	1,509	1,555	1,610	1,675	1,733	1,819	
Parimutuel net receipts	55	153	239	381	517	734	765	795	861	952	1,018	1,044
Other[c]	292	459	624	887	1,401	2,039	2,203	2,457	2,730	3,101	3,418	3,680

Source Department of Commerce, Office of Business Economics: *The National Income and Product Accounts of the United States, 1959–1965*, and *Survey of Current Business, July 1969.*

[a]Gross receipts less cash benefits of fraternal, patriotic, and women's organizations except insurance; and dues and fees of athletic, social, and luncheon clubs, and school fraternities.

[b]Billiard parlors; bowling alleys; dancing, riding, shooting, skating, and swimming places; amusement devices and parks; daily fee golf greens fees; golf instruction, club rental, and caddy fees; sightseeing buses and guides; and private flying operations.

[c]Photo developing and printing, photographic studios, collectors' net acquisitions of stamps and coins, hunting dog purchase and training, sports guide service, veterinary service, purchase of pets, camp fees, nonvending coin machine receipts minus payoff, and other commercial amusements.

books), which are bought largely to be seen; aside from the presence of symbolic intentions, of course, some objective condition may develop, such as ill health.

These difficulties in analysis do not obviate the need to isolate the internal, external and mediating factors. All three dimensions are combined in the example below.

Among the most enjoyable memories I have of Boston were the "Teleman-Vivaldi" evenings of chamber music with Henry and Ruth Littleboy. Their old home with its basement kitchen is in one of the colorful alleys up the hill from Charles Street, a few yards off Pinckney. Some of the musicians were far more capable than others, but Henry, himself a violinist of enormous enthusiasm—more of that than ability, he would admit—would rotate the violinists, so that everyone had a chance to play leading parts. Wives or friends might be sitting in the adjoining room to listen, but it did not matter whether or not there was an audience. This was an evening for amateurism, reading old music and then chatting downstairs in the basement kitchen.

The sociability could have been removed; we could have played, said goodnight, and gone home. It would then have been a little different evening for all of us. Baroque music—that is something else! Here was the core, the flavor, the charm. How often does one, these days, get a chance to play a Bach Brandenburg Concerto, or a string symphony of Geminiani or Corelli? Here we moved into the past, especially with the presence of the small harpsichord. It was a direct link between those of us, playing in a small room in Boston in 1966, with those who might have been playing in Mannheim or Leipzig or London in 1666 exactly the same pieces, with the same instruments, producing about the same sounds, followed with similar conversation.

But those who played this music in 1666 would surely have been men and women of the upper classes; none of us, two centuries later, were nobles or aristocrats. On Monday morning we would all be back in our respective jobs.

Consider our host. Henry is a researcher in the science of hearing for the Massachusetts General Hospital, a short walk down the hill. Hearing and the invention and use of intricate laboratory equipment are a constant preoccupation with him. About a decade ago Henry adopted the hobby of repairing violins. It was a natural extension of his work and his musical interest. He went to New York to work with master violin makers, read everything he found, and set up a workshop in the ground floor of his home. Little by little he demonstrated to his friends that he had the skills, until by the time I met him it was at the suggestion of the concert artist, Roman Totenberg, who had entrusted his Strad to this amateur. He "makes his living" as a scientist in the hospital, but the fiddle repairing is done at the hours he chooses, for persons he chooses (usually recommended to him by friends), and at his own pace. When Henry did a major job on my violin, for only a few dollars, he explained that this low price was to him the symbol of his purpose and amateur standing.

This was an "activity," subject to various sorts of quantification: for example, for a quartette of participants about 16 hours of time was consumed, doubled if our wives were there. The "controls" were of a special type, and very rigid, based on a notation system in which Bach, long deceased, was still telling us—not advising, but ordering—precisely how long to hold every note, at what pitch, and in what total balance *vis à vis* other instruments. We had not sought art as a leisure form to escape discipline but to seek a higher order of freedom of expression *within* a system of aesthetic order, highly disciplined. Was it a therapeutic evening? I suspect so, without wanting to grant that any of us needed "therapy" but, since this was Boston, let Freudians enjoy this interpretation. Finally, as a "construct," our leisure had elements that could easily be removed from Beacon Hill and applied to the acoustician of the General Hospital; in both cases, one could isolate the element of seriousness and skill; we "worked" on the Brandenburg with surely as much concentration as most jobs require of paid workers.

The objective or external factors in partial explanation of our Sunday evening choice were apparent: we all lived in the Boston area, we all know Henry, we were physically well, we could afford a musical instrument, we all had our instruments, and so on. On the other end of the continuum, we were all examples, no doubt, of Riesman's "inner" type, and the consensus we had in common was that composers such as T and V and B had something to say.

Finally, the mediating factors were both negative and positive: there was no winter snowstorm, which can play havoc with the playing of music on slippery Beacon Hill; there was an invitation by our hosts that had come a few days earlier by telephone (a utility not enjoyed by our counterparts of history).

Fortunately, none of us went through this process of sociological self-analysis; we got the call, packed the instrument, hunted for a place to park, and the evening proceeded.

Dynamic II: Expenditure for leisure

Another major mediating factor that may bring the external and internal factors of leisure selection into some focus is the economics of the situation.

First, we look at some across-the-board expenditures to see where "recreation" falls in relation to other expenditures. Table 6 is a total report of personal consumption expenditures from 1950 to 1970 by percentages.

TABLE 6

Personal consumption expenditures by products 1950 to 1970 by percentages[14]

Types of Products	1950	1955	1960	1965	1970
Food, beverages, tobacco	30.4	28.4	26.9	24.8	23.2
Clothing, accessories, jewelry	12.4	11.0	10.2	10.0	10.1
Personal care	1.3	1.4	1.6	1.8	1.6
Housing	11.1	13.3	14.2	14.7	14.8
Household operations	15.4	14.7	14.4	14.3	13.9
Medical care expenses	4.6	5.0	5.9	6.5	7.7
Personal business	3.6	4.0	4.6	5.1	5.8
Transportation	12.9	14.0	13.3	13.4	12.6
Recreation	5.8	5.5	5.6	6.1	6.3
Other	2.3	2.8	3.3	3.5	3.9

From this we note the following differences in the proportion of expenditures for the major items during the 18-year period from 1950 to 1968.

Food, beverages, and tobacco:	down 7.2 percent
Clothing, accessories and jewelry:	down 2.3 percent
Personal care:	up 0.3 percent
Housing:	up 3.7 percent
Household operations:	down 1.5 percent
Medical care expenses:	up 3.1 percent
Personal business:	up 2.2 percent
Transportation:	down 0.3 percent
Recreation:	up 0.5 percent

Indeed, if we go back to the turn of the century, the decreasing proportion of family expenditure for food and other basic needs from that time forward is evident. Chart 6 makes this trend visible.[15]

In Chart 7, in a more detailed view of expenditures, note that for recreation (6.3 percent) is just about in the middle of the categories from the least (foreign travel, 0.7 percent) to food and beverages (21.0 percent). Personal income totaled $747 billion in 1969. Over three-fourths was spent for personal consumption of goods and services.

The reader will immediately want to ask about the change in the value of the dollar during that time. Taking the purchasing power of the dollar from 1957 to 1959 as a base (the criterion used by the Bureau of

Chart 6

Allocation of total expenditures of urban families in the United States, 1901–1969

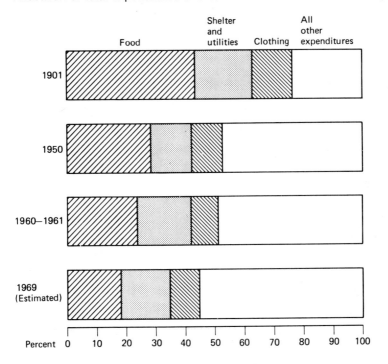

Labor Statistics), the actual value of the dollar to the consumer in 1950 was about $1.60; by 1969 it had gone down to 82.5 cents. But, of course, this constant inflation applied to all purchases, to food as well as to theater tickets. Obviously, prices went up more in some areas of life than in others; publicly owned transportation, as in New York City, held its subway price down for years, amounting to a subsidy to riders for everyone through taxes; the arts could not raise ticket prices to meet rising labor costs, they had few subsidies, they were unable to beg enough from the rich, and they are therefore in deep economic trouble now.

There is, moreover, a basic economic difference between purchases for recreation and for some other items that raises additional questions of interpretation. This is the difference between capital investment and terminal expenditures. When one goes to a motion picture he spends about two hours of his time. At the current average pay for the American worker, $3.04 per hour, and with the average ticket cost at $1.61, he has worked 32 minutes to pay for the movie. Similarly, with an average 18-inch portable TV set costing $141.48, his work to purchase the set comes to 46 hours and 33 minutes; at 1968 prices, he would work

Chart 7

Personal consumption expenditures in the United States, 1969. Total $577.5 billion = 100%

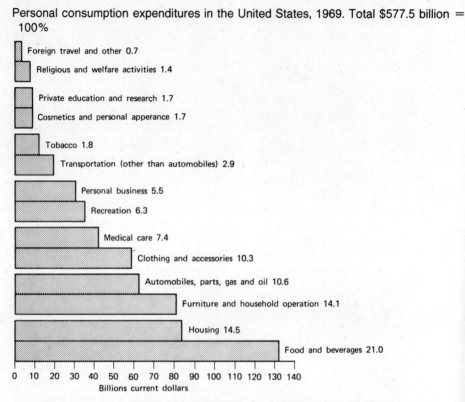

9½ weeks to buy a four-year-old Chevrolet. Therefore, when we say that these days we have more time to play, it should also be added that *less work time has been used to pay for these alternatives.* However, it is also true that the prices are going up over the years, so that the movie ticket might have been 50 cents a decade or two ago. A further complication is the fact that the investment in *capital goods*—the car or the TV set—is quite different from payment for the movie. The latter is used up, and the consumption act is terminal, in the same way as using an airplane ticket. The $141.48 spent for a TV set is no more than the cost of 88 movie performances and, of course, is used over several years. A realistic price for most TV sets, including the color and the black and white, is closer to $300, which therefore equals about 100 hours of work, or 2 ½ weeks of labor.

This kind of analysis has some bearing on personal planning and budgetary counseling, and it comes closer than any other method toward accurate cross-cultural comparisons of consumer expenditures and a meaningful concept of costs. For instance, decreasing expenditure for food and similar "basic needs" indicates, by inversion, more comparative expenditure for recreation, among other "discretionary" items; thus, in effect, the economic condition as a selective factor for leisure has lessened in its importance.

Another peculiarity of national accounting needs correction if we wish to obtain a more accurate understanding of expenditures for recreation, that is the question of what to include under "recreation." If we now examine Tables 5 and 6, recreation expenditures ($28.7 billion, or 6.3% of the total) *do not include anything for transportation, domestic or foreign.* There is every good reason to deal with travel as a separate item *vis-a-vis* consumer expenditures (12.8 percent of the total for domestic travel alone), but the student of leisure must determine the proportions of this vast sum ($59.6 billion in 1966) that is properly accountable under nonbusiness, and then to see what this does to the overall figure for leisure. Fortunately, this task was done for us in 1963.

Merely adding together (under "purpose of the trip") the items "visiting friends and relatives and other pleasure trips," the Department of Commerce study indicated that 61 percent of the trips and 70 percent of travelers were intent on leisure.

Is it fair, then, to add 60 percent of expenditures for gas and oil and for the purchase of cars (new and used) in 1963 to the "recreation" item as a whole? Three fifths of those respective items in 1963 alone came to $19.32 billion, gas and oil came to $12.8 billion; totaling that figure above, without estimating additional expenditures for recreation for food, clothing, and other items almost *doubles* the minimum figure for recreation. From $22.7 billion, or 6.1 percent of total consumption expenditures for recreation in 1963, the minimum total goes up to $42.02 billion, or 11 percent. It would be very difficult to estimate what proportion of these other expenditures (food, clothing, etc.) can be put, within reason, into the recreational expenditures to 15 to 20 percent of the American consuming pattern. Even if we settle for the 11 percent, we have a far more significant item of private and family recreation than is generally stated in statistical accounts. Indeed, if we pursued the subject of recreational or leisure content further—taxes collected on the pleasure driving, car repairs, a proportion of the almost $5 billion for foreign travel in 1967, portions of food, clothing, and education, and so on—*there can be no doubt that the total expenditure for recreation at present by Americans is up to or over one fifth of our total consuming expenditures.* This is a conservative estimate and, at a minimum— instead of the figure given by the Department of Commerce of $28.7 billion—the total for leisure comes to well over *$110 billion.*

When expenditures in this area are enlarged, as they must be to grasp the real situation, from those of persons or families to include those of communities, (for museums, parks, adult education, etc.) states, and the federal government areas, and the total transaction that American business has constructed around the recreational or leisure aspect of life, the conclusion can be reached that the total of personal, collective, and business involvement in serving our leisure amounts to well over 20 percent of our economy! Indeed, using its own calculations, the large investment firm, Merrill, Lynch, Pierce, Fenner, and Smith have estimated *$150 million* expenditure annually at present (over five times the federal estimate) and *$250 billion* by the end of this decade.

In Table 7 we look to see what happens to the family as it grows from the husband and wife to a unit of six persons or more. The expenditures most affected are food, which goes up 8.6 percent, housing, which goes down 4.6 percent, clothes, which go up 3.5 percent, and transportation, which goes down 2.5%. Proportions for recreation go up only 9 cents per dollar of family expenditure as four or more children come along.

What do we make of this last fact? A crucial factor may be that several children often will use the same capital outlay for recreation—a ball to play with, the same television set, or the same yard. Certainly, there are too many possibilities of combinations of factors, but here is one item to bear in mind later as we look more intimately into several homes.

Several answers have, then, been inherent in the data on the relative input of external, internal, and mediating factors in expenditures for leisure. Being Black in America has been a major economic disadvantage; however, income is only one factor, since his leisure expenditure is not only less but is also different as a group. Another conclusion comes out of the enormous spending that all Americans put into driving our cars—most of it, as we saw, for "pleasure." Here the external and internal conditions in the choice of leisure function as a cycle: as the population wants to get on the road in larger numbers, more roads are built, and these, in turn, encourage more travel.

The basic question, however, is whether the expenditure for "basic" necessities is down in the past decade *because* there has been a growing "internal" desire for what we used to think were nonbasic; and relatedly, whether the advertising industry (some would say the most pervasive and persuasive "mediating" factor) has found an increasing expenditure of its own resources in convincing us *that what was once discretionary (a luxury) is now a necessity*. An examination of data on advertising in 1960, 1965, and 1969 bears out this thesis. Table 8 is a compilation of amounts of advertising in newspapers by types of produce in newspapers.

Table 7
Average annual expenditures, income, and savings, all United States families, by family size, 1960-61[17]

Item	Total	Single Consumer	Two Persons	Three Persons	Four Persons	Five Persons	Six or More
Estimated number of families (in thousands)	55,307	8,390	16,660	9,920	8,935	5,783	5,619
Percent of families	100.0	15.2	30.1	17.9	16.2	10.5	10.2
Family Characteristics							
Family size (number of persons)	3.2	1.0	2.0	3.1	4.1	5.1	7.0
Money income before taxes	$6,246	$3,070	$5,676	$7,198	$7,792	$7,872	$6,863
Net change in assets and liabilities	$199	$24	$243	$238	$278	$246	$87
Number of full-time earners	.8	.4	.7	1.0	1.0	1.0	1.0
Age of head (years)	48	59	55	45	40	40	40
Education of head (years of school completed)	10	10	10	10	11	11	10
Number of children under 18 years	1.2	–	.1	.8	1.8	2.8	4.6
Percent of families							
Homeowners, all year	57	39	59	58	63	66	59
Auto owners, end of year	76	36	75	85	90	88	86
Nonwhite	11	13	10	10	8	9	17
Reporting savings: Increase	52	43	52	54	56	57	50
Decrease	42	41	40	42	41	41	46
No change	6	16	8	4	3	2	3
With children under 18 years	51	–	11	69	94	98	100
With persons 65 years and over	24	44	37	16	8	7	8

125

Table 7 *(continued)*

Average annual expenditures, income, and savings, all United States families, by family size, 1960–61[17]

Item	Total	Single Consumer	Two Persons	Three Persons	Four Persons	Five Persons	Six or More
				Family Size			
Financial Characteristics							
Receipts, total	$7,397	$3,548	$6,636	$8,389	$9,264	$9,560	$8,453
Money income after taxes	5,557	2,714	4,972	6,320	6,949	7,065	6,427
Other money receipts	81	54	94	82	89	73	82
Decrease in assets	947	615	1,062	1,004	966	1,086	822
Increase in liabilities	812	165	508	983	1,260	1,336	1,122
Account balancing difference	-186	-63	-94	-179	-304	-406	-245
Disbursements, total	7,583	3,611	6,730	8,568	9,568	9,966	8,698
Increase in assets	1,470	668	1,482	1,647	1,761	1,880	1,440
Decrease in liabilities	487	137	332	577	744	788	590
Personal insurance	299	103	248	358	405	413	352
Gifts and contributions	280	258	314	279	276	292	208
Expenditures for current consumption, total	5,017	2,445	4,354	5,707	6,382	6,593	6,108
Food, total	1,235	586	1,003	1,331	1,543	1,701	1,748
Food prepared at home	989	357	804	1,062	1,260	1,409	1,488
Food away from home	146	229	199	269	283	292	260
Tobacco	91	38	83	108	110	113	108
Alcoholic beverages	78	57	78	82	87	90	75

Family Size

Item	Total	Single Consumer	Two Persons	Three Persons	Four Persons	Five Persons	Six or More
Housing, total	1,461	863	1,335	1,634	1,775	1,797	1,581
Shelter	658	479	596	730	784	773	660
Rented dwelling	269	334	274	288	237	213	229
Owned dwelling	354	130	292	399	494	518	401
Other shelter	35	15	30	43	53	42	30
Fuel, light, refrigeration, water	249	128	227	266	302	322	311
Household operations	288	168	263	318	357	362	305
House furnishings and equipment	266	88	249	320	332	340	305
Clothing, clothing materials, services	518	200	369	597	709	772	735
Personal care	145	67	124	166	186	100	180
Medical care	340	160	345	378	408	403	352
Recreation	200	80	154	230	276	295	245
Reading	45	28	42	51	53	53	44
Education	53	9	18	67	93	97	90
Transportation	770	308	695	943	998	943	835
Automobile	693	246	612	865	915	865	765
Other travel and transportation	77	62	83	78	83	78	70
Other expenditures	111	49	108	120	144	139	115
Value of items received without expense	195	127	184	190	227	245	245
Food	15	15	12	12	16	17	28
Shelter	12	18	14	7	10	13	13
Other	168	94	158	171	201	215	204
Percent distribution							
Expenditures for current consumption	100.0	100.0	100.0	100.0	100.0	100.0	100.0
Food, total	24.5	24.0	23.0	23.3	24.2	25.8	28.6
Food prepared at home	19.6	14.6	18.5	18.6	19.7	21.4	24.4
Food away from home	4.9	9.4	4.6	4.7	4.4	4.4	4.3
Tobacco	1.8	1.6	1.9	1.9	1.7	1.7	1.8

Table 7 *(continued)*
Average annual expenditures, income, and savings, all United States families, by family size, 1960-61[17]

Item	Family Size						
	Total	Single Consumer	Two Persons	Three Persons	Four Persons	Five Persons	Six or More
Alcoholic beverages	1.5	2.3	1.8	1.4	1.4	1.4	1.2
Housing, total	28.9	35.3	30.7	28.6	27.8	27.2	25.9
Shelter	13.0	19.6	13.7	12.8	12.3	11.7	10.8
Rented dwelling	5.3	13.7	6.3	5.0	3.7	3.2	3.7
Owned dwelling	7.0	5.3	6.7	7.0	7.7	7.9	6.6
Other shelter	.7	.6	.7	.8	.8	.6	.5
Fuel, light, refrigeration, water	4.9	5.2	5.2	4.7	4.7	4.9	5.1
Household operations	5.7	6.9	6.0	5.6	5.6	5.5	5.0
House furnishings and equipment	5.3	3.6	5.7	5.6	5.2	5.2	5.0
Clothing, clothing materials, services	10.3	8.2	8.5	10.5	11.1	11.7	12.0
Personal care	2.9	2.7	2.8	2.9	2.9	2.9	2.9
Medical care	6.7	6.5	7.9	6.6	6.4	6.1	5.8
Recreation	4.0	3.3	3.5	4.0	4.3	4.5	4.0
Reading	.9	1.1	1.0	.9	.8	.8	.7
Education	1.0	.4	.4	1.2	1.5	1.5	1.5
Transportation	15.3	12.6	16.0	16.5	15.6	14.3	13.7
Automobile	13.7	10.1	14.1	15.2	14.3	13.1	12.5
Other travel and transportation	1.5	2.5	1.9	1.4	1.3	1.2	1.4
Other expenditures	2.2	2.0	2.5	2.1	2.3	2.1	1.9

TABLE 8

Newspaper advertising—expenditures for national advertising, 1960, 1965, and 1969.

(In thousands of dollars. Data are compiled on basis of actual space measurements of bulk of "national" advertising carried by weekday and Sunday newspapers. Excludes production costs) [18]

Type of Product	1960	1965	1969
Total	782,149	813,329	990,910
Automotive	196,685	239,682	286,127
Passenger cars (new)	113,963	129,748	145,778
Foods	138,000	101,968	122,115
Baking products	18,603	12,065	9,757
Beverages	21,961	17,493	18,727
Transportation	52,547	62,014	90,043
Airways	31,508	38,901	56,760
Publishing and media	48,652	59,623	71,814
Books	11,444	18,663	23,413
Radio and TV stations	22,323	29,782	36,039
Alcoholic beverages	62,276	69,781	64,740
Liquors	48,014	57,863	53,495
Hotels and resorts	20,903	25,967	31,710
Public utilities	23,340	30,877	29,066
Insurance	17,008	16,651	23,660
Total requisites	29,465	15,873	23,486
Wearing apparel	10,818	14,687	22,429
Radio, TV, and phonographs	8,620	16,929	21,768
Tobacco	35,031	10,822	18,965
Cigarettes	31,907	8,314	16,302
Industrial	16,471	14,649	18,140
Housing equipment	17,166	15,471	17,604
Household supplies	19,694	20,093	17,424
Medical	23,653	17,214	16,174
Farm and garden	9,450	10,508	12,635
Sporting goods, cameras, and photo supplies	7,395	6,232	11,708
Household furniture and furnishings	4,812	6,988	7,421
Educational	2,281	2,854	6,809
Professional and service	1,575	3,034	6,808
Jewelry and silverware	1,737	2,638	4,520
Amusements	2,167	2,648	3,723
Miscellaneous	32,313	43,121	62,021

Source   Compiled by Media Records, Inc., for Bureau of the American Newspaper Publishers Association, Inc., New York.

The increases in percent of newspaper advertising expenditures in the past decade were, accordingly, in their rank order (Table 9).

With only a few exceptions (wearing apparel and household furniture), the first 13 of the 24 items indicate advertising priority for items that can generally be called "discretionary" or "leisure-" oriented items! But the alert reader might observe, this was for newspaper advertising. What if we were to take the *total* advertising expenditure by major industries? Then we would cover television, magazines, and billboards as well as newspapers. This figure is also available. In a listing of 51 types of active corporations in the United States, with total receipts of $1,345,185, 10 types of corporations spent an average of $2 or more on advertising for each $100 of receipts. Of this group, six fall into the leisure-oriented group and, certainly, some proportion of even the remaining four (food, general merchandise, apparel, and chemicals) fall into the subject of this volume (Table 10).

Again, we see the importance of the *mediating* factor (in this case, advertising) in the selection of leisure experiences in the United States. Obviously, the profit commercial system of our life is a major (perhaps even the major) single factor in the process of "choice" (a better word might be "persuasion") into one or another use of "free" time, or at least, the purchase of items intended for such purposes.

On the international level, attempts to translate money values in respect to purchase power are beset with expected difficulties. Official exchange rates as of 1963 are used in expressing dollar values. One difficulty is that these market prices incorporate the indirect taxes on all goods and services; such taxes vary among countries, especially on such items as alcoholic and tobacco expenditures.

Table 11 is extracted from a larger table that covers expenditures for many more consumer items, comparable to Table 7.

Table 12 shows the rank order of proportionate expenditure per capita (omitting countries where no figures are given).

This, by any interpretation that goes beyond the criteria of expenditures, is an interesting result. However, in 1962, the United States and Canada possessed 235 TV sets per thousand compared to 105 in Europe, and earlier in this chapter I noted that TV is cheap in cost per hours watched during the life of the set. Yet such a fact is offset by the amount of outdoor promenading in Italy, or the amount of walking (which costs little or nothing) in other countries. Even if we accept the official proportions for recreation in the United States by the Department of Commerce for 1960—the year closest to 1962, used by Mueller —the expenditure for recreation is 5.6 percent; this raises us a little in the rank order to position 13 among the nations, between Greece and Luxembourg. Furthermore, if in all countries we were to include transportation, the United States in 1960 had almost three times as many

TABLE 9

Rank order of newspaper advertising expenditures

Rank Order	Product	Percent of Increase
1	Jewelry and silverware	1610
2	Professional and service	330
3	Education	190
4	Radio, TV	150
5	Wearing apparel	100
6	Miscellaneous	91
7	Transport	71
8	Amusement	71
9	Household furniture	54
10	Sport goods	48
11	Automobile	48
12	Hotels	46
13	Publishing	45
14	Insurance	39
15	Public utilities	24
16	Farm and garden	23
17	Industrial	10
18	Alcohol	8
19	House equipment	2
20	Food	1
21	House supplies	-13
22	Toilet	-25
23	Medical	-46
24	Tobacco	-83

TABLE 10

Percent of receipts spent on advertising, by industries

Rank Order	Type of Corporation	Percent of Receipts Spent on Advertising
1	Tobacco	6.0
2	Chemical and allied products	4.2
3	Motion pictures	3.6
4	Food	2.5
5	General merchandise	2.5
6	Photography and scientific instruments	2.4
7	Amusements and recreation services	2.4
8	Hotels	2.4
9	Other (include apparel)	2.3

passenger cars as all of Western Europe put together, and by no jug-
gling can pleasure travel be considered cheap; this should place us
much closer to the top of the list. Apparently, the answer comes from
differences in nationalization of health and subsidies for housing in
other countries, so that a larger proportion of American family expenditures goes to those items. This can be tested. Turning to items in Mueller's tables—items omitted in Table 11—note these comparisons for per
capita costs and proportions for rent and medical care.

Country	Percent of per Capita Expenditures for Rent	Percent of per Capita Expenditures for Health
Italy	8.0	4.8
Belgium	10.0	5.5
West Germany	6.1	3.5
United States	13.0	8.0

TABLE 11
International comparison of private consumption patterns, 1962[19]

Country	Total Consumption	Total Recreation and Entertainment	Per Capita Consumption	Per Capita Recreation and Entertainment	Percent of Per Capita Estimated for Recreation
United States	$348,822	$19,950	$1,870	$107	5.2
Canada	23,834	1,052	1,281	57	4.4
W. Europe	235,872	—	753	—	—
Austria	4,427	300	621	42	6.7
Belgium	8,655	649	939	71	7.5
Denmark	4,907	—	1,054	—	—
Finland	3,050	194	677	43	6.3
France	46,557	3,098	990	66	6.6
Germany, Fr.	50,950	3,815	895	67	7.3
Greece	2,851	173	337	20	5.8
Iceland	169	10	928	55	5.9
Ireland	1,585	101	561	36	6.4
Italy	23,886	1,899	476	38	7.9
Luxembourg	294	16	913	50	5.4
Netherlands	7,590	389	643	33	5.1
Norway	3,070	223	843	61	7.2
Portugal	1,929	—	215	—	—
Spain	9,294	—	302	—	—
Sweden	8,533	608	1,128	80	7.0
Switzerland	6,597	—	1,165	—	—
United Kingdom	51,528	3,483	964	65	6.6

TABLE 12
Rank order, national expenditures for recreation, 1962

Rank Order	Percent of per Capita Expenditures for Recreation	Country
1	7.9	Italy
2	7.5	Belgium
3	7.3	West Germany
4	7.2	Norway
5	7.0	Sweden
6	6.7	Austria
7	6.6	France
8	6.6	United Kingdom
9	6.4	Ireland
10	6.3	Finland
11	5.9	Iceland
12	5.8	Greece
13	5.4	Luxembourg
14	5.2	United States
15	5.1	Netherlands
16	4.4	Canada

These comparisons indicate in a small way that expenditure patterns for leisure are an important, but nevertheless a limited clue to what actually goes on by the person, the family, or the nation; not only are expenditures only a partial clue to the actual behavior, even the *distribution* of expenditures for *all* items (rent, food, etc.) are related to the political and social patterns of the society. This becomes, therefore, a major concern in a later chapter on international studies. It suggests, moreover, that this chapter may now turn to another, less measurable, but equally pertinent index of personal and family leisure patterns—expenditure of time.

Dynamic III: Expenditure of time

The availability of time for leisure is another major factor that mediates between the internal and external factors noted earlier. The reader will recall an observation from Chapter 1—that *any* activity may fall within the "leisure" patterns of the person: we must, as outsiders, see how it seems to fall into his total patterns, and we can also ask him. Yet, in dealing with data gathered by governmental or other research groups, we see that a somewhat specific category—"recreation"—is stipulated. If, within this one grouping, we see what items are officially put within it, many questions arise from the sociological view. We have already seen the last official breakdown under this category in Table 5. At the moment our preoccupation is not with the expenditures but with the items. The specialist, as always, is first concerned, if not aghast, at the broadness of some of the items. If our concern touches even slightly on the *functions, purposes,* or *uses* of leisure, why are magazines and newspapers in the same category as sheet music? Why should a boat be in the same category as a child's bicycle? What economist could be so insensitive to functions as to put the cost of a violin or a piano in the same item as a TV set? Yet, first, there must be some consensus on categories among specialists in leisure studies, and meanwhile, we cannot expect that the economists will go on sabbaticals until the consensus is reached. We are in a comparatively new field, which has the eventual obligation to make its voice heard.

On the international level, as we have seen, expenditure patterns are complicated because of the difference in purchasing power related to a given monetary index and because of the nature of the economic-political structure. A more accurate index of comparison in the selection of leisure-oriented experiences is the distribution or use of time. For this reason, cross-cultural comparisons of time use or "time-budgets" has gone so far as to constitute the most successful of all cross-cultural studies in the social sciences. Since the United States is an integral part of these efforts, we learn something about ourselves as well.

The most detailed of such comparative studies covered 12 nations and consisted of time-budget reports carried on between 1965 and 1966.[20] Data were drawn from Belgium, Bulgaria, Czechoslovakia, France, West Germany, East Germany, Hungary, Peru, Poland, the United States, the USSR, and Yugoslavia. The United States research took place primarily in Jackson, Michigan and a nationwide survey of 44 metropolitan districts with 50,000 or more persons in each. All of the material, covering middle-sized urban areas, finally resulted in about 150,000 cases (coded cards) of time-budgets, each covering one full period of 24 hours; aside from the written records kept by someone in the family, 50,000 of the families were interviewed the following day. All data were placed into the following categories.

1. Working time and time connected to it.
2. Domestic work.
3. Care to children.
4. Purchasing of goods and services.
5. Private needs: meals, sleep, and so forth.
6. Adult education and professional training.
7. Civic and collective participation activities.
8. Spectacles, entertainment, social life.
9. Sports and active leisure.
10. Passive leisure.

Specific items under the last three are listed in abbreviated form below.

8.	9.	10.
Sports events	Active sports	Radio, TV
Mass culture	Fishing, hiking	Records
Movies and Theatre	Walking	Books, magazines
Museums	Hobbies	Newspapers
Visit with friends	Art and music	Conversation
Parties	Parlor games	Write letters
Cafe, pubs, social	Related travel	Relax, think
Social travel		Leisure travel

As a whole, the findings on general matters are unsurprising: for example, those who work the longest days are blue-collar men and single women; more married men hold second jobs. Housewives spend more time cooking than employed women, no matter what the day of the week or numbers of children. Single men put far more time into cooking than married men and less on all other household activities. More time is spent with children among wives of blue-collar workers.

Classes in adult education attract more persons in professional and managerial positions, more men, and more single persons. In Eastern countries the white-collar workers spend more time than other workers watching television; just the reverse holds true in Western societies. Book and newspaper reading increases with higher occupation, and magazines have even more stratified readers, but attendance at movies is uniform among all occupational groups. Single men and women do more visiting than married people but do no more entertaining. In the United States more married than single men engage in longer periods of outdoor activities. In general, higher white-collar workers report more leisure activities than blue-collar workers on workdays.

Consider a more specific comparison of persons in Torun, a Polish community of 113,000; Maribor, Yugoslavia, with 96,000 persons; and Jackson, Michigan (United States) with 72,000 persons. Here, too, a basic conclusion was evidence for the hypothesis that "social stratification has a basic impact on the shaping of free time."[21] Beyond this, Jackson had the most time for leisure, followed by Torun and Maribor. The Jackson population sleeps the longest, and its men work the least. The Maribor men put 1.7 to 1.9 hours daily toward helping in household chores, almost twice as much as their luckier parallels in America. Housewives in Jackson were likewise the most fortunate, averaging almost six hours daily of free time compared to five hours in Torun and three hours in Maribor; it takes the Maribor housewife about three hours more every day to run her home than her Jackson counterpart.

The investigators put such differences to the availability of facilities, types of stores, presence of supermarkets, and so on. Free hours for employed women were 2.4 hours in Maribor, 3.2 hours in Torun, and 4.2 hours in Jackson. Through marriage (in spite of more time put into helping by the husband), the European women lost about an hour of free time daily, while the American women managed to retain about the same amount (4.1 hours compared to 4.2). In the two European cities, the presence of children *per se* did not seem to change the time pattern. Jackson showed quite the opposite, losing about 1.5 hours per day. Relative to the United States, there are in Europe "more deeply rooted traditions ... of long working hours in the household ... with inferior equipment and inferior organization of outside services." Furthermore, there are differences in their social position: her different place in public life, professional life, and family life, and her very different participation in cultural life.

More will be said later about television watching in American cities but, as expected, Jackson's use of TV was considerably greater among every economic level. More time was spent reading among the Europeans: in Torun "30 percent of the white collar workers, and in Maribor 15 percent of them, read books daily but in Jackson there was not a single respondent of that category in the daily book reading habit." The same held true among low white-collar workers: 26, 13, and 0 percent. Even among nonworking housewives the differences were noticeable: Torun, 38 percent, Maribor, 11 percent, and Jackson, 6%. Dr. Skorzynski, the Polish scholar, attributes these differences to the "highly different traditions of the three nations"; television arrived at a time when Poland, especially, had already developed a strong literary culture before technology arrived; in the United States, he notes, "book reading was, and even then to a rather small degree, a field limited to educated women."[22]

A more active social life was uncovered in Jackson from the time-budget studies, especially in the lower economic level; but private social visits to the homes of others are popular everywhere (in Jackson, especially among the women.) The use of cafes and similar establishments is far more a matter of national custom, especially in such places as Poland, Hungary, France, and Northern Yugoslavia. Polish women, even more than those from Yugoslavia, meet friends in cafes.

The usefulness of the comparative time-budget data to the thesis of this chapter is almost self-evident. Any broad attempt at correlations of occupation, and so forth, with activity—whether relating to leisure, religion, or anything else—is an attempt to develop a view of constants, that is, to rule out either the fortuitous or the planned mediations (respectively, meeting a friend and advertising). If we find that Americans read less over these many thousand cases, it can hardly be concluded that the television "just happened" in that survey week to carry unusual programs. TV emerges not as a mediating factor in the selection of leisure but as a basic "external condition," a fact of the American scene.

We might suspect that these constants in correlation would apply more to religious affiliation or family life than to leisure choices, since the last is perhaps more subject to change. But is it really? If we eliminate little patterns—this game for that, this travel destination for that —can we discern in the selection of leisure a pattern that is also subject to some constancies and, therefore, to projections? That is the basis of time-budget studies in this area of inquiry. As this approach becomes systematic, its usefulness grows as a source of knowledge into the values in which to look for the exploration of new values. Thus we are brought to the implications and applications of this chapter for pure science and for policy making.

IMPLICATIONS—APPLICATIONS

The chapter so far has attempted, in theoretical discussion and by extended illustrations, to indicate that a specific leisure act is a blend of external, internal, and mediating factors. From all this there are implications, both for leisure and for much else in the society. A major one points directly to the nature of mass culture, since its overall characteristic would seem to be a *maximization of the external and mediative factors and a thwarting of the personal;* that is, millions within close distance of the TV, listening to the commercials, absorbing the current tastes and products. The problem for those who strive to move the society toward more freedom in taste and thought is *to free the element of personality from the mediating agents, without sacrificing at the same time the potential comfort and advantages of such external factors as better health, affluence, mobility, and free time.*

Yet a third element of this dynamic pattern always enters the scene; if we broadly equate the external condition with the whole energy system—production, technology, and their influences—*they develop a momentum of their own, crystallizing their own values and therefore stultifying or alienating the person from individualistic challenge and creative input to the society.*

Policy Making

In a rule-of-thumb way, it might be said that government's policy for leisure emphasizes the provision of external public alternatives (museums, parks, roads, community centers); that schools, libraries, and churches exist to develop an "inner man" with a discriminating sense; and that the business and industrial world (nowadays, especially the mass media) makes its way by covering all the waterfronts: by creating new "needs" in changing men's consuming nature, by providing alternatives for him to purchase (by seasonal change within the product as well as by an enlarged repertoire of things); and by perfecting the intermediate or sales processes. Yet all of them need to know about the relationships between these three foci of leisure choice. For example, among the 27 volumes of the ORRRC reports noted above, there are detailed studies of who visits the outdoor facilities, how long they stay, their satisfaction, and so on; all this is needed as a solid basis on which to purchase lands for national parks and to service them effectively. The Madison Avenue fraternity is constantly carrying on intensive studies of the processes by which choices are made for this product or that; if Margaret Mead is right in her prediction that leisure habits and goods will be geared more and more to pinpointing of taste, the public agencies will have much to learn from private industry. But industries such as the television networks have generally carried on research through their marketing agencies composed of young sociologists and psychologists who have accumulated millions of dollars of useless research—amidst their usable studies—because the research has overemphasized the quantitative approach and the short-range view, and has neglected the dynamics involved in the choice of programs.

Of course, the private sector pays for its research and uses or misuses it. The public sector—the United States Congress, for example—often has far more data and analysis available on a given issue than it uses or that fits into the political contest. The reader need not be reminded of the disdain in which social science as a whole is held in some political quarters.

Modification

There can be no serious theory or practice in modifying leisure habits of persons, families, or even communities, unless there is a basis of knowledge about decision making. The legitimate question can be raised, on what ethical basis? Is not the underlying philosophy of leisure the idea of freedom, voluntariness, and individualism? Does not the very concept "modification" inject a false note? At the risk of severe oversimplification, one answer to this is that human action is constantly being changed, *actually*, every time a road is built or a baseball field is opened, and *potentially*, through the ongoing contacts one has with teachers, TV commercials, and Billy Grahams. The question is not change, but the *motives* of "change-agents," the *consequences* of the transformation to the person affected, and the *process or method* employed in the change.

If we apply this framework to the modification of the nature of leisure a scheme of the motivations in change appears approximately as follows, based on the categories of Chapter 1.

1. Those who wish to see more leisure take on the nature of the idealistic, in the Hellenic sense, are agents who typically represent the values of the school and the liberal branches of the church. Their assumption is a confidence in man's groping and quest for what we may loosely call the creative life. Such leisure strivings may be expected to assume the shape of consistent patterns that *develop* from the simpler to the more complex and from an "I" to a "thou" orientation.

2. Activity for the sake of activity is the model for such change agents as businessmen or of those industrialists who manufacture the things that are produced with an ethic of what has been called "planned obsolescence." Here is the whole array of fads and fashions, or of TV programming. The television as industry (thus excluding "public," "community," or "educational" TV) has no interest in idealistic goals in the use of freetime; it will broadcast Beethoven or "Bonanza" with equal dispassion, depending only on which stands up best to the audience ratings. All attempts to raise the sights of such business is naive; only pressure—purchasers' pressure and fears of governmental regulation—has any significance in such a mileau of policy making. One result is a shortsightedness in the building of audiences, because the sponsor wants immediate results; another consequence is the usefulness of quantitative research and statements of issues, and the oblivion—during conference hours of the marketing agencies—to long-range qualitative considerations. The goal is not development of audiences from simple to complex but from simple to simple, in an unending ethic of consumerism and conformism.

3. The motives of those who view leisure as an instrument of therapy and control is to change leisure either in the direction of greater effectiveness in supporting an ideology or in developing a personal independence. The Parks of Culture in the USSR provide an example of the first; less obvious are the Boy Scouts or Junior Achievers of the United States. Recreational programs in hospitals are conscious attempts in the second category; they serve the medical profession as an aid to the observation of incapacity and also in providing new tools to the patient. But politics and medicine (or psychiatry) do not subsume the usefulness of leisure as a tool: social status is another element.

4. The motivation of those who view leisure as a construct is not to modify leisure choices but to expand the range of that which is seen as leisure by its participants. The most strategic element that was proposed earlier was the full range from complete insignificance to weight. This is an enlargement that, in effect, moves our attitudes toward leisure almost full circle from a common attitude that we are really dealing in play and relaxation.

Consequences of Leisure Change

All the potential changes on the person as a consequence of modification in leisure are reducible to two: to his behavior and his values. Both subjects are extremely complex and can be only briefly discussed here.

As to behavioral change, there is no conceptual possibility of sorting out all the major or the subtle changes that take place when, for example, John Jones takes on fishing, for whatever the reason. Simple observations can be made easily enough, to be sure. He now gets up at a very early hour on a fishing day; he has substituted this new obsession for something else, such as loafing at home; in fishing, he probably goes with his male cronies, and so on. The question is, how deeply do these "changes" go? Indeed, the question raises many more questions about a conceptualization of *behavior,* a far more comprehensive term than leisure. All the social sciences are brought into play, and the reader is left to his own devices as to what school and cult of analysis he cares to work from. Should his search be in respect to new sensitivities as to beauty; to new skills, as in control over his body; to new patterns of time use, as staying up for "late, late" TV; to new use of space, as in tourism; to easier associations with other people, as in a new habit of frequenting the pub; to different associations with his children, because of the construction of a swimming pool in the yard; to attending religious services, because he read the Bible during his vacation; to choosing Florida for retirement, because he decides to spend the winter months on the golf course? All of these are evidences of behavioral change; such hypothetic listings could go on *ad infinitum.* A more controlled analysis results if, instead of starting form the dimension of behavior, we turn to some ways in which the changes in leisure can be grouped; each grouping will suggest broad implications for behavior.

1. In general we may expect there is a more significant impact on the full behavioral pattern if one leisure element replaces another than if it is added to an existing pattern.
2. We may expect a more significant impact on behavior if a new leisure element—such as an element of a mechanical invention—may contribute potentially to a larger configuration of behavior.
3. We may expect a larger impact on behavior in proportion to the complexity and ongoing developmental character of the new experience.
4. If the new leisure experience emerges in relation to a major change such as marriage, military service, migration, or retirement, the impact on behavior is more difficult to isolate, but may become a major factor in the new accomodation or adjustment.
5. The addition or replacement of leisure elements is less significant to the person's behavior in a society when change itself is a general value than in a simpler, traditional society.

These propositions could be extended, and each one, while momentarily suggesting subjective recollections, could be processed for testing under controlled conditions. This I leave to a new generation of students in the field. I turn, instead, to the third component of Level 1 in our map of issues, functions of leisure experience.

There are, of course, more than economic issues that tie leisure functions to the postindustrial society. Consider one professional group—recreationists—whose functions can hardly be further removed from business values. Traditionally, this group has concentrated its efforts on the activity-for-the-sake-of-activity function, by which time is passed and boredom is avoided. The recreationist might well raise questions about this interpretation, since his leadership does speak of meanings, spirit, team play, and (as we see in the work of Brightbill) the fulfillment of man's basic needs. Yet the bulk of recreational meetings, exhibits, and demonstrations, deal explicitly with the organization of activities. However, unlike business, this profession is mainly publicly supported and based in its training and outlook on the academic tradition. Thus, as distinct from the tendency among businessmen to seek new ways of making profit from the new leisure, the recreation leader finds it imperative that he become concerned with the place of recreation in changing values. In the United States, for example, the National Recreation and Park Association publishes a new *Journal on Research in Leisure,* and the international scene has witnessed an important interest in "sports sociology" as an integral part of the Internation Sociological Society. There can be little doubt that this profession is moving from its traditional interest in organizational and technical matters to leisure and recreation as important, if less measurable instruments and ends for man's purpose. With other professions and disciplines, it is concerned more and more with an examination of the meanings of leisure. To this topic we are taken by the next component of the model.

Chapter 6

Functions: Manifest and Latent

In a social order in which work is a central value, leisure is relatively easy to define and to talk about. Its functions are obvious. Thus, if we use the words "recreation" and "leisure" synonymously, we are thinking within industrial terms or, as I have already called it, the "kilowatt social order." Recreation for work is an historically useful concept, but the realities change as work itself is less central and may become secondary to leisure.

In the emerging social order, whatever shapes it may take, nonwork grows into a major concern. The manifest or apparent functions of leisure still maintain validity, but in a limited sense. This is where contemporary scholars still center their analysis.

MANIFEST FUNCTIONS

The clue to manifest leisure functions came directly from Chapter 2, where several traditional approaches to leisure were outlines. Functions were precisely the distinction between them.

1

First there was the Greek thought—leisure as an end. Its functions are therefore in the doing or in the experiencing. Here is where the person points to when he tells us that he does it because he "likes it." This is a higher order than any other, conceived by the upper class; therefore, as de Grazia rightly notes, "The classic ideal of leisure was indifferent to what we would call materialism," and any other external basis or criterion. The Greeks went one step further; they thought that only they, the elites, could fully comprehend such experience; they showed indifference to the foreign democratic notion "that leisure was everyone's right and that everyone could profit from it equally." As the centuries went on, the idea of the inherent, independent worth became accepted; "arts for art's sake" was perhaps the clearest example. The Greek social model of elitism kept on as a tradition and, quite literally, even 2000 years later, in such a place as the United States; to study the Greek language itself was one mark of learning for the sake of learning, and nonutilitarian education was a major symbol of aristocracy. No one had to explain the function of the classical education; it was self-evident, in the same breath as belief in God. American sociologists, nonbelievers in all such declarations except in regard to their own preoccupation—sociological knowledge itself as a value—do not rest content and, in common with their psychological colleagues, persist in trying to qualify such feelings as "I like Beethoven," with seven-point scales of liking Beethoven a little, some, quite a bit, very much, and similar nonsense. The simple fact is that the manifest function of an experience, when seen within the Greek model, is in its being, its doing—itself. When all other reasons outside of Beethoven are exhausted—such as going to a concert to be seen—then we are left perhaps with a frustrated social science but with a reality that man has always recognized, perhaps since his first encounter with the love of woman.

The great statement of this position on leisure is Josef Pieper, who equates leisure as a whole with the celebration of life; an important updated version is Harvey Cox's *Feast of Fools.*[1]

2

A second manifest function of leisure grows out of its instrumental character, also noted in Chapter 2. Whereas to the Greeks the criterion of leisure was in the act or experience—logic, political involvement, contemplation, *paidia* as a whole—the second function finds a more objective possibility of evaluation in the goals sought by those who use leisure as an instrument. These may be the participants themselves or those who—like dictators, the television industry, churchmen, or physicians—find that nonwork time of others can be used for such ends as political control, profits, public duty, or physical well-being. Now the social scientists have real clues, because there are ways of observing and measuring such matters as health or community volunteerism. We find a discussion of this on the English scene by Kenneth Roberts, who makes the significant point that industrial society has again given to the large population the time and money needed to cultivate leisure for the sheer purpose of enjoyment: "people are left with a part of their lives to use purely in accordance with their own inclinations and interests."[2]

Another English student of the subject, Dr. Stanley Parker, speaks of the instrumental functions that serve society. In the first, leisure "helps people to learn how to play their part in society; it helps them to achieve societal or collective aims; and it helps the society to keep together." Socialization is a key term for the first of these, as in the usefulness of play or storytelling. As an example of the second he notes that one aim of the industrial system (expressed in large "leisure industries") is to serve economic purposes by encouraging the purchase of leisure goods: industry, notes our discerning colleague, "needs the consuming time of workers as much as it needs their producing time." Third, leisure may promote solidarity in such matters as play and sporting activities that serve as "focal points of group identification."[3]

In 1953 Dumazedier conducted an interview study of 819 salaried persons and workers in France. He reports that practically all of them saw the functions of their leisure in opposition to routine tasks, daily chores, necessities, and obligations; the last of these was by far the most popular view and included the job and supplementary work, domestic tasks, personal care, family rituals and ceremonies, and necessary study. On the positive level, their conceptions of leisure's functions fall into three groups: relaxation, entertainment, and personal development. Relaxation, concludes Dumazedier from these interviews, "provides recovery from fatigue"; he comments that today's tempo of production, the complexity of industrial settings, and distances to work have increased "the worker's need for rest and quiet, for idleness and the aimless small pastimes."[4]

3

The third function of leisure that was verified by the French interviews was the development of personality—a willing cultivation of the physical and mental self over and above utilitarian considerations of job or practical advancement. This function and, to some extent the escape into the imaginary self, already moves us away from manifest functions that lend themselves to quantitative analysis of social science; they do, of course, profit from and contribute to conceptualization of man and his relationships to other men and to work. Indeed, as our French colleague notes, "This use of leisure for the cultivation of personality, not so common as simple entertainment, is of prime importance to the popular culture generally."[5] And there are aspects of popular culture that can and have been well studied by social sciences.

In Chapter 2, I placed the term "recreation" within this total framework of instrumental functions. Verification for this comes from statements of the profession itself. In a collective volume prepared by about 40 authorities in this applied field, recreation is defined as "activity voluntarily engaged in during leisure and motivated by the personal satisfactions which result from it," but among its products are "the values in the form of better physical and mental health and those which ... improve character and good citizenship and thus help strengthen the democratic way of life."[6] An eminent spokesman for the recreation profession, the late Professor Charles Brightbill, listed as man's needs: "to be healthy, to be free, to discover ourselves, to be wanted, to be useful, and to find our place in the universe."[7] If leisure and play feed in toward these goals, the emphasis still remains on manifest function, that is, a human experience that is observable in terms of criteria outside of itself and therefore subject to the tools of social science. But Brightbill, one of the pioneers of a broader view of recreation, was able to say of play what had not been said by the 40 authorities in 1954: "It is perhaps enough to say that *it is there,* . . . play has its own appeal . . . closely related to *human* happiness."[8] This begins to bring recreation to the philosophy of the Greeks and springboards a new security within the profession—the security that play needs no external justification but, as Huizinga and Pieper observed, is a basic human category. The recreation profession, in its relatively mature reaching, can turn fruitfully to a post-Platonic statement of E. Jordan, a philosopher of Butler University, whose works have never achieved the importance in his lifetime that they deserved. In *The Good Life* he distinguishes play from biological or physical activity, work, and reproduction.[9] These others contribute to man's sustenance, his knowledge and control over his world, and the continuity of the species. But play in the broad sense "includes art and objective forms of religion and represents the highest form that is reached by human action." Play is therefore essentially creative, going beyond production and reproduction, dealing with the "restoration of the whole individual," and thus the "essential institution-building activity of man." Its moral significance (Jordan here enlarges on Huizinga) is that play "elevates the physical acts of the organism to forms of art"; it provides experimentation of the physical "with no utility motive"; finally, since play is the "unmeditated expression of the form of the ideas and not of their content," so "action in play is the creation in purposeless activity of bodies fit for these ideal forms."

Thus Jordan from philosophy and Brightbill from recreation have provided the bridge from recreation as an instrumental modality to a moral entity able to stand on its own.

In summary, the three manifest functions of leisure identify the three approaches to the concept of leisure itself: its purpose is inherent, instrumental, or temporal. Equally important is another set, the *latent* functions. These are more difficult to pinpoint, since unlike the single thematic or homophonic orientation of the first, we come now to a polyphonic process in which the leisure function is not observable in correlations of one to one, but to a dynamic of the one (leisure activity or experience) in the many. And the *many* consists of a set of polarities, with various shades between (pianissimo to fortissimo, interspaced with

P, MP, F, MF,). The dynamics resides in the ongoing alternation, reinforcement, or conflict that is in the situation.

LATENT FUNCTIONS

Tension and resolution as a theory of human action is an attempt to say
that a human behavior can be viewed within a dialectic pattern instead
of as an individualistic, finite, or descriptive phenomenon. Folk wisdom
says this in innumerable sets or polarizations: right and wrong, up and
down, *yin* and *yang*, young and old, horizontal and perpendicular.
Social theory has its own polarities: inner-other, sensate-ideational, par-
ticular-universal, local-cosmopolitan, *Gemeinschaft-Gesellschaft*, rural-urban, individual-group, and so on.

These can be seen purely as descriptive dichotomies, bifurcations, or
opposites; then they are passive terms, although helpful in providing a
scale or range. For example, the return of a purse that I find in the
restaurant seat is *right*, and I turn it over to the management; to keep
it would have been *wrong*. The action on my part is simple, clear, easy
to describe. However, if I debate with myself, even momentarily, as my
feelings waver between honesty and potential gain, the act of returning
the purse falls into a process containing opposite goals; as observers, we
have witnessed a tension and a resolution, an internal debate. The sex
act is frequently seen as a relationship in which the subtleties of arousal
are finally released in a total giving on the part of both. Many of us have
experienced and put words to the inner debate between restlessness
and stability; for example, I find that in Tampa I miss the activity and
power of Boston, but I value the ease of life and the sunshine of Florida.

The hypothesis of this section is that the functions of leisure can be
viewed in the light of a series of dichotomies and processes which, in
their total scope, lend a character to "leisure" that is different from
religious, educational, or work institutions.[10] The sets of elements to be
discussed below are: movement-rest; freedom-discipline; play-enter-
tainment; sociability-isolation; construction-distraction; self-growth-
recreation; self-worth-self-defeat.

Movement-Rest

Leisure is closely related to concepts of space as well as of time. The first
relationship, perhaps the less obvious, has been treated in some detail
by Dumazedier and Imbert in *Espace et Loisir*. Here I deal with the
relations of leisure and movement in a more limited way. At least three
types come to mind. There is, first, the whole range of physical movement that, as in a game, is a primary characteristic of the activity-

experience. A second involves all other activities in which physical movement is present, but is subordinate: going to the museum or moving about as one gardens. Third, and quite distinct from both, is travel, whether by walking or by any carrier—car, ship, horse, or place; in these, contrary to the physical game, the body is totally transported. Very roughly put, these refer, respectively (1) to movement as a form of mastering of space, (2) movement as an instrumentality toward other ends, and (3) movement as a value *sui generis*.

Movement, also, is a term that requires a division. Its two major types are task and travel orientation. Simplified roughly, task-oriented movement is done *by* one's body; in travel, movement, is applied *to* one's body. In the first, we walk, jog, run, play tennis, move from the chair to the TV set, advance a checker on the board, stroll in the garden, or visit our friends. In the second, we are taken bodily from one physical location to another by horse, car, train, plane, or ship. Often both are combined. Stopping at a gasoline station during a vacation trip, I may leave the vehicle to "stretch"; stopping with the tourist bus at the Vatican, I will walk several miles of corridors to see its art treasures. Each of these raises pertinent issues for leisure, affecting both the personal and the public policy dimensions.

As to the first—task-orientation—a primary concern is the physical state of the person. In planning activities for children or for elderly persons, recreation leaders are directly conscious of the limits of movement. However, for all ages, the state of the body and its performance becomes a critical issue in an urbanized, automized society. President Kennedy and his family dramatized the image of "physical fitness"; in all schools this is an essential concern inseparable from considerations of the academic program. Much is heard of the "softening" of the American public. Little doubt can be held in general on this score, although there is some balancing of the whole by virtue of better medicines, the elimination of some formerly fatal diseases, and the lengthening of life. The two most used instruments for leisure in the United States are the television set and the automobile; both are saboteurs of the physical educationist's efforts.

Sports such as hunting and fishing both grow in popularity, carrying on in the leisure area the kind of physical energy that used to go toward maintenance of life. Games such as football are now great commercial enterprises that also grow in popularity and require no physical energy of the public except for its walk from the car lot to the stadium. In the history of leisure and play in the United States, outdoor sports and games went more naturally with rural or small-town life than the apartment or the suburban home.

Movement in the home offers additional issues, not so much in respect to intensive physical expenditure as to the relation of architecture to patterns of leisure use and, incidentally, of movement. Indeed, the larger issue of space enters here, an issue that enters more and more into the forefront of leisure thinking because mechanical energy can transport man to larger spaces in shorter time. In the home, however, space is more a matter of arrangement in efficiency and comfort than in the preservation of physical energy. The new leisures has led to a new architecture, implying such items as "family" rooms, "Florida" rooms, basement "recreation" rooms, television rooms, and so on. In a realistic way, some of America's history can be directly documented in the family changes revealed through such clues.

Equally important are the issues that deal with the transport of persons for purposes of leisure. Travel in the past has been traditionally for the benefit of military conquests, religious conversions, and business commissions. Tourism before this century was only for the wealthy; a century ago, especially for trips on land, even the wealthy had to undergo difficulties and dangers. It is no accident that the root of "travel" is the French *"travail,"* which implies "very hard work."

With the comparative ease of travel today and its readier availability to the masses, the range of motivations has enlarged. Curiosity, education, "change of scene," and social status are now prominent factors. Indeed, just the opposite of *rest* is the contribution of travel toward a resolution of *restlessness.* Unfortunately, the same technical forces that have amplified travel opportunities also contributed to that restlessness. Increased movement, in time free from productive processes, has beome necessary in a hurried society; furthermore, the more hurried the pace of contemporary living becomes, the wider the geographical space needed for movement grows. In this peculiar sense, both movement and rest can be therapeutic. With today's mass media, the intellectual impact has no relationship to the effort or commitment in time, money, and energy; I am sure that I saw far less of the Vatican from a personal visit than from a magnificent television "tour" with Charles Boyer.

In a previous discussion I suggested as two major types of leisure a *going to the world* and a *bringing the world to us.* There is still some reason for keeping this useful distinction in respect to our various relationships to the world, but on reviewing these ideas, I prefer this restatement: *television provides a contemporary magic whereby the viewer is both at rest and in movement;* indeed, the ideal model for commercial sponsors of television is fundamentally that of rest, to absorb the advertising. "Bringing the world to us" includes, of course, the world of material objects, from Bufferin to Buicks, as well as the views of other regions and the reports of political events.

Fourteen definitions are given of "rest" in Webster's New World Dictionary. All point to a general state of immobility: peace, ease, and refreshment as produced by sleep; refreshing ease or inactivity after work or exertion; relief from anything distressing. "Recuperation" is a restoration, to make well again; the patient may recover in part by resting under a tree or in bed, but the prescription for recovery may include activities in occupational therapy, such as arts and crafts, or walking around the room to music, or singing in a choir.

Therapeutic leisure is leisure that happens to fall into a particular sequence of experiences: it can be *after* an event such as an attempt at suicide, a bad love affair, an argument with one's boss; it might be *before* an anticipated event, such as the vacation to "get ready" for the fall teaching schedule.

Recuperative leisure is by definition more active than "rest," because it implies that the leisure episode may have a desirable effect, it may change an attitude, it will bridge a before and after—and the "after," unlike the consequences of mere rest, will be different because of the quality of recuperative leisure.

The contemporary view of leisure must include its usefulness as a tool in mental and emotional therapy. As in the case of art as therapy, there are purists who throw up their hands at any such association; but, as in the case of art, leisure is involvement made possible (as de Grazia likes to remind us) by "freedom from necessity." Involvement has its own goals and values and is there directed and directive. Art as action or leisure as action includes the restorative function, and on the priority scale of the participant—at a given moment of the day or in his life— this may be its chief value.

As to rest in its most naked sense of complete absence of purpose, leisure on this level brings to mind Charles Johnson's comment about rural life of blacks in the first third of this century.[11]

"Rural life has its period of intense work and its period of dull and uneventful calm. When the soil is being broken and prepared for crops, all hands strong enough for the plow are engaged from early sunrise to sundown . . . between seasons the most common answer to the question about how and where the children play is likely to be 'We don't do nothing, mostly just sit and talk.' "

Rest is unlike sleep in this regard; it is not a complete withdrawal; it is just short of sleep. It often turns into sleep, but whether or not sleep in any form should be counted as leisure is a moot point. Since, as Szalai points out, a person's sleeping, eating, and working altogether take up only half of his lifetime, "rest" short of sleep is probably a considerable part of that lifetime, especially in the warmer climates of the world. If recuperation is more purposeful, rest is the most passive of all leisure values and of its forms. This is the overriding quality of rest—its spontaneity or its anticipation, its usefulness physiologically and psychologically, its universality, and its classlessness.

The statistical, even the qualitative difficulty to the student of leisure is that the element of physiological rest may so often become inextricably enmeshed with other elements such as watching television. How much is the viewer really resting, and viewing TV on the side; how much is he actively viewing the program, and resting along the way? This multiplicity of activities came out sharply in all of the nations studied by Szalai and his colleagues.

Freedom-Discipline

Freedom is a highly important purpose or motivation for leisure: freedom from the toil of obtaining the necessities for life; freedom from familiar tasks, faces, and places; freedom from the clock; freedom from responsibility; freedom from family. We have already seen Germans along the Rhine in the *Fasching* season symbolically seeking freedom from themselves in their normal roles of work and status. To watch a television show is to free ourselves from the ordinary views in everyday life; to go on a vacation trip with the family is to negate, for a time and for a price, the familiar responsibilities of the same daily job, the same houses on the block, the same food on the table, and the same telephone calls from the same friends.

Leisure is also a freedom *for;* for the bullfight, for the Beacon Hill chamber music. These experiences are built on strong, positive attractions.

A few generalizations around this dichotomy of *from* and *for* apply in an interesting way to leisure. *First, as one is stronger, the other can be weaker, and yet disproportionately successful.* Example: if work is very dull, less is demanded of the evening's play; conversely, as the bullfight has a greater attraction, any other alternative will be less persuasive. The slightest leisure or form of play may be of enormous importance to the prisoner; it would seem that the recreation leader of Sing Sing should therefore have an easier time of it than his counterpart in some community center, with free men as participants. Yet there is something incomplete here. The prisoner has not come with the right spirit to his recreation; his play, by contrast, is only a change, but unfed by the nourishment that a free man can bring to his play experiences. This can be seen even in comparisons amongst those outside of prison walls. We know, for instance, that a professional man can often adjust to retirement better than others; his "play" is a continuity of what his "work" was.

What has happened, then, to our first principles? A supplementary observation suggests itself: *"freedom for" in leisure can derive through restraint.* "Through" differs substantially from "from." A classic case of this operates in the clubs or voluntary associations. The club, after all, is a fantasy in role playing. Let 10 men who a few moments ago were coequals over beer suddenly and, according to fixed expectations, go into a "meeting": one becomes the "President," another the "Secretary," and a third the "Treasurer." A formal dynamic sets in. Each man now finds his freedom in leisure through the group. It would not be entirely correct to assume that any member at the meeting has surrendered his freedom to act; he has, in fact, acquired new freedoms as long as he proceeds according to the rules. He has, after all, entered into the meeting "game" on his own volition. If the rules limit him beyond his wishes, or if—as in the case of a much larger "game," the dictatorial society—he is not in it by his choice and cannot get out, then we have another matter altogether.

Leisure, as an object of freedom, can feed into and enrich the context to which it is ostensibly opposed: it can, if successful, produce a better worker; the family vacation can contribute to year-long family relationships; our Teleman-Vivaldi evenings did not serve merely to contrast but to add a new dimension to the rest of the week.

Play-Entertainment

A classic conceptualization of "play" is given by Johann Huizinga in *Homo Ludens* (man the player, as distinct from *Homo Faber,* man the maker or worker).[12]

1. Play is a voluntary activity, never a physical necessity or a moral duty. It is not only a matter of leisure and free time, it is freedom.
2. Play is not ordinary or real life, but this is not to say that play may not be intense or serious; it is not necessarily the opposite of seriousness, and it is further outside the realm of such dichotomies as wisdom and folly, truth and falsehood, good and evil. It is marked, instead, by "disinterestedness," by being an interlude in our daily lives, an end in itself.
3. Play is secluded and limited, containing its own course and meaning; it begins and is over at a specific moment. Yet, since it becomes a tradition, it can be repeated. The dual elements of repetition and alternation are contributions to the independence of play, which further functions within limita-

tions of time and space. Play thus constitutes a temporary world within and marked off from the ordinary world.

4. Play creates order; in face, it is order. It is inside a "playground"; slight deviation from the rules spoils the game. Since order has a tendency to be a thing of beauty, in and of itself, we have the affinity of play to aesthetics. Order within play contains all the elements of beauty, such as tension, poise, balance, and contrast. *Tension* demands a *solution*, a basic cycle to aesthetic experience; rules become all-important, because deviations threaten the very existence of the play-community.

5. Last, the play-community tends to become permanent after the game is over because, in the course of playing it has become an "in-group," having already shared a common experience within an atmosphere of some secrecy, some "dressing up," some disguise or identification.

The formulation applies to chess, ping pong, pool, soccer, tennis, or volleyball—but Huizinga himself applies his concepts of play to large areas—to the arts, war, law philosophy, and science.

There has been no comparable analytic model for entertainment, in distinction to either play or art. The Oxford English Dictionary defines entertainment as "The act of occupying (a person's) attention agreeably ... that which afford interest or amusement."

From this definition it becomes clear that in entertainment the subject is being acted *on;* he receives, observes, listens, and watches. In play, on the other hand, at least as conceptualized by Huizinga, the reference is to the active participant. The dramaturgical use of "play" as in pure theater combines the performer as well as the audience. There has arisen, in the generalized judgment of intellectuals, a priority of play over entertainment: the first is "active," the second is "passive" —and the first is somehow to be blessed, the second to be deplored; furthermore, play is somehow innocent because of its association with children (freshness, excitement), whereas the entertainment is usually identified with adults (staleness, boredom). Note briefly some further contrasts between entertainement and Huizinga's view of play.

1. Play, he notes, is freedom; entertainment is controlled by others, as in the case of TV.

2. Play is an "interlude," an end in itself; entertainment is a means to such ends as relaxation, sociability, and laughter.

3. Play is marked off from the real world, with its own order; entertainment may, of course, be similarly marked off, as in a house party, but it is more informal, transitory, and subject to manipulation because it is an instrument rather than an end.

4. Play, like aesthetic experience, provides solutions to tensions; entertainment can be low key throughout, without climax, like a series of acts that follow each other in an old-time vaudeville show.

5. If the play-community—like a group of card players—tends to become permanent after the game is over, no such continuity exists among those who were related only loosely by being accidently tied to the same entertaining stimuli. The latter, like members of a movie audience, have only a San Louis Rey Bridge relationship, in the sense that Arnold Hauser speaks of them.[13]

"The millions and millions who fill the many thousands of cinemas all over the world from Hollywood to Shanghai and from Stockholm to Cape Town daily and hourly, this unique world-embracing league of mankind, have a very confused social structure. The only link between these people is that they all stream into the cinemas, and stream out of them again as amorphously as they are pumped in; they remain a heterogeneous, inarticulate, shapeless mass with the only common feature of belonging to no uniform class or culture."

Sociability-Isolation

If we are to accept the common conception of rural and smalltown life, one of its main elements is what Durkheim called its "organic" nature. As distinct from the "contractual" or secondary society, in which people know only small dimensions of other people, the rural milieu permits a person to be known as a whole. An enormous literature, both of fiction and social science, centers around such themes as anonymity, uprootedness, alienation, loneliness and, on the positive aspect, such as love, friendship, "community," neighborhood, or *Gemütlichkeit.*

All indications point to more urbanization. We may ask, therefore, whether the values of sociability and of isolation are important for the new technological milieu. If so, how does leisure serve these ends?

To start with isolation: this term is not the same as either withdrawal or loneliness. Withdrawal may be temporary,in the sense of a religious retreat, but more often the term has a permanent connotation. Withdrawal is a term of action: withdrawal to what? Isolation, by contrast, is a separation, a disengaging from others, an effort toward privacy, which may not at all result from a voluntary withdrawal: the prisoner, against his will, has been put into isolation, and so is the sick person with a contagious illness. Loneliness is one's own attitude or feeling about being apart from others, but with an idea in mind of wanting to be involved with other persons. One can, as on a fishing trip, be quite withdrawn from his friends and family without being lonely in the slightest. Conversely, he can be at Times Square on New Year's Eve and quite surely feel lonely. Loneliness has no bearing on how many people are around; isolation does, and it is an ecological more than a sociological term.

Sociability goes to the heart of psychiatry and psychology as well as sociology. H. P. Fairchild speaks of sociability as a "way of being bound to a whole and by a whole ... in a looser sense, that of the capacity of individuals to be integrated into group life. ..."[14]

I spoke of several "models" for sociability in my 1960 volume: family, friendship, and love. The family, in fact, serves as the major example of leisure that, in its purest sense, illustrates many processes. In the contemporary urban family, whether or not the wife works outside the home, the roles of father, mother, and child are generally separate in their functions. Quite the opposite is the situation of the farm family of the past, where everyone knew about or could even perform some functions of the other. It is not the economic functions that give the city family its essence; quite the reverse, it is the leisure of individuals or of the whole that becomes "a cause, a clue, and an index of sources of respect, love, interdependence, and knowledge about the other."

There is good reason for concern about the solidity of the contemporary family, with changing norms about sex and the new freedom of children. Far greater changes should be expected in the cyberculture era, when companionship will become even more the totality, when leisure becomes the major or sole essence, and functional patterns will take place in such ways as education, community volunteerism, or in ways yet to be invented.

New concepts of families and "functional neighborhoods" may be on the horizon, but whatever may be their nature—and there will be many varieties of each—sociability and isolation are cherished by many persons as they think about the future. By the first they mean that one can find himself by being with the others, pushing and being pushed in arguments, by learning to ask questions, by all the twists and turns of live conversation. By isolation they mean that there are times to be alone, to observe oneself, to become bored, perhaps, but also to feel stronger in the knowledge of self.

Friendship carries the strengths of sociability *and* isolation. Good friends are such only if they can explore each other or—even together physically—can do their own thing. Young people often have to learn this about love; that a great interpenetration of each other's values can, especially after marriage, lead to a wholesome indifference toward each other. This is a lesson that architects have learned in constructing student "union" centers: in such well-conceived buildings on the campus there is a perpetual invitation for every student to be alone and unbothered; the physical structure also encourages group structuring, formal and informal. English pubs are among the most successful inventions toward this end.

Construction-Distraction

The motivation of *construction* is used here in the sense of transforming, building, affecting, changing. We can speak of "constructive" in relation to political activity, service to the community, or adding a room to one's home; *constructing a better society, community, or personal environment.* The range is obviously wide. And yet, the "do it yourself" tendency has qualitative similarities in the building of a better home or of a better community.

As to the literal form of construction, two forms of this leisure are commonplace. In one, something is built because of interest in the construction itself. Millions of women are knitting and crocheting, in part, to have something ready as a gift to a granddaughter, but also partly because of the pleasant habit of something to do over many days or the satisfaction that comes with making something. Men and boys, in spite of TV or other distractions, are still making ship models and other things for the same reasons. There is a possibility that the return to handicrafts will show an upsurge in the decades ahead, as men and women rediscover the use of the hands and develop the patience that requires time and relaxation.

The second type of "construction" is leisure that is directed to serving the community in areas such as welfare agencies, hospitals, YMCA, or Boy Scouts, or in the more controversial level of protest marches, political activity, and other direct ways of affecting public opinion or legislative action.

Even the quieter level, generally called "volunteerism," is a far cry from what it was as late as the 1930s in the lives of upper-middle-class women. Since that time, social work has become professionalized, and the army of volunteers, which still runs into the millions of persons, is more structured, trained, and selected. The range of duties is far greater now because volunteerism has moved from assistance to poor persons toward such programs as service to students in need of special tutoring, retired persons in need of conversation and services, or communities in need of special surveys (such as a health study in Newton and an inventory of trees and historical buildings in Boston). Wherever there are artistic projects and museums, volunteers are the ministry of day-by-day chores and financial campaigning.

President Nixon established a special commission in 1970 to explore new methods of finding, training, and utilizing the special talents of volunteers. The Peace Corps and VISTA, while geared to persons who commit themselves to a period of full-time service, provide two models of federally oriented programs that bear study for shorter-range or modified free-time experiences. The church has turned to larger dimensions of leisure than merely a search for volunteers and is developing a more sophisticated analysis of leisure.[15]

Political activity—except for those in office or running for office—involves many millions of persons at sporadic periods before and during campaigns. Should not all of this be entered into the ledger of "leisure"? The construct introduced in Chapter 2 does not limit the term to light-hearted, relaxing, inconsequential activity. Even the Greek concept, *paidia,* went beyond pure use of the mind in pursuit of learning and happiness: "relaxation is not an end, it is taken for the sake of activity" (Aristotle). The current tendency of youth is not only to make itself alternately heard and then to "drop out," but, with the McCarthy primaries of 1968 in New Hampshire as a model, to participate within the system. Since this is the generation that may be the first to feel the economic impact of such revolutions as atomic energy and cybernation for economically productive purposes, its own political style will hold clues as to the restructuring of man's energies. If, indeed, major cultural revolutions in the future are caused by an elite of persons who create new social forms in time freed by machines—in their leisure—this will not be a new phenomena. Major revolutionaries of the past as well were far from the field and factory; Marx wrote *Das Kapital* in the London library.

It is conceivable that the term destruction could be used at the other end of the leisure continuum, but the gang member, as I recall from experience, does not think of himself as a destroyer. We did set out to find identity for ourselves—a quest that was important then to us as sons of immigrants. Our techniques were those of distraction—from our homes, our heritage, ourselves—in neighborhood shows, minor stealing from shops, and sneaking into movie houses.

Distractions of these kinds are as old as recorded history. A generation ago one recalls the Marxist position about the motion picture as the "opiate" of the people—their distraction from class realities. The German *Fasching* was a distraction for the medieval serfs, as it is now for their more prosperous descendants.

We all know of the Roman circuses, deliberately staged to distract the masses, or the later pageants that fulfilled the same purpose amidst earthly poverty. An interesting tale on the origins of the gypsy comes out of this form of collective psychology. It is told by the Persian poet, Firdawsi, in his Book of Kings (Shah Nameh), about 1000 A.D.[16]

"... about the year 420 before our era, Behram Gour, a wise and beneficent prince of the Sassanide dynasty (226 B.C.–A.D. 641), realized that his poor subjects were pining away for lack of amusements. He sought a means of reviving their spirits and of providing some distraction from their hard life. With this end in mind he sent a diplomatic mission to Shankal, King of Cambodia and Maharajah of India, and begged him to choose among his subjects and send to him in Persia persons capable by their talents of alleviating the burden of existence and able to spread a charm over the monotony of work. Behram Gour soon assembled twelve thousand itinerant minstrels, men and women, assigned lands to them, supplying them with corn and livestock in order that they should have the wherewithal to live in certain areas which he would designate; and so be able to amuse his people at no cost. At the end of the first year these people had neglected agriculture, consumed the corn seed and found themselves without resources. Behram was angry and commanded that their asses and musical instruments should be taken away, and that they should roam the country and earn their livelihood by singing. As a consequence these men, the Luri, roamed the world to find who would employ them, taking with them dogs and wolves, and thieving night and day on their way."

The important point is that the distractions take on *positive* qualities; the term distraction almost compels one, by the nature of the prefix *dis*, to denote a separation, a negation, or a reversal; this is the opposite of the Latin *constructs*, which comes from *com* (together) and *struere* (to pile up, build). Distraction from ugliness, proverty, or loneliness can be "constructive" and, indeed, *Webster's New World Dictionary* of 1957 denotes it as "anything that gives mental relaxation or freedom from worry, grief, etc."—thus assigning a positiveness to the term.

Nevertheless, although the bullfight or television audiences may approach their leisure choices with no attitude of negativeness, these activites are still substantially different from what is commonly known as a constructive purpose of motive. Snobbishness is to be avoided here, as in the parallel use of active and passive. For all of his caveats, David Riesman was not entirely convincing in his attempt to treat other-directedness with the same values he gave to inner-directedness. "Distraction" runs the same risk by noting here that such a "distractive" commitment as television may well be as creative—often more creative —than a shallow or misplaced engagement in a bit of community action badly conceived or executed. As Riesman says, activity is often measured by the false criterion of "lactic content."

Such terms as "constructive," "creative," "good," and "commendable," are packed with judgments and biases on the part of all of us.

When Pitirim Sorokin studied the matter of altruism, he pitted the historical cases of saints against those women of the Los Angeles area who were nominated by their friends in Los Angeles as Queen for a Day.[17] The upper-class women who, a generation ago, were welcomed by the community as volunteers in many areas of social welfare are now denied such opportunity; no more do we want the "do-gooder" to play with the lives of others. Now the constructive-oriented community volunteer finds careful constraints from the professionals.

Self-growth-Recreation

The distinction between these concepts provides perhaps the most compelling of the dialectic sets of this discussion. The term "self-growth" suggests synonyms such as development, expansion, enlargement, creation, achievement, and evolvement; it is an active, moving concept. The term "recreation," in the vernacular sense, is defined by a recent dictionary as "refreshment of one's mind or body after labor through diverting activity; play."

The recreation profession of our decade might question this limited view of their purpose. Certainly, this profession has moved very far in stressing the integrality of play to human growth. We come up against the fusionist tendency of which I will speak later; in the primitive society, play was not as often as among us a separate activity, removed from maintenance tasks, so in our emerging neoprimitive society the elements of play can be seen to penetrate work, family, and educational situations, that is, play as respite, jocularity, and interruption. There was an earlier sense of "play" that came from the Anglo-Saxon *plega*—a game, a sport, and this used to be equated with a fight or skirmish. Even the seemingly innocuous phrase, "play an instrument" originally meant to strike something. The term "plague," the Latin *plaga,* and our contemporary "play" are not unrelated. The stage "play" takes the concept much further, so that there is less of a fight than a dialogue between the symbolic, stylized action on the stage and the "reality" represented by the audience. It is in these several senses that the larger term "recreation" may be seen in distinction to self-growth.

Self-growth, as I use it here, is larger than education. The latter term, however the humanist might want to approach it, is too narrowly confined to the "process of imparting knowledge or skill" or even the broader "process of training and developing the knowledge, skill, mind, character, etc., especially by formal schooling."

Yet the scope of our communications and the range of experiences that are now commonplace go far beyond the processes defined above. Growth of self means the total interplay by which the person becomes

sensitive to his environment and enlarges his perceptions, his understanding, and his possibilities of responding. Maslow's "self-actualization" is now a standard expression in this same vein.

Self-worth-Self-defeat

Many of us in our work are engaged in ordinary taks; we sort mail, drive
a truck, or read gas meters. Yet among the most routinized workers may
be found singular hobbies or nonwork behavioral patterns that defy
prediction, as among the group of postal clerks (studied by a student of
mine) that contained a competent archeologist, a folk-tale collector, and
a talented playwright. The motivations may be many; serious studies
are needed to get at this element of self-worth. On a realistic or an
imagined level, we have the germ or the full actualization, through such
leisure, of appreciation of oneself, of some inner contentment.

On the negative side are those leisure experiences that, either in the
motivation or in the unexpected fruition, become gestures toward self-
defeat. In part this is an extension of the Peter Principle from work to
leisure—persons who move up into a complexity of experience they are
unprepared to handle. The difference is that one more easily disengages
from a leisure experience—as in the case of one who attends a museum
and finds it dull.

The result is that we find families who entertain or who purchase cars
beyond their means. As Stanley Parker has said, industry is interested
in *consuming* time, always encouraging the purchase of leisure goods
and services.[18] The cycle takes over: people are forced to work longer
to pay for their leisure: leisure becomes the determining theme of life,
and the additional scramble for dollars leads to self-defeat in a material
and emotional sense. This is contrary to the attainment of self-worth,
because it's guiding principle is often the judgment of others.

There was a built-in constraint against this type of self-defeat when
the family was the chief expression of social class position. The constraint was, of course, the knowledge of the family about itself, as evident in the kind of job, amount of money, area of residence, one's
friends, one's sexual conquests, or other indices of class. More and more,
"levels" instead of classes have become prominent, and the level of
accessibility that one has to distance, the opposite sex, education, entertainment, or things such as cars, is more individual than family in its
basis. Thus the family as a buffer tends to weaken. This is seen most
clearly with contemporary youth to whom the family now means less
and who purposely align themselves with gestures (drugs are only one
form) to symbolize their freedom from the family or, as Kenneth Ken-
niston notes, "lack of conscious or articulate involvement" with it.

Leisure as a statement of *self-worth* is a symbol of repose, acceptance of self, recognition of one's strengths and limitations; as *self-defeat*, leisure represents an urge to be other than oneself. *Self-worth* comes from the leisure that is autonomous, in Riesman's sense, calling on our own resources and not unmindful of what is going on around us. *Self-defeat* in leisure is being untrue to ourselves, imitating others, going beyond our means, skills, or real desires.

DYNAMICS OF THE DIALECTIC

The essence of the present dialectic construct is the fluctuation between termination and development. As with the preceding sets, each has its validity. And as in the others, we now face the theoretical issue: what are some of the conditions that contribute to the function of leisure within each dialectic as well as to the predominance of one set above the others?

It is not enough to stipulate a set of 12 functions of leisure, structured in a sixfold dialectic. We must ask two questions. What determines, in a given case, which of these sets of functions takes predominance, and what happens within the continuum from one polarity to the other? The two arrows below visualize this double statement of the theoretical problem.

Movement	——	Rest
Freedom	——	Discipline
Play	——	Entertainment
Sociability	——	Isolation
Construction	——	Distraction
Self-growth	——	Recreation
Self-worth	——	Self-defeat

In theological thought, this form of dialectic analysis is so important that it remains a dominant Aristotelian proof of God to the Christian, that is, nothing exists without a cause, hence if there is a something—earth, man, goodness—there is a cause, a creator, ergo a God. In epistomology (the origins of meaning and its categories), this type of thinking through contrasts asserts that no concept of "good" is possible without one of "bad," or similarly, beautiful-ugly, just-unjust. In sociological thought, the dialectic is crystallized in neither *causes* or *oppositions,* but in *relationships:* thus there can be no concept of "mother" without one of "child" or of "governor" without the "governed."

From the viewpoint taken in Chapter 4, the question raised by the choice of one element over the other in any set is whether the participant really has a choice in terms of what I have called the "conditions." These were listed as age, sex, income, work, time, residence, health, family, education, group and subculture, and cultural or historical factors. Many of these are concernably of some bearing on the choice of a bridge game, and I need hardly belabor such obvious connections: the players are adults, there is sufficient income not to work that evening, and so forth. The conditions are generally favorable for the choice. But if the "will" is there in what we call "personality," some conditions can be overcome (like playing in spite of a headache), and the conscious choice develops for this activity instead of for others that are available within the same umbrella of conditions. At this point the functional elements take over: the person "wills," "decides," "is moved," "chooses"—to do what? To (1) play bridge because it enables *play, sociability,* and *recreation,* and to (2) find play, sociability, and recreation through *bridge.* He has learned to associate these attributes and this activity, and this has happened through some circumstantial events that were described in Chapter 5 as "mediating" factors.

This process of association is crucial. One of the current associations by young people is a drug with a "trip." "Trips" differ from the relatively mild hallucinations caused by marijuana to more severe and dramatic impacts of "speed," LSD, and other drugs. Here, too, we could draw our hypothesis from the dialectic pairings, arriving at such elements as freedom, isolation, and distraction (in the sense of withdrawal). If drugs are in fashion they will be paired with functions—in the case of young people, *searchings*—that are in the climate of the times. A transference may be made from drugs to religion, or to yoga, and precisely such transfers are being made in the 1970s by youth. The clue to policy for those who wish to relate to youth is not to confuse the means (drugs) with the ends or functions. Many years ago we learned that the way to "break up" a street gang was to let the gang remain intact; gangdom was only the instrument, the channel through which young people obtained meanings such as freedom, discipline, sociability, distraction, and recreation. We are witnessing now, at the turn of the century, a serious attempt by young people to modify their purposes by a dramatic reversal of elements shown above in the dialectic elements. They seek "freedom," we say—freedom from the mores of the materialistic, middle-class values, and they do it by deviations from the norms of dress, sex, or behavior. Yet in this there is also a strong opposite, the tendency toward discipline. The young people who helped Senator McCarthy in New Hampshire were engaged in self-discipline of a high order. Similarly, the isolation that comes from the individualistic and unique experience of every drug consumer arises out of a strong symbolic identity with his generation. What was Woodstock but a dramatic demonstration of this synthesis—sociability on the high level of love, compassion, and care on the one hand and the voluntary isolation or withdrawal that comes both from drugs and from hypnosis through music?

The apparent conclusion emerges that there is no direct or inevitable straight line from function to activity. Each can be fulfilled by various forms of the other. The activities are more subject to fashions of the time; the functions sought are more ingrained, related as they are to personality and values. Furthermore, the range of activities grows, aided especially by new wrinkles in transportation and communication, but the range of values, and hence the functions of activities, has until now remained fairly constant through man's history. The "future shock" of which Alvin Toffler writes will derive from the potential changes in values, brought about by the new alternatives of action provided to mankind. We must give our attention to the approach to these new objects and new images. This, for instance, is the attraction of "sensitivity training"; it is not an activity but an attempt to expand one's openness to the world and to himself. It is conceivable, putting the matter concretely, that a community center devoted to "leisure" might be established in which no specific activities are announced. It would have an open agenda, free to implement announced intentions such as "movement," "play," "construction," and "self-growth." Innovative, intuitive, unpredictable chains of *experiences* (not activities) would emerge, so that an exploration of "movement" could lead the same group from eurythmics, to creative dance, to staging a play, to a helicopter view of traffic, to a trip across the seas. In the same way, if a university were to learn something about itself that it has never learned (being itself too busy teaching) i.e., that the curriculum is artifically cut up into a myriad of fractions, many of them serving the same functions, it might reorganize itself *thematically* to achieve the relevancy and coherence that is now often missing.

For further insights into the dynamic of both manifest and latent functions, I return to several propositions from Chapter 3, especially to discern tendencies for the future.

Propositions 1 and 2 suggest that the same leisure experience may serve different functions, depending on the time in which it takes place. The association of leisure content with time structure will be less affected on the small time scale of the day. Whatever the nature of changing work, men and women will continue to find the evening a natural time for theater or socializing. However, as long familiar days for work—Monday through Friday—become unlocked, as in the four-day workweek pattern, the association of Friday with rest may take on the same expectation of Saturday. Winter vacations have already become natural to many persons. As to manifest functions, new associations of time-leisure will take shape on the second, or therapeutic level. There still persists the guilt among many who find that they are not at work on a Friday, so that they may be heard to say, "I feel like it is Saturday."

The same feeling of guilt, as related to the *day,* will affect several sets discussed above as latent functions. Areas to watch will probably be the pairs of movement-rest and sociability-isolation. In short, time for leisure becomes not only quantitatively more but psychologically disconcerting. Freedom from work, indeed, may be easier than the break from traditional uses of certain hours, days, or weeks in the year. One of my students looked into the use made of the 10-week sabbaticals negotiated in Tampa by employees of a can manufacturer. He found that those who happened (by seniority) to get the bulk time in the summer were happier than those whose off-period came in the winter. In part this difference in adjustment came from the simultaneous vacation from school by the children; in part, however, it came from the easier perception of a "vacation" as a summertime thing—even in the relatively warm climate of Florida, which attracts tourists all year.

Proposition 21 turns to the importance of leisure patterns for family life. The discussion of this point predicted that "in the foreseeable future, leisure attitudes, uses, and roles will remain a stronger bond in the family than functional inter-relationships which were essential to the farm family." Implicitly this assigns to leisure a basic institutional function of maintaining values. Yet the importance of the family to the destiny of leisure—and of leisure to the future of the family—is that in the home we can observe the conflicts and reinforcements within each pair of functions discussed in the section above. This point will be made again in Chapter 8.

Finally, *Proposition 40* calls attention to leisure as a symbolic system that serves as a bridge between "various dimensions or forms of reality." This point will be a major focus of Chapter 15 in relation to such concepts as escape and disguise and to several psychoanalytic theories. Indeed, among the polarities that were submitted earlier in the dialectic statement of functions, "conscious-subconscious" might find a place.

Chapter 7

Meanings: Symbolic, Expository, and Epistomological

The *functions* of leisure are related to behavior patterns and categories, such as those developed in the last chapter. This is largely a sociological pursuit. The *meanings* of leisure takes us primarily into the psychological realm, since here we start with people. Social and mental systems are related but sufficiently distinguishable to have nurtured separate scientific disciplines. The specialist in leisure must take from both fields, even though neither has matured to a systematic or serious interest in the subject. It is not important that there be either a mature *sociological* or a mature *psychological* theory of leisure, but that a fusion of humanistic and scientific inquiry into leisure can develop as an interdisciplinary approach which uses, but is not limited to, college-cataloged methodologies. Equally useful to the study is philosophy, theology, economics, history, anthropology, literature, architecture, psychiatry, all the arts, and other forms of insight.

If all of these approaches to the meaning of leisure are sorted out, one might come to three major ways of digging into the subject; these I call the *symbolic, expository,* and *scientific* methods. Each has its strengths and its limitations. The symbolic approach to leisure's meaning refers to observations of the poet, novelist, and pictorial artist. The expository approach refers to a large variety of statements about leisure that may call on history, interpretations of a culture, or penetrating insights of an observer of whatever background; here we have a midway point between the first and third (the scientific), flowing over into both, and drawing on them. The scientific approach draws explicitly on studies of persons or activities that use acceptable techniques familiar in the academic and laboratory consensus and treat the leisure phenomena as rigidly as it would other human behavior.

This chapter provides examples of these approaches and arrives at a set of constructs that are broad enough to draw upon all three.

SYMBOLIC EXPRESSIONS OF LEISURE MEANINGS

Below is Marya Mannes' social commentary, contrasting the old and the new, called "A Room With a TV View," which she precedes with a headline from the *New York Times,* "Video Becoming as Standard as Baths (in Hotels)—Keeps Guests Indoors, and Spending."[1]

> *Once you traveled to change the scene,*
> *Taste whatever was strange and new,*
> *And when you got back you knew where you'd been*
> *And all the things that happened to you.*
>
> *But now, no matter how far you stray,*
> *Life is the same in every way:*
> *Scotch on the rocks,*
> *A ham on rye,*
> *And a room with a TV view.*
>
> *Once you would roam an unknown town,*
> *Drop in a bar to hear new talk,*
> *Sniff the air as you wandered down*
> *Alleys that strangers liked to walk.*
>
> *But now whether north or east or west,*
> *You're nothing more than a paying guest:*
> *Bourbon on ice,*
> *A cheese on rye,*
> *And a room with a TV view.*

The eternal matter of boredom is treated in this small gem by Nalan Hsintch of the Ch'ing Dynasty.[2]

Boredom

We can sing a different tune from the "Song of Desolation?"
The wind is sighing!
The rain is sighing!
The roseate flower of the candle is wearing itself out for another
*   night!*
I know not what is tangling up the skein of my thought.

Sober, I am bored!
Drunk, I am bored!
Even dreams refuse to carry me to the neighborhood of my love!

I go from these commentaries to another form of literature, the drama, and quote only one selection. Chekov's *Three Sisters* contains this portion of a scene that deals directly with the new meaning of work as it was evolving among the upper classes of his time.[3] One of the sisters, Irina, addresses the family physician, Dr. Chebutykim; later, their friend, Lieutenant Baron Nicholas Tutzenbakh, also speaks to the subject.

IRINA: Today I woke up, got out of bed and had a wash. And then I suddenly felt as if everything in the world made sense, I seemed to know how to live. I know everything, dearest Doctor. Man should work and toil by the sweat of his brow, whoever he is—that's the whole purpose and meaning of life, his happiness and his joy. How wonderful to be a workman who gets up at dawn and breaks stones in the road, or a shepherd, or a schoolmaster who teaches children or an engine-driver. Heavens, better not be a human being at all—better be an ox or just a horse, so long as you can work, rather than the kind of young woman who wakes up at noon, has her coffee in bed and then spends two hours getting dressed. Oh, that's so awful. You know how you sometimes long for a drink on a hot day—well that's how I long to work. And if I don't start getting up early and working you must stop being my friend, Doctor.

CHEBUTYKIN: (affectionately) I will, I will.

OLGA: Father taught us to get up at seven o'clock. Now Irina washes at seven and lies in bed at least till nine, just thinking, and looks so serious, too (laughs). . . .

TUTZENBAKH: This great urge to work, heavens, how well I understand it. I've never done a hand's turn all my life. I was born in St. Petersburg —that bleak, idle place—and grew up in a family that never knew the meaning of work or worry. I remember how I used to come home from my cadet school: the footman would pull off my boots, while I'd make a thorough nuisance of myself, watched by my mother who thought I was just wonderful and couldn't see why others took a rather different view. They tried to protect me from work. Only I doubt if their protection is going to prove all that effective. I doubt it. The time has come, an avalanche is moving down on us and a great storm's brewing that'll do us all a power of good. It's practically on top of us already and soon it's going to blast out of our society all the laziness, complacency, contempt for work, rottenness and boredom. I'm going to work and in twenty-five or thirty years' time everyone will work. Everyone.

What can literature tell us about leisure's meaning? It can focus attention on the person, the situation, or the community in ways that are beyond the tools of science; in its imagery and imagination, literature can reach depths of understanding that are enormously valuable toward understanding and that go into other kinds of dimensions than exposition or science. For example, Radhakamal Mukerjee, whose mind encompassed both the mysticism of the East and the social science of the West, summarizes the contribution of writers such as Eugene O'Neill, William Faulkner, and Virginia Woolf, who deal with the psychological realities of various states of man's "stream of consciousness." All this is vividly represented in bits of soliloquy and imaginary disputes between one-self and one-self, "in dreams and fantasies and in reminiscences and automatic repetitions of fragments of popular songs and poems that intermix oddly and freakishly with man's actual experience."[4]

If, indeed, leisure goes to the heart of man's consciousness and his values and diffuse moments of freedom and commitment, and if a central issue of man's new confrontation with his bulks of time—days or weeks on end—is boredom ("Sober I am bored—Drunk I am bored"), ennui, anomie, loneliness—then the literature of an age expresses these moods. Literature and even the ongoing soap operas on daytime television provide the models of the mass culture by which many persons find criteria of happiness or failures. The reality of such experience by association may be as strong or stronger than actual participation to the listener. Thus the literature about life of the upper-leisure classes as presented by William Dean Howells says much the same thing as Thorstein Veblen but appeals to a different audience, one that is less willing to deal with the abstract. And, of course, the intentions of the two men —who died only nine years apart—were entirely different, each arriving at comparable insights in his own way.

"It is time," as John Dewey noted,[5] "that the moral office and human function of art can be intelligently discussed only in the context of culture," but its own impact is a contribution as well as a reflection or summation of that culture. Literature, along with the other arts, enters into the study of leisure first, by *occupying* time; it stands alongside social science by *depicting* the drama of man's use of time; it enters the arena of values and of education by *dramatizing* and *teaching* values.

EXPOSITORY EXPRESSIONS OF LEISURE MEANINGS

This is the type of observation that falls between subjective literature and objective science. This middle range is where the largest proportion of statements on leisure will be found—in journalistic accounts, autobiographies, commentaries on the culture, history, and philosophy. The crucial question is not the line between imaginative and descriptive writing—who would be naive enough to say that fiction or poetry do not make true statements about man—but the line between exposition and science. Where, for example, does Riesman's *Lonely Crowd* belong? The "scientist" who cannot breathe without statistics in the air may look at Riesman (as well as Sorokin, Veblen, and others) as an "idea man." Yet Riesman's framework of personality structure has become a standard item in the sociological repertoire, as has Daniel Bell's work on postindustrial society.

There is hardly a meaning of leisure that has not been explored in the general literature. From the enormous reference to this subject, four broad types of statements seem to emerge: national, religious, social class, and personal meanings. As to the first, for example, Michener refers to bullfighting as a "ritual drama," producing "a catharsis precisely like that described by Aristotle." He quotes an unnamed source to the effect that the prologue is seen in the matador testing the bull with his cape, an "airy joy" comparable to *A Midsummer Night's Dream*. A heavy first act follows, with the preador suggesting *King Lear*. The bandilleros of the unimportant but "poetic" second act suggest *Twelfth Night*. Finally the "stupendous third act, heavy with emotion and impending tragedy, when the matador alone faces his destiny, is of course Hamlet, while the overpowering epilogue of death can be likened only to Aeschylus."[6]

One does not know the degree to which this dramatic and symbolic sense is a part of the typical Spaniard as he sees the late afternoon spectacle. It may be more, as one French-Spanish observer noted, that with the eighteenth century the uprooted masses who came to Madrid and Seville developed their passion for bullfights as "the response to a deep-rooted psychological need" to participate in public life. The "catharis" to which she refers is not in metaphors to great drama but to the intensity of resigned man who "gathers them, strains them to paroxysms, breaks them by an abrupt relaxation, knots them together once again, breaks them once again, to the rhythm of the bull's charge and retreat, charge and retreat"—destroying the sensitivity of the watcher.

A classic of insight into leisure's meaning from a religious point of view is found in Joseph Pieper's *Leisure: The Basis of Culture.*[7] In it the Swiss philosopher asserts that "one of the foundations of Western culture is leisure." Its proper understanding requires that we set aside "our prejudice that comes from overvaluing the sphere of work." This over-emphasis had come from Kant's conception that the good is normally difficult. Pieper adds to this: "the highest moral good is characterized by effortlessness—because it springs from love."[8] Contemplation goes with leisure and may therefore be spoken of in the same breath with play. The divine wisdom, according to Proverbs VIII, is "always at play, playing through the whole world."

Pieper draws on St. Thomas Aquinas to show that effort is not a necessary cause of knowledge but may be one of its conditions. As a further argument that effort can be separate from value, we see that even the Christian concept of sacrifice or discipline is not based on suffering *qua* suffering but is concerned with "salvation, with the fullness of being, and thus ultimately with fullness of happiness".[9]

Then Pieper considers leisure in relation to the liberal arts, since the true function of the intellectual worker in his social system is to be found here. Again Aquinas is brought in: "The liberal arts, then, include all forms of human activity which are an end in themselves; the servile arts are those which have an end beyond themselves, and more precisely an end which consists in the utilitarian result attainable in practice. . . ." Not everything is useless, notes Pieper, "which cannot be brought into the definition of the useful."[10] Work does not exhaustively define the world. Man is more than a worker if he leads a full human existence.

Approaching a positive conception of leisure, Pieper begins by distinguishing it from acedia (A-Kedos, or not care), since *sloth* is one of the seven deadly sins—a capital sin from which despair and other conditions follow. Idleness is the utter absence of leisure; indeed, it renders true leisure impossible. Real leisure is, first, "a mental and spiritual attitude," not simply a result of external factors, such as spare time, a holiday, a weekend, or a vacation. Its characteristic attitude must be one of nonactivity, inward calm, and silence: not being "busy" but "letting things happen." Other qualities are given for true leisure: "a form of silence," a "receptive state of mind," the capacity for "steeping oneself in the whole of creation," a certain happiness that comes from recognition of the mysteriousness of the universe and the recognition of our incapacity to understand it.[11]

Second, true leisure can be viewed as a contemplative "celebration," because it leads man to accept the reality of the creation and thus to celebrate it. Consequently, feast days and holy days "are the inner source of leisure."[12]

Third, leisure is opposed to the ideal of work as social function. A chronological break in work time is still part of the world of work. Leisure is not considered a "restorative, a pick-me-up, whether mental or physical. . . ." Following Aristotle's view, then, leisure steps beyond the ordinary world, touching on the superhuman life-giving power.

Finally, Pieper deals with the practical question, how can man be brought to this view, how can he be saved from work as his exclusive interest? For his answer, Pieper goes back to his conception of "celebration" as the source of leisure. Here all of its elements combine. The basis of celebration or the feast is "divine worship," and thus we arrive at the ultimate attainment of leisure. There is a divine *time*, as there is of space.

"In divine worship a certain definite space of *time* is set aside from working hours and days, a limited time, specially marked off—and like the space allotted to the temple, is not *used*, is withdrawn from all merely utilitarian ends."[13]

Another classic of expository writing is Veblen's relationship of the purposes and meanings of leisure to social class. Whereas Marx had argued that each social class develops its own way of life (its own culture and morality), Veblen sought to demonstrate that the lower classes emulate the higher. Of what, then, does the upper class consist? To be one of the upper class means more than the possession of wealth or power; these must be made visibly evident for all. What results is a high self-evaluation based on esteem from others.

In our discussion of personality the elements of social role were indicated. The circle, according to Veblen, is clear-cut, since the wealthy associate with each other, living a life in which leisure becomes purposeful activity; their purpose is to give to other circles of men a public accounting of their time. Their function is to become expert precisely in those skills and arts that go beyond spare time, that go on during the working day of the working class, and that require dress or other equipment beyond the spending power of the workers. Their status and, consequently, their conception of themselves as persons, comes from the ease with which they undertake such productively useless activities. Part of that ease is wrapped up in the manners that characterize the rich in social intercourse. All together, "these are the voucher of a life of leisure."[14]

The publicly noted waste of time, then, is the principle on which good breeding is evidenced. The visible male servant—the larger and more powerful the better—is one such tangible evidence: servants to do physical work and to exhibit are an obvious example of luxury spending.

Yet not all of one's time can be spent in playing polo, riding to hounds, or being driven through Central Park. The year is long and the lower class is not always there to see. Some accounting must be given of private time by the rich. *Immaterial goods* and *quasischolarly* or *quasi-artistic* activity form such public evidences of continual and substantively useless activity. Others are the study of dead languages, cultivation of the arts, games, sports, ownership of "fancy-bred animals," or activity in charity organizations, drives, and clubs.[15]

If all this is *conspicuous leisure,* then *conspicuous consumption* is another side of the picture. Time is spent on productively useless activity and money on a superabundance of things.

The guiding motive behind all this is self-satisfaction and position through esteem accorded by the have-nots. But is this all a mythology, a fantasy created by those in power? Clearly, it is a motif deep in the life of all, says Veblen, since the poor themselves seek to emulate the rich. Here, perhaps, is the core of Veblen's sharp irony because, unlike Marx, he offers no solution.

Veblen made the public aware of waste, as Riesman notes.[16] Veblen's contribution to institutional economics was to outline the latent functions of the system. In relation to leisure, a parallel can be seen between Riesman and Veblen. Both (more explicitly in the case of Riesman) are telling us something about groupism, about conformity. To Veblen, one *class* seeks to emulate the other and is sensitive to judgments by the other. To Riesman, one *person* seeks to be like the others and tunes in his "radar antennas" to the judgments and behavior of others. In the largest sense, both authors speak out for freedom of person and group so that they may be true to themselves. In contemporary America it is indeed a paradox that on the one hand the individual tends to conform to what *others* do, thus surrendering some freedom, and on the other hand, judging by the possession of things as well as control over leisure time (which can, indeed, be uselessly spent), *all* classes are now potentially free.

SCIENTIFIC STUDIES OF LEISURE MEANINGS

The nature of "science" could, at this point, interrupt the text at great length. The traditional view is that the indispensables of science, as Professor A. B. Wolfe noted four decades ago are, "(1) a body of observed facts, (2) established generalizations, principles or laws, the result of previous scientific work, (3) the fundamental laws of thought or logic."[17] In the course of discussing system in the ideal of science, Cohen and Nagel distinguish this from "common sense," which is content "with a miscellaneous collection of information."[18] However, sharp differences have developed in the methods and, indeed, the traditions within the scientific community that are familiar in such dichotomies as empiricism and rationalism, neopositivism and antipositivism, induction and deduction, or quantitative and qualitative. As one writer notes, empiricism is "an attitude-complex characterized by the utmost faith in the senses, firm belief in the power of observation . . . and belief that scientific conclusions should never get beyond the realm of extrapolation. . . ."[19] In rationalism, on the contrary, "the criterion of truth is not sensory but intellectual and deductive. . . . It is preoccupied with conceptual schemes, constructions, and logical manipulations." Several instances of the first are presented below in the study of leisure, followed by an example of the schematic or rationalistic.

A Dutch study is addressed to the feeling of "well-being" related to drinking and smoking habits. Evan Gadourek reports his sample survey of 1382 persons made by himself and students of psychology and sociology in 71 municipalities.[20] About 150 questions were used on the degree of "cultural involvement" and attitudes to smoking and drinking. A full battery of statistical techniques were employed, including Stuart Chapin's social participation scale, a component analysis to measure general satisfaction and psychological conditions, and a factor analysis applied to 34 variables.

Some of the theories tested were that the habits of smoking and drinking are adopted in adolescence "as an ostentatious affirmation of their own maturity, manliness or independence," or that anxieties, worries and personal *anomie* or disorganization lead to more drinking. Of every 10 men in the Netherlands, 9 smoke; and 4 out of 10 women smoke (17 cigarettes daily among men, 3 among women). Most smoking takes place in social contexts, confirming the "social role" theory of proving oneself an adult. Small correlation was found with neurotic tendencies or inner tensions, with the more "feminine" occupations (to appear as a "man"), or with parental norms. Interestingly, heavy smokers knew more about the harmful effects of their act but accepted the information less. The increased intensity of the habit among smokers who dread cancer is one of the paradoxical findings of this study.

The regular consumption of liquor in the Netherlands is far less common, only 9 percent among all adults; 18 percent never drink at all. A large part of the population therefore has some association with alcohol.

Men drink less as they become older (not women, however); young men usually are the beer drinkers, over weekends in cafes and restaurants; married men, at home entertaining friends. More consumption generally is found among Roman Catholics than among Reformed Church members. No association was found with theories of "escape" from material or emotional cares, and little association was found with higher income. "Social pressure" is a positive factor on drinking that is not to excess. Again the "social roles" theory was confirmed, with younger men showing their independence; "group-forming, social function of the consumption of alcohol persists in later life."

The chief value of this intensive study is to show that whereas in the past drinking may have been primarily on an individual level of motivation and meaning, we are now witnessing "the process of a further development towards a rational society in the sense that the average citizen is learning to control his impulses and channel them socially"; the purpose of drinking is not intoxication, but "a kind of ritual, or gesture of hospitality." What we have then, is testimony that smoking and drinking can be viewed less as leisure activities in themselves and more as supplements or visual and mental elements within a leisure social milieu.

Confronting another scientific issue, Robert Havighurst of the United States and Raymond Aron of France agree that the general meanings of leisure and of work are about the same: for example, sociability and fulfillment or the feeling of being needed by others.[21] Stanley Parker of London, however, put this question to about 200 persons in England who are employed in business and service occupations. In replying to the question on their reasons for enjoying leisure, they had several choices in answering: "Because it satisfies the interests that you *would like* to satisfy in your work, because it is satisfying in a *different way* from your work, or because it is *completely different* from your work?"[22] Most replies favored the last attitudes toward work and leisure. Parker's general conclusion is that "those who find work more demanding of their abilities are more likely to be socially or intellectually active in their leisure than are those who find work less demanding."[23] Different meanings are ascribed to leisure even within one occupational group. Among manual workers, especially those with relatively high skills, 73 percent associated leisure with freedom.[24] The last three chapters of his recent volume are especially recommended to students of the field. Here develops his theory of work-leisure relations, with the following conclusion based around his major concepts, given in parenthesis:

"A person who sees that the parts of his life are integrated, each one affecting and being affected by the others (wholism) is likely to have an extension pattern of work and leisure and to live in a society—or at least in a social circle—in which the spheres of work and leisure are fused (identity). On the other hand, a person who sees the parts of his life as separate segments comparatively unaffected by each other (segmentation) is likely to have either of the other two types of work leisure relationship *or* he will have a neutrality pattern of work and leisure . . . fairly self contained."[25]

CONSTRUCT: CONVERGENCE OF APPROACHES ABOVE

The "rationalistic" example of meanings in leisure was referred to in Chapter 2 as an epistomological conception of leisure. As stated below, it is a hypothesis that the world may be approached through faith, knowledge, or symbol. Each is an organizing principle of life, thought, and behavior; each is simultaneously a clue to personality and—as we will see later—the basis for a category of leisure of types of substances. I have referred in other writings to these distinctions as the assumptive, analytic, and aesthetic.[26]

The *assumptive* source of knowledge is the kind that reaches into past generations. It is therefore believed, affirmed, legendized, poetized, dramatized, embraced with enthusiasm, prayed to, immortalized in song, and reaffirmed in salute.

The teacher, in such a case, is the transmitter, preacher, policeman, and propagandist. He reveals, reminds, and orders that which is already established. He is the guardian of thou shalt's and thou shalt not's. He has been delegated to the authority of morality, ehtical order, and social control. Assumptions need not be without validity and imminent logic; they are highly important and, as far as possible, are indoctrinated to new and powerless generations of children. One thinks of religion and philosophy as preeminent models for the assumptive approach to life.

The *analytic* source of knowledge is best illustrated by the sciences. It is a knowledge based on objectivity, evaluation, examination, doubt, tests, and experiments. Within this model one does not permit himself to be totally committed to conclusions as does a fanatic believer; he is a sort of *Luftmensch*—always stepping back from the world to look at it. Enjoyment is incidental to understanding, whether it relates to a flower, a woman, an idea, a political system, or a beautiful city such as Paris. The observer here cannot permit himself to admit "This is what I like." As scientist he must ask, "What is it?" "How do we know?" The laboratory is one workshop for such questions, although men have made notes on the stars long ago. The case study and IBM code cards are familiar tools for the social sciences, although George Bernard Shaw did very well in his plays without either.

The educator in this type of knowledge is a fellow explorer, interpreter, and midwife to the birth of new data among his students. He has no need to apply his knowledge, leaving that to his assumptive brethren; he is fundamentally an amoral man, as all social scientists must be. He is a subversive of this society and, therefore, of the educational system, because he takes seriously the half-belief that the student should be taught to think for himself.

The *aesthetic* kind of knowledge is based on the essence of originality in putting together things, objects, ideas, sounds, forms, and time and space relations in ways that have not been done before, but on the principle of beauty. It is not that creativity alone deals in symbols, since the others do so. For example, we symbolize many aspects of life, as in the prayer (assumptive) or in the hospital's antiseptic smell (an image of the analytic). The assumptive way of knowing depends for its strength on conserving, stabilizing, repeating, and ceremonializing; the strength of analytic knowledge is therefore a shock to those who cannot afford to have their notions challenged. The aesthetic attempts to view both stability and change in terms of a subjective norm through the creator's own perception and experience as a trained, sensitive, courageous, individualistic, and confident person.

Analysis and assumptions of many kinds enter into the aesthetic or creative process. But it has added a third element—subjectivity—whose essence, by definition, is that it cannot lend itself to generalization or objective verification. The nature of the aesthetic as an art is that it is undefinable in any other terms of communication or meaning known to man. This is its strength and reason for being. The educator in creative fields has the function of inducing the proper atmosphere of liberty and craft, imagination and restraint, originality and respect. He displays the masterpieces of others. He systematizes the requisite skills. He finally evokes the unpredictable resources of his students so that they may exercise their own limited perceptions of the world and thus know themselves and the world in greater depth.

Thus we have three distinct perspectives or frameworks for approaching the world, knowing it, and organizing our lives in it: *living* in it by referrents to cultural indoctrination, *understanding* it by extrapolations that go beyond history or cultural boundaries, and *boring into it* from the special view of the imaginative individual. These overlap, of course, and within a given context, all may be found together, as in a cup of coffee that simultaneously denotes fellowship (assumptive), chemistry and economics (analytic), and good flavor (aesthetic); or a room that includes a visual statement of purpose, expense, and harmonious arrangement.

These three complement each other; as each expands, it contributes to the others: for example, the expansion of science today sharpens and enlarges philosophical issues. More important, they serve each other while remaining independently valid. Language in its broadest sense serves all three, yet both science and art develop their own language communications, in the dictionary sense and in the private sense of professional exchange.

The relationship between the assumptive, the analytic, and the aesthetic provides a clue to the difference in the symbolism attached to each. It is a relationship that has many sides; we could, for example, designate the first as *moral,* as a dominant force for social control; the scientific is fundamentally *amoral,* with its dominant value one of social detachment; the aesthetic stands as a *supramoral* factor, with a strong tinge of social replacement. But space does not permit an exploration of this clue. Let us look, however lightly, at two other relationships: revolutions of social *role* and of *time.*

The roles within the institutionalizations of the assumptive are primarily those of conservators—parents, teachers, governors, policemen, lawyers, and the like. The priest may stand as an overall umbrella of all these figures, a protector from the rains of change. Temporally, of course, his vision is turned to the past.

The scientist emerges as our major image-figure of the analytic. He is the contemporary, unbound by precedent, using it only when viable for a better understanding, for understanding is a nondynamic term, free from tendencies of the past or of growth. The scientist is firmly ensconced in the present moment of time.

The artist, alone of the three, is completely a man of the future. Paradoxically, his work and values represent a rich continuity with creators of all past generations, but it is uniquely a continuity always with other men who were also men of the future *in relation to their own time.* The creative process (granted we know little about it) is surely a conceptualization and a realization of a becoming . . . a transformation, a growth. Every bit of art, if genuine, is new in some element; if repeated, it is not a creative, but a repetitive, conserving, reaffirming act. The innate urge and crystallization toward newness, freshness, or "creativity" in the large sense is therefore unpredictable even to the creator, and understandably upsetting to guardians of the familiar. It both requires and produces men who, in contrast to the past, have the courage to make their own Heaven. We will recall Otto Rank's thesis, in

Art and Artist, about the relationship between art and death, or art and immortality.

"their generally high intelligence, experience, their freedom from crippling inhibitions, their esthetic sensitivity, independence in thought and behavior, abundance of creative energy, commitment to creative endeavor, and an unceasing search for solutions to increasingly difficult problems that they have set for themselves."[27]

These are terms that speak of forwardness and future-mindedness.

Assumptive insights and controls are the heart of societies where traditions are dominant, as in primitive societies. They are stronger yet, when, as in the long history of Medieval Christianity, the traditions are rationalized by ideologies, routinized by rituals and implemented by the social roles of defenders of the faith. To be sure, strength and necessity of justifying the present by the prior is fully operative even today; even in the space age, very much of our thought and behavior is predicated on nothing more substantial than the "shell of custom."

The thrust of the assumptive is backward in time; the term we often use in political life is conservative. The term has never been defined more congently than by Professor A. B. Wolfe.[28]

"Conservatism, generally speaking, is simply that system of sentiments, that mental attitude, which causes the individual to accept with equanimity and approval things-as-they-are ... which desires little if any change, and which opposes with vigor any proposal for radical transformation ... Conservatism, if it could have its way, would thus stand still, maintaining social relations, and processes, thought, belief, and culture practically as they happen to be at the time."

This term speaks of more than a political attitude and, if the conservatism approach provides the central theme of a persons relationships, this theme includes leisure as well. We often hear of the person who is "conservative" or "cautious" at a game like bridge or, conversely, "wild" and "unpredictable," and without hesitation we associate his character in the game with his general character. Contemporary social psychology supports this folk truth. One current term for the unity is "syndrome"; another is "configuration." What is provided for us is a rough prediction of his attitudes or behavior in a new situation.

The main problem consists in knowing how consistent that syndrome is, as in the case of David Riesman's "inner-directed" type. Riesman described this person before the era of the hippie, the New Left, or the current use of drugs among the young. An outsider might say these are hedonistic in the direction of their values—living as though each day were their last—but I am not convinced: the alienation is not hedonistic, a commitment to joy but, instead, to a highly individualistic experience removed from the reality that is proclaimed as shallow and middle class. This generation, so suspect by America's political conservatives, is actually a new, dramatic *conservative* force in American life. Truth, as they see it, is in simply *being*. They have no program for reconstruction but turn inward in a mystical gesturing, aided in many cases by drugs. The drugs incapacitate them for simultaneous or subsequent creativity; although one hears of artists who obtained new insights into light and color, no one has yet announced new social insights from such experiences heretofore unrevealed to man.

Yet, in their nondrug periods of behavior, many of these same young persons are social reconstructionists, whether as critics in demonstrations or as activists. Looking at their elders, we often see that businessmen and other political conservatives will embrace new fads, new gadgets, and new games in their leisure. There seems to be an off-guardedness in leisure, when barriers are down and inconsistencies are admissible. A consistent conservatism would suggest that the person in his leisure will do what is being done by others, whether in sports, travel, or other accepted forms. Yet, as Reisman indicates, he may seek to "escape" *upward*, as through the arts, or *downward*, through cheap novels and gambling. The other-directed person also finds leisure a useful means for self-change. Tastes are changeable for both through play.

For the conservative, leisure is an avenue toward liberalization as well as a means for affirming his values. This may be one reason that the American businessman does not read much outside of business journals; he avoids contact with a literature that spells out the need for human instead of business values; in his social world he is equally at a loss with academic people.

The analytic approach to the world may be equated with the scientific attitude. It was defined by A. B. Wolfe as "faith in the universality of cause and effect. . . ." According to this approach, what we ought to know is infinite, what we can know is finite, and what we do know infinitesimal. The basis of such an attitude is that science and the world must be deterministic, not a realm of whim, but of dependable mechanism, observation, classification, and analysis, or else "we might just as well look for the sun to rise in the west any day, a Bermuda onion plant to yield oranges one day and potatoes the next, or an angry man to be reasonable."[29]

If, then, the assumptive attitude toward that leisure is used fundamentally to preserve the world as it is, the analytic stance would find that leisure can be a device for understanding instead of believing; the space age, for example, has induced an enormous interest in astronomy, physics, geography, and all related disciplines or technologies. Here, too, it is possible that one set of insights induces another, so that conceivably many persons who had lost their religious faith have been led by exploits in space to embrace a theology as, in the reverse, many whose theology was earthbound through Genesis are now confused.

In general, those who are attuned most faithfully to exploration and understanding of the world are not theologically oriented; they neither fear nor embrace contemporary artistic or political creeds simply because they are contemporary; they are aware of the avant-garde but also of the wisdom from the past. *Leisure for such persons is a means toward accomodation to the changing world;* in travel, they do not ignore Rome but may go on to Tel Aviv; their shelves can hold Pope as well as *Portnoy's Complaint* and, free from current fads, they may turn to the former for their more "proper understanding of man."

The aesthetic approach to the world is future-oriented, as I noted earlier, but this must also be understood in the sense of personalism. The person who creates—whose leisure may be partly devoted to painting pictures—is engaged in self-growth, in the discovery of himself as he depicts the world. Inner discovery is an entirely different dimension from either of the two forms of insights discussed above, since they were focused on the world as object—one with a higher regard for the past, the other with a desire to know the present. *Leisure for those persons whose emphasis is on the creative is not limited to personal growth or expression alone, but the use of the artistic channels to change the world.* Thus radicalism as a political or social force has always displayed a close interest in the arts interpreting these tendencies in a particularistic setting.

This section has spoken not of a category of leisure activities but of insights to the world through leisure. The inference is that *if* leisure is conceived as an increasing aspect of man's life that results from new time, new affluence, and new access to the world (through literacy, mass media, travel, etc.), then our concern is larger than categories of leisure behavior. Our purpose must then be to view leisure as a means through which one can view the world more completely.

Relation of Insights to Types of Activities-experiences

The assumptive type of relatedness applies whenever we engage in an activity that is a complete statement, such as playing a game, fishing, taking a trip, watching television, reading a book, or visiting a friend— the list is infinite. No explanation is needed, no further rationale; the activity speaks for itself. Why are you reading a book? Why are you visiting your friend? These are unnecessary questions, even though *this* book or *this* friend is not worth much. Each page read, each visit made, each fish caught by an individual verifies a pattern long engrained and accepted. No bravery is required and no individuality is asserted. It is an immersion in the world as it is. Illustrations of this are seen in the functions listed on the right side of the sets shown in the last chapter: rest, discipline, entertainment, isolation, distraction, and recreation.

When, however, we turn to "analytic" illustrations of leisure, we enter a potentially more upsetting enterprise, both to the society and to the person. Here we have the general momentum of the reading, as an example, and the issue becomes the *content* of the reading. Here we turn to the analysis of the population explosion that comes to us over television, and immediately the simple item "watching TV" becomes a item of far deeper potential social change.

It would seem that the aesthetic approach turns us naturally to art as the content of leisure—art either as a creative act or as a set of experiences to enjoy. And this is true in part. Yet the core of the aesthetic is not art works but the process of creating; but does creating limit itself to painting pictures? Maslow speaks of creativity in homemaking. He equates the aesthetic to the need for "self-actualization," which develops and is fulfilled only after the "lower" needs—physiological, safety, belongingness, love, and esteem. Actualization can come from transforming block dwelling into a community as well as from turning rough motifs into a musical composition.

Joining a protest movement offers some potential access to transformation of the society, yet one may question if this really can be called a part of the "aesthetic" insight; can this be realistically translated into leisure activity or experience? The clue to this apparent perceptual difficulty is to be found in the symbolic element that is crucial to the concepts of aesthetics. The protest, as at Berkeley or at hundreds of campuses throughout the world in recent years, must be divided into two parts; that part that is real, shaped by events or by plans; this part is political, and any differentiation of human activity should not be called leisure. It may occur during the free time of the student, between hours of classroom attendance. But not all free time is leisure; free time merely sets one condition within which leisure may develop. The second part of the campus protest may be what some students of crowd behavior call "expressive." In this sense the person may come to watch, almost as he would watch a parade. Parades, as on July 4, are engaged in symbolic behavior with the main purpose of affirmation (the assumptive), whereas it is the *onlookers* of the protest crowd who are engaged

in the symbolic by observing the form of group action without participation in the substance or the reality. At the moment of change from
the role of onlooker to that of active participant, there may be a behavioral index, such as moving closer to the center of action or joining in
the chants and songs. This moment may be a fine line, surely, and yet
the importance of it is legally recognized and may send the person to
jail. The crucial issue is *intent*. The federal law judges conspiracy or
participation in rioting and violence on this term. The police do not
know and hardly care whether the individuals in the crowd *intend* to
be a part of the action or are there as onlookers in their free time, but
the student of leisure is not a policeman as he seeks to sort out motivations. The point is that (1) a phenomenon such as a riot may bring one
in his free time to look at the crowd; (2) he may, in that crowd, change
his motivations and become an agent of change; (3) his leisure has
become activist so that the crowd itself was transformed by him from
symbolism (the crowd as a metaphor for "excitement") to instrumentalism (the crowd now as a channel for transformation).

So the action or transformation may develop from a form of leisure
and move into a more direct engagement or confrontation with the
reality.

Putting it another way, when one becomes involved in political activity, we had best refer to it as leisure only in that aspect of it which
Huizinga calls play. The playing we do at politics is leisure; so are the
playing we do in the hospital as a Ladies Aid and the playing we do at
selling tickets for the local symphony.

The term playing was applied by Huizinga to religious, legal, family,
and even military activities. It has nothing to do with how serious one
is; the player in a game may be very serious indeed. What it means is
that the *substance* of the activity may be viewed as one category and
the *meaning* in another. Thus—as in our "TV" evenings on Beacon Hill
—the leisure element was inherent in the totality of thinking about,
anticipating, recalling, and enjoying the musical experience; the playing *per se* as a violinist was exactly the same process as though we were
members of the Boston Symphony. It is the context—the symbolism of
being in the home of my friend instead of being on the stage of Symphony Hall before paying listeners—that made the difference; the first
was a playground as an interact between other experiences, the stage
would have been a workspace. Indeed, if in the course of the amateur
evening we had started to quarrel and had broken up, then the whole
dynamic and intention would have been defeated, just as in the opposite situation, the Symphony should theoretically not engage in "horse-
play," as it often does during a Pop Concert with Arthur Fiedler; but

then neither the audience nor the orchestra have come with a classical worker-consumer model in mind.

Questions for Tomorrow

In *Proposition 6* of Chapter 3 the matter of *modifying* meanings "toward more depth and personal growth" is raised in relation to "capable leadership." Furthermore, *Proposition 12* defines the major function of a leader as insuring that the participant in leisure "may go beyond the limited expectation or meaning he brought to it." Part of this need to define the leaders role comes from the fact that, as *Proposition 32* points out, leisure as a class symbol is fading, so that we may expect not only change in leisure but confusion as well.

Yet here is a sore point that permeates much of the attitude among laymen toward an attempt—such as this textbook—to analyze the matter. "Leave us alone," I am told. "What I do with my leisure is my own affair. Don't plan it for me. Don't be concerned with my meanings as I watch TV or drink or do anything else." It is a legitimate plea; *freedom,* we like to say, is the epitome of leisure.

The question is taken on by the Englishman, Ralph Glasser in his provocative *Leisure, Penalty or Prize?* What evidence is there, he asks, "as to the validity of the arts and crafts movement's claim that leisure time creative activity really does supply a person's emotional needs?"[30]

"Is there indeed a hierarchy of leisure occupations in terms of the extent of this emotional benefit derived from them? Does handwork at, say, pottery or weaving really rank higher in this respect then say, spending one's time at drinking or bingo? . . . Is there some formula for creative fulfillment in leisure time, which is equally fitting and effective for all grades of ability, intellect, perception, spiritual capacity?"[31]

To supplement these questions, Glasser points to the growing suspicion of the intellectuals who, under the guise of progress and science, "appear to have collectively led us all astray." Universities, the font of the emphasis on intellectual values—"the higher things," "great literature," and so on—themselves include people who are "every bit as narrow, petty, scheming, unscrupulous, backward looking and apparently unsuccessful in personal relationships as anybody else."[32] Indeed, whole societies that had been regarded as models of "high culture"— notably the Germany of Kant, Goethe, Bach, and Beethoven—were found capable of crimes unknown before in history. "The same people who swooned with Schubert and Schumann, Heine and Rilke, who called themselves heirs to world culture, and whose language provided the word *Weltanschauung,* were the same who forced the tortured inmates of their bestial concentration camps to give orchestral concerts on the parade grounds of degrading death, while their fellow prisoners were whipped along in their doom-laden servitude, and finally to their death and incineration."

The question of *values* and their cultural foundations will be treated in Chapter 14, and there, too, the suspicion of intellectuals and their elitist values will be seen in such writings as Eric Fromm. Yet whatever one's position on the origins or validity of values—democratic or aristocratic, personal or class-based—the issue of *meanings* remains, since even in the immigrant community of the 1910s and 1920s in which I grew up we had leaders undertake to give us the meanings of leisure experience as building blocks in a structure of social concerns and socialist construction. The "social" devices we attended, sponsored by the Workman's Circle, included groups arranged in explicitly political mimes, with prizes awarded to those that showed the most originality in depicting the ills of the sweatshop and capitalism or the advantages of democratic strategies instead of communist terror. Our fathers were already caught up on the American dream eagerly accepting technical advances, which meant jobs and comforts, and later, cars and TVs; just as our children, half a century later, take these comforts for granted and turn to leisure as a natural expression of *themselves.* Glasser writes:[33]

"This concept of the critical human need to express personality in these ways is a residual variation on the theme of the natural man; but here the emphasis is on the idea of a *creative* link with nature, with the source of life, almost as if in doing something formative with our hands, working upon basic natural materials, we were *giving something back to the universal life force, and in so doing joining ourselves* with it."

This is the sense behind *Proposition 52,* which speaks of "depth and challenge" for the leisure of tomorrow instead of in the mere growth of variety. The purpose of the epistomologic scheme of insights to the world was therefore provided not only as a guide to the actual observation of how leisure experiences can be given perspective in analysis but also as a foundation for guidance to leadership in the light of new conditions.

Although illustrations and insights have been provided along the way, one intention of these four chapters has been to provide the tools for analysis that can now be useful for the variety of contents of the next three levels.

PART 3
Clusters
of Relationships

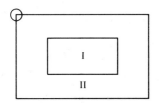

Chapter 8
Person and Family

GENERAL CONSIDERATIONS

The temptation is strong to call the family the most decisive factor on the leisure of its members. Yet large numbers of children and youth, in every ghetto, find their models and leaders among peers in the street, leaders of the gang, or culture heroes of the moment. On the other hand, the large majority of children will obtain, from the general style of life that they see in their formative years, a general impression of what is natural: they see books and magazines; since the middle 1940s, they have seen a television set; they take vacation trips with the family; friends come into the home; conversations take place. Or the reverse may be the case: no trips by the family, no reading, no friends. Values in general are crystallized, but amidst others of the family, as distinct from the context of work, school, or church, the child observes human relationships in their freest, most unguarded, and continuous context. Except in psychiatric terms, the family cannot hide or submerge the spirit and essence of tensions, frustrations, and enmities, or of respect, inviolability, and love between its members.

In his early years, at least, the child is heavily influenced by the tools of play, as well as by the general life-style of his family—his toys, his early friends, his yard, the type of neighborhood, and the location of the home in relation to such community facilities as playgrounds, parks, beaches, and theaters.

In a reverse analysis, leisure is more and more a powerful influence on the family. The unity of the farm family came from the functional relationship of colleagues and fellow-workers, each with his responsibilities—his identity, the knowledge that he was needed. Conversation was quite easy and could be almost eliminated amidst the common concern with mundane matters of weather and the condition of the sick cow or the price of wheat. That type of unity disappears in the city. Now father works away from home; mother goes her own way; children have no chores that have to be done, because machines do most of the dirty work.

Now if there is unity and mutuality in the urban family it comes from play together, as on a vacation, or from respect for the play of each other. And the most difficult and penetrating play of all—conversation —is often underminded, supplanted, and destroyed by distractions from the airways.

Thus, in both dimensions, the family remains the strategic unit it always has been.

Furthermore, each member of the family, in his choice and use of leisure, is affected by the conditioning factors discussed in Chapter 4: the health, sex, and ages of others in the family, their jobs outside the home, the level of income and education or the religious affiliation. As we will see in Chapter 9, the Negro, Indian, Spanish-American, Jewish, or other minorities may provide unique factors within the family, both from traditions of the group and from its relationships to the society.

After our preliminary gropings with the "nature" of leisure in Chapter 2, the reader might now assume that for discussions of the "family," by contrast, there is a clear consensus. This is far from the case. As Morris Zelditch, Jr. points out,[1] the most obvious definitions are clearly unsatisfactory. He quotes a famous definition by the anthropologist, A. P. Murdock, based on analyses of 250 societies, that four elements must be present: "a social group in which sexual access is permitted between adult members, reproduction legitimately occurs, the group is responsible to society for the care and upbringing of children, and the group is an economic unit at least in consumption." Yet even this set of elements cannot be identified with such a concrete unit as the nuclear family composed of parents and children, since numerous and important exceptions can be seen in the Israeli *kibbutz* (where children are raised outside the family), in China with its extended family, and in other numerous cases in which one or more of Murdock's list of characteristics are carried on primarily by agencies outside of the family.[2] This point —what is a family?—is close to the topic of leisure. It is not an academic secret that the family, here and in other societies, is going through significant changes: in the social roles of mothers, fathers, and children, in the new assertions of youth as to their rights, in the "lib" movement among women, and in the family's relationships to work and to consuming patterns. Indeed, a major conclusion of this chapter will be that leisure patterns of the family are both a critical clue to the nature of these changes within the family and a crucial pivot or variable in creating new relationships between family and community.

However the family is defined by the specialists, a general, common-sense view of family as generally perceived (parents and children involved in Murdock's quartet of characteristics) is basic to the conditions of leisure discussed earlier. The relative importance of these is changing, as in the new *access* that women of today have to leisure alternatives. But fundamentally, the person is housebroken into leisure do's and don't's as he is into other areas of life. He learns, in good part through the influence of the family, how to play, eat, speak, behave, wash, dress, or cook. His peers enter into the process, but in large part the choice of neighborhood, the kind of home, and the amount of money and time emanate *from* the family. As Kenneth Roberts of England notes:

"Despite the growth that has taken place in large-scale organizations catering specifically for leisure interests, the family has remained the most popular group in which people choose to spend their free time. For this reason the roles that individuals play within the family have a much stronger influence upon the structure of their leisure than any of the social roles that they play in the wider society."[3]

A substantive difference in the closeness of family and leisure may be drawn between the small-town, pre-World War II American family and the contemporary family after 1945. In the first case we have a simpler, more rural, less crowded, relatively uncomplicated, Model T-Ford society. In such a view—stereotyped, to be sure—the family constituted a natural content for social activity, for family visiting (before baby-sitting), for an interaction between generations (as in a picnic), for the absorption of leisure as fragments of time between chores that children (as well as adults) had to do around the house. Between helping mother to hang the clothes, bake bread, sweep the floor, or deliver newspapers (because the money needed, not to develop "character"), there were only fragments of time free for any member of the household. Professor Walker claims that the housewife today is still as busy,[4] but the question is not busyness, but busyness for what. Columnist Tom Wicker recently pointed to this difference.

"... it seems to me that one of the major problems for younger people in the country today is that they don't have anything useful to do. When I grew up, not too many years ago, in the South ... [if we] didn't bring in the wood and coal at night, my family didn't keep warm. My children don't have anything useful to do."[5]

Since the arrival of television, after 1945, together with urban family life-styles in general, the family has become a consuming agent; home is a place from which workers (often mother as well as father) come and go; it is a frozen-food cooperative, a bedroom to hold itinerant bridge-players, a headquarters in which a TV tube becomes the Muezzin's recorded call to the mosques of prayer, play-court jestery, sports events, war reports, and the harems of an updated Sultan-like TV master of postmidnight talk. Play, partnership in adventure of mind and in body become primary values, suggested in the "personal column ads" in newspapers and periodicals. An example of this is seen in a few classified ads from the April 8, 1971 issue of the *New York Review of Books*.

PERSONAL

PH.D. DEGREE STUDENT in N.Y. area—single, 27 years old—seeking intelligent female companion to concerts, theater and movies. NYR Box 3290.

SEEKING WARM GENUINE relationship with intelligent, sensitive man who welcomes the richness of sharing and knowing another person. Professional woman, 32, works with children, intellectually and human-istically inclined, interested in literature, music, ideas, people, outdoors. NYC area. NYR, Box 3396.

MAN 39, unencumbered desires meet woman same 25–40 incensed by U.S. destruction of Indochinese and concomitant decay American life consider possibility emigrating Canada. Minnesota. NYR, Box 3466.

WOMAN WITH LOVE OF MOUNTAINS, woods and country streams; European sensibilities, reative interests, 32, seeks warm, perceptive man with active interests and dreams to share. NYR, Box 3443.

DECENT, SENSITIVE, LIFE-LOVING, (POSSIBLY) HANDSOME AT-TORNEY, 40, seeks lovely woman, similar qualities, 20's–low 30's, special person, to love. Please reply in depth. Photo welcome. NYR, Box 3435.

BLACK POET MALE, 37, New England area, seeks white female 22–30, unattached, Taurus or Cancer, for meaningful relationship. Must be sincere. NYR Box 3303.

GILES (serious hip intellectual) 29, handsome, tall seeks female Grand Tutor friend and patron. NYR, Box 3440.

CUTE CALIFORNIA GAL wanted as mate for young, intelligent male advertising executive in early 20's P.O. Box 664, Lodi, California 95240.

UNUSUAL ENGINEER—with diverse interests, art to flying (tall, bald, presentable, divorced and suddenly 50) seeks catalyst to reactivate life. If you are attractive, unfettered, youngish, versatile, independent but feminine, and would like to explore and share—(NY, NJ, Phila. areas) —please write with phone. NYR, Box 3445.

PROFESSOR 35, 5'11", 140 lbs., definitely no social lion or outdoors-man, seeks well-educated woman, 30–40, Philadelphia or NY, who appreciates intellectually active, gentle, emotionally responsive males. NYR, Box 3448.

ARTIST, humanist, skier and tennis player, trimly sixtyish and conspicu-ously younger in appearance, outlook and vitality; seeks gentle woman of comparable youthfulness to share the compassionate con-cerns, creative interests and sensuous delights of mature com-panionship looking toward remarriage. Southern Connecticut. NYR, Box 3452.

MICHIGAN GRADUATE STUDENT, 26, mature, ardent humanist, seeks creative and sensitive female, 23–30+, to share in redefinition of self and senses. Permanent. NYR, Box 3413.

WALL ST. LAWYER, philosopher, aesthete, 23, seeks bright, beautiful female for liberty, equality, unity. NYR, Box 3454.

MEN: Get erotic mail. Personal handwritten letters, $5 per page. Please write; I'll answer in kind. Kyla. NYR, Box 3457.

PHOTOGRAPHER/WRITER, 29, affectionate, intelligent, athletic, seeks warm, intelligent, attractive female for walks on beach, museum and cinema, outdoor trips, good involvement. P.O. Box 60228, Terminal Annex, Los Angeles 90060.

FEMALE MEDICAL STUDENT, 26, who loves dogs, horses, outdoors, philosophy, the arts, Blake, intellect, the irrational; seeks sensitive man to share laughter, warmth, dignity, friendship, love. Philadelphia. NYR, Box 3460.

YOUNG ENGLISH TEACHER, 55, divorced, 6', retiring June wishes attractive, sociable, unencumbered woman under 50 as companion on leisurely, modest automobile tour of Mexico or Europe off season. NYR, Box 3463.

MEDICAL STUDENT, 26, seeks female cellist who likes Mozart, Tur-genev, *Die Frau ohne Schatten,* Julia Child, and I. F. Stone. Minneapo-lis, NYR, Box 3465.

AGE ROLES AND TIME

Proposition 30 of Chapter 3 notes that time as a psychological element in leisure "is geared closely to age roles, and its increase on redistribu-tion could have tangible effect on the conception of such roles and their associated expectations of behavior."[6] *Proposition 3* simply states that at various stages in the life of a person as well as in various types of activities "time carries different images."[7]

Dr. P. Maydl, director of the European Center for Leisure and Education in Prague likes to say that a major philosophy or goal in his country is for people to "be young at all ages."[8] Nevertheless, the goal does not imply that the men of 70 will feel life as he might have at 17, for then life is not worth living; because—as Shaw noted—"youth" is often wasted on young people, the ideal is the zest of youth blended with the wisdom of experience. And the actual disparity in attitudes, especially when several age perspectives are to be found in the same house, becomes a more and more complex issue in contemporary family life. Our attitudes toward time (*Proposition 3*) are related to our roles, and these roles are changing (*Proposition 30*).

Clear roles of mother, father, and child prevail in the simpler society: father plows, mother cooks, the child gathers eggs; or father hunts, mother weaves and raises children, the child hunts with father and watches younger children. That model is long gone. In urban society, father may be puttering in the garage, mother may be working in an office or attending a women's lib meeting, and the child may be visiting friends or baby-sitting. Away from the farm, and with increasing freedom from the clock as a major synchronizing element for the functioning of work roles, TV remains as the major consuming time-unity in the home; even that will eventually disappear as the family will be able to purchase or rent a casette-TV show and put it on the set to fit their moods instead of watching scheduled TV.

However, the major characteristics of time for leisure in the decades ahead will be bulk-time, and it is to this aspect of time that we must relate ages and social roles. Consider the difference between a family "vacation" and a "sabbatical" for the head of the family. The term "vacation" can be traced easily to the past participle of the Latin *vacare*, "to be empty"; this relates directly, as *Webster's New World Dictionary* (1957) notes, to "the state of being free from work, activity, etc.; inactivity; idleness." A family vacation, in this sense, is a collective act of disengagement from working for father, sewing-dishwashing-house-cleaning for mother, or schooling for the children. This is not difficult and involves only the decision of how and where this change from commitment to emptiness can best be made. Here is when the conditions spelled out in earlier portions of this volume enter: the amount of money, time, size of family, health, place of residence, and so on.

A "sabbatical," on the other hand, is "suited to the Sabbath," not just to rest, but to *worship* and set aside not by the conditions of work, and so on, but by the Fourth Commandment; it's essence is not a release from, but a commitment *for*. Most universities have learned that this release of some of its faculty for either a full year (with half pay) or a

half year (with full pay) should not be automatic, but should be re-
quested and justified with some positive personal project for the period.
It is too early to judge the success of the fifth-year, 13-week "sabbatical"
among United States steel workers; if there is good reason to question
the ritualistic pattern of work from 9 A.M. to 5 P.M. Monday through
Friday, there is equal doubt about vacations and sabbaticals coming on
clocked schedules set by an outsider.

The four-day workweek, a pattern that will become popular and
much discussed in the 1970s, can have a considerable impact on the
family by shifting the synchronization of interrelated leisure roles from
a psychology of vacation or *release* to that of sabbatical or *commitment.*
*The three-day "weekend" is only the beginning of what could be a
revolution in our use of, and even our mastery over time.* As the period
for leisure becomes more of bulk and less of fragmented quantity, the
quality also is affected; Saturday (the most flexible day of the traditional
weekend) is normally a time for this, that, and the other: an hour to dash
out for a visit, a quick game of tennis, and so on. As the weekend
enlarges, alternatives open for more sustained activity, such as trips
away from home. Eventually, as the potential develops for nonwork
periods of months or even years at a time, a real generation gap could
develop so as to shake the traditional family to its roots. Younger members of the family require more variety within a given time span; older
members normally require more comfort, as in travel; and, in any case,
the family plans for a three to six month sabbatical will bring to a head
all of the individual desires or needs based on former patterns. The
situation will be aided (or aggravated) by the more and more favorable
attitude toward keeping schools open during the year for reasons of
good economic management; this policy, of course, frees the family
from always arranging its vacation or sabbatical plans around those of
the child.

Looking further into the future, the *kibbutz* pattern for raising children outside of the home could become a pattern for family life toward
the end of the century.[9] It could provide the ultimate compromise for
maximum flexibility in use of time by working adults and could solve
the question of reconciling age and role patterns with work and nonwork cycles.

A second part of the relation between time and age roles and attitudes is the question of what the economist calls "trade-offs." Given a
theoretical parity of all ages toward receiving more maintenance with
less effort, we then arrive at a new question for research and for the
life-styles of individuals. Will the younger, middle-aged, and older person generally show a greater interest in income, goods, and services or

in time? As he leans in the second direction, the expenditure pattern revealed in Chapter 5 will become radically changed. The trade-off of income for time will then mean a relatively smaller amount spent for shelter, clothes, food, and furniture, and more for items of recreation such as travel and reading. However, expenditures may become a less accurate index of leisure than they are even now; the observations of the youth with the turn into the 1970s seems to be a negation from spending for recreation to some sort of throwback toward self-reliance in leisure and entertainment. The throwback appears, in part at least, to recall the depression days for many of us; the difference is that we may be approaching a preindustrial model of recreation with a postindustrial material base. Some data for this conclusion are present if we relate the variable of age to one example of a preindustrial leisure prototype—the theater. Professor Herald Swedner of Lund, Sweden, has gathered audience data in the United States, England, France, Norway, Finland, Denmark, and Sweden over a 10 year period. He finds that "the frequency of visits to the theatre is usually highest in the 20–29 year age-group," and also that "the frequency of visits to the theatre begins to decline markedly with in increase of age...."[10] At any age, of course, his findings coincide with audience studies by Zweers and de Jager in the Netherlands and with Baumol and Bowen in the United States, that the theater goers (or art and music lovers) are a very limited minority of the population.

The question that is new to our time is whether this minority, generally young segments of population, will go the way of prior generations as they age, or whether the values of present-day young people will persist as part of a permanent assertion of new goals. Research is unable to deal with this with certainty, perhaps the central difficulty of all futurology, We may, however, look briefly at the generations of the family.

The Child

The White House Conference on Children in 1970 was held separately from the sessions on youth.[11] This was perhaps a potential advantage from a substantive view. *Profiles for Children* established a statistical review of pertinent data for the several thousand delegates. For example, children born today are coming into a world in which the world's population may well be 8 billion by the time they are 40 years old. The most rapid annual rate of growth is in Asia (excluding China and India), followed by Latin America, India, Africa, Oceania, mainland China, Canada, the United States, the USSR (at about the same rate) and, last, Europe. The population of the United States, 205 million in 1970, will go up about 20 million in this decade. In 1980, as pretty much in the 1970s, one out of every four Americans will be under 15; in 1970, we had 55 million children under the age of 14; with 4 million births a year, near 100 million children will have in this decade gone from some or all of the stages from birth to 13.

Over 87 of every 100 of us are white, more than 11 are Negro. Our population is highly concentrated in nine states, with 70 of every 100 Americans living in urban areas—more Negroes than whites in proportion to their population.

The proportion of families below the federally defined poverty level is largest among Negroes and farm families—greater in the southern states, and there more than twice the proportion of black families found nationally. (see Chart 8)

Chart 8

Proportion of families in the United States below the poverty level, by race and residence, 1969

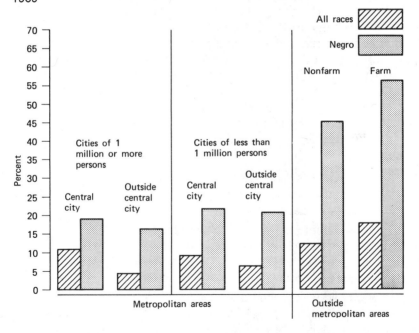

For all Americans, our rising affluence (excluding inflationary factors), according to Commerce reports released on August 20, 1970, is unmistakable: in 1969, 40 of every 100 households had incomes over $10,000, with 15 going over $15,000. At the other end of the scale, 16.2 families of every 100 earned less than $3000 in 1969, a drop of some 600,000 families in one year. The median income (half earning more and half earning less) was $8760 for white households in 1970 compared to $5290 for Negroes.

This general data was reflected in the working papers of the White House Conference on Children, held in November 1970. "Forum 21" was called The Child and Leisure Time. Its working paper stated:

"Most of the leisure activities currently available for children primarily benefit the affluent; we have not yet recognized that certain leisure opportunities are essential to all children. . . . A commitment to leisure —in fact, the very existence of leisure—requires the prior satisfaction of the basic needs of life, but leisure for the poor is too often simply ignored rather than made a part of a multi-purpose program."

Even among the poor, as the report notes, the urban child has more advantages. Since the national conference is held every 10 years to establish goals and recommend policies, a set of necessary steps were outlined toward the goals of setting priorities, correcting attitudes, eliminating institutional obstacles, and encouraging a diversity of programs. These recommendations called for more planning and financing of agencies on all governmental levels; the joint use of facilities and leadership by multipolitical areas; cooperation of public and private agencies; the creation of a national Leisure Services Administration to plan and coordinate all federal recreational agencies; and more mobile facilities to bring facilities to where the children are.

Of special pertinence here are the questions posed by the working paper for research.

Are there sufficient quantities of quality leisure time activities available in the community that are specifically geared to satisfy the unique social and psychological needs of children?

To what extent do prevailing physical, social, and economic environmental features in a community shape the leisure-time activity patterns and preferences of children and what can be done to accentuate positive features and overcome those features that are negative?

How should leisure-time activities for children be structured and presented to provide optimal childhood education for subsequent adolescent and adult leisure interest and skills?

To what extent and for what purposes should community-based human services and organizations develop and support a structured program of leisure-time activities for children?

What impact does the lack of meaningful and constructive leisure time activity have on the child, his family, his community?

In the light of earlier discussions in this chapter, we can raise additional questions. Central to all is the issue of the directions toward the postindustrial restructuring of time and work. The nature of social change is the primary dimension that must be added to the questions above. For example, how can the schools become prepared to respond to the flexible work and nonwork patterns that are becoming possible in their varieties of alternatives? What components within the present curriculum are expandable in view of the larger needs for what may be described as humanistic and aesthetic experiences instead of for a preparation in earning a living? What do we know—what do we need to know—about leisure attitudes and experiences that cut across the generations within the family?

As a consultant at the Washington conference that acted on the working paper noted above, my remarks to Forum 21 touched in part on these larger issues.

1. Leisure for children will be directly affected in the 1970s by the growing time among segments such as factory and office employees. The work week, now averaging below 40 hours per week, can go down—if the worker and his unions want it so—to about 35 by the end of the 1970s; this work time will be structured differently in many industries, as we see already in the four-day workweek that is spreading. In the longer run, this tendency could result in half a week of work, half a month, or even half a life-time, as in the military. This flexibility could create flexible school sessions, winter vacations for the father, more family time, and increases in adult education.

2. The major trend in television structure that will affect us all eventually—since almost everyone now owns TV—will be the technology by which the child and all of us have access to programs at our own time. This is on the way through simple techniques. Until then, television is in its infancy as a social and personal tool. As to use, we know that the average 3-year-old child has already watched the screen as many hours as are needed in class time to obtain a college degree. We may, with security, anticipate a continued growth of educational TV in this decade. "Sesame Street" has put the commercial imagination to shame. We must recall that TV came in 1945. Children who were 5 years old then are 30 now and, in many cases, raising their own 5-year olds. Therefore, it is only in this decade, starting literally now, that we can observe in a longitudinal way the lessons to be learned about this revolutionary tool.

3. The leisure of black children is affected by all of the resources and conditions that shape the lives of all children—such as playgrounds, family income, health, and clean air. In addition, we may anticipate that this minority will

use its leisure more and more to deepen its knowledge about its own history and circumstances. As the economic struggle is gradually matured, we may expect that the American black will turn further inward to examine his goals and to achieve the identity he desires. This, historically, takes place largely through symbols of expression. Anything that can further the arts, as such a symbol—the folk arts, the traditional fine arts, and literary or film expression—will be constructive. Observations of the American scene in all the arts indicates a maturing creativity in the 1970s and 1980s and can be given a base among the young children of this group. This, obviously, also has implications and some parallels for all children. What it means is that the mass or popular culture, despite academic and professional art criticisms, has already moved far toward a more mature inner America. The public schools might therefore be pinpointed as one major hope in furthering the noncognitive forms of learning, turning to such programs as Dorothy Maynor's Harlem School for the Arts and other programs within the National Guild for Community Schools of Music and Arts for models of philosophy and accomplishment.

4. In housing projects for the poor as well as in middle-class homes, architects and neighborhood planners will, in this decade, pay more attention to play areas, leisure resources, home facilities, traffic patterns, family rooms, and the like. Leisure, like life itself, is affected by space distribution and symbolism. We anticipate more sensitively to this, although architects and planners need guidance.

5. An enormous development in all phases of outdoor recreation may be projected. The ORRRC predicted an increase of 50 times in the use of some Midwest areas. The encouragement of camping, hiking, or other approaches to making the outdoors an integral part of the child's life are in line with all projections on the use of time as well as with values traditionally held by all men. This suggests a strong alignment of leisure interests with the environmentalists and conservationists. On a local level, it also suggests the use of children, during their free time, as participants in the fight on all forms of pollution; this also provides one new form of commitment and service by children at a time when at least some of their restlessness stems from a lack of functional roles.

6. With the rise of population in American suburbs and other indices of family values, we may anticipate a visible rise in crafts, in a leisure preoccupation with making or repairing the home or with the making of small objects within the home. This may lead to a creative interplay by the child between toys and nontoys such as tools and simple objects. This tendency among adults is clear, indicated by large expenditures for tools or garden seeds and equipment. Schools, community centers, and the family itself might be addressed on this point. The deeper implication of this is to put the intellectual emphasis of the school into a new perspective and to achieve a renewed balance between the rural and urban or the hand and the mind.

7. Travel of all kinds may be expected to increase as long as economy moves. The relatively comfortable financially will expand in their physical outreach

as the world is continually brought to them by the media. Indeed, television and travel represent this duality of bringing and going to the world. American children, beyond the present hopes of children elsewhere, have access to both. Education for leisure can safely project increases in physical as well as armchair travel.

8. The decade will undoubtedly witness an enlarged concern with handicapped children, whether in the home, the hospital, or other institutions. Our insight into mental and physical health turns us more and more to a synthesis of medical, physical, psychological, and play modalities. This will be one growing research area in this decade.

Youth

To the play-recreation-leisure theoretician or leader in activity, youth inevitably becomes the most difficult age segment. This is the period of transition from childhood into young adulthood. We, together with other societies, continue "rite of passage" and "confirmation" ceremonies to note publicly these progressions: the high-school graduation, the *bar-mitzvah,* the eligibility to vote at 18. However, as the expected behavior of the young people in their traditional role has changed, these artificial lines have come to mean less. In part this has resulted from the changes in adult role and attitudes toward themselves; the world faced by young people in a far different world than it was several decades ago.[13]

It used to be that the purpose of "youthhood" was to grow up to responsibilities; this fundamentally meant to make a living. Early in life the child on the farm became an integral part of its economic operation; until the Depression the child in even our village and town homes had functions to perform. Then, with the advent of numerous social changes, all of which paved the way toward a consumer-oriented society, the adult world turned to youth as a model for the image of activity and the capacity for play. This groping for a complete acceptance of play or "happiness" (in the hedonistic instead of the Aristotelian sense) was fed by, and found affirmation in television, professional sports, and increased gambling; furthermore, the increases in time (such as a free Saturday and the longer vacation) were brought about in good part by labor negotiations and became declared objectives of organized workers. But everyone, even antiunionists, adopted the similar goal of the freer life.

The same social, technological, and political transformation affected blacks, Asiatics, Africans, Catholic congregants, retirees, and women; that is, the general breakdown in traditional ways of living, making a living, or thinking about either. Youth did not *cause* these changes; they grew up in them, were fed by them, and inevitably contributed to them. The "alienation" of youth is as inept a phrase as the "strike" of a laboring group; in each the action is only an integral part and a reaction to a total situation. All of the values are under reconsideration by all of the society, but youth is in the most exposed, delicate, and strategic position, precisely because its role is to grow up from being a fresh convert to the heritage of the past to a functioning member of the present.

But already the adult world (especially since World War II, Hiroshima, Korea, Vietnam, civil rights struggles, and the space age) had begun to raise serious questions on national and personal morality and conscience; the church was no longer accepted as a guide by many; political leaders could not be trusted; the schools adjusted only in nervous pulsations, like providing more science courses. Youth had no familiar institution to turn to for counseling. It turned inward, to itself, along the way picking up teachings and phrases—from Mao, Senator McCarthy, President Kennedy, Updike, Marcusse, Jesus, Thoreau—and from this eclecticism, youth acted rationally and irrationally, in the system and outside the system, with flowers and with rocks, maturely and childishly, with drugs and with Peace Corp enlistments. Yet whatever it did, the central core has been a reexamination of our collective values. The closest institution with which young people inevitably had to tangle was the home; next was the school.

In the home, the first battle was for communications—to be heard and to be treated with some respect. The odd clothing and long hair became a symbolic bond of communication *across* families and communities; attacks on these outward symbols merely affirmed and strengthened their necessity.

Leisure—even the word has been so used in militant circles of youth —came to be one center of everything, since it summarized the independence of men from toil for the sake of toil, goods for the sake of goods. If abundance in *things* had, for the adult world, become the epitome of the capitalist order and its value-center, then its symbols, such as a bank in Santa Barbara, had to be bombed. If extended labor led to suburbia, then the suburban youth (as in "The Graduate") went into communes and developed antiwork attitudes as reactions against swimming pools. If complexity had become the obvious order of family life, then "Love Story" swept along the longing for simplified emotional loyalties.

The Vietnam war served as a major example of the stupidity of their elders but, in the university classroom (of which the masses and the media have little knowledge or understanding), the questions of youth have gone much further. And here it has become evident that the traditional relationship of the young person and his family to the world of values has been reversed. The family was, roughly, the person's buffer, barrier, gateway, and introduction to the world. From father, the women and children obtained their class status; his work determined not only the income but the total life-style. One major reversal took place when radio and TV brought the world into the home, injecting other models and values; a second injection toward change was the opening from the home to the world by the car, travel, and wider reading and education. Now we have the third change—the natural fruition of the earlier two—in which the familiar family becomes divided, unsure of itself, and expressing both the "inner" and the "looser" morality, yet greater love: more divorce, yet marriage at earlier age; more contact with the whole world, yet moves to the suburbs and their relative privacy.

Finally, note the central position of leisure in all three stages: the world coming into the home, the family going out to confront the world, and the adjustment (or confusion) in the home itself as it seeks to manifest both tendencies—to be private and public, disinterested and interested, pluralistic and integrated. At this point we confront the largest meanings of leisure in the actual, "practical," pragmatic level. The family, not the factory, school, church, playground, voting booth, or theater, is at the heart of the issue; it is in the family, a far more informed and responsive institution than ever before, that all of the issues of values converge. Here the usefulness of the four-day workweek or the preretirement plans will be applied. As to youth, the family has not proved useless; it is the key area for observing what the rush is all about, what goods are used for, and whether happiness is served by the gods of increasing *productivity* and the sages of *paidia*.

The Adult Woman and Man

The adult family person, it would seem, is singularly freed from his children's leisure patterns in the United States of this century: TV serves, among its other functions, as a reliable baby-sitter; the child is heavily influenced by his peers; schools have taken over instruction in physical activity, such as games; teenagers, in many cases, own or drive cars; and the total social pattern has been toward independence for each member of the family.

Yet there is evidence that the American family is far from an atomized and weakened unit. Television itself has brought the family together, at least in a physical sense, although we know little as yet about the precise effects. The automobile has made it possible for the family to spend long periods of time together, in camping or touring situations that are close and that spread over long periods of time.

The issue, presented this broadly, is subject to many interpretations and needs refining for scientific purposes. We might ask, for example, what is the comparison of free time among working and nonworking women on a worldwide level, or comparisons of men and women in general; some observations from Szalai's 12-nation study will be presented in Chapter 11. Dr. France Govaerts of Brussels has produced a major volume, *Loisirs des femmes et temps libre,* which awaits discovery by the women's lib movement as a gold mine of insights on the comparative subordination and slavery of women.[14]

Yet the overall issue that still returns as the major one is the general life-style of the adult, whether centered in the home or in outside employment, in relation to both the younger and the older generations. And the impression remains; it is a life-style that has become freer to find its own expression in the past half century. It is a dual freedom, emanating from external and internal conditions.

Externally, the adult has been freed from long hours of employment and of home chores; automation has been the key in both cases. We cannot forget how enriched the American woman has become with enough energy at her constant command to equal 85 to 90 male servants. If she continues to find herself busy, it is in the self-assignment of other tasks not directly related to the hard-core maintenance of life, shelter, and clothing.

Internally, the basis of relationships among adults in the home is interpersonal instead of interfunctional. This has developed also from the greater literacy of both men and women and from the consciousness of personal relationships that has accompanied a growing awareness of social science. Much of the fare of television, the movies, and magazines (not only those addressed to women) deal with this theme. In addition, the freedom from both young people and from the aged in the home has been encouraged by movements from within these subcultures. Although only 5 percent of Americans over 60 live in nursing homes or other institutions, the bulk of the 95 percent are not with their children.

The impact of these freeing tendencies on the middle generation has been to raise questions, as seen especially among women in their forties: who am I, what am I becoming? Men of this age are in the professional prime, and they are too busy to ask the question; women have been gradually freed by then from chauffeuring their young and waking at night to heat bottles of milk. The questions of self-being press on them, unless by then these women have been killed of creativity, curiosity or self-esteem. Alcoholism is among the alternatives among those who can afford it financially, and it is the chief drug that is easily available and socially acceptable by polite society to negate the need for more constructive leisure forms.

The Elderly

In other centuries as well, including the Eastern European area, the traditional family of three or four generations is breaking up. The grandchild is now more likely to see the grandparent when one visits the other. The grandparent is more likely to play with the third generation than to teach it how to play.

If we define the elderly as those over 60, there are 27 million elderly in the United States. About 60 percent of the total are in good physical shape to do what they want, within reason; 60 percent are not working. Gallup's polls reveal that about the same percentage are willing to volunteer in some community activity but are rarely called on. The large majority of the elderly do not live in institutions but in some family situation or alone. Increasing numbers find their way amidst their peers, in such planned communities as "Sun City Center" in Florida or "Leisure World" in California, where they find a variety of organized activities. As one survey notes, the "little old ladies" are not rocking on the porch; they are more likely to be on the golf course, in the swimming pool, trumping their partner's aces, planning the next party, or participating in club activities. Many American cities have special programs for the elderly in tax-supported community centers such as "Senior Citizens" and "Golden Age" clubs or numerous nursing homes run by churches, unions, professional organizations, and entrepreneurs.

Overall, leisure patterns of the elderly have been less studied than their problems of health, income, and housing. The 1971 White House Conference on Aging, by comparison with its predecessor of a decade ago, paid more attention to leisure as a fundamental approach to the development of meaningful new roles and values. It seems apparent that basically the elderly participate in the full range of alternatives open to all ages, influenced—as is everyone in his own situation—by income, background, and the like. Instead of the familiar practice among policymakers in the past to add up the unique situation of the elderly as an accumulation of disadvantages, the trend now is to build services for and with the elderly on the basis of *accumulated advantages,* such as their wide experience and freedom from responsibilities.[15]

Many new programs have been instigated with federal funds under the Older Americans Act but operating on state and local plans and including the use of day centers, clubs, informal education, and volunteer services by aging persons to their peers and to younger people (e.g., the highly successful "Foster Grandmother Program")

The Older Americans Act, begun in 1966 as one of President Johnson's Great Society programs, has funded over 1000 projects, including about 250 multipurpose facilities that always include recreation. Centers such as Little House in Menlo Park, California have become models for all-purpose recreation programs that are planned and directed by the members. The Institute for Retired Persons, begun at the New School for Social Research in New York City in 1962, provides a full college graduate program. Dr. Ruth Glick heads the Institute for Post-retirement Studies at Case Western Reserve University in Cleveland. In Orlando, Florida, a full concert season is presented by a symphony of 75 retired musicians whose careers had been with major professional orchestras of the nation. Many local tax-supported recreation departments, numbering more than 3000 across the country, now include special centers or organized programs for the elderly as an integral part of their function. A major force among the elderly themselves is the American Association of Retired Persons, with offices on both coasts; its membership is open to anyone over 55 years of age. An excellent bimonthly magazine, *Modern Maturity,* reflects a close concern with leisure activities alongside its interests in health and other areas. An equally important journal, *Harvest Years,* is issued monthly under private auspices.

Historically, the uniqueness of the elderly in relation to leisure is that they have experienced more directly the social panorama suggested above: a loosening of social class, the mixing of populations, the release from a work ethic, large internal migrations, the spread of art and literacy, the growth of public services, and the companionship-oriented family; they have lived through major wars, a great depression, rising costs, and the birth of cars, planes, television, and astronauts. From a time when many of them carried water from the well, they see a life now in which the middle-class American woman occupies an automatized-feudal castle, beset with ongoing jousts between time-saving (dishwasher, telephone) and time-consuming (TV, radio) servants. The single major pivot between them and the young is television, which all generations use widely. If work is materially reduced and leisure correspondingly evolves as a major orientation for all ages, this medium for developing and carrying out new social and personal values may see leisure forms that are based in new commitments to personal growth and to public service; these tendencies are already discernable in the protestations and values of the young.

Several recommendations are reproduced from the 1971 White House Conference that are most pertinent to the present discussion.[16] I omit the supplementary implementation statements, as well as recommendations that came from the 17 "special concerns sections," dealing with areas such as "rural older older people," the "poor elderly," "aging and blindness," and "aged blacks."

RECOMMENDATION 1. Society—through government, private industry, labor, voluntary organizations, religious institutions, families, and older individuals—must exercise its responsibility to create a public awareness of changing life-styles and commitments in a continuous life cycle. Together they should discover and implement social innovations as vehicles for older persons to continue in, return to, or assume roles of their choice. These innovations should provide meaningful participation and leadership in government, cultural activities, industry, labor, welfare, education, religious organizations, recreation, and all aspects of volunteer services.

RECOMMENDATION 2. Program efforts to meet role problems and to create new role opportunities should be designed to serve all segments of the older population. Priorities should be determined according to local and individual needs; special effort must be made to include persons who might otherwise be excluded—the impoverished, the socially isolated, the ethnic minorities, the disabled and, the disadvantaged.

RECOMMENDATION 3. Society should adopt a policy of preparation for retirement, leisure, and education for life off the job. The private and public sectors should adopt and expand programs to prepare persons to understand and benefit from the changes produced by retirement. Programs should be developed with government at all levels, educational systems, religious institutions, recreation departments, business, and labor to provide opportunities for the acquisition of the necessary attitudes, skills, and knowledge to assure successful living. Retirement and leisure-time planning begin with the early years and continue through life.

RECOMMENDATION 5. Public policy should encourage and promote opportunities for the greater involvement of older people in community and civic affairs and for their participation in formulating goals and policies on their own behalf as a basis for making the transition from work to leisure roles. Society should reappraise the current life-style sequence of student-worker-retiree roles and promote role flexibility.

RECOMMENDATION 9. It should be the responsibility of the federal government, in cooperation with other levels of government, to provide funds for the establishment, construction, and operation of community-oriented, multiservice centers designed for older citizens. Industry, labor, voluntary and religious organizations should assist in the planning and implementation.

CASE STUDY METHOD

The preceding general observations about the several generations need to be brought into some totality, that is, into a "real family." Thus the case study emerges as an important tool for students of leisure. However, it is essential that those who employ this method must also be clear about what their method can and cannot achieve. This is the method by which a person, a group of persons, a family, or even a whole community is observed closely, and the time factor is covered either by actual duration of the observation or by historical recollections of persons and the use of documents. I do not refer here to "cases" such as written records kept by social agencies; these may have value beyond their original welfare purposes, but they were not intended for later research and are therefore generally too sparse. I refer, instead, to "insight-stimulating" examples, such as those that provided the basis for Freud's theories, or the set of personal documents collected by W. I. Thomas and F. Znaniecki, which laid much of the base for personal documentation in social work. In this method, one attempts to obtain sufficient information to explain both the unique features of the case being studied as well as those that it shares with other cases. In the study of the individual, this may involve an extensive examination of his present situation and his life history.

Any one or a combination of factors may be the determining explanation for leisure patterns (or for their absence) in the family: father works at night, so his children must play outside during the day; grandmother lives with a family, limiting the amount of travel of everyone else; the Jones family is wealthy, a fact that does not fully explain but certainly enters the explanation of their deep-sea fishing; for this young family, the central fact is that the husband attends the university. More difficult, but no less crucial, are the "internal" factors that point to clear explanations: the wife's fear of strange places, the attitudes or aspirations that develop from one's poverty or life in a small town, and so on.

Such findings may come from partial, descriptive bits, or from more complete accounts ending in a hypothesis to further additional study. First, several examples of the first are reproduced portions from the fourth edition of the famous Michelin Guides, titled *Chateaux of the Loire.* In a section on "country and chateau life" the visitor is given this vignette of leisure.[17]

"In the fortified castles of the 10th and 11th centuries living conditions were rough. The whole family lived, took their meals and slept in the same room on the first floor of the keep. This could be reached only by a ladder; it was barely light there at midday and the wind whistled through the narrow loopholes. In spite of the logs blazing on the hearth, the walls ran with moisture; there were no carpets, but straw thrown on the floor. A table, bed, a few chests, stools and wooden benches made up the scanty furniture. Monotonous meals of meat roasted on the spit and vegetables boiled in the pot hanging over the hearth were cooked in the fireplace. The pewter tableware was rudimentary.

The people of the castle lived shut in among themselves. As the lord was often a man of limited intelligence, the time spent in the house seemed to him desparately long. He thought only of getting out; he would hunt, skirmish with his neighbours and welcome the great adventure of a crusade with joy. His wife would fall back on endless needlework or sit at her spinning-wheel.

The smallest incident—a passing pilgrim, a begging monk—was an event. The arrival of a juggler, a *trouvere,* a wandering poet and storyteller—or a minstrel made a festival. Simple conjuring tricks, the noise of a hurdy-gurdy, the thin note of a flute, a tune on a lute caused transports of delight. Interminable poems were listened to all day with rapt attention.

Chateau life always meant many idle hours. Varied amusements were in demand. Indoors, the inmates played at chess, spillikins, dice and draughts and, after the 14th century, at cards. Out of doors the men played real tennis, bowls and soft-ball; they also practiced wrestling and archery. With tournaments and tilting, hunting remained the great lordly sport.

Dwarfs entertained the women and children; at court, the jester cheeked all and sundry, including the sovereign. Festivals banquets, balls and masquerades were frequent. Performances of the Mysteries drew audiences of nobles, bourgeois and rustics. The public were insatiable: after having followed the innumerable unravellings of a drama for 25 days on end, they were sorry to hear the last verse spoken."

Contrast the chateau style of life with a contemporary Florida family described below. (I have left the paragraph just as it came to me, for it suggests, alas, that the student might profitably spend some of his free time learning something about the use of his native language.)

"The B. family are much like any average group of children that you would imagine. They heave (have?) their play friends. They have their toys and games, and Tommy has school. Children in this category are probably much easier to classify than their parents. Mrs. and Mrs. B. are found in the home from Sunday night to Thursday night. Friday and Saturday night you are probably going to find them gone. The television set is on about 16 to 20 hours per week. This will vary with the season, for Mr. B. is going to watch more television during football season than any other time of the year. The set is usually turned on at 6:30 to catch the news, and probably stays on till either 10:00 or 11:00 P.M. During this time neither are glued to the set, but appear to be quite loose. Either or both can be in the room with the television set on and still be quite involved with a novel. . . . They also play cards. This is a sometimes sort of arrangement, and not a iron-clad bridge game. Mrs. B. also bakes, and antiques furniture. She says she enjoys it, and it is very beneficial. I might add that while I was in the home I had the pleasure of trying some of her choclate cake, and found it to be quite goo. This seems to be what activities that seem to be home oriented. . . ."

The enormous difference between such families emphasizes, indeed, it demands a hypothesis drawn from the fourth dimension from the model of Chapter 2, to the effect that it is the social order *in its totality* that provides the dominant leisure style in these contrasting cases, specifically the degree and type of isolation/contact with the rest of the world. All of McCluhan's work serves leisure studies in spelling out these differences in communication.

Now we turn to two other family studies that, in their contrast, bring to mind another type of hypothesis. Both are taken from student papers. The first is a summary made by a son of the life-styles of his mother and father.

MOTHER	FATHER
50 years old	51 years old
Weak heart	Chronic alcoholic
Housewife, works as a waitress on Sunday in the tavern	Operates a tavern
Watches TV evenings, with a friend in their home or our's	Watches TV sports only
Goes to drugstore Friday or Saturday night with friend, talks; shops with same friend	Hunts and fishes often, especially duck-hunting; spends much time and money on this
No hobbies; sews out of necessity; used to drink and drive the car alone (does neither now). Has four friends. Goes to baseball games alone	Stays at tavern often after hours to talk. At home: sleeps, eats, watches TV sports, reads papers, leaves when these are done or not available

In contrast to this report, I quote from another student whose father is a research chemist near Chicago, and whose mother collects antiques and reads much. The parents were educated abroad. The home, as one might expect, contains many items that are useful for a large variety of leisure experiences. She writes:

"My parents, read constantly the journals of the American Chemical Society, Society of Philatelic Americans, American Philatelic Society, Chicago Philometer Society, Illinois State Archeological Society, Archeological Institute of America and all pertinent information in *National Geographic, Life, Readers Digest,* and *Scientific American.*

I have deliberately not mentioned specifically the *institution* of philately in our home. This is because this hobby plays a dominant role in our leisure time.

My parents had an interest in this hobby since their childhood, but it wasn't until December of 1952 that it became the largest consumer of leisure time. This began when my brother and I both had the mumps and complained of nothing to do. Mother remembered having a few stamps in an old box and thought we could mount them in a book for diversion.

The thorough and active participating in philately spread through our leisure time like wildfire. It was a frenzy to provide ourselves with multitudes of catalogues, albums, mounting equipment, tweezers, and of course the professional advice to begin properly. . . .

Immediately this activity served to solidify the family. Discussions were constantly held to discuss everything from a field of specialty and how the money should be invested to the trivial problem of mounting."

She goes on to speak of the new friends they made from their correspondence about stamps; one new friend from New Zealand called on them; they joined clubs; and through new friends they developed other interests; they had to remodel their home to accommodate their collection. She then summarizes: "I believe we found a closer psychic unity . . . something to escape into . . . all of our needs for creativity and individuality . . . new friends and new knowledge."

The two cases above present a remarkable difference in the degree of closeness between husband and wife. Yet there are undoubtedly vast differences among families with a chemist father as there are among bartenders. The hours of work required in both cases is a decisive factor, especially if this can be combined with the variable of aspirations or values that attract persons to these respective fields. The scientist has enough troubles when his hypothesis contains multivariables, but the task is far more complex when the variables move on different levels of quantifiable possibility.

The first two "cases" (chateau life and today's Florida) moved toward the broadest type of hypothesis—cultural milieu—and therefore require historical data. It is the sort of problem that makes the American sociologist uneasy and therefore moves the student of leisure more properly into the types of cultural studies associated with Sorokin or Riesman. Of a far different order is the following description of daily life in the home of a former student, written by Miss Irawan Chulawat, who lives in Pattant, Thailand. The feeling one derives of life in this southern region is of stability and precision, of strong family and community cohesion.

"Between 5:00 and 5:30 A.M., the mother arises and makes a fire in the small clay stove, washes in the river, and then prepares breakfast.

At 6:00 the children, and usually the father, get up. During the plowing and harvesting season the family rises at 5:00 A.M. and starts to work in the fields as soon as possible. An older child stays home to care for the younger children and to look after the house.

The children's first job is to feed the chickens and then take out the buffalo and give them hay. At 6:00, the mother squats at the entrance of the compound and awaits the monk who calls for his daily rice. Upon their return, the children wash their faces and hands and brush their teeth. While awaiting breakfast, the father putters about the house, checking his fishing rod or perhaps taking a quick look at some rice in a nearby field.

Breakfast is at 7:00 or 7:30, and the family eats together. After breakfast, children play about until 8:30, and then are off to school by foot or boat. The mother washes the dishes and pots, puts up the mosquito nets and rolls the sleeping mats out of the way, then sweeps the house and compound.

About 9:00 the farmer may go to do the shopping. If the father is hiring out or busy in the fields, the mother or an older daughter does the shopping.

At 11:00 or 12:00 they eat again, usually unheated leftovers from breakfast. During school, children are fed three times a day.

After the noon meal, the entire family naps unless there is urgent work to be done. Small children are forced to take a nap for an hour or two every afternoon. Mid-morning and mid-afternoon are the usual times for visitors to call and, of course, in the early evening after the work is done. If a visitor arrives, tea is offered as well as betal or cigarette paper and tobacco.

In the late morning and late afternoon, people gather at the stores, or sit at the small sala (place in the temple) and chit-chat. To a much more limited degree this also occurs on their way to or from work.

If there is a celebration in the village, the entire family attends.

Entertainment divides into six categories: gossip and conversation, games including gambling, wat (temple) festivities and life crises festivities, radio, and extra-village entertainment.

Chatting and gossiping probably occupy the greater part of the villagers' leisure time."

I turn now to a more detailed analysis of the Hanson family. Here we will find materials for analysis that move in all directions at once: (1) conclusions about a particular case and observations that reach out in application to others; and (2) "external" and "internal" factors.

On a small mountain in western Massachusetts, an elderly couple has built a large, modern home and almost everything inside. Mr. Hanson comes from a line of expert Danish woodworkers. The family, with two sons and a daughter, had lived in Greenwich, Connecticut and Rochester, New York; they moved to the Beckett, Massachusetts area to get away from city "hubbub," and to protect daughter Rhetta (whose childhood illness had caused a speech defect).

After several years in the Beckett area, the Hansons bought several farms adjoining their own and became interested in the mountain they now occupy. It had become a favorite spot to climb. There was one tree on the top of the mountain, and much of the small flat area consisted of rock. By this time they had purchased three contiguous farms; then Mrs. Hanson decided suddenly one day to have a home on the top of the hill.

First came the blasting of rock, four feet down. Then the lumber had to be cut and hauled up the hill. Mrs. Hanson worked side by side with her husband on all phases of the project. This was done in the family's spare time, since Mr. Hanson was holding down construction jobs in nearby towns. As many others have done in building their own home, the Hansons constructed a livable basement into which they could move. When they did move to the hill, to settle temporarily in the basement, living was far from uncomfortable. The room came to the considerable length of 105 feet with adjoining bedroom and kitchen. Here the Hansons lived for six years, with only a framework above them for the house that was yet to appear. Two factors delayed further building: Mr. Hanson's illness and an option for possible purchase by a lime company. Finally, the Hansons decided to forego the possibility of sale and proceeded with their project: "family tensions" had developed, "and were not worth the money." In 1967, four years later—when I visited—the job was mostly finished. The main living room, a master bedroom, and a workshop outside of the home were still to be built.

Why can this project be discussed under "leisure"? Many families have participated in the building of rooms, even of whole houses. In other cases, as well, the project is a part of "leisure" if more than utility or construction is involved, that is, more than a saving of money, or an inability to find builders. With the Hansons, building is not merely an extension of his skill with his hands, but a major binding force that reminds us of William Morris in its philosophy. I was shown a wooden box that they had constructed on their honeymoon. The building and, on her part, the making of the rugs and other items inside, has been chosen as their way of life in preference to social visits. As she observed, "It's nice to have lots of friends, but you don't get anything done. If I'm making a big rug, I can't drag it up and sit and talk." They "don't bother with nobody," and seldom attend church. They watch television in the evening "to keep up with the times."

"I sit in my bed at night and I crochet or embroider and I look over my glasses at TV and my husband will sit right alongside of me and I'll say, 'Oh, look over there, the lamp is like mine, or there's an old wheelbarrow like mine. . . .'"

She went no further than the eighth grade and, because of illnesses, sometimes attended school no more than six weeks of the year. Her husband had one year of high school, plus night work at the Pratt Institute in Brooklyn many years later to study architectural design. Building things as a hobby is a natural extension of his work, but he brings the elements of play into his work: "When you make something a drudge you might as well give it up." His traditionalism extends into a critical attitude toward the methods of labor unions: he believes in and has worked with apprentice carpenters; too many young men of today "want to start at the top." Less vocal than his wife and less open in his expression of a way of life represented on this hill in Massachusetts after their life in Connecticut, he nodded his head in obvious agreement when she said, "I can walk around the house and look out into the space. You don't get tired of looking."

"I'd call this a hobby," he noted, waving his hand at the home. "I enjoy doing it." Should one's hobby be necessarily related to his work? Not necessarily, he thought; every man "should have something to take his mind off what he's doing. A doctor or a lawyer should have a hobby that takes more physical activity." However, in his own case, he does not read except materials relating to his work or to the building of his furniture in the home. He considers playing cards—a favorite pastime in the nearby community—a waste of time; he does occasionally chat with friends in the village nearby. Sometimes he attends the town meeting, but he has never run for public office; he is known as the town "Republican."

Do they have a strong feeling that a husband and wife should do things together, based on their experience? "Yes," he replied,

"I think they should do things together, whatever it is. Make it a partnership, that's the way I always felt. I think there would be a lot more happiness."

Mrs. Hanson broke in here.

"They should also work with the children. Our children were right with us, making benches, cutting lumber, like a family picnic. It was play."

Does their attitude toward cooperative activity extend to the community level? There is only one Negro family in Beckett; the man is a construction worker. Mr. Hanson: "I've known nice people who were colored. But I'm not going to have someone tell me that I have to have them. This I don't go for." The area is mostly Catholic and becoming more so. This doesn't bother the Hansons, who feel, however, that the ecumenical movement is "not right." Summarizing the matter, they shared the sentiment that she voiced, "You've got to have your choice."

There is a piano in the home; the old-fashioned phonograph is not much used. I saw few paintings in the home; the Hansons have never attended Jacobs Pillow, the world-famous dance center a few miles away, or Tanglewood, summer home of the Boston Symphony. He hunts, and keeps his guns hanging on the wall.

The contents of each room reveal the time and family commitment over the years. All the lumber for the house came from one tree in order to keep the same texture that was filled, cut, and prepared by the Hansons. All the rugs, bedspreads, quilts, towels, and pillowcases were sewn, knitted, or braided by her, aided by her daughter and mother; the latter is 81, and lives a bit down the hill. Mrs. Hanson made some bedspreads waiting for children at a time when she drove a school bus; one such piece took a full year. Rugs are made from old pieces; dolls found in various rooms are hand crocheted. She goes from one piece of work to another for diversity—"if you work at one thing you get sick of it." Most of her creative activity is reserved for winter time, and is done in part down the hill several hundred yards "to keep my mother in the house. I walk down every morning or go down in my snow sled, and I stay there until noon-time. Then I come home to do my housework and cooking."

The mother also helps in making wreaths that are sold at Christmas time, mostly by December 1st, to deer hunters. "Mother has to be included, because if you put an old person aside . . . right now she's out picking blueberries." Mrs. Hanson does not know what price she would place on her rugs; she does have many quilts stored and may open a shop someday if they decide to sell and move elsewhere.

A major reason for leaving Connecticut over 20 years ago was the desire to protect their daughter, who, at an early age, had a serious speech defect. "I said if she's going to roam around, she's going to have nobody making fun of her." The family could not afford doctors and began developing their own methods for teaching the child how to speak and read; the daughter is now a division manager at Sears.

"She could have been married at least four times. But I always sat her down in the chair and I didn't say, you can't do this, it's got to be this way or that way. I just showed her—how *he* likes this, *you* don't care for this. Are you going to sit home while he runs out to get this?—this skiing that *he* likes to do? You don't care for skiing. Of course I never let her ski, for fear she'd bang her head. I love swimming. Nobody in the world loves swimming more than I. But I gave it up because I wouldn't go to the beaches with her. There are things you have to do.

Now she's married to the right man. He is older than she is, but age has nothing to do with your happiness. He has a business; she loves to meet people. She has 3,000 chickens, 1,500 fruit trees. She's in Seventh Heaven, and she's working hard. Work is nothing if you're happy doing it. Sunday we went out and picked 700 eggs. You get dirty and the chickens swat you in the neck, but she likes it, I like it. They really get along."

This case study properly ends on a sermon by Mrs. Hanson: one conclusion from the case is the self-consciousness that emerges throughout the interview: the use of construction on a family level (three generations) to inculcate and maintain a closeness and a sense of worth. The questioner must be careful to check whether this response was called forth and emphasized by the nature of his questions, remindful of the interviewer who asks 30 questions, 25 of them on sex, and concludes that the "subject seems to be preoccupied with sex!" In this case the moral issues seemed to emerge naturally from questions that could have moved in other directions. Relating this observation to concepts of leisure discussed in Chapter 2, the building, knitting, gardening, and so on, were a means—consciously realized and in part selected—as well as an end; in the first sense, the therapeutic element was there, even literally on the medical level with the daughter, but not on the "recreational" level of getting Mr. Hanson ready to go back to "work" on Monday mornings.

One may wonder about the degree to which Mrs. Hanson (the more extravertive of the two) is carried along in recent years by the reputation that she enjoys among the residents for her handiwork. This reputation can feed into a compulsion, suggested by her crocheting at nights in bed during TV shows. However, the matter is not explained by the Hansons' need to simply keep busy since, by severely limiting their social life, they have consciously selected to keep busy by building and overfurnishing. The aesthetic sense noticeable in the separate objects —quilts, rugs, drapes—is not matched by an overall sense of interior design, because the home is packed with objects far beyond aesthetic need or proportion to space. Thus every room, every corner, is a visible symbol of the virtues of togetherness, self-reliance, self-image. An aesthetician would be fascinated to arrange all these objects in a chronology of creation and, from this retrospective vantage, come to a judgment of the family's aesthetic growth. Yet there is a legitimate question whether "growth" in the realm of primitive art and artifacts is subject to familiar criteria such as increasing complexity or insight. In respect to imagination, judged by variety, this home houses a very large array of ideas in the objects, as seen in patterns, color combinations, and ingenuity.

Returning to the Hanson case as illustration of a method, it is apparent that an economic approach (e.g., through expenditures) would be naive except as a part of the whole: one could, for instance, refer to expenditures for tools and materials, but immediately the strangeness of the purchases would require a social inquiry. If one takes the position of Steffan B. Linder that *time* must be considered by the economist as a scarce commodity, he is led to wonder why economists have in the past ignored this social perspective.

However, even if all of the data on the Hanson family were reported here—I have used only a fraction of my notes—the case study approach, like expenditure and time studies, has its limitations in coming to major issues of personality and family.

FINAL OBSERVATIONS

It is clear that the destiny of the family will, in good part, derive from trends in leisure. The reverse is equally true. For this reason, if no other, there is a surprising lack in the discussion of leisure in literature on the family and, indeed, in the larger area of "social work" or "social welfare." The outlines are clear for such needed work. Already, in the level of time budget studies, tourism, outdoor recreation studies, and mass media inquiries, much is known indirectly about family behavior. What is needed now is a direct approach by scholars of the family who can proceed, as it were, from the inside and go outward toward these correlations. From the "inside" we need sensitive, qualitative observations of the kind that are made by novelists, buttressed by quantitative and objective research.

One place to begin is with the flexible work patterns that will be touched on in Chapter 12. Anticipating somewhat, what happens to parental-child relationships when the father works four hours a day, or a "normal" day of eight hours but for half a year? After all, our experience with consecutive months or years of free time usually comes in retirement, when children are no longer a primary consideration. The nonworking wife, we know from international studies, now spends *more* time doing housework on weekends than working women do. What happens, then, with new nonwork patterns for the men, especially if work schedules may change from month to month, or with seasons and moods?

One other issue will be suggested that deserves far more than superficial investigation. It is the question of the quality of family life. As long as the husband's role was primarily to maintain the family as an economic unit, he was excused by general consent. It was she who was most concerned with the life-styles of children, and she who provided the cultural and social atmosphere of the home. Yet the general trend is for her to be freer of the home and for him to be freer of work. A more equal, cooperative concern is therefore possible for the leisure dimension as the central indicator of the successful family. Such potentials as flexible work periods, desires to travel, and other leisure preferences are new clues of the future on the decision to have children or on the choice of mate.

The future of the family has begun noticeably to move from its legalistic, moralistic, traditionalist, and economic foundations to more amorphous, unpredictable, personal and cultural relationships. Here lies its new dangers and also its new opportunities.

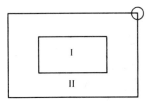

Chapter 9
Group and Subculture

The group is a number of people who have some physical or social identity. There is no scientific criteria in either the objective level (size, sex, or space limitation) or the subjective (communications, knowledge of each other or degree of homogeneity).

Obviously, much leisure is carried on by groups, as in a baseball game or a class of adults. Common interests, such as sports, help *create* groups; thus the group itself is both an *instrument* and an *end* of leisure. The sciences that are concerned with groups, such as social psychology, have much to say about leisure. Conversely, students of leisure may have something to say about group behavior.

The definitions of subcultures are equally ambiguous. On the physical level one can speak endlessly of "teenagers," "youth," "retirees," "blacks," "Catholics," "professors," "Parisians," and so on. In each case we can think of real people who live near each other, are of similar age or stage in life, or share a common racial, ethnic, or educational background. But, as in the category of groups, the term "subculture" also refers to subjective unity. Leisure is affected by both the objective and subjective aspects of subculture, in some cases more than in others; and again it may itself function to unify—or to dissipate—a subculture by its meanings and symbolic qualities.

The plan of this chapter will be to distinguish several themes and related patterns of leisure behavior, applying them to groups and to subcultures.

THEMES	LEISURE BEHAVIOR
Purpose	Telepractic-dynamic
Structure	Formal-informal
Control	Regulated-traditional

The examples of each will, wherever pertinent, be seen against the accumulating backlog of analyses from earlier chapters.

GROUPS

The sociologist E. T. Hiller listed the following elements of a social group: (1) some uniting interests or goals are accepted by the members; (2) members "become values to one another for various reasons"; (3) members are given functions "which are integrated in a manner suited to promote the interests of the association"; (4) relationships among members are regulated by norms, "such as customs, mores, and expressed rules"; and (5) tests of admittance are applied "in keeping with the united interest."[1]

Another sociologist, Florian Znaniecki, spoke of social circles of individuals to satisfy their specific needs. In a limited local community, he noted, "such a circle is always small enough for the individual to identify personally everybody who composes it and for the participants to subject his interaction to social control."[2]

Hiller and Znaniecki, colleagues for many years at the University of Illinois, independently developed the concept of *social roles* as the basis for observing social relationships.

Such explanations of human behavior as "human nature," or other psychological, biological, or metaphysical explanations attempt to explain our behavior by what we *are;* the Freudian approach and its offshoots seek to explain man by his subconscious, his very early training, his instincts, and his complexes. However, the theater provided other social scientists with an analogy from the make-believe of the "stage" to the actor-audience setting in "real life."

Sociologists and social psychologists who became aware of this analogy adopted the term *role* (eventually with the adjective *social*) and applied it to individual participation in social life. They concentrated, first of all, on the individual's representation of his own self. Baldwin, Cooley, and Mead emphasized that this representation is a product of social interaction and communication: that is, the individual imagines and conceives himself to be the kind of person that he believes others judge him to be. Park and Burgess, in their *Introduction to Sociology,* defined the term *person* (following the old Latin meaning of the word *persona*) as "an individual's conception of his role," and showed that an individual tends to behave in accordance with this conception. A few years later, they and other investigators pointed out that the particular person plays various social roles in his various groups, just as an actor performs different theatrical roles.

The elements of social role which Znaniecki uses are (1) social circle, (2) function, (3) status or esteem, and (4) concept of self.[3] These, together with the interrelations from one's roles in many groups provide the student of leisure with essential tools with which he can distinguish one activity or experience from another. The role concept embraces both the social and the psychological dimensions; it is especially crucial in understanding the passage from work to nonwork situations. I apply them first in the informal-formal group distinction.

Informal-Formal Groups

All elements of the social roles are relatively flexible in the informal leisure situation. In the home party, for example, persons meet who, for the duration of the party, freely shed their normal roles as policeman, clerk, teacher, or minister. Conversation turns quickly from one topic to another. No discussion is prolonged or, if it is, not beyond a certain point of seriousness in which excitement or offense can prevail. Aside from a purposeful lack of content in the party, there are factors of manners, good taste, and tact.

We have in sociability both a decided freedom and a consciously observed limitation or control.[4] It is a control that arises out of consideration for persons *as persons*. The host's chief function is to create the group, then to maintain this quality of sociability. One technique he/she adopts is to select members of the group by mentally matching them, anticipating who might force his opinions or favorite topics of conversation or who might simply not like other guests.

When a content is provided—entertainment, song, serious discussion —then the informal and unorganized group, no matter how momentarily, takes on the aspects of a political group, or an audience, with such role functionaires as debaters, entertainers, group fools, jesters, sages, or teachers. However, there are devices used by the host to insure a successful affair, although he is not necessarily aware of what he is doing. He will provide refreshments to break down reserve and make the extended conversation more difficult, or liquor that at once dulls the mind and stimulates spontaneity.

The social circle of the party is temporary; it has, of course, some awareness—in upper-class affairs, that is a major input—of who its participants are and why they are there. In New York social gatherings this flexibility is noticeable and often puzzling to the outsider. Those parties are often matters of business, occasions for developing "contacts" and "connections," especially if the participants have the same interests such as theater, writing, or public relations. But where social honesty prevails, in or out of large metropolitan centers, the social gathering brings together persons who have temporarily surrendered work roles. Your momentary companion in conversation was a clerk, or social worker, or teacher—or was he? You had discussed a recent book, and had forgotten to ask—and why should you? Of course, in the great majority of social gatherings that are taking place every hour in some part of the world, social partners know each other well enough, including the work that each does, but the wine in Heilingenstadt or the fried chicken in Topeka are designed to supplement friendship that, as Hiller noted, is based in this setting on the person as a person, on "intrinsic evaluation" of one another.

Unlike the work role, rewards of the leisure role in the party fall into the general sphere of relaxation, entertainment, or change of routine, discussed in Chapter 7. Unlike payment for work, personal satisfactions are less measurable yet, since we often make the decision whether to work or to socialize, we bring evaluations into the social situation; however, the success of a party or other leisure experience is measured subjectively not against a nonleisure alternative, but against the expectation we bring with us to the experience. This is why it was necessary to include the element of "pleasant expectation" into a formulation of leisure.[5] In the more formal association and in the category of "telepractic" leisure later in this discussion, I will suggest that there are situations in which one's leisure "performance" and rewards are evaluated by him more strictly than in his work; this is seldom so in the informal activity.

Similarly, one's "concept of himself" has a flexibility in the informal situation of family member. Conversation is the major activity of informal groups and serves the participant in learning to know himself. Mead, to whom Znaniecki refers, stressed the importance of communications in the group process—"through the development of significant symbols," accomplished "almost entirely through the development of vocal gestures. ..."[6] Indeed, argued Mead, "That is the process of thought. It is taking the attitude of others, talking to other people, and then replying in their language."[7]

Thus it is that conversation within the informal gathering is one way in which persons find out what they think on issues of the day; yet the home party is largely successful if it avoids arguments or intended concentration or serious potentially divisive matters. "Inasmuch," wrote Georg Simmel, "as in the purity of its manifestations, sociability has no objective purpose, no content, no extrinsic results, it entirely depends on the personalities among whom it occurs. But precisely because everything depends on their personalities, the participants are not permitted to stress them too conspicuously. ... Tact, therefore, is here of such peculiar significance."[8]

Simmel introduces the term "social threshhold" as the point at which content or subjective aspects enter the scene.[9] We have here a relationship in which each person acts as if all were equals; this is not a lie, any more than art or play are social lies. It becomes a real lie when the ostensibly self-contained phenomenon is a deception played for ulterior purpose.

It would seem possible for empirical research to construct scale measurements or observations of two factors: first, one's interest in people *as people,* apart from their extrinsic valuations; second, one's level of personal security when confronted with verbal thrusts and explorations. With these it may then be possible to predict, hence to check, the behavior of types of persons in an atmosphere of sociability. Kurt Lewin's comments on national character types will be recalled; he notes that the stranger can break through to the American person quickly but then finds it hard to get at his core, his deeper thoughts or feelings; the German person is more difficult to know at first but, once rapport is established, he will bare his inner thoughts.

A relationship exists between sociability and our American value of "individual personality." There exists a general feeling that individuality is something of an assertiveness. To be "one's self" is not easy, since it implies "standing up" against pressures for conformity. To have individuality is to be relatively free, either in leading or in following, in originating action or in responding to someone else's prior action. Yet individuality comes not out of self-isolation but exactly the opposite; its test is among other people.

It is, of course, true that many feel a lack of independent thought, or of the "inner resources," fundamental to individuality. They may be at home in the momentary or fragmentary relationships that are proper at a party but quite lost in the open scrutiny of persons in this situation. Although, as Simmel noted, there is no *content* in sociability, no content is needed between two people for one to uncover the second as shallow or dull, which even small talk may reveal. It has often been remarked that Americans have lost the art of conversation; if so, it is both a result of less sociability and a cause of it. Lewin's observation of our ease at getting to know other Americans on the surface, but seldom going very far, would seem to result naturally from concentrations of population, from persons rubbing shoulders with many others, but never for very long.

The presence of the mass media in America is a second factor in producing a paradoxical situation. Although listening or watching movies, radio, and TV does reduce the actual time that people may need to talk to one another, it also serves to provide topics of conversation that are safe and inconsequential, hence not threatening to the conversants.

Formal leisure groups are sometimes spoken of as "instrumental," as distinct from the "expressive" gatherings discussed above. The associations that are explicit play groups, such as a team that bowls, plays baseball, or makes music, will be treated later under the category of "telepractic." Here I consider the association in the more vernacular sense of voluntary groupings that are often, but not necessarily, committed to accomplishing something for the members (as in a book-review club) or for the community (as in a move against pollution). Just as sociability is a relationship with a minimum of content other than interest in persons, association is characterized by content, by a common interest that is more important than people. Hence more structured roles will be expected. The interests, with accompanying sentiments about them [(1) dogs; (2) be kind to dogs] may center on almost anything from a shared hobby such as collecting stamps to a shared political belief.

Contrary to many who assert that most Americans are lonely, living anonymous lives removed from the interests of others, the facts point to a nation of joiners.[10] As a shrewd observer of American life, Donald Bell points out:[11]

"There are in the United States today at least 2,000,000 voluntary organizations, associations, clubs, societies, lodges, and fraternities with an aggregate (but obviously overlapping) membership of close to eighty million men and women. In no other country in the world, probably, is there such a high degree of voluntary communal activity, expressed sometimes in absurd rituals, yet often providing real satisfaction for real needs."

Arnold Rose points out that although no international comparisons of membership exist for voluntary associations, if the United States does lead, there may be a legal reason:[12]

"The First Amendment to the United States Constitution specifies the right of all citizens peaceably to assemble and the courts have always interpreted that to mean the right to form free associations. On the other hand, democratic countries like France, and Italy have had a history of restrictive legislation with respect to voluntary associations, and still other democratic countries, like Great Britain and Switzerland, have never put either encouragements or restrictions into their laws."

It must be noted that sociability can easily arise (or the reverse) in an association. Millions of persons who met during World War II through a joint interest in civil defense, as volunteers for Red Cross activities, or in the military itself have remained friends on a purely social basis. The Ku Klux Klan serves as an example in reverse, a case in which a program for social action resulted when bored young men, sitting around, looked for a source of excitement.

FUNCTIONS AND ROLES. Voluntary associations provide many functions, quite aside from their contributions in relation to the explicit interest. It is here, for instance, that millions of microscopic political structures are created, so that agencies for leadership and for "followership" are achieved. An army of "presidents," "sergeant-at-arms," and so on, is to be found in every town, city, village, or hamlet. Millions of cards are mailed every month by "corresponding secretaries," and perhaps millions of dollars are collected by treasurers across the land. These are offices created partly on a functional basis, of course, to keep the group machinery going and partly as a device for involving many persons. As much as we must say that these offices find the men and women to occupy them, so, too, men and women deliberately create these responsibilities in order to have something in which to become involved, to achieve some status, to exercise power, and to feel important. Within the perspective of the Tuesday Study Club, decisions that are taken by officers or members are as important and dramatic as those made by the President of the United States and the Congress and, indeed, occupy more of their attentive and anxious interest. Matters of fame, significance, drama, importance, or reputation must always be seen against the respective mental world that is involved. Certainly, the leadership experience to be found in decision making or in the small political manipulation within leisure time associations is an important training center. From such political "sandlots" come the "big leagues."

Another function of voluntary associations is to provide a meeting place for people whose ideas or interests are similar. Thus, especially in a large city, primary groups are made and vicinal proximity becomes less significant than in a smaller community.

Third, as a member of a club or group with a goal, one's leisure takes on direction and the perceptions of constructive living. This is especially needed by persons who feel guilt at wasting time or doing nothing. A deep psychological, perhaps even a religious, sense of duty or ethics enters here.

Personal growth and information are found in voluntary associations. Yet it must be added that in the arguments, bickerings, intrigues, electioneering, and enmities that also characterize such groups is to be found the nourishment that makes life interesting to many people. Leisure activity, in this sense, is also constructive, if that word is used generously. Shared struggles and defeats, as well as common victories, provide solidarity as well as factionalism.

In summary, the association as a form of leisure goes far beyond the stated objectives of the group. The organization or role grows largely out of the tradition and circumstance of the group. A local Masonic lodge has its hierarchical pattern already established for it. Elaborate study, followed by tests and probationary periods, is prescribed to graduate its members into various "degrees."

In many associations, perhaps less in the Masons than in others, there is a correlation between role position in and out of the group. A member is more likely to be elevated within the association if he has, in "normal" life, proved successful according to general societal standards. Persons are members of several groups or social circles; although these circles do not provide a uniform status across the board, the key role that is recognized by the society (banker, teacher, millionaire) often finds its way or its reflection even in the world of play and associations.

THE FUTURE OF INFORMAL AND FORMAL GROUPS. In a consideration of the future of the formal and informal groups for leisure, a significant matter for research is on the types of persons who turn to either group. In one such study, Professor Arthur P. Jacoby of the University of Alberta interviewed 94 persons who were members of one or more groups.[13] In summary, he found that more persons are inclined to join expressive groups through the influence of other persons; leaders in such groups are relatively new in the community and not as well educated as leaders of instrumental groups. Members of instrumental associations are more likely to vote and attend church.

Jacoby also assumed—in his first hypothesis—that the expressive group, more than the other, provides those satisfactions that come from "primary" relationship, that is, that arise from personal fellowship. Jacoby was surprised to find that this applies also to those who join instrumental (action-oriented) groups. He tested his hypothesis by comparing the number of married and unmarried persons who belonged to each, and also persons who lived alone, and concludes that "It would seem that the individual is motivated to join the instrumental association because he believes in the cause which the group represents; how he first makes contact with the association, through personal or impersonal media, is relatively unimportant."

This suggests the question as to whether *commitment* or *concern* to public issues may increase as new social forces lead us toward the post-industrial, or what in Chapter 2 I called the cultivated society. Concern and commitment are the heart of the instrumental or formal group; the increased time, literacy, mobility, and communications that have become available to the masses would imply that we have more access to public issues and to the tools for expressing our concern or joining in the action.

Indeed, the past decade has seen a remarkable rise in concerns, commitments, and action by persons who in the past were quiescent. Evidence comes from women now in the lib movement, students, minorities (including Spanish-Americans and Indians as well as blacks), the elderly, workers who for the first time have moved into unionism (teachers and airplane pilots), groups of poor who have exercised influence within urban renewal programs, demonstrations against war, and activities to protect the environment. All of this represents a direction in leisure of the United States that is by far the most dramatic in the short run and significant in the long run for leisure activities. Some scholars of leisure and many participants themselves will argue that these are not "leisure" activities; they seek to transform the society. Yet, in the past, the historian has found it agreeable to speak of political activities (or "public service") of the *elites* as a natural phrase in describing how they used the time freed for them by lower classes. The Greeks, whose concept of *paidia* still permeates the philosophy and conceptualization of such critics of democratic values as de Grazia and de Tocqueville, included service to the community. If young people were tied to the farm or factory, they would not possess either the literacy or the material base from which they can join movements. The same type of women who look askance at me when I ask what they do in their leisure—"Leisure? I have none,"—seem to have the time to join the Kate Millets and Betty Friedans in meetings and mimeographed rooms.

Furthermore, the trend toward informality has penetrated traditional guardianships of manners and formality: this is seen in the relative ease in addressing recent strangers by their first names. The scrutiny to which important figures are subject in television has lessened the distance between the more and the less "important" persons in the community. Feudallike distances tend to disappear when, as in a Florida trailer camp, one's new acquaintance in a campsite crawls from under your trailer and in good humor asks, "have you ever had a millionaire fix your car before?"

What is being projected here is that the complexities of contemporary times have also induced a directness and simplicity that is often overlooked. The directness is in the new *alternatives* that, for example, are inherent in suburban life—and this is the direction that emerges clearly from the 1970 census: the alternative of being left alone by neighbors or of being involved with others.

In short, the ease of moving into both informal and formal groups for leisure is greater; indeed, the lines between them may be lessening, necessitating new categories, especially with the universal presence of television to muddy old concepts such as primary-secondary. McCluhan awakened us all to the need for new analytic tools of social distance and of access to the world.

In my own studies of groups, stemming in good part from observations of the symphony orchestra, I have had to develop personal categories to explain groups that either live, organismic-like, or those that approach a goal or "crisis." Hence the division into *telepractic* and *dynamic* groups that, unlike the informal and formal, seems to become more distinguishable as a tool for describing our current leisure scene.

Dynamic and Telepractic Groups

With this division I come to a stress on the life of the group based on its purpose and content instead of on structure. Every student of social groups is aware of categories that call attention to such characteristics as composition, permanence, functions, interests, structures, cohesiveness, and sanctions. These categories, and in essence many of the analyses related to them, stress the static nature of group life inherent in the familiar term structure. Yet a group is more than structure. As a dynamic "synthesis of social roles," interrelationships within the group may change so sharply that a substantially new group will emerge. This dynamic process of transformation goes on in a family as children and parents grow older, as someone leaves the home, as father loses his job. Yet, in both cases, family and congregation, a new direction or goal is not sought; change is inevitable, but it is not consciously embodied as a desirable aspect in respect to more or less specific ends.

There is another kind of group whose function is not just to survive, but whose entire activity is consciously geared to a future event, experience, or even crisis. A military unit drills for anticipated battle; an athletic team looks ahead to its "meet"; a worker's union directs its energies toward negotiation or strike; and a group of actors rehearses for its public performance. Often, the "enemy," the "public," and the "opponent" are known in detail, and plans are shaped accordingly. Indeed, the very day and hour of the "crisis," "meeting," or "show" is often known, if not arbitrarily selected. These facts color such aspects of group life as the selection and training of members and the presence of objective criteria for evaluating success.

In a previous work I have applied the scheme to associations, games, and arts, and observed in some detail the workings of a symphony orchestra.[14]

THE FUTURE OF DYNAMIC AND TELEPRACTIC GROUPS. An easy parallelism may already have occurred to the reader: between the Greek conception of leisure as an *end* and the *dynamic* leisure group; conversely, between leisure as *instrumentalism* and the *telepractic* group. Such a neat construction cannot always conform to the facts: an organic family may be involved in leisure of quite a meaningless kind, such as playing a game; "togetherness" as a family ideal may then have been served, but that could have been accomplished in many other ways. On the other hand, an amateur string quartet rehearsing reasonably well on a Beethoven quartet—a telepractic situation—is relating itself to significant *end*-experience.

One might use a baseball game among boys to show that such a group —telos-oriented, organized, explicitly recognized—can be either an end or an instrument in the dichotomy described in Chapter 2. In the United States when we were boys, baseball used to be played on empty spaces, with a minimum of organization, no supervision by adults, our own balls and bats, and sometimes our own rules; if someone had to rush home to perform a chore, he left; if someone came along unexpectedly, he would go to second base or wherever he was needed just then; a rough score was kept, but every game was its own end; for the next game we would again rechoose "sides." The game was played for fun; it had no other purpose. Now, throughout the country, there are Little League teams, well organized, wearing suits like professionals, coached by adults, keeping accurate score, with players chosen or substituted on ability, carefully scheduled for competitions within communities, and ending in local, regional, national, and even a *world* series. On the same page that reports the World Series results of the National and American Leagues, the 1971 World Almanac reports that the 24th annual Little World Series was won by Wayne (New Jersey), defeating Campbell (California) by a score of 2–0 at Williamsport, Pennsylvania. So far-flung has this movement become that the champions the year before were from Taiwan, and from Japan before that. The criticism often heard in American recreation circles, especially among professional leaders is that these activities have become the psychological gratifications for parents, and that a large uniform industry pushes its interests.

If, then, the dynamic (or living) and the telepractic (or performing) groups can be either ends or means, another level of significance must be sought that is relevant to the social transformations of our time. Such a level is that of function. The thesis that seems tenable is that among the functions discussed in Chapter 6, three are particularly served by the telepractic type of activity: *sociability, growth,* and *discipline.* Those that seem to relate closely to the dynamic group are *freedom, recreation,* and *construction.*

SUBCULTURE

A subculture is a somewhat homogeneous or identifiable group within a larger and more comprehensive culture. Such groups may be large or small; they may be bound by ties of religion, ethnic origin, historical accident, significant location, or occupation. To be a Roman Catholic, Seventh Day Adventist, "bobby soxer," black, Jew, Southerner, New Englander, Bostonian, or New Yorker means that in these identities one may have motives of attitude and behavior that cut across traditional indices of class.

For example, the division of faculty and town may be a very real one in the mind-life of the college community. The intellectuals within this town-gown structure are generally less rooted in the region. They are cosmopolitan in outlook, critical of material values, and subdivided into specialties and social strata that lack intercommunication. Yet these campus and noncampus groups do not imitate or envy each other; they may shun one another; they exist side by side, dependent on one another and independent as well.

Subculture can be distinguished from *minority group* or nationality. Minority refers to social power. In terms of number, the minority may be an actual majority. With its limited power, the minority is kept out of favored positions or denied access to facilities or opportunities taken as a matter of course by the majority. This minority may possess very little cohesion within itself. In subcultures a "we" feeling is more than a reaction to treatment and results from self-recognized elements of identity.

From the scientific standpoint the subculture is important to our subject if significant connections can be drawn to uniqueness in leisure; from a humanistic view one could hold that the presence of subcultures provides some basis for pluralism in life-styles. From a political and social policy level, leisure issues—such as program planning in community centers—may be designed to serve the particular traditions and desires of segments of our population. All will be touched on in the following section.

Telepractic and Dynamic Subcultures

As they were used earlier with smaller, face-to-face groups, a telepractic or subculture exists positively, consciously, purposefully, and at times militantly.

In my 1960 volume I compared the Jew and the Negro subcultures.[15] Since those words were written, the Negro has gone through enormous political, economic, and psychological struggle. Universities everywhere have established "black studies" programs, or "Afro-American" studies. Here, on the campus, the most far-reaching of all changes are taking place, as the economically poor Negro student finds himself alongside white students, both confronting common issues of youthful alienation from the larger society, but coming from highly different family, community, and educational backgrounds. Outward symbols of behavior among the black students change quickly, as David Gottlieb notes among even black youth of high school ages who, under the federally funded Upward Bound program, are placed on college campuses, usually for special summer programs.[16]

"Upon arrival the typical pattern is for a quick abandonment of the old life style and the acceptance of the perceived college student culture. Obviously initial changes will be limited to the more visible aspects of the self. Plaid bermuda shorts replace shiny tapered trousers; madras summer caps are substituted for felt hats (an important part of the ghetto peer culture); pipe smoking replaces cigarettes; and there is obvious pride in the wearing of a shirt which carries the name of the college attended. No matter how brief the contact with the college it does appear to have some impact. University staff working with these students are impressed with how quickly new behavior styles are acquired. Changes occur not only in dress but there is an acceptance of the traditional with respect to how college students behave in the classroom, how they study, and how they are responsible for their living quarters. Although there is a tendency for some university officials to look to these same students when there is a theft on campus there is little evidence that they have been guilty of stealing or vandalism. On the contrary there is a general feeling that compared to typical students the Upward Bound enrollees conduct themselves as gentlemen. Other staff note with some surprise the fascination these adolescents have with words and the obvious desire to expand their vocabulary. Desire to become an integral part of the student culture includes involvement in a new set of leisure time activities. These same students will attend and enjoy concerts, foreign films and theater presentations."

In no case, notes Gottlieb, has he found any student who comes from poverty in the ghetto to say that he wants to stay poor and in the ghetto. Their aspirations for the "good life" come now from the television screen. They want jobs with a future, but they also want everything symbolized in the nonwork and leisure patterns of the "typical" American family—nice neighborhoods, lawns, summer vacations, good clothes, and education for their children.

In contrast to all of this, the Jewish subculture is "dynamic," that is, it lives its course, assimilated sufficiently so that its need for militancy or purpose is gone in the former sense. To recapture that purpose he either goes to Israel or buys Israel bonds, but that is a vicarious, even if deeply felt purpose. There is, as always, a large amount of community that absorbs time of both men and women, as in local chapters of Hadassah (a women's group primarily concerned with hospital work in Israel) and B'nai Brith (a men's group devoted to local and national programs). This type of "leisure" serves a social and communal purpose, it deepens friendships, and it consumes time, but its intensity is far less than comparable activity a generation ago or among other minorities now. Its leisure, on the broad scale, is assimilated into that of the mainstream of American life, whereas a "telic" subculture uses its leisure more consciously as a tool for attaining a self-identity and pride, as well as for concrete political or social goals.

The leisure roles of persons in these subcultures correspond to the dimension of telepractic or dynamic. In the former, leisure roles are more clear-cut and definable. For example, we may say that the youth of our time in history is more homogeneous than it had been; in addition to the delineations between the generations that are found in all societies, youth of our day is at the same time more aggressive and more attacked. Even with the youth segment, the "hippies" (in appearance to begin with), provide themselves with a physical indoctrination that symbolizes a cohesiveness; their major role in leisure is a reversal to conversation, human contact, and nature. Drugs supplement this rural withdrawal into magic and primitivism. The escapism through drugs has not yet led to any creative breakthroughs in art, literature, science, or thought in general. The leisure role of youth is perhaps close to the Greek concept that has already been described, and in its value of life as *being,* there are connections both to Western existentialism and to Oriental mysticism. Yet the bursts of action, either physically or within the political process, make the leisure roles of this segment the most difficult for all to assess. Its importance cannot be minimized, since young people already have the material base. Their leisure—their full life-style—is an indictment of forms of leisure that spring directly from this material abundance. If they follow the evolution of former generations, they will "relax" and accept the dominant values of middle-aged persons, and their leisure will then be more predictable and controlled by commercial forces, social status, and by what Charles Reich calls Consciousness II.[17] An opposite situation is seen in a consideration of the poor.

Subculture: The "Culture of Poverty"

Of the 200 million persons in the United States in 1971, almost 7 of every 100 (13½ million) are on public welfare. Not so well known, or expressed, by political critics of welfare is that 90 percent of these "cases" are women and children, the blind and the disabled. Following a television documentary on hunger in this country and another on the conditions among the poor and the migrant workers of Florida, there was a cry among some persons in very high office that these documentaries were inaccurate and misleading, because they failed to show "progress." It is, indeed, difficult to believe the fact that—as by now officially admitted—hunger does exist.

Frequently, discussions on leisure in America come to this question: are we not "really" talking about the middle and upper classes? Can leisure be an issue of any importance—or an issue at all—among those who lack the necessities of life? To this there are two types of responses: (1) to treat poverty as one of our "conditions" in the conceptual scheme of Chapter 4; (2) to examine the indigenous or characteristic of what Oscar Lewis called the "culture of poverty."

A lack of goods, services, or money may, given a specific situation, be more or less important for analysis of leisure than other "conditions," such as health, where one lives, his age, family situation, and education. We also assume for our present purpose that the poor, the middle-incomed, and the rich may, in fact, have similar tastes and may on occasion be doing quite the same thing: watching a comedian on television, parading on Main Street, or fishing in the same stream. The problem then, is to note the types of leisure activities or experiences that depend directly on the possession of money or credit.

It is evident, first, that in a community such as New York City, which has a very wide range of income among its population, there is a large range of opportunity for anyone, because they are supported by taxes or, in any case, free or almost free to all. This includes the use of public parks, free concerts, beaches, museums, the general life of activity to watch in the street, sandlot ball games, attendance at television broadcasts, community centers, and adult education facilities.

Every American city has similar possibilities. If a child of a poor family —or an adult—does not use these opportunities, it may be because he cannot afford transportation, he does not know about them, or he lives in a psychological milieu where certain types of places or experiences are strange to him. The last of these will be treated in the next section. Restricting ourselves to cost alone, it can be said that the poor in America as a whole are not completely deprived of a variety of opportunities for leisure. Television, for example, is owned by 98 percent of all Americans.

We have, however, 20 million or more persons who are in families with incomes averaging less than $3000, which by any standard for a family of four persons, is poor.[18] It is therefore evident that although television may be a "necessity," other types of expenditures for leisure are limited or prohibited altogether: cars, sports equipment, musical instruments. Their purchasing power for such items is nil, as is apparent from Dr. Gabriel Kolko's study *Wealth and Power in America* for the relatively affluent year of 1957.[19] For that year, 44 percent of our households lived below maintenance levels established as guidelines by the U.S. Bureau of Labor Statistics; over 25 percent lived below the "emergency" limit. Furthermore, many of them live in communities where little or nothing is provided for youth or adults, where schools are not opened at the end of the school day for recreational uses. Among Southern Negroes, as Myrdal reported some years ago, the church provided the setting in which group life was lived outside of religious or work. Budget studies reveal that a higher proportion of blacks than whites goes to such activities.[20]

Yet any expenditure studies of leisure among the poor—or anyone else—are to be regarded with suspicion. Sociology has not yet been able to do more than itemize and perhaps describe. It has contributed little to explaining, or more important, to catching the inner spirit of the quality of life among the poor. For here we get into the difficult matter of capturing the paradox of being poor in an "affluent" society; on the one hand, of not having access to goods, services, time, health, or other "conditions" of leisure that are taken for granted by others, and on the other hand, of constituting a "subculture" of positive values that emphasizes people and provides its own set of values and a pattern of behavior. St. Claire Drake paints one vignette.[21]

"The 'Ghettoization' of the Negro has resulted in the emergence of a ghetto subculture with a distinctive ethos, most pronounced, perhaps, in Harlem, but recognizable in all Negro neighborhoods. For the average Negro who walks the streets of any American Black Ghetto, the smell of barbecued ribs, fried shrimps, and chicken emanating from numerous restaurants gives olfactory reinforcement to a feeling of 'at-homeness.' The beat of 'gut music' spilling into the street from ubiquitous tavern juke boxes and the sound of tambourines and rich harmony behind the crude folk art of the windows of store-front churches give auditory confirmation to the universal belief that 'We Negroes have 'soul.'' The bedlam of an occasional brawl, the shouted obscenities of street corner 'foul mouths,' and the whine of police sirens break the monotony of waiting for the number that never 'falls,' the horses that neither win, place, nor show, and the 'good job' that never materializes.

The insouciant swagger of teenage dropouts (the 'cats') masks the hurt of their aimless existence and contrasts sharply with the ragged clothing and dejected demeanor of 'skid-row' types who have long since stopped trying to keep up appearances and who escape it all by becoming 'winoes.' The spontaneous vigor of the children who crowd streets and playgrounds (with Cassius Clay, Ernie Banks, the Harlem Globetrotters, and the black stars of stage, screen, and television as their role models) and the cheerful rushing about of adults, free from the occupational pressures of the 'white world' in which they work, create an atmosphere of warmth and superficial intimacy, which obscures the unpleasant facts of life in the overcrowded rooms behind the doors, the lack of adequate maintenance standards, and the too prevalent vermin and rats."

This relaxed pattern, in the past, has been sufficient to carry the group along. It is a pattern that does not make demands on the larger society. But then, two related factors emerged: the fight for civil rights in the 1950s and the penetration of television into homes of rich, middle class, and poor. Never before had all segments of a large society been so collectively exposed to comedians, sports heroes, social commentators, motion pictures, and selling campaigns. Leisure consumption, thus brought into almost every home for two decades or more, crystallized a new poverty, that is, one with an aspiration for goods and other life-styles that was not only expressed in words, but dramatized and embellished in every program and TV commercial by experts.

The direction of leisure among the Negro community has also moved inwardly and outwardly. On the one hand is the "inner" socializing, the church life, and the total complex of organization aimed toward community improvement and the struggle for civil rights; on the "other level" we find the striking dominance of the Negro athlete in the sports scene, his literature, his actors and entertainers on TV and in films, and the ordinary participation in all facets of leisure (fishing, touring, reading, and watching TV, for instance) in which he shows tastes as everyone else.

If the arts be taken as one criterion of this "inner" and "other" orientation in leisure, we hear the gut music—soul; in dance we see a free and spontaneous modernism; in their theater there is a folk-expression of race history; in black painting there is a realism grounded in conservative, descriptive symbols.

These efforts have found in the ghetto a dramatic potential by which the poor can be encouraged to bring creative insights into a self-examination of themselves and thus contribute to the general culture, as in this fresh bit of writing by a student of Herbert Kohl in a slum of New York.[22]

"Once upon a time there was a pig and a cat. The cat kept saying old dirty pig who want to eat you. And the pig replied when I die I'll be made use of, but when you die you'll just rot. The cat always thought he was better than the pig. When the pig died he was used for food for the people to eat. When the cat died he was buried in old dirt. Moral: live dirty die clean."

We need now to move in two analytic directions: (1) the relation of the leisure of a subculture to elements of group life discussed earlier in the chapter, and (2) the relation of groups and subcultures in leisure to other conceptual elements discussed in the propositions of the third chapter.

Subcultures and Group Life

Implicit in the conception of a subculture is not only the statistical or historical fact of common characteristics, but the more subjective or psychological fact that communications exist within the subculture that reflect the objective characteristics. For example, we can arbitrarily discuss "youth" as a subculture from a statistical level—such as age and presence in schools—but we could also do this with all those who, on a given Thursday at 8 p.m., watch Bonanza on television (describing their median age, residence, occupations, marital state, etc.). It is the reality of the one (youth) that a convergence exists between its objective situation and its intercommunications on more than one level. The 'Bonanza' audience, which is a segment defined by the scientist, has no other characteristic communication among itself derived from this one fact.

Among the elderly Jew, blacks, youth, businessmen, physicians, or professors, there are social groupings, friendships, intermarriages, characteristic conversations, and forms of play that are sometimes based on the marks of the subculture.

It is clear, from the earlier discussion, that the term "social role" goes farther than one's *work* role. We have "roles" in each of our settings—in the family, the church, the political party, or the game. Even to be a member of an audience, sitting quietly in a dark theater, is to fulfill one's role, with legal, moral, and social restraints and values in the situation. E. T. Hiller has talked of one's work as his "key-role," which often influences many other patterns of behavior. But the meaning of much in contemporary life is that work, the stage for playing out one's key role, becomes less crucial as the varied activities in nonwork tend to bring other roles into greater prominence. The businessman may talk more about his success as a golfer than as a cigar seller; the black activist may be far more involved emotionally with his off-work commitment to the NAACP than to his job as a carpenter. What often happens, then, is that *our present leisure roles are related more and more to our membership in our subcultures instead of to our work roles.* So important for the future is this new fact that it might be proposed as one useful indicator of the so-called postindustrial society. A thesis in Chapter 18 will be that this term is misleading in that if we set up our "indicators" or criteria, we will find that these are not *necessarily* the consequences of the industrial society. And, indeed, the proposition above is useful only if we apply it to the masses of today. In this historical sense, we are reviving a fact of life that pervaded preindustrial societies. In those former periods, the nonwork patterns of the farmers, the residents of courts, the castes in India, or of students among the "ivy colleges" of pre-World War I American or English colleges were heavily influenced by social class or caste traditions or religious differences and associations.

One example from modern American life is documented by Ferdinand Lundberg in his volume *The Rich and the Super-Rich.* Indeed, as his description of their "social clubs" makes clear, it is the solidifying factor of sub-cultural consciousness—being members of this exclusive grouping—that becomes the springboard of "work" (business dealings) instead of the reverse.[23]

"The private clubs are the most 'in' thing about the finpol and corp-pol elite. These clubs constitute the social control centers of the elite. There is at least one central club of the wealthy in every large city—the Chicago Club, the Cleveland Club, the Houston Petroleum Club, the Duquesne Club of Pittsburgh, etc. These are all imitations or outgrowths of earlier Boston, New York, Philadelphia and Baltimore clubs, which were imitations of English clubs. But the New York clubs are now the most important because the big money is centered in New York and the leading New York clubs include the wealthiest of the out-of-towners and many foreigners. . . . It should not be thought that the top clubs are purely sociable haunts where the rich idle away the time, although such is the impression conveyed by Amory, Wecter and the long line of cartoonists and satirists who have shown elderly members snoozing over newspapers in the windows and who have derisively quoted club nincompoops. The clubs, one may be sure, enjoy being mildly derided as centers of futility and senile naivete. As they say in spydom, this gives their serious members a good "cover" for serious purposes. . . . The clubs are the scene, at least in the preliminary stages, of some of the biggest deals in the capitalist world."

This subculture of the very rich extends, of course, into all aspects of their lives, including control over the young through both education and marriage. This explains the origin and character of some American "preparatory" schools and of their colleges. I spent a year as Academic Dean at one such college in New York State; responding to changing times, it had in recent years gone consciously from a "finishing school" to an attempt toward becoming a respectable institution of learning. In some ways the girls were becoming subversives of their upper social class, as, in their seminar discussions, they identified more and more with the youth in the changing world, but largely—as in their dating and marriage with Yale and Trinity boys—they carry on the mores of the very rich, as expected by their parents.

On other class levels as well, the subcultural elements override the work or student roles. In 1971, objecting to some policies of the University of Florida in Gainesville, the black students withdrew as a bloc during the school year. We need not spend time here on whether the meetings among these black students to determine their stance was "leisure." This is a fruitless and theoretically outdated issue, for no activity per se is "leisure." Instead, each experience or activity must be viewed in the life and momentary pattern of each person. Some blacks in every community are at this very moment meeting and discussing racial problems and strategies whose motivations include social transformation and also the same personal response and communication that, in a happier time, might go into an athletic team; just as, in contrast, many American Jews are at this moment engaged in reading for pleasure, driving, and watching TV aimlessly—time that a generation ago might well have gone into a meeting of the B'nai Brith to discuss local anti-Semitism.

There is no way of "proving" that these important aspects of social transformation are "leisure." I have already, in my conceptualization of Chapter 2, and as far back as 1961, included the "full range from frivolous to serious" within the scope of leisure. The Greek's emphasized the latter; American folklore has centered on the former. A small observation is relevant: the strategy of introducing songs, entertainment, and food as an inducement to many of these meetings. An example was provided by Johann Huizinga and Jacob Burckhardt in their analyses of war, religion, art, festivals, and other major expressions that produced a convergence of "play" and utmost seriousness.

Burckhardt discusses the Mysteries which, with the Procession, constitued the ecclesiastical forms of festal display.

"In the public squares, in the churches and in the cloisters, extensive scaffolds were constructed, the upper story of which served as a Paradise to open and shut at will, and the ground floor often as a Hall, while between the two lay the stage . . . representing the scene of all the earthly events. . . ."[24]

No expense or trouble was spared to make the performance and representation as perfect as possible. There was, on these occasions, the clearest merging of churchly and secular motivations among the populace for whom they were intended. Indeed, special occasions for these productions included princely weddings and other social affairs as well as religious days. For example, records Burkhardt,[25]

"We are told that a learned monk celebrated his promotion to the degree of Doctor of Theology by giving a representation of the legend about the patron saint of the city. Charles VIII had scarcely entered Italy before he was welcomed at Turin by the widowed Duchess Bianca of Savoy with a sort of half-religious pantomime, in which a pastoral scene first symbolized the Law of Nature, and then a procession of patriarchs the Law of Grace. Afterwards followed the story of Lancelot of the Lake, and that 'of Athens.' And no sooner had the King reached Chieri than he was received with another pantomime, in which a woman in childbed was shown surrounded by distinguished visitors."

Subculture, Leisure, and the Conceptual Scheme

Finally, what is the overall place of subculture in relation to other components of the map of leisure propositions in Chapter 3? As in prior discussions, I confine myself to the impact of or upon the time element alone.

Proposition 14 observes that time divisions are related to leisure patterns of subcultural groups. One distinction here is the difference between those subcultures, religious or otherwise, that place man's faith into some Heaven, or a future in which all aspirations, including that for leisure, will be attained. Sebastian de Grazia puts his finger on the change that occurred when this comfortable belief became infected with the work ethic.[26]

"At a point in the history of Christendom a particular confusion appears. Political and religious ideas, time on earth and timelessness in heaven, merge and blur into each other. The Calvinists helped mightily to put living on a slanted plane if not to cast it out in a vertical thrust. Their version of the Kingdom of God was of one that must be built into the New Jerusalem by man's efforts here on earth. They thus excel in temporal striving toward atemporality."

Proposition 18 suggests that the "choices of leisure which are heavily influenced by the sub-culture . . . are more deep-seated and permanent than those affected by social or friendship groups." This statement is tautological, as Dr. Susan Ferge noted after reading it during our conversation in Budapest. It has value only if the social or friendship groups cut outside the subculture. This is a possibility more likely between religious than racial groups; that is, in a given population we are more likely to find Jew and non-Jew or Catholic and Protestant friendships than white-black friendships. In spite of increasing contacts between the races during the daytime, these practically cease after the school or the workday. But, to test this proposition, the scientist would have to establish his criteria for "deep-seated and permanent" and then locate actual or hypothetical conflicts between membership in a group or a subculture. Perhaps the crucial matter here is that of history. In their immigrant periods, ethnic groups were well established, friendships were formed within such larger segments as the German, Polish, or Italian. Thus their leisure had maximum relevance to their foods, types of humor, and traditions. With assimilation came intrasubcultural friendships, intermarriages, and jobs that mixed people during the day. The proposition can be more useful if rewritten on a dynamic level, *leisure groupings that represent a crossing of ethnic or other subcultural lines reflect either common interests or proximity and present a force in the further diminution of subcultural differences.*

The validity of this rewritten statement can be seen in race relations efforts; a subproposition may be further studied in the light of policy: *that the uses of leisure or play techniques are as useful, or more so, than policies that concentrate on work or schooling relationships.* Work and school roles freeze images of the person; play roles are flexible and voluntary. There is a qualitative difference between four men fishing together instead of working near each other on a factory assembly line. In this sense the recreation leader on the playground or community center should be considered as a highly strategic person in community relationships. It is a policy mistake in community budgeting or programming to relegate this profession to a subordinate place in priorities.

It is by no means the case that when two people from differing backgrounds get along in play each has given up some of his pride in origin; under ideal conditions, each understands the other more, and may, indeed, feel freer to "be himself." What happens is then expressed in *Proposition 22: leisure can be used as a social device to maintain and nurture social and ideological pluralism as well as to provide an integrative or assimilative vehicle among subcultural groups.*

One wonders if even the mentally retarded child—considered as part of a subculture—cannot be treated in larger part by a recreation program that is conscious of its power. The "pluralism" in this instance is achieved by acceptance of the condition by parent and society. Professor Betty van der Smissen of Pennsylvania State University summarized this view in a conference devoted to recreation research.[27]

"The effectiveness of utilizing play activities is being recognized by programs for the mentally retarded in both the institutional and noninstitutional setting to increase motor coordination, to enhance intellectual stimulation, and to facilitate socialization of the retarded."

Van der Smissen notes some research on the importance of the physical setting in research on the impact of recreation activities. "What," she asks, "is there about the camp setting that seems to make the mentally retarded and the person afflicted with cerebral palsy respond?" She recommends more study on the relative impact of sizes of spaces, interior decoration, air comforts of ventilation, heat, and so on, and architectural barriers in relation to effects of these on the outcomes from the activity engaged in.

These suggestions apply, of course, to other groups and subcultures as well. Perhaps the decisive advantage of play over work and educational settings, for affecting group relationships, is the flexibility of settings—the tavern, the picnic or camping ground, the fair, the community center, the street. This dynamic aspect of the environment as it influences human relationships has been of increasing concern to those in mental health. The community as a leisure environment has for centuries attracted the thinking of philosophers, welfare workers, and city planners. As a potpourri of interests and a storehouse of things the community has been a setting for heterogeneous groups and subcultures. In the sense that the community—a Florence, a Boston, a Dubrovnik—itself takes on a homogeneity and a unique setting, in itself its populace becomes a subculture. We turn to the community and the region as a component in the conceptualization of leisure.

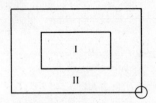

Chapter 10
Community and Region

Two conceptual frameworks meet in this chapter, the spatial and the behavioral, as suggested in *Proposition 15: the new resource of time enlarges the concept of community and transposes it from a geographical to a psychological and cultural entity.* A more accurate statement, perhaps, would be that time is not responsible for the change (as suggested by the word "transposes") but contributes to the change.

In a previous work I related leisure to the concepts, *Gemeinschaft* and *Gesellschaft.* [1] The present chapter moves from rural to city, suburban, megalopolitan, and regional life. The last section provides a comparison of one tourist region with another, Florida and the Dalmatian coast of Yugoslavia.

RURAL LIFE AND LEISURE

By 1955, according to Professor T. Lynn Smith, there were already 102 tractors for every 100 workers on American farms. Our rural technology was also observable in hundreds of thousands of grain and bean combines, corn pickers, machines to pick cotton, and airplanes to sow, fertilize, and spread insecticides and fungicides. As machines came, people were less needed, so that in 30 years, ending in 1965, the number of farm families fell from a little over 8,200,000 to less than 4 million; similarly, the total number of farm workers dropped from 9,855,000 to 3,650,000, and hired laborers were reduced by more than 56 percent. If farmers are divided into various economic levels, lower-class farm families dropped from 26.8 to 19.8 percent of the total; lower-middle-class families dropped from 23.2 percent to 19.8 percent; and those above this level—those most prosperous—*increased* from 49.9 to 60.4 percent. This represents in part a migration of millions of poorer farmers to the city. There they "have found the welfare rolls to be a substitute for the economically marginal activities they once carried on in agriculture. As a result there has been a profound change in the class structure of society in the agricultural portions of the United States." [2]

This rural "class change" not only affects the free-time life of farmers, it also creates a profound difference in work itself through scientific techniques and technology. Modern farmers represent a higher literacy and smaller families than their predecessors, and a life-style affected by transportation for personal use and by television. They both go to the world and they bring the world to themselves. Some years ago a student told me that she comes from a "middle-class" Illinois farm family; on further questioning about her points of reference, she told me that on many Sundays they all climb into father's airplane and take off for California! That stretches the point, no doubt, but it says something at least for her immediate area and the image of one farmer's daughter about halfway along in the century.

Furthermore, with the growth of large urban areas and their constant transmission of urban images to the farms, the rural resident's image of the world is now formed and dominated by urban life. Indeed, one observer of rural-urban patterns in industrial societies, Professor Gideon Sjoberg, states categorically, "One can no longer speak of rural-oriented regions, only of urban ones." [3] The "mass society" reality permeates farms and towns as it does the larger communities.

Among other changes, this means a change in the kind of produce sold to the cities, but also the purchase of urban goods by rural persons. As Sjoberg notes, in traditional towns of England and France this has brought the end of traditional handicrafts. Yet the "moral fiber" argument on behalf of rural values persists, based on the person-to-person relationship that is associated with simple life, honesty, and a no-nonsense attitude toward social change. In its recreation, which is still untouched by television—such as, the county fair—the patterns of a century ago still persist, with its rodeos, spelling bees, country fiddlers, and log-rolling contests. All of this falls under what I have referred to in Chapter 7 as leisure which is oriented to an assumptive view of the world. Such leisure verifies the world as it is. Its selection is based on the conditions that are indigenous to rural life, although the ease of transportation and use of mass media have gone far to lighten the limitations of distance; the fortuitous circumstance that may affect the choice of leisure—called the "mediating factors" in Chapter 5—are less likely in rural life. Among the sets of leisure functions, the most applicable in rural life is the contrast of sociability and isolation.

If isolation is sometimes the condition of rural life, it becomes a value worth seeking out and paying for among the city person whose entire existence is hemmed in by many persons, most of whom he does not

know or want to know. This search for privacy through physical isolation becomes more difficult in the United States by the decade. Camp-
sites become more crowded and citified with urban comforts.

If we accept this as one social function of leisure—to serve as the
preserver of traditional values and the instrument of new values—then
we can look on the condition of characteristic space as the content in
which both preservation and innovation can find expression through
leisure. The full range of meanings must be potentially fruitful: the
assumptive, analytic, and aesthetic (creative and innovative). We seek,
in short, the advantages of *Gemeinschaft* and *Gesellschaft,* linked by
the analytic ability to know one from the other. Since the city has always
been the chief context for the analytic and aesthetic, we need to see
what has been its attraction.

URBAN LIFE AND LEISURE

Cutting across the history of cities and their many types, shapes, sizes,
locations, and purposes, at least four major characteristics stand out in
relation to leisure.

The Variety of Persons

For studies of leisure, "variety" refers to differences in ages, incomes,
races, ethnic and racial origins, aspirations, personalities, education, or
anything else that influences tastes, degrees of restlessness or stability,
perspectives toward the world, and what is frequently called "vital"
versus "dull" persons. This full range—however the particular culture
defines such differences—is to be found in Paris, London, New York,
and in other cities that produce and attract differences.

Just the presence of this variety is in itself an element of high importance. It obviously means that we can expect to find here a wide range
of interests, audiences, listeners, and participants. In the socialist countries this variety may not be expressed in as many consuming patterns
as in countries where a profit-minded business economy not only seizes
on special markets but constantly develops them. On the other hand,
in the latter societies, business is also interested in the mass market, and
this may neutralize the distinction.

The Variety of Facilities

This follows both from the fact of mere numbers as well as the
heterogeneity of backgrounds. Manhattan, Kansas, in contrast to its
predecessor in New York, has no need for multiple museums, concerts,
sports events, theaters, broadcasting stations, libraries, gambling

houses, education courses, or a host of other possibilities. Yet, in the one, population 1,540,000—as well as in its namesake of population 27,500 —a cycle develops: variety attracts residents, more residents demand greater variety. Within each category—museums, theaters, etc.—there is specialization, that is, not only theater, but burlesque, off-Broadway, arena theater, and X-rated pictures. Finally, the large community can contain larger or more spectacular facilities than the small community: Lincoln Center for the Performing Arts in New York, Madurodam in the Hague, or the Prater in Vienna. Their parks often include open areas for sports, tennis courts, zoos, pools for swimming or for sailing boats, and picnic areas. My own interest in music started from attending band concerts in the Milwaukee's Lake Park, especially in watching Mr. Percussionist dismantle and store his gleaming chimes.

Plato pointed out that the seacoast towns of Greece were expectedly creative because the heterogeneity of their populations and constant visitors or mercenaries insured a hearing for new ideas. Vincent Smith, the historian of India, shows that the same process holds for the interchange of ideas among whole societies. "Experience proves that the contact or collision of diverse modes of civilization is the most potent stimulus to intellectual and artistic progress. . . ." [4]

The old stereotype that a larger proportion of political liberals are in urban areas does not stand up to recent studies, but the hypothesis still has not been contradicted that the larger community offers a more conducive arena for the exercise of liberal thought or its consequences in social change. If we recall the types of leisure that follow from the aesthetic or transforming perspective (as distinct from the assumptive and analytic), it would appear a reasonable proposition that these will have more outlet in the larger community.

The Bridge to the Outside World

The large community provides this bridge for purposes of leisure in three ways: (1) by the possibility of access to relatively strange styles of behavior through the presence of varieties of people who also reside there; (2) by the presence of visitors (such as persons or groups of entertainers and performers); and (3) by the relative access to images of the world through mass media and literature.

This takes us beyond the concept of the community as a "storehouse"; it looks at the community as a *link*. An example is the airport which, in transportation theory has until recently been considered only within local terms; more and more, transportation is seen as a regional or national system, with the local community as only one point within it. Again, when major highways went to and through the center of a city we had a localized, limited concept; now—for functional as well as cost-of-land reasons—the "freeway" is free of such parochialisms as it winds its way beside the cities, oriented to a wider concept of travel.

The Heart of "Life" and "Excitement"

This is the consideration that attracts the young; when translated into noise, traffic, and confusion, this drives them out in middle age; the older citizen, once more in need of contact and a milieu, is again fed by this fare of stimulation. Some more than others can translate this into words, as Alois Svoboda has done for Prague, Senche deGramont for Paris, and John Gunther for a score of cities.[5]

But the city is also a potential block to leisure experience. Its largeness and complexity becomes a confusion for some. Both terms—size and complexity—are relative. Withdrawal may take the form of literal escape into one's visible and familiar neighborhood, or it may be a psychological withdrawal by the minimum of interest in what it offers in resources. I have met at least one native New Yorker who, already in her 30's, has never been on Ellis Island to climb up the Statue of Liberty, and there are no doubt thousands who have not been to the Metropolitan Museum. This is not just a matter of taste—for climbing or museuming; with the plentitude of opportunities, it is "too much trouble" to go; for some, the knowledge that these possibilities are there is enough. The distance, traffic, or danger are all realities or just convenient excuses. Mixed with this is the sense of loneliness, impersonality: "no one will miss me" if I don't go, unlike the small town sense of personal commitment or involvement. This, of course, ends up in a circle; one *can* be anonymous in the large city, and thus it becomes a self-fulfilling prophecy when it is acted on by further withdrawal.

The presence of racial or ethnic groups, if they are a force or symbol for mutual separatism, adds further to the disuse of leisure possibilities in the complex city. As I noted in the last chapter, the subcultural delineation of leisure can be a reality: the black may choose not to go somewhere in the expectation he will not be wanted in the given park, theater, or public event.

This array of factors are not clearly the "good" and the "bad." Actual life is too complex for such simple dichotomies. Mixed in with all of this are one's moods, tastes, changing friendships, and the nature of one's work. How do we manage a fact, immeasurable in scientific terms, that living in New York City in *itself* gives many a participation in "life," a personification of power, a feeling of being "where the action is?" That, in itself, borne out by the walk in Central Park or Brooklyn Heights, is a recreational romance. It is a *milieu,* a backdrop for activity

—or for inactivity that, because of the atmosphere, is more than inactivity. But in driving through Prince Edward's Island, Canada—a greater contrast can hardly be imagined—we met young people who are so happy in (to them) *this* self-sufficient milieu that they seldom if ever leave the island, even for social reasons.

Within cities there are institutions whose function it is to work within all the barriers and the potentialities for leisure: one such group are the commercial enterprises—such as theaters, gambling institutions, dog and horse races, pool halls, and sports events. Among them, sports teams, although organized purely as business-for-profit ventures, serve as vehicles for public joy and despair. Brooklyn as an identity to its residents is unknowable without the Mets in baseball, nor is Green Bay now an organic unit without its Packer football team. Boston has not only its baseball, football, ice hockey, and basketball teams but, for the artistic element as a leisure pursuit for audiences, there is the Bostom Symphony. Similar attitudes are evident among towns throughout Europe in relation to soccer.

On the public side, a recreation department exists in most cities as a tax-supported agency that has, in the past several decades, gone far beyond the organization of sports and games. One direction has been the structural fusion in many places of the "recreation" program and the "park system." Here, in concentrated form, we get the synthesis spoken of at the beginning of this chapter: time, space, and behavior. The meaning of parks for the large city is a subjective matter, with the physical plant as an objective statement of the variety and direction of its interests.

For example, the variety of recreational possibilities in the New York parks is suggested merely by this index and directory for the 1967–1968 season: archery ranges, baseball diamonds, bathing beaches, bicycle paths, boat basins, boating, bocci courts, botannical gardens, bowling greens, bridle paths, carousels, children's gardens, coasting areas, cricket fields, cross country, fife and drum rehearsal areas, fishing areas, football fields, forum areas, golden age centers, golf courses, pitch and putt golf, golf driving ranges, handball (three-wall courts), historical points, hockey fields, ice skating, kite flying, model airplane flying fields, model yacht ponds, museums, music groves, nature trails, picnic areas, pony tracks, recreation centers, regatta courses, riding academies, roller hockey, rugby fields, running tracks, skiing, ski slopes with artificial snow, softball, little league, swimming pools, outdoor theater troubadour areas, wildlife refuges, zoos, and aquariums.

A closer look at the activities themselves would reveal the excellent performances of Shakespeare in the parks by the Joe Papp players, all professionals, as well as park concerts by the New York Philharmonic, and filmmaking by children. This wealth of opportunities, including almost 2500 tables and 5000 benches for picnicking, serves about 8 million people. Other cities have excellent park systems—Philadelphia, Los Angeles, Portland (Oregon)—that offer programs comparable to their needs, but the people who need such public facilities the most generally live in neighborhoods that are deprived of sufficient recreational open space, especially for children.

The situation becomes more serious in its disproportion as American large city cores are inhabited more and more by blacks as the whites move to the suburbs. The recreational and leisure issues of the "inner city" have come to be recognized as closely related to health (mental and physical), housing, education, and family life. In some ways that recall the impact of "settlement houses" on immigrant families in the first three decades of this century, the "community centers" of today are contributing to residents in the slums of today. Leisure activities in those centers (e.g., Karamu House in Cleveland) sometimes reach a high level in areas of athletic and artistic participation and performance. The National Guild of Community Schools of the Arts grew out of the settlement house concept: in over 60 schools in the United States and Canada, a rich program of instruction is provided in all phases of music (sometimes in other arts as well) for children in poor areas who can afford little or no tuition. Following some severe outbreaks in black areas of Los Angeles, New York, Newark, Detroit, Milwaukee, and other communities in the summers of the late 1960s, various efforts in several leisure directions can be credited with rechanneling energies toward creative purposes. The work of Bud Shulberg with young writers in the Watts area in Los Angeles and Katherine Dunham with the dance in East St. Louis are cases in point.

Yet a contemporary discussion of population clusters must deal with the interpenetration of urban and rural *styles* of life that are becoming more important than the demographic classifications based on population density.[6] An area that illustrates the new tendencies is the region from Washington, D.C. up to Boston. The geographer, Jean Gottman, has carefully analyzed this area in his book, *Megalopolis*.

MEGALOPOLIS AND LEISURE

Gottman notes that the familiar pattern of the "pull of the cities" has been modified by a growth of rural-nonfarm areas, or farming that exists in what are really suburban conditions, as agricultural production is less and less a matter of land space.[7] The new competition is not between farm land and urban growth but between wooded land and cities. Even in this megalopolis of 30 million persons that includes, aside from Boston and Washington, such large cities as Baltimore, Philadelphia, and New York, half of the entire area of megalopolis is still woodland. In Connecticut, for example, woodland has increased in the past 100 years from one third to two thirds of its total. Tilled land, of course, has been diminishing, but wooded areas for multiple uses has actually been expanding east of the Mississippi. Around the big cities, woodland has been used for conservation of water supplies and wildlife and for recreational activity. Where the wealthy city residents had access to natural areas away—but not too far away—from their interests in the city, more middle-class adults and children have had access to public lands for fishing, walking, camping, and simply being in the countryside. Thoreau has never been forgotten in the United States and, assisted by the youth movement, has become more influential than ever. The antecedents of the present development are worth examining briefly if we are to understand the importance of leisure in this eastern megopolis as a rural and urban phenomenon with ever increasing interrelationships.

As in Europe, the aristocrats of America, after the 1760s, also enjoyed the real and symbolic advantages of life in the countryside. Such fishing villages as Nahant and Swampscott became suburbs of Boston and Lynn for the rich. This practice spread to other states along the east coast, and eventually the "resort" populations often became full-time residents.[8]

Thus developed the unique regional sprawl; no other section has a "comparable role within the nation or a comparable importance in the world"—in politics, economics, and cultural life.[9] Our concern here is with the recreational uniqueness of this region.

One factor is the interpenetration of rural and suburban parks. State and county parks are numerous but of recent origin. New York State is especially notable for its many state parks: Long Island alone has 13, and one third of its shoreline is publicly owned. A system of hotels, cabins, and boat basins enlarges the functional use of these state areas. Connecticut, even by 1955, had 16 state parks with over 20,000 acres, almost 15,000 acres in county and township parks; Massachusetts, since 1936, created 26 state parks of over 1000 acres each. Gottman sees the demand for parks increasing in this megalopolitan area as a whole.[10]

The popularity of hunting in the megalopolis illustrates the growing use of the countryside for recreation in an 18-year period from 1938 to 1956 (see Table 13).

Obviously, the problem of land and the supply of game are major issues for hunters. Fishing also increased by tens of thousands of permit holders every decade. The degree of restocking for this leisure activity

TABLE 13
Eastern megalopolis: hunting licenses, 1938–1956[11]

	1938	1956
New Hampshire	50,000	87,000
Massachusetts	71,000	118,000
Rhode Island	8,000	13,000
Connecticut	27,000	55,000
New York	650,000	976,000
New Jersey	128,000	168,000
Pennsylvania	606,000	932,000
Delaware	16,000	19,000
Maryland	63,000	148,000
Virginia	136,000	382,000
Total	6,899,000	14,462,000

leads to Gottman's observation that hunting and fishing are very much a product of man's own work.[12] Indeed, far from the region being a "natural" environment that only has to be saved from pollution, the planning for outdoor recreation has become a complex problem.[13]

Not every "region" in the United States consists of a large population congregate now referred to as a "megalopolis." The dozen or more of the latter take in such areas as Gary-Chicago-Milwaukee, or the huge composite to the north and south of Los Angeles; and, in each case, the major asset for leisure is the interplay of rural and urban facilities and life-styles. The primary tool for all of this has been the car, but it is the larger term, transportation, that will determine the future of these areas.

For the bulk of Americans, the resolution of leisure as conserver and as innovator of values will take place in the suburban context.

SUBURBS AND LEISURE

It is possible now, in the United States at least, to consider the new suburb as the self-sufficient living center, augmented by its neighboring metropolis as a gigantic leisure tool—for its restaurants, night clubs, major theatrical and sports events, museums, and so on. In the past 20 years, according to HUD (Department of Housing and Urban Development), 63 new planned communities have been built in the United States, with areas of 1000 or more acres; however, these have been primarily residential. The most discussed of these is now Columbia, Maryland, which was farmland only a few years ago; it now holds 8000 persons, and will grow to 100,000. Reston, another new village near Washington, D.C. covers almost 7500 acres; its private developers also hope to provide their own economic base. These, however, are still satellite cities in the economic sense but, for purposes of leisure, except for the larger purposes noted above, they are already self-sufficient. As a recent report in the *New Yorker* indicates,[14] "They are no longer mere orbital satellites. They are no longer suburbs. They are broad, ballooning bands, interlinked as cities in their own right." This is the outer city. The report notes that in 1940 our suburbs held 27 million people, or 20 percent of all Americans; the number now is 76 million, or 40 percent of the total. These, however, are not isolated suburbs, but are often used as a "system." As one resident of California notes, "I live in Garden Grove, work in Irvine, shop in Santa Ana, go to the dentist in Anaheim, my husband works in Long Beach, and I used to be president of the League of Women Voters in Fullerton." No doubt she or others could similarly check off a similar intrasuburban division of tennis, golf, theater, clubs, and football games.

Lewis Mumford points out that the suburb goes far back in history. "All through history" he notes,[15] "those who owned or rented land outside the city's walls valued having a place in the country, even if they did not actively perform agricultural labor: a cabin, a cottage, a vine-shaded shelter, built for temporary retreat if not for permanent occupancy." There are the examples from Greece, such as the location of the great medical center and sanctuary a mile or so outside of Cos,[16] or the location of monasteries and universities (Oxford and Cambridge) away from the large cities. In the case of the latter, Mumford suggests that the "luxury of space" intensified the town-gown antagonism.

"The early appearance of the suburb points to another, even more important fact: the life-maintaining agencies, gardening and farming, recreation and games, health sanatoria and retreats belong to the surrounding countryside, even when the functions they fostered spring from the town's needs or deficiencies. By the eighteenth century, it is true, the romantic movement had produced a new rationale for the suburban exodus, and the increasingly smoky and overcrowded town provided a new incentive. But it would be an error to regard suburbanism as a mere derivative of this ideology, for it had older, deeper roots. What needs to be accounted for is not the cult of nature that became popular in the eighteenth century, affecting everything from medicine to education, from architecture to cookery, but rather the obstinacy with which people had often clung for centuries to a crowded, depleted, denatured, and constricted environment, whose chief solace for misery was the company of equally miserable people. . . ."[17]

In more recent periods, Mumford argues, this ideal was successful as a "nursery for bringing up children" but, as a whole, the suburb succumbed to the "temptation to retreat from unpleasant realities, to shirk public duties, and to find the whole meaning of life in the most elemental social group, the family, or even in the still more isolated and self-centered individual." [18] Leisure, he claims, took over, becoming in the suburb the serious business of life; an "overspecialized" community, with a commitment to compulsive play as an end. Leisure, much as work itself, becomes in the suburb what it has become in the city: beset by mass production and mass consumption, producing a similar environment that is "standardized and denatured." [19]

We have in Mumford's discussion several common threads that have woven through much critical writing on both suburbs and on leisure in our complex society. First, he is historically and theoretically right in associating the concept of space and freedom. Space became a literal matter, more and more at a premium in the city, and also a symbol of the rich who could afford it. The uniqueness about the suburb is its new accessibility to the masses. Indeed, the move to the suburbs was the dominant population tendency of the 1960s in the United States—a direct expression of (1) the new abundance, (2) the increasing recognition of urban problems, from insecurity to dirt, and (3) the better transportation to work, or willingness to take the time. But there is another reason, contrary to the observations of Mumford, as well as some sociologists who have been equally critical of suburban noncreative living. And that is a twofold observation; one, it is now impossible to think of the suburbs as a unit separate from the parent city, and two, some doubts about the observations of suburbs by sociologists on the matter of creative potentials.

On the first: suburbs, because they generally contain more expensive homes and therefore include a larger proportion of educated persons, provide an audience to the central city programs, whether of sports, arts, or adult education; they also purchase a relatively high proportion of books and magazines. My own suburb, near Tampa, has a proportion of 30 percent college graduates among its men and 19 percent among its women; granted, this is high because of many university faculty. But place the members of the museums of Cleveland, Philadelphia, or Boston on a map, and note where they live. Furthermore, the creative elements of the parent city, such as classes for adults, are going more and more to the suburbs in extension classes. Thus the creative traffic, as it were, goes in both directions. New York may be another case; having been on its subway trains in late evenings, I understand the Brooklynite's desire to remain home after the workday in Manhattan.

The second observation goes to the charge of suburban conformity. In Brookline, near Boston, as in Cambridge and Brockton, there are excellent community orchestras, numerous painters, and poets. Mumford lives in a magnificent countryside area about a half hour drive from Poughkeepsie, New York. In almost every small town down the Hudson to New York, there are creative individuals and activities. I have played chamber music, with excellent and enthusiastic musicians, in Poughkeepsie; only some players were part of Vassar College. Some groups, as in Millbrook where we lived, specialized in "play"; this in a feudal area with the very rich still embracing the fox hunt and its attendant socializing, but Bennett College also provided the area with concerts and lectures on a high level.

I recall recently riding through some Romanian villages with Professor Albert Frances of the University of Timisoara; just as I commented about how life might be sterile and nonproductive in these villages (we had just passed some sheep on "Main Street"), he informed me that this particular village had organized a chorus and dance group a century ago that is known throughout the country. Perhaps we are easily led to judge others by terms of convenience passed along and quoted from one book to another.

The important point is that it is work that generally serves as the dividing line between the suburb and the central city; leisure is the link between them; it is the spectacle, the sports, the theater, that is sufficiently compelling in the one direction, and the more private play, with family or friends, that moves us in the other.

Some classic studies of leisure only several decades ago were possible within the confines of the community. One was *Middletown,* an inquiry into Muncie, Indiana, by the Lynds in the 1920s and 1930s; the other was *Leisure: A Suburban Study* by Lundberg and his associates of Westchester County, New York.[20] Neither has been exceeded since as good social science efforts; but, with the advent of television and the further development of transportation, it is hardly possible now to think of communities or regions aside from the national and world picture. In this spirit I turn now to a comparison of three areas: the Boston community, a Florida region, and the Dalmatian coast of Yugoslavia.

THE REGION

West-Central Florida

Florida as a whole is now the eighth state in the nation in population and the first as a tourist and retirement area. In 1970 about 23 million tourists came to the state and, with the opening of Disney World in

1971, an additional 11 million visitors came in 1971. Thus the 8 million permanent residents are in the unique situation of relying heavily on the popularity of outdoor advantages—sun, warmth, water—for their economic vitality. The public or commercial developments that help attract tourists (marinas, golf courses, beach facilities, compsites, etc.) also equip the residents beyond the level of their own needs.

The region to be discussed in some detail is in west central Florida, covering four counties: Hillsborough, Pinellas, Sarasota, and Manatee. Three of the counties lie on the Gulf of Mexico. The permanent population of this region was 1.3 million in 1970, with about 3.4 million tourists. By 1985 about 3.1 million residents are anticipated, with 8.1 million tourists. The number of employed persons will go up from 312,000 to about 617,000. A superb new airport in Tampa, together with an auxiliary airline to Disney World (60 miles east) will play their part in the projection of tourists. Although, in 1968, less than 3 percent of the 2629 square miles in the region was "recreation" land, fully 68.4 percent of the area is still not developed, with less than 20 percent of the total in farm use. Urban area comprises less than 13 percent of the total, and 13.6 percent of urban area consists of parks and open spaces.

The steady demand on recreational facilities is intensified by the high number of retirees who are attracted here because the warmth reduces the cost of living. Florida has almost 1 million residents over 65, leading the nation in its proportion of this older generation; the population of semiretired and fully retired, 65 years or over, will increase over 120 percent by 1985. Since many older persons live on Social Security, the income level among residents of the region is pulled down, and came to only $2348 per capita in 1965; however, this figure shows an increase of 3 percent higher than income growth in the state as a whole or for the United States. Within the region, Hillsborough County had the highest per capita income.

The percentage of foreign-born adults in this region is similar to that of the nation. The percentage of nonwhites in the region is about 12 percent; this is 7 percent below the Florida average, but about equal to the United States as a whole. Because of the proportion of elderly widows, Pinellas County has 116 females to 100 males; 107 is the average for the region, or 3 per 100 females more than the national average. Demographic figures indicate clearly that in this region, as the population increases, it will become ever younger and older. Present and projected age distribution for the region is seen in Table 14.

The crucial group in the table above is the large anticipated expansion of the 15–24.9 group, and the 65 or over group, which will increase

TABLE 14
Tampa–St. Petersburg age distribution, 1970–1985[21]

Age	1970	1975	1980	1985
0–04.9	109,843	133,836	184,150	245,376
5–14.9	225,269	255,504	337,365	446,181
15–24.9	220,745	292,776	333,054	379,852
25–64.9	638,231	837,157	1,109,932	1,489,183
65 or over	244,980	306,987	391,526	504,386
Total	1,437,068	1,826,260	2,356,027	3,064,978

over 50 percent in the same period. This fact, as a report of the Tampa Bay Regional Planning noted in November 1968:

". . . will make great impacts upon education, transportation and other public facility systems in the region. Also, as efforts are made to accommodate the future needs of this type of population, the resulting high degree of competition for available land and public revenues may cause new approaches of development programming to be sought."

Leisure facilities will obviously be directly affected by the increases of youth and retirees. To take education as an example, the past 10 years have seen significant development. Saint Leo College, north of Tampa, has become a four-year institution. Three other institutions have all seen birth: New College in Sarasota, Florida, Eckerd College in St. Petersburg, and the University of South Florida (19,000 students in 1974) in Tampa. Junior and community colleges have grown up in addition.

The history of this region provides clues to its present. Transportation to and from this region was available in the nineteenth century on the water; fish were plentiful for food. Agriculture developed here in a natural way. Only as late as 1884 was a railroad line built into Tampa, connecting the region to the North. Tourists came who were wealthy, such as those who came by railroad directly to the door of the famous hotel built by a railroad magnate, nicknamed "Plant's Folly," an unusual building that is now the University of Tampa. About the same time a physician in the Midwest said in a public talk that St. Petersburg was the best place for older persons to go and thus started a migration of retirees.

Private land developers caught the spirit and began to feed it. As elsewhere in the state, in recent years the government has judged against major developers whose spirit unbalanced their sense of ethics. The balance of land to water, a crucial interraction in space use for this region, was further upset by filling in shoreline with land on which more houses were hurriedly built. However, so heavily developed is water frontage now that only about one tenth of 90 miles of shoreline is accessible to the public.

From the sites in America's northeast and southeast, we go far off to the beautiful Yugoslavia coast.

Yugoslavia's Dalmatian Coast

Dalmatian values are part of a long national history which at one time distinguishes all Yugoslavs from their western or their Baltic neighbors and also unites them—if we can speak of a nation "united" that includes Serbs, Croats, Montenegrins, Bosnians, Slovenes, and Macedonians. But it is a nation that, for 1000 years, has resisted foreigners; the Turks occupied parts of it for 500 years; and Tito's dissaffection from the USSR is known to all.[22] Rijeka alone—to take a city in the Yugoslavian littoral, at the northern tip of the coast—was taken over by the Austrians in 1466; Diocletian, who died in 313 A.D., is buried in the castle at Split. Nevertheless, in these old areas, too, family life is changing; young people want to move to the big cities, and the mass media are bringing in ideas from the outside. Furthermore, radio programs come to this area from many countries of Western Europe. An effort is being made to preserve the traditions. In Dubrovnik we saw an excellent program by young people from the city; all parts of the nation were represented in the folk songs and dances. In Varna, Bulgaria, we had attended a magnificent performance by a professional group as well as by groups from towns and factories. Leisure, as much as industrialization, is therefore instrumental in creating change—in tourism, mass media, and the attraction of the city for youth; on the other hand, leisure, as in the case of folk art, is also an instrument for identification with the past.

Perhaps the duality of land-water *use* and their *availability* through environmental agitation is implicit; but, in Europe, the natural affinity of these issues has become explicit in both government and volunteer action. In Germany, for example, where an acreage equal to that of Munich and its environs is being urbanized every year, the recreational movement led by the late Opel, the automobile magnate, is also a conservationist movement. The enormous project that is currently underway in Yugoslavia's Adriatic coastline is a model for an attempt in planning on the dual level of saving the area and preparing for its future use. Up and down the 1000-mile Dalmatian coast a coordinated plan is being developed that will include all aspects of economic, political, social, education, and recreational life. Professor Miro Mihovilovich of Zagreb has headed research in the preservation of recreational space and general potentialities for parks, tourist facilities, motels, and historical areas.

Comparisons

Some observations can be made about regionalism, urbanism, and rural values in regard to leisure by some comparison of these three areas: (1) the east coast of Megalopolis, (2) the central Florida region, and (3) the Dalmatian coast of Yugoslavia.

1. Both Megalopolis and the Dalmatian coast are over-coming a pro-urban orientation.

In the United States case, the growth of cities was an accepted goal until recently when the feeling developed that as the city becomes larger, it is more dangerous, more polluted, more difficult to manage, and the scene of guerrilla warfare; its central areas need rebuilding, its play spaces need enlarging, its whole meaning needs rethinking.

The city's poverty, once hidden, is now exposed; its frictions are recorded on television; its mayors are now national figures, sometimes national villains. The city is often a center for housing armed camps when, as Mumford says, its purpose should be to "unite the forces of life and given them a fresh expression." Our planning, writes Jane Jacobs, has not been to rebuild, but to "sack" our cities, amputate neighborhoods, and uproot their people.

Philip Hauser, in his 1968 Presidential address to the American Sociological Society, spoke of our population "explosion" and "implosion" as profoundly altering our whole social, political, and economic mechanism.[23] This authority in population projects noted that in 1800 less than *3* of every 100 Americans lived in cities of 20,000 or more. Now that number is over *20* and, by the end of the century, the percentage will more than double. He argues that this growth of cities will further raise the proportion of blacks, who half a century ago were 73 percent rural and now are 73 percent urban. The frictions will continue from their sense of rising aspirations and the end of that time when people, here or anywhere in the world, will settle "for second place in level of living"—in housing, income, education, or political rights.

Cities such as New York and Newark are in one stage or another of bankruptcy, ongoing inefficiency, and crisis. The life that they often provide is referred to as the "rat race." The move to the suburb, our most dramatic population change of the 1960s, is apparently an escape from the central city of congestion, dirt, noise, and impersonality. The suburb has become the halfway point from urban to rural, at its best drawing on the strength of vitality and withdrawal, at its worst a strung out succession of streets and gasoline stations.

The eastern countries of Europe, in new attitudes about leisure and population or spatial policy, must be placed against the socialist philosophy that had more or less taken urban life as its model. Professor Gideon Sjoberg notes that, based on Marx, "the leaders in Communist countries have usually taken a strong anti-rural stand. For a number of decades in Russia, and today in China, the formation of an industrial-urban order has been considered the main goal, and the political leaders have instituted policies intended to destroy the traditional peasant way of life." [24]

There is reason to believe that a serious change has in recent years taken place in this regard. In spite of—perhaps because of—the movement of youth to the large urban centers, the peasants have resented the urban elite, as evident in the revolutionary movement of Mao Tse-tung among peasants. The general dissolving of collective farms in Yugoslavia, as well as some similar tendency in Poland, is a break from values of the large group to the more traditional individualism of the farm life-style. In my discussion with scholars in Romania (who are close to highly placed policy makers), I was impressed with the fact that the official population policy is to enrich village life with more electricity, schools, and cultural programs; that one motivation, aside from economic policy, is to preserve the rural tradition and its values. With new communications, the spread of television, and possibly the realization that large cities are the centers of innovations (political and otherwise), the Socialist societies may have to turn more and more to a consumer orientation in economics and to its symbolic counterpart, that is, a pluralism of contemporary and traditional values.

As much as anything else, the new attitude toward tourism as an economic boon has been responsible for the reorientation toward the countryside and its traditional ways of life. One impressive example is along the Black Sea in the Delta resort area down to Mamaia and Constanta in Romania, and from Kavarna and Varna down to Nesabar and Burgas in Bulgaria. In Varna alone, for example, within the past 10 years the government has constructed a hill complex of over 40 hotels, plus an array of nightclubs, restaurants, and other services that go with its superb beach. This complex, entirely unlike Miami Beach, preserves the natural environment. It is rapidly becoming a convention center for Eastern Europeans and will eventually attract world groups.

The Dalmatian seacoast has gone far in preparing itself for tourists, from the walled city of Dubrovnick to Split and up to Sibenik and Zadar.[25] This coastline is a part of the nation that is between Western and Eastern Europe in a political sense. It has gone far toward the balance of urban and nonurban orientation in its leisure. Belgrade and Zagreb will always exert their presence as magnets for the young as cultural leaders. The division of states, and especially the tensions between Croatia and Serbia, will always contribute to a preservation of indigenous art, costume, and localized play traditions.

2. Each of the regions—Florida, Metropolis, Dalmatia—has a stake in characteristic values related to leisure.

The values of the Florida region are generally hedonistic. Leisure is the basis of the economy; history—although there is a small interest in the Spanish heritage—is nonexistent for most tourists. The impending changes will take place in the complementary growth of educational and artistic activities; these were clearly on the way in the 1960s, with the addition of colleges noted above. For the first time, in 1971, the state legislature contributed some funds to save the state theater in Sarasota. Retirees will become more and more well-educated. In 20 to 30 years, this could become a new model of fusion between the Sensate and the Ideational, to use Pitirim Sorokin's terms. But that is an ideal; the facts suggest that educational and aesthetic forces face an uphill task.

The megalopolitan area more often, and the Boston area particularly, is a traditionally work-oriented area in comparison to resort regions. The New England region, although not lacking for nonwork commitments, relies on the image of hard work and the Puritan ethic. True, its retirees seek to escape its cold weather, wind, and snow; its young, if not captured by status of prestige colleges, move to the southeastern states for vacation and often stay the year for college work. Yet the characteristic of leisure in the megalopolitan area, good weather or not, is the variety of alternatives that come with community size and complexity. The life-style is more tense and complicated. With this, in part related to it, is a lesser trust in one another, and an inside instead of an outside life—suggesting more impersonality. Leisure may be more meaningful than in warmer regions because the sunny day, coming less often, is more celebrated. Technology will increase in such places, but the "leisure society," as Aristotle or Bellamy visualized it, will not emerge easily, if ever. Furthermore, the worker always will be plainly evident to prevent a full conversion to the image of a Ft. Lauderdale.

Regions such as Dalmatia fall between a Boston and a Bradenton. On the one hand, the fishing villages know hard work, on the other, they are close to folk tradition, which also plays hard; they know life in its full range of joy, awe of nature, tragedy, and survival in the face of challenge from external enemies. Play and work, pageantry and ritual, puritanism and basic pleasures, the full meaning of male and female roles—these are fundamental and coexisting qualities here. The evening korso in Dubrovnik or Split or Kotor are both freedom and control, as young and old, night after night, carry out a 1000-year-old expression of community at its best, adventure, subtle communication, accountability, self-entertainment, and control—all in one.

Thus, in a way, the Eastern European society as a whole may turn out to be the most interesting of the three types of cultures under comparison. Let us expand the concept to include Latin and South America, Asia, and Africa—the Third World. They see Western Europe, well along toward computerization, television, automation, and Americanization; they see America already suffering severe pains from abundance of things and soon, the overabundance of time. Communities of the Third World still have a solid foot in the values of yesterday as they prepare for tomorrow. Florida no more has the chance to plan for tourism from a philosophy of preservation; its mindless sellout to the tourist and landbuyer's fast dollar is now history. But the Black Sea, the Adriatic, the China side of the Pacific, and parts of the Mediterranean are still controllable. Tourism in these areas, and leisure as a whole, may still borrow comforts from the new technology and maintain the uncrowded, unhurried spirit left in only a few Western oases, such as Vienna. It is in such cultures that an episode in the new leisure will be worth watching. The New Englands may already be too conscious of leisure as well; the warm states have had heaven defined by Howard Johnson and Eastern Airlines. Will the community of the newer societies provide us with a middle-ground, a postindustrial or cultivated society of peasanthood and *paidia* at their best, in a new programmed mix?

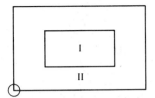

Chapter 11
Nation and World

Motion pictures, radio, and especially TV are designed for national masses, bringing the whole nation into our living and bedrooms.

The opposite of this is going to the nation for leisure—the second major form of leisure in the United States. For example, until the "energy crisis" of 1974 became acute, about 6 of every 10 trips by car were for "pleasure"; the past few decades have seen Americans riding farther across state lines with better cars, speedier highways, and more time; attendance at national parks has shot up.

But the most important influences on leisure are the factors implicit in the nation's historical development, its values and traditions.

GENERAL CONDITIONS FOR LEISURE IN THE UNITED STATES

1. *American leisure patterns reflect the history of a nation that grew up without a rigid carryover of the European or feudal principles or systems.* Just the opposite prevailed as our basic ethos: the principle of egalitarianism and the general trend toward looser distinctions of social classes. Even the South never developed an aristocracy to equal European ruling classes.[1] It would be naive to overlook the great disparities of wealth among our classes or the distances and styles of life that —actually and symbolically—have been present in dress, housing, travel, family patterns, and the rest. Nor need we blind ourselves to the current struggle of the black population, which points out social and economic division. Yet even with this caveat, our social structure has had a fluidity that was especially dramatized in the history of immigrants; one generation in time was often enough to see a leap from "Old World" father to a "New World" son, in the full sense of what these terms meant. Leisure, as a symbol of Americanization and of social class, served instrumentally and as evidence of progressive leveling.

2. *Regional differences in our leisure reflected the immensity of the country as well as its history of successive frontiers.* Our territory in

1790 was 888,811 square miles; in 1960, it was 3,628,150 square miles. Our shoreline along the Atlantic coast (15 states) comes to almost 29,000 miles; along the Pacific coast (5 states) it is over 17,000 miles. Between these great borders of water are great plains, forests, mountains, lakes, rivers, deserts, huge metropolitan and over a dozen "megalopolitan" areas, with 30 million people in the most populous (from Boston to Washington, D.C.); an enormous variety of types of beauty on the land or kinds of skies. The Southern tradition, the Middle Western, the Southwest, the Northwest—these are regions whose distinctive traditions extend into leisure patterns as in other areas. If the instruments of leisure—television, e.g.—have leveled these differences, producing a homogeneity (a mass culture) then, in fact, this standardizing force has removed our pluralistic origins and become a source of *change.* If the leisure pattern has served, on the other hand, to accentuate or preserve traditions and regional meanings, it has been a source of *stabilization.* Undoubtedly, leisure has contributed in both directions.

3. *Leisure patterns in America have been related to the heterogeneity of our population—a factor that, in turn, is a part of the immigrant waves.* A rough chronological sequence of immigrants reveals this succession: English, Jewish, Balkan, Slavic, Mexican and Latin American, Filipino, Middle Eastern, Oriental.

Many of those groups brought with them, and have kept in some degree, basic likes and ways from their heritage, whether in food, attitudes toward family, or values about education and religion. As in the case of regional differences noted above, leisure has undoubtedly been both a force toward integration and pluralism.

4. *It was as hard workers that our immigrants came to this country; in common with our administrative and business activities, our rural values and our youth orientation, the work ethic has been strong and is basic to all considerations of attitudes toward nonwork and leisure.*

There may be a question as to whether, in degree or in kind, attitudes toward work differ substantially from the United States to other nations or cultures. It is the combination of contributing factors noted above that makes so forceful an American tradition. Especially notable is the first of these: attitudes of the upper levels of workers—administrative and proprietary—who, if anything, often put more hours into their duties than their own employees. Thus a crucial element of traditional class lines is absent. Hefty inroads have been made into the work ethic, proceeding in a gradual evolution of urbanization, working for others and unionization, spurred by individual dramatic acts such as Henry Ford's momentous policy of $5 a day for a five-day week. Nevertheless, as Gunnar Myrdal notes at length, the American's behavior and his creed can be at great variance without his awareness of the paradox.[2] It is undoubtedly true, as Ozbekhan argues, that projections into the future must take into account the changes in values that will evoke new contexts; thus, he notes, the future is more than an extension of the present.[3] On this issue—the ethic of activities in work and expectations of rewards from work—hinges the major doorway into the path toward postindustrial society.

5. *Activism in various forms—physical mobility, restlessness, even violence—contributes another dimension of the American tradition that is manifest in leisure.* One index of our mobility in the United States is the proportion of the population now living in a *state* other than the one in which it was born; this was as high as 20.6 percent as far back as 1900; by 1960 over 26 of every 100 Americans had left their state of birth. The comparable movement from one's *city* of birth must be enormous.

The "restlessness" of a people is a concept that applies psychodynamic analysis to a study of national "character"—admittedly a difficult task; yet social science has moved not only toward more empirical types of analysis but also toward such loose terms as "anomie," "rootlessness," "anxiety," and "alienation." One trend feeds into the other, as we find the same scholars gathering highly specific data on crime only to be content with very general explanations taken from the less precise literature of psychoanalysis, psychiatry, history, or philosophy. Considerations about leisure face the same duality. How can we explain the fact that in 1963 alone 45 million Americans took at least one trip of 10 or more nights? Many explanations, given reasons and motivations, existed. But among them was some degree of a need to be moving, to change "scenery," to recharge one's "batteries" by confronting the unfamiliar.

Violence has many relationships to leisure; most familiar in American history were rural games, rowdiness from drink, and the physical contact from such sports as the prizefight or football. Most recent is that aspect of campus disorders or civil disorders in the community that— as a form of parasitism on the real issues—give rise to a leisure of mass entertainment by witnessing mass movements and becoming involved in contagious action.

6. *The rise in mass literacy through democratic education becomes a more and more key element in the leisure of this country.* A few basic facts illustrate the growing proportion of school education. From 1920 to 1960, we find a rise among those in school from ages 14 to 20 (see Table 15).

TABLE 15

Proportion of those 14–20 years in age attending school, 1920–1960

Age	1920	1930	1940	1950	1960
14	86.3	92.9	94.8	94.8	95.3
15	72.9	84.7	87.66	91.4	92.9
16	50.8	66.3	76.2	80.9	86.3
17	34.6	47.9	60.9	68.2	75.6
18	21.7	30.7	36.4	39.8	50.6
19	13.8	19.8	20.9	24.7	32.8
20	8.3	13.1	12.5	17.9	23.5

These percentage growths appear in graph form in Chart 9.

The changes in Chart 9, most apparent between ages 16 to 20, reflect many influences: new attitudes, laws, affluence, urbanization, greater competition for better jobs, and loans for college education. An even more pronounced tendency is to be found in adult education, which has been described as "the largest and the fastest growing segment of American education." After noting the difficulty of obtaining reliable statistics in this field, Professor Malcolm Knowles indicates a startling growth. "Rough estimates placed the total enrollment units in all forms of adult education activity at the 15 million level in 1924, around 22 million in 1934, close to 30 million in 1950, and almost 50 million in 1955."[4]

Two levels exist between the relationship of adult education to leisure: (1) adult education as *an end* in itself as a major form of leisure (a statement that needs to be broken down by analyses of kinds of courses, etc., and therefore the purposes, motivations, and commitments in time); (2) education obtained by the adult that serves as an *instrument* for use in other forms (e.g., a course in how to listen to music or how to prepare for a trip abroad).

7. *The social class levels of participants in community transformation are undergoing radical change, creating new areas for significant leisure involvement.* Gone are the days in which the upper classes are the primary volunteers of the community. To some degree, within the ethnic communities of our cities, there always were natural leaders who served as liaison with City Hall. These leaders, as among the Italians in Boston, began to speak for a larger following with increased integration. In recent years, there have been two dramatic episodes, still in full swing: the Civil Rights movement among blacks and whites—more recently the blacks on their own—and the purposeful inclusion of the

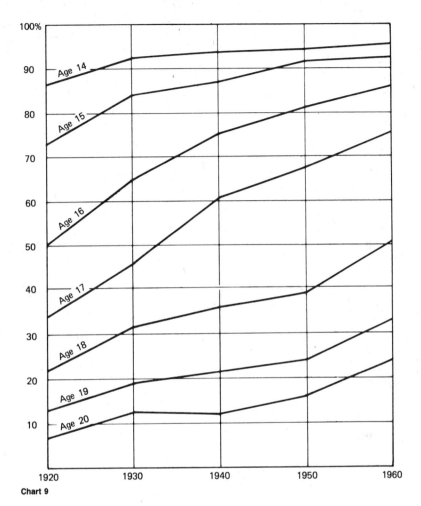

Chart 9

Proportion of 14- to 20-year olds attending school, 1920–1960

poor in urban renewal, OEO, and other programs of the Great Society program under President Johnson. Of course, behind both movements there were many years in which all levels and interests had learned to engage in direct action.

The sociologist, Jesse Bernard, has commented on the former days of "class leadership." In her 1949 volume she notes,[5] "In general, then, the poor, the uneducated, the minority group member, the mobile, the timid, or the person with a heavy load of personal or family maladjustment is not likely to have either the desire or the facility for impressing his will on the community either directly or through an organization. ... The privilege of leaving an impression on community life is, it appears, an upper-class prerogative for the most part."

When participation and power are tested and tasted, they become permanent values; we may safely project a continuation and deepening of community participation. In addition to existing social factors, such as conflict, cybernation will intensify the need for finding personal commitments within contexts other than traditional work and for inventing or enlarging opportunities for civic involvement. One impact of the civil rights struggle already has been to pull many blacks into the public arena who, while rejecting the application of "leisure" to their constructive efforts, are literally engaging in such activity in nonwork periods.

8. *In contrast to Europe, the private business sector in American history has been a more and more important factor in affecting activities, attitudes, and tastes for leisure.* In the days of rural or small-town life, leisure was primarily invented or given shape from the inner resources of family or village life, as in social exchange and festivals. A series of developments from the bicycle to the automobile, and presently climaxed by television, has altogether created what is often called the "mass society."

A crucial question, which the private television industry enjoys raising, is whether there are characteristics imbedded in the society, so that the producers of "Peyton Place" and "Bonanza" are simply providing what the public wants. Cause and effect can never be accurately isolated or measured. American business—book clubs, organized sports, or mass media entertainment—are responding to and influencing taste. They are tastemakers and taste caterers. In the latter sense, the leisure fare that is catered is not necessarily destructive or devoid of quality. Occasionally, excellent motion picture shows or "specials" on TV remind us of the excellence that is possible under the profit economy. The point, however, is that with such rare exceptions as the defunct "Bell Telephone Hour," education or quality are not primary goals of business.[6] The leisure dimension of American life, inasmuch as a portion of it is dominated by goods or services provided for financial profit, is *efficiently served* instead of *purposefully elevated.*

9. *Alongside the dependence on commercial provision of leisure content, the public sector has also grown as a major instrument for leisure, and it will continue to grow in importance.* One use of public funds, on the municipal and county levels, has been the development of a profession of recreation leaders who function in such settings as playgrounds, parks, camps, and community centers.

Indeed, the Congress several years ago engaged in significant observations and forecasts on the use of the outdoors; by every indication the needs in this regard will increase enormously, with an impact on American leisure patterns of the utmost importance.

10. *A growth has been evident in the artistic life of America, including professional, community, and educational levels, with a positive dimension of present strength and future potential for leisure purposes.* Critiques and defenses of "mass culture" in the United States hinge on the validity or the overoptimism of this statement. There are other categories for productive leisure than the arts, of course. Yet they provide one crucial index of the present state of leisure and of its future, since they revolve around inner experiences of the audience or consumer as well as the favorable social conditions for the creator. In spite of evidence of "mass" manipulations by the nature of influences from Madison Avenue, Hollywood, or community pressures, the possibilities for more "creative" uses of free time in the future are visible from tendencies in the United States since the turn of the century. On both the amateur and professional levels, standards have gone up; in the arts, because of such as factors the movement to this country from Hitler Germany of important pedagogues and creators, the availability of records and picture reproductions, the "jet" journeys of live performers, the general rise in literacy, and the growth of a public school art and music program. Most of all, the arts have been opened to all segments of the population.[7]

11. *One general fact that influences all aspects of leisure in the United States is the magnitude of our productivity, affluence, and potential through cybernation.*

Why then, was this statement not placed at the top of our list? Because, in spite of its importance to any consideration of leisure, the economic base must not be exaggerated as *the* deterministic factor. Sorokin's summary of the matter still holds up 40 years after its writing. Sorokin states the essence of the economic theory: it "determines all other social phenomena in the causal chain . . . it is 'the starter. . . .' " To this he replies:[8]

"It is evident that such conception cannot be accepted: factually, such factors as geographical conditions and biological drives inherent in man appeared and operated earlier than economic factors . . . we cannot say that among man's inherent drives or instincts there is only an instinct for food, or even that it is the strongest. . . . We cannot even claim that man is an economic creature and always acts economically as it was supposed by the classical economists."

We should be cautious in considering even the "work ethic" as an economic drive. The whole weight of industrial studies for several decades has been to undermine that assumption. What we learn is that it is the social, the human structure, the work situation, that constitutes its satisfactions.

Leisure in the United States is an issue now because of the *attitudes* behind our gadgets, our production, and our inundation of techniques. Thus it is an issue that affects all economic levels, not only those who "have." That is why, as the Europeans see the moral factors within the transformation of attitudes, leisure has become a matter of higher priority in their social science and in public policy. We turn, then, to some considerations of European societies.

EUROPE: ECONOMIC GROWTH

First, there is the dramatic and rapid economic growth, especially in Western Europe since World War II. A few figures come to the heart of the matter. Countries of the European economic community moved up in their industrial production from 80 in 1950 to 203 in 1963 (using an index of 100 in 1953); meanwhile the United States went from an index of 82 to only 136.

During the 1950s, this expansion was especially notable. In that decade, for instance, boom conditions were evident everywhere as per capita output rose by more than a third. Italy's gross product went up about 64 percent and France, the Netherlands, Switzerland, and Spain shot up between 45 and 50 percent. These remarkable spurts in growth leveled off in the 1960s, but the realization in terms of affluence in private life had by then become well ingrained.

A further comparison of economic development in Europe and the United States is the rate of relative growth in output per employee, based on total civilian employment and real gross product (see Table 16).

TABLE 16

Growth rates of output per employee, selected periods, 1913 to 1968[9]

Period	United States	France	West Germany	Italy
1950–1968	2.5	4.8	5.2	5.4
1950–1960	2.2	4.8	5.9	4.7
1960–1968	2.9	4.7	4.4	6.3

A further evidence of change is seen in the reduction of hours in the work week. Table 17 shows several examples.

This is the basis of a second reason for our interest in the European picture. In Western Europe, far more than in the USSR, the new affluence was realized in visible consumer goods and in the comfort of services. This varied among the countries. Again turning to the crucial decade, 1950 to 1960, the highest gains in personal consumption, including the instruments for leisure, took place in the United Kingdom, Switzerland, France, Belgium-Luxembourg, and the Scandinavian area. With only 42 percent of the total population of Western Europe, these countries had more than 7 of every 10 automobiles, 6 of every 10 telephones, and 53 of every 100 radios.

More so than in the United States, the ownership of automobiles abroad is most sensitive to economic differences among these countries. I have not been able to ascertain the approximate proportion of miles or expenditures in which the European and Englishman drives his car for "pleasure." In the United States the figure is 60 percent; my suspicion, purely from impressions gained abroad, is that the European percentage is higher.

Almost three quarters of Paris residents leave their city for summer vacation, and Dumazedier's report on Annecy and France brings out full data to illustrate the trend in the Frenchman's use of vacations, movies, television, books, and education.[11] Has the world—he asks, really entered a "civilization of leisure"? Yes, he argues, after a recital of man's persistent attachment to work, and the presence of slums and hunger. "First things come first"; yet his observations of daily life for the French person and the family convince him that the postwar affluence in Europe (and, of course, even more in the United States) has created

TABLE 17
Reduction of weekly work hours, seven western countries, 1960-1963[10]

	1950	1963	Reduction in Hours
Austria	44.4	42.5	1.9
Germany, Federal Republic	48.4	44.3	4.1
Ireland (1953-1962)	46.2	43.8	2.4
Netherlands	48.8	46.6	2.2
Norway (1950-1962)	44.4	41.4	3.0
Sweden (1950-1961)	41.6	38.4	3.2
Switzerland	47.5	45.4	2.0

the visible problem of *cultural democratization,* which now takes its place alongside the issues of political, economic, and social democracy.

National Ownership

In contrast to our own political structure, European mass media and travel facilities are in whole or in part within the governmental structure. Administrators of these services are closely aware and deeply concerned with the public reaction—whether to television progress or to train service. Leisure patterns and facilities are therefore inseparable from top-level policy research and judgment. In Amsterdam, for example, Dr. V. Zweers until recently directed the Boekman Stichtung, carrying on research in the sociology of the arts.[12] One would strain to find more than a few individual scholars in this field in the United States, much less a government-funded organization. Dr. H. De Jager's study of the Utrecht Symphony audiences is another example of Dutch work in this field.[13]

INTERNATIONAL RESEARCH

In probably no other field of social science research has there been as much activity and success as on the leisure issue. This has already been explained implicitly in the high priority the subject holds among many nations. From an organizational point of view, it was possible because (1) the subject contains both statistical and interpretative issues (such as relationships to ideology), permitting the participating scholars to concentrate on the first, or "neutral" aspect; (2) the issues are such that comparative observations and even interpretations—as on the nature of impact of the mass media—are valuable and even applicable across national lines. Furthermore, the field happened to count among its members some leaders who could seize on the international milieu that has permeated all the sciences since World War II.

The first of these comparative surveys directed by Dumazedier emerged in 1956 from a meeting at the World Sociological Congress held in Amsterdam; in this study were representatives from Belgium, Finland, France, Italy, Poland, Yugoslavia, Federal Germany, Austria, England, Israel, and Switzerland. Numerous sessions were held, then, beginning with one in Annecy, France, in June 1957. This group was concerned with a comparative study of the problems of leisure according to different technical levels and different social structures in industrial civilization. For example, there were common questionnaires of leisure practices and needs applied to random samples of population; studies of groups as they were engaged in leisure; a *"quantitative and qualitative* study of the effect of popular educational organization;" and historical studies covering a half century to observe trends. Dumazedier's stress on the normative stress of this international group (evidenced also in the work of his own staff at the Centre d'Etudes Sociologique in Paris) is noted in the statement, "We propose that our work contribute to research into the democratic conditions necessary suited to sociocultural planning in industrial societies." Dumazedier's own work in Annecy as well as his broad conclusions from the internation studies are to be found in his volume *Toward a Society of Leisure.*[14]

The present study that Dumazedier directs included originally scholars from France, West Germany, Sweden, Switzerland, Czechoslovakia, Canada, and the United States. Each is examining the leisure pattern of its own nation by going back into the history of the past, and by what the French call "the technique of prevision" i.e. selecting from among those projections for the next two decades those that seem to be most desirable for "planification," that is recommendations for public policy.

Simultaneous with these substantive studies within and across the cooperating countries, Dumazedier's group is also developing the techniques for storing its information in a project known as CISDOL. In a 1974 Toronto meeting a cooperative plan was developed with SIRLS, a computer program of the Faculty of Leisure Studies, University of Waterloo, Ontario; the Canadian group will organize and distribute the data.

The program that Dr. Szalai organized is the Multinational Comparative Time Budget Research Project, an unprecedented cooperative effort among research groups of Belgium, Bulgaria, Czechoslovakia, Federal Republic of Germany, France, German Democratic Republic, Hungary, Peru, Poland, United States, USSR, and Yugoslavia. The research was carried on between 1965 and 1966.[15]

The time for intensive study in each case was a complete 24-hour day, with a written record to be kept by the person of everything he did in chronological order, the precise length of each activity (doing "nothing" was recorded as an activity), the location of everything done, and with whom. An equal distribution of all days in the week was arranged (some persons reporting on their Monday, others on their Tuesday, etc.). In each of the countries, unusual periods were avoided, such as vacations, peak agricultural work, seasonal feasts, or unusual weather. On the day after the written report was kept and returned, the subject was interviewed in his home, the data was checked and, if necessary, completed, so that the full 1440 minutes were accounted for.

Altogether, the study ended in 150,000 coded cards of precise information from the 13 survey sites and from nearly 30,000 interviews. This mass of data was classified into 66 basic tables and 27 categories of "principal" activities. These studies provide us with the most intensive statistical data ever assembled for any of the respective countries, enriched by the comparisons across national lines.

What, then, are some of the early results? Tentative results cover: (1) comparisons of leisure among men and women; (2) influences of urbanization and industrialization; (3) general comparisons of working and nonworking time; (4) differences in leisure between days of the week; (5) the use of mass communication media.

Clear distinctions exist for working and non-working women. Both are at a disadvantage next to man; the first are overburdened, what with work and home duties; and labors of the latter are "under-estimated and their existence is much more drab than that of man."[16] Yet the study reveals that considerable differences result from the degree of economic and social development. Generally, however, nonworking women devote more time to housework on weekends than working women do, except in the United States.

In spite of great differences in the level of industrial development among the countries studied, results show "a remarkable homogeniety in the general proportions of time-budgets," extending not only to time spent on sleeping, eating, or washing, but even to time allocations among different population segments and use of days in the week. Perhaps the most interesting difference is that the general average of free time (every day) is somewhat more in the United States, but less for nonworking women than it is in the USSR. Nonworking women spend from two to four hours more in housework, one hour more for self care and sleep, one to two more hours for leisure. However, the free time of nonworking women is "less than or just equal to that of *working* men."[17] Time put into housework differs more according to countries than the number of children (a variation of four hours of the 24 compared to one half hour). Since nonworking women are more likely to have a lower level of education and have less money, it appears that the additional free time of nonworking women is devoted more to such items as resting and conversing than to reading, theater, or even to TV.

A general similarity among all the countries for actual amount of time spent going to and from work is less a reflection of types of transport facilities than of the time available for the journey—available, one gathers, in the sense that the worker is willing to surrender other activities (as evidenced by living in a suburb). The general average of time for the trip to work and back varies from one half hour in the USSR and Yugoslavia to one hour in Hungary; in the United States it is 30 to 70 minutes for 52 percent of American workers.

Night work on a regular schedule makes for more free time; afternoon work decreases free time in all countries.

As to the use of free time, the research directed by Szalai and his
colleagues provides an interesting comparison of time given to study in
relation to all other activities. The percentages are shown in Table 18.[18]

As might be expected, the distribution of activities during the week
derives from the pattern of working people. Leisure on Sunday is only
partly a day of rest, with increased leisure of four hours for men, three
for working women, and two for nonworking women. Saturday is almost a normal working day in the Eastern countries, so that the character of Sunday depends largely on the uses of Saturday. Going to church
takes considerable time only among a "tiny minority" in Eastern countries; television takes twice the time given to it during week days (four
hours in the United States, three for the French). The mass media
(defined as radio, television, and reading) consume most free time of
working people everywhere.[19]

One result of the cross-cultural study will undoubtedly be a number
of independent volumes by some scholars who participate in the comparative program. One such volume has already seen publication,
Women and Leisure, by Dr. France Govaerts, of the National Center
of the Sociology of Work, a part of the University of Brussels.[20] Her
excellent study has combined the international data with her own theoretical framework.

Dr. Miro Mihovilovich of Zagreb has conducted research on women
and family life that cuts across six or more nations, East and West.[21]

It is a gratuitous pleasure to ponder as an individual the directions
that international research might take. It is obviously easier for these

TABLE 18

Time used for study: Result of 13-nation study; five communities

	Private Study, %	Attendance at Courses, %
Pskon[a]	24.4	3.5
Kazenlik[b]	24.4	7.9
Torun[c]	24.0	2.4
Jackson[d]	8.1	3.5
France	5.1	2.2

[a] Near Leningrad, USSR.
[b] Center part of Bulgaria.
[c] North Central Poland.
[d] South-central Michigan, United States.

projects to succeed if they remain close to objective data. Yet, as Professor Zygulski of Warsaw has argued at several international meetings, a substantive, historically based examination of leisure can result only if there is some conceptual scheme large enough to encompass various epochs, and (the more difficult qualification) that it encompass countries in various stages of industrial, social, and political development.[22] The Szalai studies, important as they are, leave these issues to each interpreter. The Dumazedier group will face these issues as it moves from its data to the development of "indicators" for the "postindustrial" society; but it will need more than economic orientation, since these are the easiest.

One of the themes that will run through Chapters 16 to 19 is the "neoprimitive" fusion of roles and institutions that seems to be emerging: for example, the difficulty, even in the United States—where separation of government from the marketplace is a fetish—of ignoring the industrial-military-political complex. On a more visible level, the American home is another example. It also has been a strategic center for the understanding of American life (in common with families in all cultures) but all the more now because its character has changed from a producing to a consuming unit. In the former capacity, the more it produced, as on a farm, the more all of its members were business colleagues, fellow workers. As machines and electronics took over in the home, and as this became more and more a city family, its members related as partners in play. This "play" was not necessarily organized; its elements penetrated the nature of conversation, sex relations, mealtime, vacation trips, use of community facilities such as parks or art events, and the like. Margaret Mead and others have analyzed the merging of roles—father now joins in shopping, mother joins political movements; but there is also the merging of community and family in the satisfaction of human needs. There is really little difference between a Pacific Islander, who prays, makes a fierce mask, or goes to war, and a Manhattan Islander, who prepares his sales pitch, presses his suit, and calls on a prospective client to sell TV advertising. If we can speak of "fusions" in the first, and therefore call it "primitive," it makes equal sense to recognize "fusions" in the current scene, and call it "neoprimitive." Nomenclature is not the issue; the fact is that among the fusions of our time, that between work and leisure is of crucial importance.

Thus transcultural studies can focus on fusions of roles and institutions. Automatically, this brings the "underdeveloped" nations into the model of study. The Dumazedier group has already recognized this gap, and began to explore it in the Varna sessions of 1971 with a special meeting on "leisure and preindustrial society." At one of the United

Nations sessions several underdeveloped nations have asked for such studies, in part to help them avoid the observable impact of industrialization on traditions, in part to prepare for mass media and tourism. These countries embrace both the primitive and feudal models on which *Proposition 56* of Chapter 3 is predicated; "The general meaning of leisure to the conquest-primitive societies is a oneness with nature." This suggests that the international studies must be very cautious that they do not fall into the evolutionary trap of equating postindustrial with higher, or even with characteristic elements that emerge only from industrial.

A basic condition that has brought all nations to a concern with the goals and qualities of their lives is the growing availability of energy. To this topic we turn.

PART 4
Cultural Systems

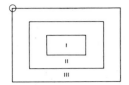

Chapter 12
The Energy System

The placement of economic influences on leisure within the "map" of issues in Chapter 3 has several implicit assumptions: (1) that the dynamics of leisure as an institution (level I) draw on and influence a large number of types of disciplines; (2) that the location of the "energy system" amidst other components of the cultural level makes it more certain that we will view the economic as only one of many factors; (3) that the proper emphasis is therefore drawn to relationships instead of to deterministic or unilateral factors; (4) that the use of the term "energy systems"—already defined as "the total production and control of resources used or available to the society together with attendant attitudes, motivations, rewards, and deprivations"—moves us toward the institutional or cultural economics known to Adam Smith and to Karl Marx.

Putting all this together, we must interrelate two quite distinct matters that are simple to state in a gross way, but that constantly become confused; *one is the energy that is needed to keep the society going—the "system" and the "people"; the other is the set of ideas and attitudes about that energy.* Another way of distinguishing these is the economic *event* and our mental *construct* about the event. This chapter will indicate the changes in both and the problems caused by those changes; a third concern is types of solutions or at least of approaches toward solutions. The question is whether the first two, in their confrontation, lead naturally to traditional solutions, or whether a Caesarian operation is needed to give birth to innovative ideas and new social forms.

ENERGY FOR MAINTENANCE

The change of economic processes is related to systems of class, slavery, nationalism, religion, family, community, age groupings, and ideologies; evidence is found in numerous writings. One is Max Weber's famous thesis on capitalism and the Protestant ethic; another is Thorstein Veblen's essay on conspicuous consumption. Davis, who writes of nationalism as a force of economic change,[1] states that it is a "*sine quo non* of industrialization, because it provides people with an overriding, easily acquired, secular motivation for making painful changes, as National strength or prestige becomes the supreme goal, industrialization the chief means." A contemporary classic that relates the economic process to a wide array of conditions and ideologies is Gunnar Myrdal's *Asian Drama;* in his preface, Myrdal notes his "increasingly firm conviction that economic problems cannot be studied in isolation but only in their demographic, social and political setting."[2]

England was the center of the nineteenth-century expansion of energy. With only 2 percent of the world's population, she provided at one period over half of the world's productive product. Coal and iron became the major commodities of the world, making possible the locomotive.

Yet before the end of the century the United States and Germany had out-stripped England in steel production. This period also brought a new era of the huge industrial concern as the organizer, producer, and distributor of energy into consumable products. Political power became a tool of this technological innovation and application; thus, as the circle began to close toward the mysteries of atomic power during World War II, the state became a prime decision maker, financier, and organizer of energy. The net result was a transformation so radical that the energy system can no more be considered as an economic matter alone. Economics of our time, closely related to every social, technological, and political trend, can no longer follow a pure or "classical" model; it is inevitably institutional or holistic, deriving its dynamic—as Robert Theobald notes in the very title of one of his recent books—from an "economy of abundance."[3] It is, however, not an abundance based so much on ownership as on use. The *possession* of money or the ownership of things is no more the primary criterion of wealth, but has been replaced by *access* to energy or to experiences (the first as means, the latter as ends). Furthermore, it is the topsy-turvy nature of this access that has outdated class lines and that is at the root of new values.

Persistence of Old Attitudes

Yet the old ideas die a hard death. Here, for example, is a homely essay that summarizes old attitudes. It is titled, "What is Work?"

"Work gives order to life. It is the basic background upon which all the patterns of life's progress are woven.

Work is a never-ending giver of knowledge and opportunity. It is a winding stream upon whose banks something new may be seen each day.

Through work, man finds his own level. As some are content with the fruit on the lower branches, so will some grasp the largest fruits.

Work is our personal contribution to others, as theirs is to us. The house in which we live and all its conveniences . . . the food we eat . . . and the clothes we wear . . . these, and infinitely more, do we receive and give through the common bond of work.

Work has no boundaries, nor is it confined to the strong. Yet, all work is important to the worker. The child, carefully building a castle in the sand, or the aged woman sewing on a quilt—these are as much examples of work as the blacksmith pounding sweat-drenched iron, for all work begins in the heart.

A man's work can be as subtle as a poet describing the fragrance of a single blossom, or as awe-inspiring as men awaiting the thunderous roar of a space vehicle leaving the launching pad.

But whatever the work . . . if it is honest work, performed with all the pride, skill and integrity of the worker, then the world will be a better place because of it."

Does this statement come from the last century, or this? Why was it written? Who are its intended readers?

On my honor, it comes from the "editor's corner" (one Martin Buxbaum, affectionately referred to by himself as Bux) of a small monthly publication issued by the Marriott Corporation, prepared for "our guests" in a string of American motels! The little journal put out by Bux is named, oddly, for a bedroom readership, *Table Talk*, subtitled, "For Your Entertainment While Visiting Us." Few of its readers are in the motel as part of a working assignment; comfort instead of work must be uppermost in their minds. The date, incidentally, is March 1969.

A summary of the Protestant ethic that Bux typifies has been provided by Ariano Tilgher. "The methodological discipline of professional work binds into a strong sheaf the scattered forces of the soul, frees man from doubts, anxieties, preoccupations, and sets the soul moving in a fine powerful rhythm which tends to perpetrate itself because of the very joy it gives . . . it gives him at all times, the divine joy of creation. . . ."[4] *Work therapy or control* has been described by Sebastian de Grazia as a follow-up of the Reformation. It was only the "right and moral thing to do," but also something that is "good for you, a remedy for pain, loneliness, the death of a dear one, a disappointment in love, or doubts about the purposes of love."[5]

Yet there is a wide range of evidence, covering all periods of history, to indicate that if we strip away the need to work for sheer maintenance of life, man is not by his "nature" or his "soul" impelled toward more and more productive work as an end. One type of evidence comes from primitive societies on a contemporary group living in the Kalihari Desert of Africa, where the workweek seldom goes beyond 19 hours, where material wealth is seen as a burden, and everyone is as rich—or poor—as everyone else. There are no clear property lines and unemployment is high, sometimes reaching 40 percent (not because the society is shiftless, but because it believes that only the able-bodied should work, and then no more than is necessary). Food is easily gathered. Everyone seems to be comfortable, happy, and secure.

Among the Romans, 109 days, nearly one third of the 355 days of their calendar, were unlawful for political and judicial business, since they were festival days; the total work segment of the year then came to about 2160 hours.[6] French workers on the higher strata (intellectuals in government capacities) worked about 2500 hours per year in *1800*, and over *3000* hours in *1950*. In thirteenth-century France, some craftsmen received 30-day vacations annually and another 141 days off, or about 2300 hours per year.

Was it different after the "Protestant ethic" took over? Long after the Puritan attitude should have hardened, we are told by some historians, the Industrial Revolution could not easily count on it. Wilensky and Lebeaux note that in the early days of that development, the peasant had to be *pushed* into factories almost literally, by such coercive measures as laws on vagabondage, the economic destruction of small villages, and long-term indenture contracts supported by penal sanction.[7] The latter device is still in use in Latin America and in Portugese West Africa; head taxes, payable only by case, are used in British West Africa, Uganda, Northern Rhodesia, and New Guinea. Direct coercion found a classic expression in the slavery system in the United States and elsewhere. Forces and motivations that encouraged white immigrants to come to our shores, especially from 1880 to 1914, were combinations of poverty, programs, and political persecutions—not the need to keep active or to ensure "order to live."

Writing of the nineteenth-century England, the historian S. Pollard notes that because of their habits in the agricultural way of life, those who formed the potential workers for the factory system that came first to England were "men who were non-accumulative, non-acquisitive, accustomed to work for subsistence, not for maximization of income." The problem of changing these ways and attitudes "was new, and called for as much innovation as the technical inventions of the age."[8]

Since these accounts have been documented by intensive research into work after the Reformation, one is tempted to wonder why so much has been made of the "Puritan ethic." Indeed, a case emerges from these illustrations for the position that with growing computerization, man's "need" to work beyond the call of the checkbook is an exaggeration and reflects not so much the need to work as the emptiness of nonwork. "Work," in that case, has as its motivation mere activity. Indeed, the possibility arises that if the proper conditions develop, man's "nature" is *more* flexible than the post-Reformation mythology leads us to believe.

The question is, what are the "proper conditions" for a rerighting of values? Is it possible that with the approaching possibility of widespread material comfort, always augmented by new machine energy, the worker will want to go back to the more carefree, less regulated life that prevailed before the Industrial Revolution? That will be difficult, many say, since man has by now been caught up in a vast complex of keeping busy, wanting more goods, and—as economic goods increase—becoming part of the middle or "harried class."

LABOR NEGOTIATION, TRENDS, AND COMPUTERIZATION

In the past century the workweek has gone down from over 70 to under 40 hours. One of the dramatic moments in that reduction was Henry Ford's policy announcement of the five-day, $5 a day week.[9] A week later, Judge Gary of U.S. Steel stated drily: "God decreed that we work 6 days and rest on the seventh, and by God—that's enough rest!" Now 45 years later, workers under the U.S. Steel contract get 13 weeks paid vacation every fifth year—on top of regular vacations. The recent Chrysler-UAW contract calls for getting ready to install a pilot four-day week. Riva Poor's book, *4 Days, 40 Hours: Reporting a Revolution in Work and Leisure,*[10] notes that about 11,000 employees—usually in small companies—are trying some formula of squeezing the typical 40-hour workweek into a new combination of time structure: Samsonite luggage makers work 38 hours, Monday through Thursday; in Everett, Mass., employees of Kyanize Paints start at 7:00 and leave at 4:30 with no coffee breaks; a firm in Cushing, Oklahoma, keeps open seven days, but each employee works only four; a retail tire company in Los Angeles works Thursdays through Saturdays, when sales are best.

Almost everywhere the reports are favorable from workers and employers alike. As a *Wall Street Journal* report summarized the evaluations in a dispatch of October 15, 1970: "The workers love it, which is less than surprising. . . . What is surprising, though, is that the employers love it, too. The four-day week . . . increases productivity, decreases absenteeism, boosts worker morale and cuts worker turnover."

The 40-hour week itself is undergoing serious reconsideration. Mutual and Metropolitan insurance companies are both trying the three-day week for their data-processing staffs (40 hours and 460 men, respectively to maximize use of expensive computers). Sylvia Porter puts the challenge of new time to the worker in her column of February 16, 1971. "How will you handle yourself when '5–40' gives way to '4–40' and then swings into '4–32'?"

Basic to the new order of life and its resultant attitudes is, of course, the fact of computerization.

Whatever its technological or social impact may be, no one denies that automation, computerization, or cybernation (a combination of the first two) is expanding in quantitative use. By 1970 about 1 million Americans were employed in some aspect of the computer business. Since 1966 the number of programmers has grown from 100,000 to 175,000; the number of systems analysts has grown from 60,000 to 150,000. In 1955 there were about 200 computers in service; 15 years later the number stood at about 85,000 in the United States alone, with perhaps 210,000 by 1980. Yet the first system, UNIVAC, was delivered to the Bureau of the Census as late as 1950; by now the federal government alone uses 17,000 such machines. As time goes on, construction will be more standardized, cheaper, and amenable to programming by language closely resembling English or standard arithmetic notation. According to figures provided by the Belgian Centre d'Analyse et de Programmation: "between 1960 and 1968 the number of computers for commercial, technical, and scientific purposes increased 14-fold in the United States, 28-fold in Europe, and 100-fold in Japan. At present Europe possesses one-quarter of the number of computers of the United States, and Japan one-fifteenth. Recent statistics give the following figures and estimates (Table 19).[11]

This goes on as human labor becomes more and more expensive, as competition from European and Japanese economies becomes sharper for the United States, and labor-industry negotiations become more sophisticated.

In a detailed discussion of the technological revolution taking place, the former principal scientist of the Systems Development Corporation, Robert H. Davis, foresees that component cybernation in industry will be the rule, not the exception, and many plants will become organizationally cybernated, making it possible to predict product demand, taking into account such factors as seasonal variation, to control inventories of raw materials, to produce, inspect, and store finished items,

TABLE 19

Computer growth, 1959–1970, and estimates to 1980

	United States	Europe	Japan
1959	2,034	265	11
1960	3,612	479	37
1961	4,528	801	103
1962	7,305	1,450	220
1963	11,078	2,170	416
1964	15,867	3,413	767
1965	22,495	5,018	1,164
1966	29,142	7,634	1,624
1967	39,516	9,543	2,302
1968	52,000	13,200	3,500
1969	68,000	21,000	5,100
1970	85,000	30,000	7,500
1975	170,000	110,000	41,000
1980	240,000	200,000	110,000

and to bill customers. The entire operation will be coordinated by a single computer.

In the summer of 1970, I.B.M., which controls over 70 percent of the United States market and over 90 percent of sales in Western Europe, was unveiling its "fourth-generation" computer, reported to possess a new degree of integrated circuitry, unlimited memory, and dramatic improvements to provide access to four times the storage of data in one half of the operating time. Already, reported William D. Smith in the *New York Times* on May 24, 1970, the world's *fastest growing* industry, which will in a few decades become the world's *largest* industry, has moved up from total revenues of $975 million in 1970 to $12,225 million by 1970; anticipated sales will be $24,430 million by 1974.

The application of automation varies among the industries. In the mid-1960s, one survey indicated that among the 32,000 American manufacturers who employ over 100 persons, over 21,000 were already using some automatic control and data-handling systems. Two thirds of equipment, machinery, and metal-working plants were using such devices. But across the board, the question arises of the ability of major industrialists themselves to understand what is happening.

Among those who have emphasized the impact of automation and computerization, economist Robert Theobald predicts that within a decade we can expect that tens of millions will be either unemployed, on public welfare, or on public works programs. The long-run displace-

ment of works on this magnitude, he states, "is no longer really controversial among those who have studied the impact of automation and
cybernation."[12]

One research organization, Resources for Future, Inc., projects this
new time picture in Table 20 (including moonlighting).[13]

I submit that over and beyond all this, *the hour in each successive
decade is worth relatively more in its potential;* thus the comparison of
hours "income," like that of dollar income, is only part of the story. The
60 minutes in 1900 was physically the same as in 1970, but one had less
access to distance, friends, images of the world, or anything else that has
extended our reach into places and experiences. Inflation makes the
dollar less useful, and the hour is affected only as there are less dollars
to buy transportation, communications, or other tools of leisure. But
practically all Americans already had a TV set by the mid-1960s, and
over 25 percent of families had two sets. As to cars, it is only a calculated
mythology that cars should be changed every few years; inflation does
not deny the consumer a car; it simply sabotages the Madison Avenue
hawkers. It is worth restating the basic fact that our new measure of
wealth is *access,* not dollars and not hours. The "old" dollar could buy
more than today's dollar, but there was less to buy. The "free" hour is
not only greater in total quantity but in its possibilities as a content for
experience, and it exists in a freer psychological and sociological content.

Need for new attitudes

In view of the trends in facts and in attitudes noted above, time, in its
subjective or even in its metaphysical senses, has recaptured the attention of those concerned with the meaning of our whole era. For example, J. B. Priestly, in his important book, *Man and Time,* ranges widely
into such matters as the various approaches by astronomers, physicists,
parapsychologists, and dramatists.[14] He examines the writings of John
William Dunne and spells out his own "feelings, intuitive ideas, vague

TABLE 20

Weekly work hours, 1955–1970, with projections, 1985, 2000

	1955	1970	1985	2000
Hours per year	2070	1950	1860	1790
Weeks per year	49.6	49.2	48.9	48.6
Hours per week	41.8	39.6	38.0	36.8

impressions," and "personal encounters" with time. He distinguishes the three types of time—for he who simply passes or lives it, for the "contemplative slower-up," and for the "creative speeder-up": in the second, man becomes less than himself, in the third, his personality vanishes altogether. The correctness of Priestley's distinctions is not important; what he submits is a personalistic view of man who, although locked into certain external elements of his environment, adapts these elements to his internal functions. These elements of the world's necessity, or—to use Berdyaev's phrase, the "world given us"—are to be penetrated and adapted if "meaning can break through meaninglessness."

In just this sense, we can approach the energy system *for the first time among large masses of men as the tool for freedom* and for passing "beyond the boundaries of the given world." The size of this new "tool" is seen in a simple comparison. In the eighteenth century *80 percent* of the population had to grow food, spin, and weave their course clothing in the winter. Today, in the United States, *10 percent* of the population produce so much food that millions are on a slimming diet; although sufficient food for millions goes down the drain daily and much is exported to needy countries, a considerable part of the harvest even then has to be stored every year to "protect" the farmers from ruin.

Among the most articulate of those who anticipate in these major social and economic transformations based on the new energy and control systems is economist Donald Michael.[15] He draws a picture of the future and its problems, when most of the "routine blue-collar and white-collar tasks that can be done by cybernation, will be." Most of us, even though better educated, will not understand the new world; "good-thinking" computers will be operating on a large scale, presenting a new interplay between government and science; a small segment of the population will relate to these machines on top levels, having been trained from childhood "as intensively as the classical ballerinas."

"But the rest, whose innate intelligence or training is not of the highest, what will they do? We can foresee a nation with a large portion of its people doing, directly or indirectly, the endless public tasks that the welfare state needs and that the government will not allow to be cybernated because of the serious unemployment that would result. These people will work shorter hours, with much time for the pursuit of leisure activities."[16]

As Michael speaks of the change in values and power in such a society, he can see that the former life of private recreation may carry on, indifferent to public responsibility. "This indifference, plus the centralization of authority, would seem to imply a governing elite and a popular acceptance of such an elite."[17]

Amidst this dialogue, the view that I take as the base for both theoretical and policy construction is that what we are faced with is a series of new *alternatives.* The quantitative basis for this has been best expressed before a Senate Committee on Aging by Juanita Kreps, a Duke University economist.

If one supposes, as she notes, that we were to hold the per capita GNP constant at $3181 and take all of our economic growth in free time, the workweek could go down to 22 hours by 1985, or we could work a full day for only two full weeks of the year, or we could retire at the age of 38.[18]

Dr. Kreps summarized the choices in a more recent statement before the same committee; the two questions, she notes, are, "one, how much of your growth would you take in the form of leisure as opposed to taking it in more goods and services? And two, how would you have the leisure distributed through the life cycle?"[19]

Need for New Values in a Flexible Life-Style

Noone has analyzed the technological society and its values more succinctly than Jacques Ellul, the French sociologist-lawyer-theologian. The given world that has befallen us is the technological society, *La Technique,*[20] which has always been present to some degree even in primitive and preindustrial society; but, in former eras, it existed in only narrow and limited areas, among men who had little time to devote to techniques, and in societies where there were other, more comprehensive values. Now, writes Ellul, the technological society is characterized by *automism,* so that man accepts the mechanical as superior to the nonmechanical; by *self-augmentation,* in which anonymous accretion of invention replaces the inventive genius, and by *monism.* With monism, writes Ellul, technical phenomena become a whole. No one element can be grasped in isolation. The whole is objective, having no end: technique creates the automobile but does not define its precise use; no "purpose" or "plan" is progressively realized with the new combinations of techniques. "There is not even a tendency toward human ends." The phenomena is "blind to the future," with no internal or inherent goal. The only choice man has is to use it according to technical rules or not at all. Techniques are not to be confused with machines (as Lewis Mumford has done), so that an army of men illustrates the principle of technical monism with a relation to efficiency, not to ideals. Indeed, the destructive possibilities are preferred by the state and are far simpler to evolve for criteria of efficiency, as in the use of atomic energy.

This tendency will become stronger, especially through the agency of the state. State and technique "buttress and reinforce each other in their aim to produce an apparently indestructible, total civilization."

In the milieu described by Ellul, work by the person is not necessarily the ideal; he is talking of the acceptance of expanded appetite for things. If we assume that the mission of the humanistic community is to attempt to break through such a technological Frankenstein, one of its issues for discussion must be, first, the relation of man to productive process (to *things*), and second, of man to man (to *humanistic values*).

Ellul apparently thinks that humanistic values can replace man's present obsession with the materialistic, technological, value-free world. As American sociologist Robert A. Nisbet emphasizes,[21] the French critic is also a theologian and is not to be confused—as he appears to be by the American left—with other technophobes. This point is verified by John Wilkinson, who translated *The Technological Society* into English and who emphasizes the religious nature of Ellul's solution. In this regard, Ellul shares common ground with Pitirim Sorokin, Arnold Toynbee, and Oswald Spengler, much as he differs in his analysis.

For us, the question takes on a new form: it is whether the new elements of leisure, which to a large extent grow out of the new techniques, can become the link between the preindustrial and the postindustrial?

Ellul has some observations about leisure. First, he states the case for leisure as a source of humanistic values as seen by its proponents: by "Christian employers" who hold that through leisure the worker can regain a personal life and psychic equilibrium; by sociologists who want maximum conditions for self-development through reduction of work hours; or by technicians of labor, such as Georges Friedmann, the eminent French industrial sociologist, who had concluded, "In a leisure more and more full of potentialities, and more and more active, will be found the justification of the humanistic experiment."

Not so to any of them, replies Ellul. Leisure itself is no different from the environment in which it finds itself. On the contrary, it is "literally stuffed with technical mechanisms of compensation and integration."[22] It is not free time, but "mechanized" time, exploited by techniques and as exploitative as work itself. We see the evidence of all this when modern man is left alone; he has been molded and adapted. The creative persons and gardners are only a fraction of those who, free of work, do nothing. The melancholy fact, Ellul concludes, "is that the human personality has been almost wholly disassociated and dissolved through mechanization."

Yet it may be that *the major potential impact of cybernation may well be to create the favorable work psychology and structure of the preindustrial society.* In the preindustrial structure or rural work structure, no matter how long the hours, the worker was free of major work characteristics of our own time. He was free of the complex structure of the contemporary plant symbolized by the time clock, in which every worker depends on the presence and productivity of others. This reaches its climax in the assembly line but is evident in all plants of any size. He depends on the structure and it depends on him; this is hailed as a value by the company in the name of loyalty and identity. In the case of business, the young executive is evaluated in good part by his —and his wife's—allegiance to this value. The emphasis is consciously as much on the work *group* as on the work *content.* However, when the work itself becomes impersonal, its social structure is also in danger of becoming diluted. An example is sometimes seen in those offices (governmental or private) where there is evidently no regard or commitment to the tasks that are to be done, and the morale is low. I have observed this in rehearsals of symphony orchestras, where the *esprit de corps* went down with a poorer conductor, and accordingly, a lower level of work resulted. A striking illustration comes from a report in *Fortune* for August 1970. Absenteeism in the Baltimore plant of GM has gone up from 3 to 7.5 percent in the past four years. About 5 percent of the hourly workers are out every day. On Mondays and Fridays, says Judson Gooding, the rate of absence is twice that. Tardiness has increased. "The deep dislike of the job and the desire to escape become terribly clear twice each day when shifts end and the men stampede out of the plant gates to the parking lots . . . some assembly line workers are so turned off, managers report with astonishment, they just walk away in mid-shift and don't even come back to get their pay for the time they have worked. . . ."

Of course, the "astonished" managers enjoy their own jobs; they are not bored, as are the assembly-line group. Nor are they in a work slot comparable to a "jail-cell."

"They (the managers) don't have to put up with the boss, the foreman or the office manager, those names which stand for constraint, compulsion and social discipline in our society. It's not just the hippie communards who've aspired to independence; it's every guy who's wanted to be his own boss and tried and failed by sod busting in Oklahoma or by running a gas station by the side of an Interstate. For a lot of people the difference between a good job and a rotten one that deprives a man of his pride is whether he has to punch a time card, whether he must take his coffee breaks at a prescribed time, whether he'll be questioned about too many trips to the toilet."[23]

Indeed, the managers have lost their hold on management. The computer, which came into full view about 1950, began to free man's mind and energy from clerical and management tasks; these machines produce things directly, but they began to supervise, monitor, control, and prepare inventories. The men who created, understood, or programmed these machines quickly became a new breed in business and industry. As Toffler notes—solid-state physicists, operation researchers, and engineering specialists—men are assuming a new decision-making function. Whereas in the past they merely consulted with executives who were responsible for decisions, now the managers do not know enough to run the plant or the business.

From the employer's point of view, there are unique advantages to all of this. First, he has employees whose life-styles are not subordinated to work, but for whom work is only one element in a larger range of commitments. Now this work and his leisure are more and more arranged in the sequences *he* wants, and he will give the *best* of work hours to his employers. The labor unions will require a new point of view as well. American unions have centered on purely economic concerns for their members, but now they find that this affluence confronts a basic shock of infiltration by machines; thus the unions must think through their functions in a potential postindustrial society. This is basically a society in which income (by present consuming standards) reaches $4000 per capita, in which abundance instead of scarcity becomes the prevailing reality, in which technology is controlled as well as accepted, theoretical knowledge of the university replaces materialism of the business community as the source of values, and internationalism assumes the central focus for increasing ranges of interests.

The flexible life-style is the outward form in which the elements of the post industrial order can find expression and can provide maximum conditions for both management and labor. I have already suggested an "hour bank" as only one approach in facilitating such life-styles. Its theory is based not on working "overtime," but in banking the extra *hours* instead of the earned money; the money that is earned—for the first four hours of work—is sufficient for all purposes of livelihood and even of savings. The hours, such as hour 5–8 of the day, are entered into a ledger. They can be redeemed at any time, now or 20 years from now, in either comparable money or in time. Let me illustrate with a simple case.

Let us say that a labor union has negotiated a 4-hour day, which amounts to 968 hours over an 8-hour-week workyear. Worker "A" is in a trade that currently pays $12,000 per year, $1000 per month, $240 per week, or $10 per hour. He chooses to work 8 hours every day; thus at the end of one year, he has either $12,000 or 968 hours in the bank. He can choose to leave these increments there for future withdrawal, and each draws "interest," that is 5 percent interest on 968 hours would be 48.4 hours. He can draw on his money at any time, just as he always has; to draw on his hours, he must give notice to his employer for such time ahead as the labor contract would stipulate, such as 30 to 60 days. After two years, assuming the same pattern continues, he would have 9680 hours plus 484 hours "interest," or a total of 10,164 hours saved. He could use these hours in approximately 10.5 years of "retirement," or any fraction thereof. He could return to school, travel, return to his job, or redeem some of his savings for a car or a second home.

Throughout all of this, the modern plan in money has not been violated or changed in the slightest. What has been added is a possibility of (1) breaking up the work period into a variety of patterns, or (2) retiring at a much earlier age.

The crucial question remains: if Worker A can work for $12,000 for a 4-hour day, by working 8 hours he essentially holds down two jobs for $24,000. If there is no "hour bank," as at present, what has he lost? When he has saved enough dollars, he can still retire earlier or take off on a trip. There are, however, several uniquenesses that enter the situation with the double alternative of money or hours.

1. The possibility of "borrowing" on hours is that the debt can be paid off by future work time, insured him by his present employer. The bank takes no more risk than it does now.
2. The possibility that the worker has of taking long periods of time off with the contractual assurance that he can go back to work.
3. A considerable morale benefit for the employer, knowing that his employees can take a break in their work when they are in psychological need of rest or a change of activity.
4. The possibility for the worker of adapting his time to the plans of his family, as for vacations or extended trips.
5. The possibility of early retirement, with the added increment that when an hour is taken in lieu of the $10—or whatever the prevailing wage scale—the hour has become inevitably worth *more* as the dollar goes *down* in value.

These advantages, especially the last, will not be immediately grasped by either employers or managers. Nor does this simple presentation lose sight of the numerous details that would have to be worked out, industry by industry.

The overall advantage of this plan is to combine the theory of the *guaranteed annual income* with that of *guaranteed flexibility of lifestyle.* If such a plan were experimented with, its success would depend largely on the self-education of labor, management, and government.

Another type of innovation is not aimed at banking or storing work hours for the future; the "flextime" pattern that began in 1967 in West Germany is now practiced by 150 companies there (half a million workers) and by 500 companies in other European countries. The advantage over the 10-hour day that comes with the four-day workweek is that under "flextime," as one writer describes the plan of the London and Manchester Assurance Company:[24]

"head office staff can skirt peak travelling hours, take short or extended lunch breaks, and fit in personal daytime appointments without having to fabricate a headache. The company's doors are open from 8 A.M. to 7 P.M. And provided that the staff are at their desks during the "core" time—ten A.M. to noon, and 3 P.M. to 4 P.M.—they can now flex their 35-hour week to mediate between their personal and work requirements. The hours worked are recorded and totalled on a four-weekly basis, with credits or debits of up to ten hours being carried over to the following month."

The demand of labor unions reflect the tastes and needs of their members; I suggest that it is the *bulk time* habits that will, in the future, play the large role in the old question as to which has the greater appeal, more leisure or more pay. Here, too, the worker of today has access to both, but the turning points in favor of leisure are several: (1) the worker's increasing experience in using bulk time, (2) improvements in transportation opportunities and comforts, and (3) the general instability and cynicism about the future in view of wars and other crises. An additional element, physical and emotional health, was illustrated recently by a Norwegian medical study that concluded that the five-day week "fails to provide a relaxing weekend and that people need longer vacations." The recommendation was made that the established legal vacation of one month should be lengthened to five weeks for workers over 40, six weeks for those over 50, and seven weeks for persons over 60.

We can, if we want to, work toward flexibility in work and nonwork patterns. However, the acceptance or rejection of creative visions are influenced by the values and the organization of our social system. It is to this subject we turn on our conceptual scheme.

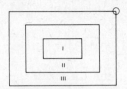

Chapter 13
The Social System

By treating leisure as an institution, we have two commitments in analysis: its internal organization and structure and its relationship to other systems of the society. Similarly, we can examine the church as an institution, even with the large variety of denominations, sects, or systems of belief. In leisure we also have a variety of subsystems. Sports is one subsystem, the use of the outdoors is another, and art is a third; the parameters of each are no more difficult to define than those of the Pillars of Fire, Jehovahs Witnesses or, indeed, the Catholic Church. If a critic of this approach to leisure is concerned with the impermanence, the transciency of many "fads" in leisure, we have in both the arts and sports as much tradition, as many religious bodies—as many heroes, saints, and sinners—and as many followers.

First, what is a social system? This, obviously, is a term that applies to a far wider range of analysis than leisure. It is distinct from the energy system, which is describable in respect to the production of wealth from the soil and manufacturing, or from the biological system, which sets the potentials and limits to our bodies. The social system deals primarily with the interrelations of man to man; it relates to the biological and energy systems in that our social system (class, as one example) may be influenced by the amount of material wealth or by the pigmentation of one's skin. But the wealth or skin color in itself has no meaning; the meaning comes from attitudes within the cultural system, including its social patterns and symbols.

In some ways we are each *born into* history and tradition as a part of the community, region, and nation. History is an abstraction, a collective memory that is employed differently to support social relationships, as different as the memories of the members of the Daughters of the American Revolution in America or of the sabra in Israel. Those groups have no contact with each other, because they belong to different cultures. Protestants and Catholics, on the other hand, often exist within the same culture and social system. No matter what the *origins* were of Catholic-Protestant struggles, the social reality is that children are born today, as in Ireland, to one or another of these groups with consequent implications to their friendships, marriages, attitudes, and street riots.

In some ways we can *choose* some elements that underlie the social system, such as the amount of education beyond the legal minimum, the religion that we adopt, or the social level of those we marry. For example, the nature of the work we choose is more than a way of maintaining ourselves. It opens and closes doors to various kinds of people, attitudes, and characteristic behavior, becoming a basic explanation of the social system in which we live.

In some ways we are in a given social system for no other reason than the *determination or definition of other persons;* this is the case of the "inauthentic Jew," to use Sartre's term, or of the black in America, or of women who—by the conceptualization of men instead of by any inherent incapacity—are denied high careers in arts, politics, or education.

These are several ways to become a member of a given social system: by birth, choice, as a by-product of our work, or by the will of others.

Each institution—*marital, economic, political, educational*—draws on human relationships in a different way and adds its own uniqueness to these relationships. Notice how quickly the men who have just been drinking together informally at a bar suddenly, as they convene in a "meeting" of Legionnaires, take on refined behavior—as president, secretary, treasurer; the man who only a few minutes ago came from chatting with his favorite newsboy puts on his robe and, as a judge, has the power to jail a proven murderer. The interests of the Legionnaires and of the law decidedly colored the type of conversation and action in these situations; conversely, antecedents of the social system had something to say about who is a Legionnaire, a chapter president, a judge, and a criminal. The tools of social science that are useful for observing these changes in relationship (before-during-after the meeting and the trial) are concepts applied systematically to a specific situation: social roles, communications, norms, and values.

In the discussion below, illustrations of roles, communications, and norms will be interwoven as they are applied to the leisure typology.

I hold no brief for the five major subsystems of leisure listed below: physical, intellectual, artistic, sociable, and practical. They are currently being employed in the comparative data of seven nations under Dumazedier's—and more recently—Prof. P. Bosserman's chairmanship.

The outline of subheadings under each in the present chapter are:

Typology
I. *Physical*
  A. Play
  B. Travel
II. *Intellectual*
  A. Understanding
  B. Production
III. *Artistic*
  A. Enjoyment
  B. Creation
IV. *Sociable*
  A. Communication
  B. Entertainment
V. *Practical*
  A. Collection
  B. Transformation

I. LEISURE SUBSYSTEM I–A: PHYSICAL PLAY

The two examples to be used here are opposites: one is fundamentally public and outside; the other is private and inside; the first can involve many persons, the second involves the smallest social group—the dyad. Although both have long histories, the first is generally held to be a leisure "good," the second is often condemned, in its leisure form, but continues to flourish. I speak of games and of sex.

Sports—Games

Games may hold their attraction precisely because the roles of players are often closely delineated. If anyone is unsure of his function in society as a whole, let him become a football quarterback, or a basketball guard, or a goalie in soccer. In each case his general function is clear, and precise observations can be made to evaluate how well he performs. Not only his success, but that of the whole group of players—if it is a team play—can be measured by its victories and defeats.

The game world is generally a conservative one. With minor variations, baseball is still the baseball I knew as a boy. Its roles, therefore, are so well ingrained and its inherent controls are so widely accepted that three strikes are an "out," whether the player is an Al Capone in Alcatraz, a Hank Aaron in Milwaukee, or a sandlotter anywhere.

The team, in sports and the arts, may have a "style" of its own, so that the role of the shortstop is not standardized, but it is still carried on within the general specification of how a shortstop differs in function from a second baseman. Deviations from this acceptable function can be accepted by the circle of players only to a point, even in an amateur or leisure framework. When the same role is performed professionally, as in Aaron's case, there are several trained umpires who are present to serve as authorities to interpret the rules and, in case of doubt, to pull out a rulebook for reference.

The satisfaction of games, in even the leisure context, is not to violate the rules or norms, but to see how successfully the roles of batter, pitcher, and so forth, can be played *within* the system of regulations. The amateur may be as proficient as the professional, but his role is executed more in the spirit of immediate satisfaction and fun and less in the professional spirit of accountability, commitment to win, and play for financial reward.

The communications among game players exists on two levels, the performance itself and the attitude or "spirit" that is brought into the situation. As to the first, there is no substantial difference between leisure (amateur) and work (professional) game playing: the communications are, in both cases, the vernacular and the symbolic. The former consists of cognitive exchange, "throw the ball," "serve the deck," "third down, four to go," which is understood by players and watchers alike; the latter is communication without words, such as advancing a base when the next player at bat hits a ball.

There is an important element of normative behavior in the game that is even more pronounced in leisure games and sports, especially when these are manifestations or symbols of class consciousness. This is the element of mannerism, as in the fox hunt. "Sportsmanship" is the watchword, with the emphasis on how the action takes place. In his well-known satire, *The Theory and Practice of Gamesmanship*, Stephan Potter instructs us on how to take advantage of the slogan, "the good gamesman is the good sportsman." He advises us that against a stupid but strong opponent who suspects you of being unsporting, "extreme sportingness" is the thing, and "the instant waiving of any rule which works in your favour is the procedure." But against the introvertive, cynical type, sportingness will simply be wasted.[1]

"Sportingness," seriously considered, is the set of values that have been brought into the play situation by such clichés as the "spirit is what counts, not the winning." The familiar argument that recreation for youth will keep them off the streets and reduce crime is usually advanced with an implied formative creation of "teamsmanship" (read as "citizenship") by virtue of the colleagueship or collective concern with the game. In this sense, those who argue for games as ethical articulations believe in some mystique of transference. It is somewhat odd that the same theory of transference is not admitted when we turn to the subject of extramarital sex: we do not say, at least publicly, that such sex as a form of leisure produces a human warmth that carries over to one's family life.

There is a second side to games and sports—the roles of spectators. The rise in their numbers in the United States is impressive for the past 20 years, as seen in the following table from the *1970 Statistical Abstract of the U.S.A.*

TABLE 21
Rise in spectators to sports events: 1950–1969[2]

Activity	Unit	1950	1960	1969
Major league baseball	1000	17,659	20,261	27,498
Professional basketball	1000	NA	1,981	4,427
College football	1000	18,962	20,403	27,626
Professional football	1000	2,008	4,153	9,334
Professional boxing	1000	3,800	5,902	8,110
Horseracing	1000	29,291	46,887	68,099

[a] NA – Not Available.

These rises in spectatorship did not reduce the numbers of participants in games and sports. For instance, while attendance at professional baseball went up in the two decades from about 17.5 to 27.5 million, participation in amateur softball went up from 8 to 19 million in the last decade alone; and the number of golfers grew from 3.25 to 9.5 million from 1950 to 1969. Nor must we forget the additional millions who watch all of these spectacles on television or listen to radio accounts.

We are dealing, obviously, both in the United States and in other nations, with a significant phenomena. The leisure of a Brooklyn may, in the standings of the Mets, affect the mood of the populace as much as war victories affected Sparta of old. The impact of sports on the life patterns of families during the TV schedules of football was illustrated several years ago by the many complaints when the network had the temerity to start a special production of "Cinderella" before the game had finished. Cities such as Green Bay are known nationally only for the team that represents them. In Europe, soccer occupies a similar status and, if anything, attracts even a higher interest in sports, sometimes to the point of spilling over into international politics.

The role of the sports enthusiastic "fan" or follower is far from passive and gives us more evidence that the active-passive dichotomy is useless. His moods alter with the fortunes of the teams he supports. "*We* won today"—not a paid team of workers who are hired by a firm in the business of making money from baseball or football; neither management nor team usually have the slightest interest in the community, and members of the team are bought and sold purely as business investments. But the image of the team remains as an ongoing symbol to the public, with individual heroes who emerge now and then to lend aura and enlarge this world of worship, myth, and fantasy.

The practice of gambling on teams and on such sports as horseraces hardly gets into official estimates of expenditures on leisure, but serves to lock people into a deeper commitment as active publics.

Finally, Dumazedier has spoken of fantasies that are played out in leisure, such as the amateurish guitar player who hears himself as Segovia. This probably occurs as frequently in sports as in the arts. Indeed, except for the business aspect of professional sports (which includes a large coverage in special journals and in the daily press) the roles played by publics are substantially fantasy roles. An artificial competition is concocted between artificial teams (i.e., with no generic homogeneity) *as if* the end result—who wins today, or at the end of the season—will change the course of history. Because this fantasy is heavily institutionalized with its symbols, its officialdom, its rules and traditions, and its characteristic dress and speech, it becomes the whole, real world to many persons.

But to describe this as a world of fantasy is to speak as observers; it is acted on and altogether becomes a reality in relation to other portions of the person's life. Leisure, for such a person, is not a peripheral element; the Packer fan is most alive during the season; if he is unable to turn with equal fervor to other sports fantasies, he finds that the rest of the year is simply an interlude. For him sports is an end, and he knows its regulations, its scores, its great figures, and its history as well as he knows his religious books and rituals.

Nevertheless, the social system of this reality is unique only in its emphases, not its independence. The roles of amateur players and publics relate, for instance, to conditions of leisure laid out in Chapter 4. There must be time, health, and the community in which the games are played or the mass media over which the vicarious experience is attained. The fantasy aspect of the game has permitted leakages in the nonplay social system, so that black men found the game to be the single most accessible route to fame and wealth among the white publics. Furthermore, the artificial rules of the game are stronger and more universal than the rules of human relationships: no Supreme Court decision was ever needed to declare the three-out policy for baseball among players of all races!

In another form of attachment to a physical type of leisure, sex, only direct participants are involved.

Sex as Leisure

The common attitude, after Christianity dominated the discussion, was to treat sex as instrumental to childbearing. In that sense, the discussion properly fell into the family as an institution. This is less so, as sex and sin became psychologically divorced, and as sex and pleasure were becoming synonomous. A great deal of sex takes place—it always has—outside of the married couple's bedroom, and its primary purpose is not to procreate. It is a leisure activity-experience by any standard.

Sex experience, in or out of the family, represents the ethos of its time. One hears today that old morality is crumbling, with such extreme examples as commune living and "wife-swapping." The most basic biological and social roles are the stuff of sex—maleness and femaleness. Indeed, familiar sex-marital categories such as single-married-divorced are decreasingly viable—the subculture, for example, of the "formerly married." In Denmark a bill has been introduced to allow group marriage. It is widely known in Florida, which leads the nation in its proportion of retirees, that many unmarried elderly couples live together to overcome regulations of social security; according to studies, sex does not disappear in such cases.

The norms of the relationship in sex are reflections of the culture, the group, or subculture of population within the culture, the personal tastes or sexual vocabularies of participants, and the degree of commercialism that may be present.

In prostitution we have an unusual role relationship, because one of the partners is at work. In most games—such as golf or baseball—where professionals are involved, they are paid to entertain a public. The communications of sex, as a whole, rely more on gestures that symbolize various phases of the "game" than on words. These cover such matters as behavior before and after the sex act, the length and intensity of the act itself, deviations from the traditions as known in that milieu, and the attitude toward oneself as a person that Znaniecki considered a basic aspect of role.

Price alone dictates a relationship of prostitution to social class and income levels. The 4000 prostitutes in New York City subdivide themselves. The "call girl" commands $50 for a half-hour of her time, and as high as $1000 for a "bachelor party" or orgy. Lower in the pattern are the 40–50-year-old women ("dumpers"), heroin addicts, and girls in the $10, $15, and $25 "trick houses."[3]

This form of leisure for men, more than any other in modern times, is the target of the law. Gambling, in contrast, is far more widely practiced and condoned by all levels of population and officialdom; its difficulties do not spring from the inherent nature of gambling, but from its close associations with crime and bribery in high places. Some states, like New Hampshire and New York, decided to legalize the lottery and use the money for educational purposes. No one has yet suggested this for prostitution. European bawdy houses in past centuries were erected beyond the boundaries of cities, although not far from the walls. A solution of sorts was achieved by the Nazis, who simply shipped undesirable women of this profession to concentration camps; the official class, as Bassermann notes, "did not need professional harlots . . . they helped themselves by direct application to the various Leagues of women and girls."[4] Today, in the United States and in European nations, the system for meeting the sex needs of men outside wedlock as a leisure pursuit is decentralized, permeating all parts of the community. With the "new morality," lines between amateur and professional relationships are more and more difficult to define and legislate; one is no more conspicuous, harmful, or beneficial than the other. Upper classes, government officials, businessmen, and the military have always exercised this leisure pursuit away from home with both amateurs and professionals. Its professional aspects have "lost all meaning" as an "abject and disreputable trade."[5]

SUBSYSTEM I-B: PHYSICAL TRAVEL

As part of the social system of leisure, tourism has been the most important of the physical activities. Restlessness, of which I spoke in Chapter 6, combined with the impact of TV, has created an industry and a way of life that has penetrated leisure, as it has migration in jobs and places of residence. Tourism, pleasure travel, nomadism—or whatever its name—is contrary to social stability; this is the chief social effect of this type of leisure; it is also the chief result of new forms of energy, and was the chief leisure victim with the "energy crisis." As long as the land remained man's chief source of maintenance, travel was limited, rootedness and stability were dominant. Leisure, especially in the use of bulk time, was made possible by production of goods by industry; in turn, as the appetite for more time is fed by trips away from home, home itself becomes a weaker social and psychological force. Ongoing migration from the farm to the city is a revolution in work and energy; the subsequent migration from the city to the country is the pastime not of workers but of gentlemen whose work is sufficiently dispensable. Fishing for food is quite different from fishing for fun and symbolizes several centuries of social change. Perhaps 21 million Americans per year will leave the country for many leisure motivations in the early years of the 1970s. Barring wars or continuing inflation, this number is bound to rise.

The dichotomy of outside-inside is a fundamental one to leisure with the car and the TV set as their respective instruments; but the car has not only taken space for conversion to highways, it has also created a demand for special spaces to get to, such as the national parks. Sixty years ago the American covered about 1600 miles per year, including all of his walking; today he may travel 100 times that with his car alone. The miles we drive as a nation have multiplied six times faster than our population in the past 25 years.

The role of the amateur traveler stands in contrast to such professional travelers as missionaries, businessmen, soldiers, educators, government officials, airplane or train crews, bus drivers, and the like. These all have roles in travel that are relatively clear to themselves, their work circles at home, and generally to those whom they approach. What of the tourist? Is he in a foreign land to see, to study, to compare, to escape, to brag, to buy, to be excited, to consider moving his residence? His own motivations are often unclear to himself, but find expression in such phrases as "liking to travel," "see new places," "I've always wanted to," or "change from the familiar." The nature of his role, to himself, is that he is here today and gone tomorrow. There are two types of roles, as I pointed out in an earlier writing:[6] that of the "comparative stranger," who leaves home only in body, and that of the "empathic native," who takes only universals from his own background as he sincerely tries to perceive and to understand other cultures. In either case, however, the tourist stands to gain: if he looks at poverty in India, he takes color slides of bodies lying on the street in the full knowledge that he will soon leave and be back in his American (or West German, or English) home. If he is an understanding traveler, he finds more and more people who will go along with him on the next trip or who will watch his slides.

Less familiar is the issue of the traveler in Georg Simmels' view, "who comes today and stays tomorrow, the potential wanderer, so to speak, who, although he has gone no further, has not quite got over the freedom of coming and going."[7] He speaks here of the person who is a relative stranger who—like the American businessman or soldier in West Germany—represents the union of nearness and remoteness. He has fixed himself in the new environment, but he is not accepted as a permanent emigré; for instance, he does not own land; he can be expected to possess a certain "objectivity," which combines concern and indifference, but does not necessarily negate sympathy; he may become a confidant, since we sometimes disclose our inner thoughts to strangers; he is relatively free of local conventions, submitting them to "more general, more objective standards, and is not confined in his action by custom, piety, or precedents."[8]

These observations of Simmel are more apt for our time, 50 years later, because with the mobility of residential patterns, there are millions of us who have moved to communities far from our first homes, and even to far-off areas that we adopt as permanent or temporary home.

SUBSYSTEM II-A: INTELLECTUAL UNDERSTANDING

One conclusion from the 12-nation study of leisure is the considerable number of adults in the world who spend a portion of their free time studying. We will assume here that study includes the elements of some prolonged period of time, generally (not always) some guidance or teaching, and some unity in subject matter. This construction ignores subject matter, because anything may qualify.

The role that applies is that of *student*. Age, of course, is of no relevance, nor the presence of books, laboratory equipment, or other academic symbols or equipment: one may study the life of ants in the field. The process of studying may include writing, as in the preparation of a seminar paper. But to distinguish studying from the category below, creating, I will assume that studying rests primarily on receiving knowledge, whereas creating emphasizes its production or discovery.

The role of student implies a teacher only in a manner of speech. Even in the traditional class situation the teacher as a person has given way to situations in which there are supplementations—the library of books, TV cameras, movie projectors, programmed learning machines, and so on. The teacher, in the general thrust of contemporary education, moves into the role of resource person, colleague with a team-teaching concept, and a copupil with the student. If we think of a *professional* relationship between student and teacher, the ideal, in lip service at least, has always been that of the *amateur* learning process. That is, the amateur spirit is the ideal in such a model as the folk high school of the Scandinavian countries. In that model the adult students decide to band together to study whatever is of interest to them; they then have access to a teacher who is made available by a central education office of resource centers.

The ideal of amateur study for the adult is understandable. He starts with a strong motivation to learn; he proceeds at his own pace; he may join with others interested in similar subject matter; he brings to his new action a life time of experience; his approach to his teacher, if there is one, is not of a captive student but of a voluntary devotee. He may be sitting at home, preparing his assignment for a course in social problems, reading books, writing short stories, painting, or comparing political doctrines. . . . I have watched Professor Jim Schwalbach of the extension Division of the University of Wisconsin address an outdoor group in a small resort town, pointing to pictures on display outside of a hardware store, offering his judgment of the canvasses painted by amateurs of the area. In Copenhagen I spent an evening with 22 men and women in an elementary school; they were listening to Strauss' "Elektra" on records, with explanations by an opera singer who had arranged for the class to attend a performance in southern Sweden the following week.

Czechoslovakia has developed a comprehensive program to train adult educators in a plan called the Standard System. Begun in 1962, a large variety of opportunities are provided in general adult education, popular arts, public libraries, museums and local history, and the care of historical monuments.[9] Opportunities are also given to trained volunteers to work with professional teachers.

One of the monumental examples of free time devoted to acquiring literacy was the Russian experience after 1917. For example, between 1927 and 1937 the number of illiterates and semiilliterates who received systematic instruction rose from 1.5 to almost 8.5 million. Many graduates from schools for literacy entered secondary schools for adults called Facilities for Workers, with the purpose of preparing working class people for college work. These, according to A. M. Ivanova of the Academy of Pedagogical Sciences, played an important part in the development of Soviet intellectuals.[10]

Basic education for adults—to provide the tools for literacy—is the great need and the present thrust of adult education in the so-called underdeveloped countries of the world, and it explains in good part the active interest of those regions in leisure planning and trends.

In the United States as well, full and semiilliterates have also become the core of constructive leisure programs. A recent summary of ABE (Adult Basic Education) indicated that in early 1968, of 400,000 adults enrolled, three fifths lived in urban areas and had incomes of less than $3000 per year.[11] Obtaining new or better jobs was the motivation in only one third of the cases; most persons wanted to improve themselves. The typical student (over 56 percent) was white and female; 55 percent had a job. Over 46 percent were between 24 and 44 years of age. There was about an equal proportion of adults in the various educational levels, 1–3 grades, 4–6, and 6–8 grades. This $30 million program is a partial answer to those who ask whether leisure has pertinence to poor persons. Nine federal agencies, in addition to the U.S. Office of Education, have administered programs for undereducated adults; these include the Office of Economic Opportunity, the Bureau of Indian Affairs, the Air Force, the Veterans Administration, the Immigration and Naturalization Service, the Bureau of Prisons, and the Department of Labor through its Manpower Development and Training Program (50,000 trainees in 1967).

In sum, the social system of the "amateur specialist" in education is closely related to the social system of the fulltime student. The circle of the latter is more structured, since it is a school for full-time students. The association in the school for adults can be more honest in that adults are free of the need often seen among young people to prove themselves, to compete and, consequently, to show less than their best. The major similarity is in the social role. There is no amateur approach to Plato or Shakespeare. There are, to be sure, differences in commitment created by conditions such as time. But the wisdom of these thinkers is indivisible, and the leisure pursuit of each permits of sincerity, commitment, and personal growth.

SUBSYSTEM II-B: INTELLECTUAL PRODUCTION

The characteristic of intellectual creativity within the leisure situation is relative isolation. In this sense it comes close to the creative process in the professional community. Nor is the actual doing different in quality between the two spheres: the serious amatuer who writes his first novel goes through substantially the same process as a craftsman; lacking the time or experience of the professional, he may not be as skillful. But not being responsible to a public to cultivate its financial support, the amateur benefits from a freedom to move in his own directions. For this reason, the first novel of new writers is often their best. Eric Hoffer, the philosopher and former longshoreman, has maintained his freedom of thought in a succession of volumes by disassociating himself from "intellectuals," of which he is himself one; even then, his chief contribution is his first essay, *The True Believer.*[12]

The norms that direct serious leisure intellectual activity are precisely those that dominate the professional scholar in the university—the search for truth, the canons of rational thought, a knowledge of what others in the field are doing, and so forth—but what distinguishes the amateur philosopher, novelist, poet, or scientist is that his preoccupation *may* persist over time and end in a contribution, but it *need* not: no career is involved, no basis for supporting one's family, and especially, no hard judgment is awaiting from one's professional colleagues.

The question remains, is the realization of this goal the indicator of most value to the observer of leisure? Here we go back to the various conceptions of leisure noted in Chapter 1. Those who subscribe to the Hellenic approach, stretching in its proponents from Aristotle to de Grazia, would agree with this general statement of goals. As de Grazia writes:

"Felicity, happiness, blessedness. Certainly the life of leisure is the life for thinkers, artists, and musicians. Many of the great ones, though seldom attaining it, have throughout their lives given signs of their passion for it. Throughout their biographies runs an attempt to get more free air than the surrounding atmosphere held for them. For that matter, though none of us may ever have been able to live this way, most of us, too, perhaps, have had moments when we felt close enough to get glimpses of a truth—that could we have more of the way of life, we would also have more of the truth."[13]

SUBSYSTEM III-A: ARTISTIC ENJOYMENT

Four major subdivisions of the arts as a social process are: creators, distributors, publics, and educators. Here we will look at the members of publics and those creators who perform this role within the leisure sphere. Table 22 is a summary of performances from 1955 to 1972. It indicates that in the 17-year interval, the number of Broadway shows did not increase substantially, and opera performances went up, as did the number of concerts by symphony orchestras; expenditures for concerts went up from less than $14 million to well over $70 million.

Toffler, in 1964,[14] estimated that 35.5 million Americans play an instrument and 40 million try their hand at amateur painting now and then. He concludes that *30–45 million* (out of 185 million total when he wrote) may be classified as "cultured" persons; that is, they listen to classical music, attend concerts, plays, operas, dance recitals, attend

TABLE 22

Performing arts—selected data, 1955–1972[15] (For season ending in year shown, except as indicated)

Item	1955	1960	1965	1967	1968	1969	1970	1971	1972
Theater, legitimate, New York City[b]									
Broadway shows	72	76	77	82	87	80	76	68	78
New productions	58	58	67	69	73	67	62	45	53
Performances	8,917	9,214	10,000	10,152	10,056	9,672	6,865	9,427	9,650
Off Broadway shows	41	114	86	91	79	99	106	126	111
New productions	41	100	75	80	77	118	88	110	94
Performances	1,883	6,803	6,637	6,326	5,140	5,828	8,819	7,227	7,143
Opera companies[c]	543	754	732	918	622	623	648	685	715
Performances	3,217	4,232	4,176	5,487	5,222	4,629	4,779	5,246	5,723
Orchestras[d]									
Symphony	1,029	1,226	1,385	(NA)[a]	1,441	1,441	1,441	1,450	1,463
College	240	250	290	(NA)[a]	298	298	298	300	300
Community	761	933	1,032	(NA)[a]	1,020	1,021	1,021	1,023	1,023
Urban	(e)	(e)	(e)	31	36	31	24	22	31
Metropolitan	(f)	18	38	48	59	63	72	76	81
Major	28	25	25	28	28	28	28	28	28
Musicians	2,079	(NA)	2,216	2,465[9]	2,396[b]	2,512[9]	2,513	2,539	2,521
Concert played	2,257	(NA)	2,987	3,658[9]	3,984[b]	3,976[9]	4,349	4,508	4,487[i]
Attendance 1000	4,900	(NA)	6,750	8,303[j]	8,229[h]	8,176[9]	9,020	10,587	10,702[k]
Gross expenditures $1000	13,888	(NA)	27,700	41,245	46,123[9]	51,746[9]	58,753	66,269	70,749

Source Except as noted 1955–1965, William J. Baumol and William G. Bowen, *Performing Arts—The Economic Dilemma* copyright, 1966 by the Twentieth Century Fund, Inc., New York)) thereafter, supplied by Mathematica, Inc., Princeton, N.J.

[a]NA.–Not Available.

[b]Through 1970, comprises new musicals and plays, revivals, special productions and presentation of special companies and visiting foreign troupes. Beginning 1971, data from New York Times, *Closing the Record Book*, annual; excludes presentations of foreign troupes.

[c]Comprises high school, college, other amateur, and professional companies. Beginning 1971, data from Central Opera Service, New York, N.Y., *Directory of American Opera Producing Organizations*.

[d]Source: American Symphony Orchestra League, Inc., Vienna, Va. For years ending Aug. 31. Orchestras other than college are principally defined by their annual budgets: Community, $100,000 prior to 1967, $50,000 thereafter; urban, $50,000–$99,999; metropolitan, $100,000–$500,000. Metropolitan includes a few orchestras operating on budgets over $500,000.

[e] Classification began in 1967.   [f] Classification began in 1958.   [9] 27 orchestras reporting.   [h] 26 orchestras reporting.

[i] Includes 899 ensemble performances by orchestra member players under the orchestras' auspices.

[j] 25 orchestras reporting.

[k]Includes 574,000 attending the 899 ensemble performances shown in footnote i.

305

museums or galleries, read about the arts, or participate in any of the arts as amateurs. He includes the millions of children in school or home who consume the arts. This comes to between 15 and 25 percent of the total population. In 1970 terms, with the present population of 205 million, Toffler's estimate would come to bring these numbers up to 32 to 51 million.

The state of the arts is, indeed, crucial to an assessment of any culture and to the observation of innovations and directions of the culture; for the United States, especially in relation to its future impact on other cultures, the arts deserve closer attention than they have been accorded among social sciences. These observations cannot overlook the importance of artistic life in the schools and colleges or on the amateur level of communities.

SUBSYSTEM III-B: ARTISTIC CREATION

Differences between the amateur and the professional have already been suggested. The force of the school arts program has been its emphasis on "general" music and art, that is, treating them as subject areas that contribute to the growth of the person instead of as preparation for a career.

In the adult level, the arts, including creative writing, are favorite preoccupations among the 18 million or more in the United States alone who pursue some form of weekly adult education. In 1960 Carol Pierson and I had occasion to carry out a national survey of adult education and discovered that experiences in creating were being provided under many sponsorships, including business, industry, labor unions, high schools, colleges and universities, many forms of summer workshops and institutes, governmental agencies (federal, state, municipal), settlement houses, community centers, churches, nursing homes, libraries, art galleries and museums, and correspondence schools (such as Famous Writers).[16] To take only a few instances, the Toledo Museum of Art offers adult classes in design, drawing, painting, crafts, ceramics, sculpture, and graphics—and art history and appreciation; the museum also holds free music classes and concerts, a circulating library of records, books, and thousands of colored slides on art.

The amateur creator has, in fact, never enjoyed the advantages that he enjoys today. In almost every community he has orchestras to play with, theater groups to act in, and exhibitions to display his pictures. Counts of symphony orchestras generally go into more than 1400 and, in many of these, there are combinations of professionals and amateurs.

SUBSYSTEM IV-A: SOCIABLE COMMUNICATION

The purest example of sociable communication is that of two persons in face-to-face conversation; the use of a telephone to master distance is already one step removed, but nevertheless more direct than a written relationship.

A "sociable" communication is not one that revolves around work, domestic chores, or such functional relationship as clerk-customer, teacher-student, judge-lawyer, or policeman-speeder. We refer, instead, to a relationship that manifests the nature of leisure itself, that is, a self-determined communication that is seen as sociable by the participants themselves, that is psychologically pleasant, that can be frivolous or entirely serious, that exhibits characteristic norms and restraints, and can move in the direction of simple recreation, of personal growth, or of service to others. It is, of course, possible to engage in sociable conversation even during a work period. Leisure is not a limited, self-defined activity, and no better illustration of this can be found than the subsystem of communication.

There are two forms. One is the so-called communications of the mass media. Motion pictures, radio, television, and written materials (magazines, newspapers, books) are *unications;* they lack the element of "com," or *with.* These all fall more properly under entertainment and are discussed there. The other form is the writing of letters; such activity, aside from letters or parts of letters that are utilitarian (such as those for business), fall into the leisure institution as a whole and, among many persons in all literate societies, consume a noticeable period of time.

It would seem that the general pace of urban life leaves less time for letter writing, but we have no evidence for this. Indeed, postal mailings go up by the decade. The crucial item would not be the quantity but something closer to intent, mood, and the pace of writing. For instance, the Korean and Vietnam wars have meant separations of sons and friends, and correspondence has followed. Our general mobility as a people, even in peacetime, has also necessitated letter writing; another factor is the increasing number of sons and daughters in colleges and universities away from home.

If the time spent in communicating by letters may, indeed, go up with the kind of life we lead, the same may hold true for oral communications. A central factor may be our increased urbanization, with people living and working together. Affecting the matter is the amount of free time we spend in watching TV, which limits conversation in the room and travel by car away from home. There are many problems here that suggest closer analysis and research: classifications on types of conversations, lengths, degree of the thematic development, and so on. There is the additional problem of "extension," by which television seems to limit conversation during the program, but may subsequently provide topics for conversation *about* the preceding program. A still more difficult research problem was faced by Szalai and his associates, who recognized that we often do two or more things simultaneously: one or both may be in the realm of leisure and the other, something else (talking while punching a press at work). This research group settled for a tabulation of primary and secondary activity, with primary as the activity that was mentioned first. Maria Lazar of Bucharest has been working with three simultaneous actions.

In spite of these problems in methodology, several generalizations may be considered.

1. *Oral communication is both the simplest and the most difficult of leisure subsystems.* It is simple, as made evident by the millions of persons everywhere in the world who at this very moment in time are engaged in talking for no utilitarian purpose—in twos, threes, or larger groups, in homes, on streets, in pubs, in village squares, on park benches, in street cars and buses—simple, because it is a "natural" thing to do, to pass the moment, ease the trip, find a response, comment on something or other, overcome one's loneliness, or make one's opinion heard.

It is difficult because of the problem some persons have in maintaining or developing a theme of conversation, or a fear of becoming involved with others, of feeling insecure in discussion, of hesitation in revealing one's opinion when controversial subjects enter the conversation, of revealing ourselves as unknowledgeable, or of saying the wrong thing.

Closely related to sociality is its facilitation or lubrication through the use of alcohol. Alcoholism frequently goes to excess, as seen in the huge number, perhaps over 10 million in the United States alone who are confirmed, pathological alcoholics. Because of its acceptance as an integral part of the social scene among the most respectable circles of every community, there is a refusal by the culture to admit that the problem exists, even in the face of the indictment of marijuana heard by the same establishment quarters that nurture alcoholic drinking. But social drinking in excess plagues many societies today, such as the Yugoslavs. It is safe to say that any *examination of leisure as a social form of exchange cannot ignore alcohol and alcoholism in the forefront of concerns for private counselling and rehabilitation as well as for public policy.*

2. *Oral communication as a subsociable system in leisure is a clue to the general social systems of class, religion, family roles, and work.* Here we come again to the closeness of leisure to all aspects of life. Hence the somewhat tautological character, remindful of *Proposition 18* in Chapter 3. Social class and other divisions have much to say about who communicates with whom and, in turn, these divisions are reinforced by the communications. But this truism only supports the view that this form or subsystem of leisure, perhaps more even than the other subsystems already discussed, is one of our best clues in understanding the total society. The reason for this is that the two or more parties to a conversation confront each other as people, even more than if they happen to occupy the same train or to fish in the same stream.

SUBSYSTEM IV-B: SOCIABLE ENTERTAINMENT

The entertainer does respond in part to his audience, but fundamentally it is a one-way communication; no serious violinist would cut Bach's "Chaconne" in half because of a restless audience. Thus there is an historical social system that affects the roles of the performers; for example, they are generally classless (*entre tenir*—to be held between). There is a social system that, as in the price of a ticket, controls who can become a member of the audience. But the dynamic of the theater performance, unlike that of the dinner party, is less directly related to the norms and roles of the present. In a controlled society, the censor has already insured that no political applecart will be upset; in our society we rate our movies on a scale of potential moral disturbance, and are free to ignore the "X" movies. The television show goes into every home, so that sponsors go far out of their way to offend no one. In these ways our entertainment is prepared with normative values in mind, and the public views it from its unique background and bias. TV requires the least effort in preparation and is therefore prepared for a mass common denominator. As the proportion of two TV set owners rises (it is already over 60 percent) the industry may move toward pinpointing its programs, thus recognizing the divisions of sex, age, and taste within the family. An even more direct reflection of the roles and values of the family is imminent in the selection of TV programs with the emergence of casette and taped systems.

SUBSYSTEM V-A: PRACTICAL COLLECTION

The term "practical" refers to that which is useful, workable, and immediate as distinct from "theoretical." At the end of leisure that is practical we have something to show for it. This is one motivation for the hobby of collecting. Indeed, a significant effort and expense goes into the collection of stamps, coins, dolls, beer mugs, buttons, bottles, rare books, spoons, antiques, baseball cards, paintings, figurines, greetings from other ham operators, autographs of notables, rocks and stones, shells, bells, old cars, phonograph records, hunting trophies, gems, and chess sets.

In many cases, as among coin and stamp collectors, there exists a well-understood set of norms; there are conferences, exhibitions, journals, experts, foibles, fables, and personal friendships based on common interests. Some collections, such as baseball cards, are important to young boys; some, such as antiques, appeal more to older women. Collection has a long history; in its most sophisticated form we find that art museums go back to the Romans, when Marcus Agrippa, deploring the dispersion of many works of art to country villas of the rich, urged a public policy for showing of pictures and statues.[17]

Leisurely looking at collections, as well as the critical examination by experts, became at an early stage—as it remains today—a mixture of motives, from pure pleasure to a concern with the economic "cost" of artistic work.

Eventually, under the influence of the humanists, art works became a source of insight into the culture of their origins, and it is on this dual level that a genuine tradition of art collections has affected leisure: (1) art as a source of personal pleasure and (2) art as a commentary about artists and their times. In the first sense, leisure exists through art in the Hellenic sense noted in Chapter 1 as an end that needs no further justification; art as social commentary or sociological clue is instrumental. Vasari, Alois Riegl, and Heinrich Wofflin were analysts of the second.

The amateur collector, the *dilettante,* developed among the middle classes in the sixteenth and seventeenth centuries, but the public museum as we know it came in the eighteenth century. The Louvre, for example, became nationalized in 1793 when it was converted to the Museum of the Republic by the revolutionary government; the National Gallery of London began in 1824, and the National Gallery in Washington in 1937.

The revolution in museology in recent decades has been to make of such institutions a potent educational force, above the original function of collecting, preserving and displaying. In the process their range in content has also expanded to include folk arts, archeology, prints, furniture, industrial design, special displays for children, concerts, lectures, extension services, classes, picture rentals, casette-guided tours, TV broadcasts, and publications. Among the foremost examples of the museum as educator for the masses is the Museum of Modern Art in New York; the Israeli Museum in Jerusalem provides a classic example of diverse styles and contents in a highly dramatic complex. The magnitudes of attendance to museums is seen in the following total for only one year taken from the UNESCO Statistical Yearbook for 1968 (Table 23).

Historic houses, private properties, and gardens have become additional resources for visitors.

The private collector—of anything, but including art objects—plays a relatively solitary role. This form of leisure may encompass other persons or it may not. The collector has no moral commitment to educate either himself or someone else; he may or may not communicate with other collectors; he may or may not follow traditions, whether in pursuing antiques of one culture or another. However, as a public client or devotee of the public collection, one's leisure hours are devoted to an historical role as lover of art and as participant in an open celebration or pageant. The collection has been brought together for him by professional persons, and a major attribute is not only that it *is* there for him to use, but the *awareness* of its presence, whether or not he actually uses it.

TABLE 23
Museum attendance in five countries—1968

	Museum Visitors (Millions)	Number of Museums
United States	188	1900
Russia	75	966
Japan	43	259
France	16	438
Czechoslovakia	14	415

SUBSYSTEM V-B: PRACTICAL TRANSFORMATION

We come, finally, to the social system of those who, in their leisure, seek to *change* the world or a small bit of it. In this sense it differs from all the other subsystems described above. The intellectual *contributor* may have an impact, but it is indirect, as with the artistic creator. The "practical transformer" is someone who, in his leisure, directly undertakes to change a *thing*, a *person*, a *social institution*, or *some familiar pattern of organization.*

The transformation of a *thing* ranges from adding a bedroom, making a piece of furniture, cutting one's lawn, or participating as a concerned citizen with some aspect of urban renewal. Participants are the do-it-yourselfers who make objects, build houses, and sometimes become known as the "handymen" of the neighborhood. They make ideal farmers, janitors, and "maintenance" men and often begin with a boyhood knack for taking clocks apart and (sometimes) putting them together. These are the Wright brothers and the Edisons. The breed, with its fundamental quality of curiosity and a search for the root of mechanical processes, was active and useful on a grass roots level when more of us lived on the farm or in small towns, and before the age of standardized products. Some of these persons are still around; technology ultimately depends on them; MIT classrooms attract them, and they are epitomized in the astronauts.

The transformation of *persons* is one of the most common of all leisure forms; it is found in gossiping, advising friends what to do and what not to do, and serving as informal or folk psychiatrists and physicians. The popular "sensitivity" sessions illustrate the group pattern. Here we have the perennial issue: "Are these leisure sessions, or are the motivations not far deeper?" Again we see that leisure can go very deep; experiences are, more often than not, complex syntheses of many purposes and many levels. The therapeutic form of leisure implies that the result of play, social dancing, and political rallies can, indeed, have implications for change in some aspect of health, emotions, or total personality.

The ultimate illustration of leisure as a transformation of persons is in *education* as a social institution. That is its whole purpose—transformation in the sense of growth or development. Is it rash to think of the educational experience as a whole an experience in leisure or in its preparation? It would have been rash when children were being trained to work and to develop proper attitudes related to work in a fairly unchanging society. This is less and less the case. Below the level of specific skills, as in bookkeeping, medicine, and law, education has become more concerned with the *personality*, with *principles* (as in the new math) and with *insights* into the world, for the way of life to be faced by its students is no more a self-evident expectation. New life-styles, less work minded and more life minded, are evident.

The social system of education as a leisure enterprise involves human relationships, values, and norms unlike that of other leisure. What is present now in education that directly relates to leisure is the course or experience that has no utilitarian purpose—literature, the arts, history—and the perpetuation of self-growth and curiosity. Illich and others claim that the school is so structured that these are killed. To the degree that this is the case, education is preparing for the tasks of work and for insuring the *status quo*. Schooling, of course, is not necessarily synonymous with education. It is in the schools for adults that the "education" level is often apparent, due, first to the accumulated life experience as a base, and second, to the voluntariness of the situation. It may be, if and when the schools for children recognize and react responsibly to the meaning of a leisured society, that the philosophy of the adult school, especially the Danish tradition of the folk school, will permeate downward, with a result in greater flexibility. These adult schools have a long tradition that will, indeed, be strengthened for the purpose when even the work-training element is diminished because (1) there will be less need and (2) industry will undertake more and more its own retraining as part of the adjustment to cybernation.

Leisure as a transformation of institutions or *social organization* can be indirect or direct. Its indirect function may occur when someone joins a club that—let us say, the Rotary—becomes active in some new legislation. Its direct form occurs when one decides to help change the city or the "system" by joining a political party. History is full of its revolutionaries—French, American, Russian—who met in the basement hideout after work hours. The history of the Ku Klux Klan—the first one—goes back to young men in southern towns, bored with little to do, creating safe fun by harrassing minorities. Even those registered students who are the campus radicals, if they are to maintain their standing as students, must attend their meetings and paint their posters outside of class hours.

The social system of such agents of change often brings together persons of differences in background for whom the goal of transformation is the common bond. Demands of their time may be heavy. The discipline or the feeling of commitment may so reduce the element of freedom to get out that the leisure characteristic may be eliminated.

SUMMARY

The institution of leisure is composed of many social systems. Indeed, the nature of these individual subsystems—roles, values, norms—may provide the core of the activity itself, being as important as the external behavioral phenomenon. Thus the simple desire to be with friends can result in going to a bar, to an adult class, or to the beach, but not to retiring to one's bedroom with a book. From the socio-psychological view, therefore, the bar, the class, and the beach may provide the same function and are alike for the purposes of leisure, no matter what the statistics or time-budgets tell us. The choice of the milieu in which the friends gather is important, not from the standpoint of function but of symbols, such as the attitudes of one's parents toward the bar. But the choice of friendship is a question of values. This becomes our next topic.

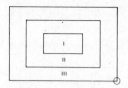

Chapter 14
The Value System

In a rough sense, the energy system is a way of describing what a society has as its material base, and the social system indicates how it is organized beyond this base. But no matter what may be the nature of this material base—agriculture, industry, or atomic power—there are choices to be made as to what people *want and do;* not all farmers live in the same way, even in the same geographical area, and certainly not in comparison with farmers of other regions and cultures. The same obvious statement applies to businessmen, nobility, peasants, or unskilled and skilled workers.

By values, therefore, I will refer here to *the goals and rationales that serve as the ideological basis for the selection of leisure actions.* Robin M. Williams, Jr., a Cornell sociologist, defines values as *"modes of organizing conduct*—meaningful, affectively invested pattern principles that guide human action."[1] They are conceptualizations; they are charged toward action, they are important; they do not provide concrete goals but, instead, criteria by which goals are chosen.

Thus we may speak of whole configurations or philosophies, such as hedonism, existentialism, rationalism, or pragmatism; these are, then, subsystems within the more inclusive term, "value system." On a general level, Barzini has written about Italy, Gramont about France, Michener about Spain, Sampson about England, Benedict about Japan, and Mead about the United States. On a more specific level, Robert Lynd and his associates spoke of specific examples of values in their two studies of Muncie, Indiana.[2] Finally, there are the priorities held by individuals, which reflect their own temperament *vis á vis* these larger value factors of their environment or milieu; one famous example is the Thomas and Znaniecki classification: Philistine, Bohemian, and Creative. The first is at home with conservative ways and might attend the church picnic; the second likes to be up with the latest fads and might spend the evening learning the current dance craze; the third goes his own way and might use the same day to read a new novel.

At this period of history, man's values have become the most important issue that unites philosophers and social scientists; that is, the nature of values in a changing society and their necessary reconstruction or adaptation. For this purpose philosophy and social science need each other. As Florian Znaniecki wrote, "to realize any philosophical ideal, nonevaluative scientific knowledge of culture is indispensable"; but, we might add, an awareness by social science of its own assumptions is also necessary, and this is not a scientific or objective but a philosophical pursuit. Gunnar Myrdal states that, "every study of a social problem, however limited in scope, is and must be determined by valuations. A 'disinterested' social science has never existed and never will exist." Social science has therefore failed to produce a more mature understanding of leisure because, clinging to its value-free ideology, it cannot assess the current trends in leisure without some criteria. Under that condition the studies end up largely either as *inventories* (time-budgets), or as correlations between such items as age and activity. Conversely, the critiques of leisure that have been most insightful and significant have come from philosophers (or other cultural observers) such as Aristotle, Josef Pieper, Lewis Mumford, Bertrand Russell, or broadbased sociologists such as Sorokin, Riesman, Ellul, and Dumazedier.

Both approaches are needed in an understanding of leisure: (1) surveys of present attitudes toward leisure that determine choice and (2) a consideration of the values needed in the changing society.

It is possible to speak of values in leisure on two levels: the *microscopic* one in which we observe a momentary or isolated choice—such as a motion picture over a social visit with friends, and the *macroscopic* level in which a general style or configuration of values is identified (hedonism, existentialism, pragmatism, etc.). Their respective usefulness is seen in relation to the various conceptions of leisure noted in the second chapter.

Humanistic: Here the macroscopic application of values applies in its full sweep. Those who advocate contemplation, education, service to community—*paidia* in its totality—are talking of a way of life, an overview, a set of attitudes that consistently is concerned with knowledge, art, and thought for its own end.

Therapeutic: Here we have a mixture of the scale in values. If we look at leisure as an ongoing instrument of health, we have invoked such values as the human body or form—a priority among the Greeks, among medieval man (as warrior), among the Nazis, but decidedly less among automobile-oriented industrial societies.

On the other hand, there are momentary choices when a particular form of leisure is chosen to suit a mood, a friend, the weather, a special TV program, and so on.

Quantitative: Here there is an absence of concern with values of the subjects studied; these may be inferred by the observer through the patterning of the choices.

Institutional: Values are a primary element when we speak of institutions, and indeed, it is to incorporate the conception of values that this approach is adopted. The familiar reference to leisure as "idleness' or "relaxation" illustrate the macroscopic reference, as opposed to the "discipline" and "divinity" of work.

Construct: Activities-experiences constitute one element of the construct submitted in Chapter 2. This permits momentary decisions that have little use to the observer until they are fitted into a series of patterns.

For a more detailed inquiry of values as they relate to leisure, my approach will be by the levels given in Chapter 2. The purposes will be to uncover how each of three levels—institutions, clusters, and cultures —reveals something about (1) the influence of values on leisure and (2) the influence of leisure on values. As in the past, I will recapitulate several propositions from Chapter 3. There it will be recalled, a value system was defined as the *nature of priorities and the process of judgment by which the person, the group or the society chooses its interests, and according to it creates patterns of belief, faith, and behavior.*

LEISURE: INSTITUTION AND VALUES

Leisure institutional dynamics is the interplay of conditions, selections, functions, and meanings. Under conditions (Chapter 4) we discussed age, sex, income, work, residence, education, and time. Although each is useful as an objective fact, and each can be measured, each is also related to attitudes of the culture in which it exists. In our society, youth itself is a value providing a basis for a cosmetics industry; to be a woman is to be expected to prefer opera more than men; to be rich carries the seeds of the value of conspicuous leisure and consumption; work, itself man's major source of identity, colors the guilt or the guiltlessness of nonwork; to be a Parisian or a Bostonian carries a meaning including an interest in cultural matters; to be educated implies an interest in leisure that leans toward intellectual forms; and the presence of free time *per se* may be a value for some, as among those who desire retirement. It makes little difference whether the associations suggested above are all actually the case. The fact is that "objective" conditions carry meanings in the culture: to be old in Japan is not the same as in the United States.

Yet in all cultures, associations or bridges exist between institutions and social structures on the one hand and the predominant values and ideologies on the other. The reader needs only to recall some outstanding examples of the literature along these lines. James Leyburn, in *Frontier Folkways* states:

"A frontier may be broadly defined as that region on the outer fringe of settlement where pioneers are forced, for the sake of survival, to make new adjustments to a raw environment. It is a region, it is a process, it is even a state of mind."[3]

Robert S. Lynd and Helen M. Lynd, *Middletown,* Chapter 17 to 19, and *Middletown in Transition,* Chapter 7 is another example; here the authors note in detail how leisure is conditioned by the physical environment of the city and by the rest of its culture.[4] Crucial to the local culture is what the Lynds denote as the "Middletown spirit," or its full range of beliefs, such as that "sex as given to men for purposes of procreation" or that "it is pleasant and desirable to do things as a family," or that "red-blooded physical sports are more normal recreations for a man than art, music, literature."[5]

Robin M. Williams, in *American Society,*[6] lists the major value orientations of this country as achievement and success, activity and work, moral orientation, humanitarian mores, efficiency and practicality, progress, material comfort, equality, freedom, external conformity, science and secular rationality, nationalism-patriotism, democracy, individual personality. These, both singly and in their consistency are integrated into the history and institutions of the society of which he writes. An even more ambitious attempt is found in Max Lerner's *America as a Civilization.*[7]

Max Weber's *The Protestant Ethic and the Spirit of Capitalism*[8] is a classic statement of the close relationship of religious ethics to social and economic organization. What he sought to judge, as in his study of China and India, was whether the general character of the social structure was more or less favorable to the development of Western institutional patterns and values.

Frederick J. Teggart, in his *Theory and Processes of History*[9] shows that new values and mental change follow on "the collision of different groups," as in coastal towns, here confirming Plato's thesis.

The evidence is everywhere, as sociologists of knowledge point out, that values do not float down to the society from on high and influence the shape of the society but, as F. S. C. Northrop demonstrates in *The Meeting of East and West,*[10] that the broad values are (1) partly the manifestation or crystallization of many historical and institutional forces and conditions and (2) partly the shaper of those forces.

This is quite different from the approach that, as in the work of Talcott Parsons, looks for generalized "patterns-variables" that apply everywhere regardless of the social differences below them.[11] The departure from such a position by social scientists is evident in the way we have by now forgotten the once popular "four wishes" of W. I. Thomas: the wish for new experience, for recognition, for mastery, and for security.[12] An extreme instance of this view that a few ideas determine everything is the statement that "values determine the choices men make and the ends they live by."[13] The overly simple determinism of ideology is no more acceptable than that of economics. Since conditions carry social meanings, it follows that as the character of these conditions are altered, the values themselves may radically change. Work provides one illustration. Work, everyone seems to agree, is not only a job, a means of livelihood, it is a *good thing* in itself. It is a goal as well as a means; it is a strong value.

The validity of this value was easy to maintain when several conditions prevailed, such as the necessity to work and the influence of a supportive, influential institution such as the church. Indeed, as a generalization, any value seems to require, for its ongoing acceptance, both a need rooted in some current condition and a relationship to one a more other dominant values. For example, the value that Robin Williams calls "progress" seems to lean on the *condition* of literacy and on the larger value of social change. The idea of progress, like that of the work ethic, did not exist universally or firmly, as anthropology tells us in studies of primitive societies. Nor, if we look at youth of today, does the work ethic cling on as many have supposed. According to a recent poll,[14] 63.7 percent of college and high school students in the United States think that the four-day workweek will become general in the next 10 years: according to a study of college students reported in Peter Sandman's *The Unabashed Career Guide*, they listed the following as source of satisfaction for them (Table 24).

TABLE 24
Projected source of satisfaction for students

	First Choice (%)	Second Choice (%)
Family	55	35
Leisure	23	20
Occupation	14	37
Other	8	8

Further evidences of changing attitudes toward work are so obvious that they hardly need belaboring: the acceptance of longer vacations and shorter workweeks are illustrations. The *need to be needed* continues, but that it a different thing. Indeed, a whole division of both psychology and sociology has developed in the past 25 years to deal with this distinction. One vital change has been the transfer of increasing human effort away from work that makes things to work that serves other people. This change was emphasized in the 1963 Manpower Report of the President. From 1947 to 1962 the proportion of American workers in goods-producing industries dropped from 51 to 42 percent. Government employment was the largest gainer in the growth of service occupations, moving up in the same period from 5.5 million to 9.2 million employees. Whatever one may say about the growing demands on government or the growth of white-collar jobs in general (outnumbering blue collars since only 1956), we must note that the expansion of services was not, in some cosmic revelation or fiat, ordained to equal exactly the loss of employment in goods-producing jobs. There is no doubt that much of the enlarged work in serving man was invented simply to absorb people. A small example is the modern elevator, which carries unnecessary operators to press buttons as the mechanized locomotive still carries excess (but unionized) workers. Featherbedding is not unique to transportation; the whole service economy is overmanned by a collective symbolic featherbedding, and this overblown reserve of manpower can be pricked by the pins of automation anytime a depression sets in.

Yet those who are disengaged or disemployed by technology in industry—perhaps 2 million per year since 1950—could not surrender their deep-rooted value of work so quickly: *the move toward service jobs is a transition from serving others to serving themselves.* As supermarkets dispense with human checkers near the doors, the checkers will one day find themselves outside except when they buy goods; telephone operators long ago began to find automatic gear for which they were not needed, and they went home to call their friends. More service jobs can and will be automated. Then we should expect another transition, from service jobs to—what? The new issue, therefore, is whether the new umbrella of the *what*—we are calling it leisure—can provide what phases I and II (work and service jobs) provided beyond the source of maintenance: the need to be needed, to be a going part of life around us. Reich's Consciousness III has a rough analogy, but I will not push it here. His II joins with the III—leisure—in that it comes along in part as a natural *extension* of I and II, and in part as a unique sort of freedom that looks back with some critical observations of I and II, and with a new mind-set of its own, striking out in new directions of its own.[15] At the risk of repetition and beating the same horse, I submit these skeletal observations; they may also move us somewhat forward.

1. Leisure is on the verge of becoming itself a dominant value, and one measure or indicator of the postindustrial society.
2. Leisure as a value springs from the emergence of new technological conditions, the weakening of religious supports, and the democratization of economically free time.
3. The chief technological change leading to leisure as a dominant value among the masses has been the assembly line, followed by progressive automation, with a dual impact: (a) it reduced the relative economic output of muscle in relation to machines; (b) the machine substitute tended toward an increasing impersonalization of the time.
4. The industrial revolution, especially in its advanced stages, removes the worker from the whole product, just as the size of the large companies removes him further psychologically from an interest in the company.
5. The simultaneous industrial and marketing forces create an expertise in planning and selling a product and in programming the consumer. This expertise is converted to creating leisure goods and services to take up the slack time that it had created by producing and selling assembly-made goods. Thus the creation of time itself as a value is given substance by the selling of goods and services that require time to use: cars, vacation tours, camping equipment, and the like. Thus *the value of work* (a rationale for commitment to production) is balanced by *the value of leisure,* both now promoted by comparable marketing techniques.
6. The reverse of point 5 also takes place: as leisure becomes a value, and as the businessman seeks to identify that value with the consumption of his products, the growth of the value has a material impact on the economy; that is, the presence of more cars and highways causes a need for some more time, and increasing free time spurs the use and manufacture of more cars and highways.
7. Point 6 suggests that the values of work (production) and of leisure-as-consumption (through purchases) are simultaneously supportive or reinforcing and antagonistic or in opposition. Indeed, this is a resolution to be faced in the next few decades, and the presence of the problem is itself one indicator of the postindustrial society: how does the advanced technological society strike a balance between the pragmatic need or psychological desire to make, produce, work and the equally strong desire to spend, enjoy choose momentary activity, that is, to be "free"?
8. Three models of leisure values emerge from point 7 that in their resolution over the next several decades, will affect the destiny of work, leisure, the private economy, and the range of governmental functions.

Model A: A leisure devoted largely to purchase and use of goods and services paid for by the person; such as cars, tours, TV sets, and casettes. It may be called the *Good Housekeeping model.*

Model B: A leisure that is minimally dependent on purchases and generally based on activities-experiences such as walking, gardening, and conversing. Call it the *Thoreau-ian model.*

Model C: A leisure dependent largely on tax-supported services, such as the municipal golf course, museums, parks, playgrounds, and the library. Call it the *Shavian model.*

Model A feeds the private economic system; such leisure is consonant with business interests, as in the classic Ford rationale for the five-day workweek. Private industry is aware that its reduction of hours is accompanied by higher production per dollar investment in machinery, and that the familiar indices of "manpower production" are more and more meaningless. What is crucial to industry—here the managers are not yet generally aware—is (1) that the leisure as a general value is vital to their interests, but (2) that Models A, B, and C are reinforcing as well as competitive. That is, those persons who utilize Model C will want more time, and some of the increase will inevitably end up as Model A.

The *Thoreau-ian model* of leisure values is counterproductive. The hippie communes, for example, hardly need subscribe to Consumers Union for purchases. I witnessed a demonstration of this leisure value in the Montmorency II Conference on Leisure, which I attended as the American observer in September 1971. In direct confrontation were those, symbolizing Model C who proposed a Canadian Council on leisure to help coordinate many public services across that vast nation, and those of Model B, who spoke for the new generation of nihilistic, anarchistic, existentialist youth. The latter seemed to represent the Quebec secessionist philosophy; as an outsider I could not be sure of the respective force of secessionism or of a cosmopolitan youthful impatience with government bureaucracy, whether on matters of planning leisure or planning anything else. At any rate, they spoke eloquently for a minimum of leisure "planning," and for a maximization of small groups whose leisure experiences would be intense, immediate, noncommercial, and creative.

The *Shavian model* moves toward socialism. Already, if Ralph Nader, Ferdinand Lundberg, and others are right, we have "corporate socialism," with large companies such as the Pennsylvania Railroad and Lockheed unabashedly seeking tax funds to bail them out; "leisure socialism," might be said to consist of the whole set of facilities, from the Yellowstone National Park to the local public library. This represents the ultimate alienation from the private economy, not only literally rejecting its array of goods but figuratively encouraging higher taxes. A small example of such perverseness takes place every time one turns off his TV to read his book just as the commercial comes on.

We will recall Ellul's concern with the ongoing, autonomous, organic life of technology and its values. He is saying, in effect, that the producer of such a society goes right on to be a planned consumer; he has no choice.

"Leisure time is a mechanized time and is exploited by techniques which, although different from man's ordinary work, are as invasive, exacting, and leave men no more free than labor itself . . . it is simply not the case that the individual left on his own, will devote himself to the education of his personality or to a spiritual and cultural life."[16]

Since youth, says Ellul, man has been relentlessly "adapted." What or who is to be his guide in finding creative expressive? Employer? Administration? Labor unions? The answer, if there is one, is not in leadership from these or other external sources, but from the presence of other values which, in spite of the power of Ellul's argument, exist within the totality of values and may emerge more prominantly as a response to technology. For this examination I turn to the second level of the conceptualization.

LEISURE CLUSTERS AND VALUES

Chapter 2 grouped four sets of clusters: person-family, group-subculture, community-region, and nation-world. Each provides a fairly concrete source of values that are free of economic values; most of the following discussion will deal with the person.

In their rationale for permitting and encouraging polygamy, the Mormons developed the theory that the heavens are filled with infinite numbers of unborn angels; the birth of a child provides each angel with a corporeal form. In a rough analogy, Wiener, the father of cybernation, used to say that the heavens were filled with "signals," and that each of us has to choose which of these signals we hear and make part of us. Put in a third way, the air is filled with assumptions or values that can become guidelines for the goals sought by every person and the norms he therefore will apply in reaching those goals. The problem becomes, therefore:

1. What are the values that are overwhelming and difficult to ignore (these would best be dealt with under *nation-world*)?
2. What are the values that emanate from middle-range sources that affect some, but not all of us? These would best be dealt with under *group-subculture* and *community-region*.

3. What are the values that are most personal and are associated with what we call one's personality? These I deal with immediately.
4. Most important, how does leisure as a value enter the conflict of the personal, independent, individualistic versus the group, the conservative? In what does leisure serve as a barometer, even if not a resolution of this conflict?

One familiar approach is to identify personality "types"; this implies a leaning toward some values more than others. Again I turn to the Thomas and Znaniecki classification: Philistine, Bohemian, and Creative.[17] The first is hardly able to develop new attitudes; he is accessible "to only a certain class of influences—those constituting the most permanent part of his social milieu." The Bohemian's character remains unformed," open to any and all influences, for some of his temperamental attitudes are unrelated to each other constituting an unstable and unsystematic set." Creative Man is settled and organized, and he "searches for new situations to be defined simply in order to widen and to perfect his knowledge or his aesthetic interpretation and appreciation; or his aims may be 'practical,' in any sense of the term—hedonistic, economical, political, moral, religious—and then the individual searches for new situations in order to widen the control of his environment, to adapt to his purposes a continually increasing sphere of social reality."

There is the suggestion here of the type of person who might, in his leisure, move toward those activities-experience that, in Chapter 7, were called the assumptive, aesthetic, and analytic. But it would be straining at artificial constructs to push this correlation too neatly. Let it simply be suggested that the Philistine's values are conservative, his leisure has been fashionable over a long period, and his choices will not upset his circles nor their opinion of him. The Bohemian will follow the latest fad, more like Riesman's "other directed," and is the target of latest models in cars. The Creative Person, like Riesman's and Sorokin's "autonomous" type, is flexible and rational, and the hope of those critics of mass conformism.

The Philistine, as Toffler suggests without using the name, is the accessible victim of "future shock." Emotionally or mentally he is unprepared to adapt himself to rapid change. He does not believe it. The computer to him is just another machine, as the atom bomb is another bomb. As he considers time and its use, he is busy, and sees no problem; Bohemian man also sees no problem, except to keep up with the current fanaticism. The problem of this classification is where to put rebellious youth of our day, because they are less flexible than they think. Those who drop out (as through drugs) are less Bohemian than the familiar artists through the centuries who were, in fact, open souls; indeed, these artists were not only open to new trends, they had the craft and sensitivity to create and thereby contribute.

Leisure among the young of today, who are its most visual images—those whom the police of Amsterdam arouse every summer morning with water hoses—is an unwelcome symbol among the older generation. It is a symbol of the value that older persons associate with sloth and irresponsibility. On a deeper level, the leisure that is inactivity among the young is a protest against activity for its own sake, which the young see among their parents. It is an autonomy in being a statement about their technological world. It is a value not as a positive entity or end, but leisure as a nonvalue, an affirmation of the useless to dramatize the futility of useless nonleisure.

The difficulty with this analysis is that "youth" is too varied for neat generalization. There is a need to look at personality of any age, to delineate types, syndromes, patterns, and miniconstructs. Adorno and his associates did this in their famous studies of authoritarian-oriented girls in California. A useful illustration of this technique is a schematic of personality "paths," suggested in 1947 by Charles Morris. He attached no names, simply numbering the seven as Paths of Life.[18]

Path 1: In this life-style the person takes part in his community to appreciate and preserve it. "Life is to have clarity, balance, refinement, control." One avoids great enthusiasm for anything, indulgences, easy friendship. Restraint and intelligence are all-important.

Path 2: One should go it alone, value his privacy, simplify his life, concentrate on one's self, avoid living "outwardly," focus on himself.

Path 3: Other persons are most important. Affection for others is the main thing. Avoid great concern for oneself, restrain his assertiveness, help other persons.

Path 4: Enjoy life; important matters are abandonment, spontaneity, delight, openness with others. Be alone a lot, "have time for meditation and awareness of oneself." The good life requires both solitude and sociability.

Path 5: Merge with a group; "enjoy cooperation, and companionship, join with others . . . for the realization of common goals." Live with gusto, enjoy the good things of life.

Path 6: Be constantly active in physical action and adventure. What one does is important, not how he feels. Progress is important, not just dreaming of the future. "Man should rely on technical advances made possible by scientific knowledge."

Path 7: All of the above have some merit. At various times take something from all of them. Enjoyment, action, and contemplation should exist in equal amounts. Cultivate flexibility and diversity; develop some detachment.

We all recognize parts of all of these within ourselves or our friends. These vignettes or constructs of life-styles each suggest characteristic leisure activity, but what is important is not a series of hypothetical or real correlations; instead what is important is that the type of leisure in each case falls naturally within a personality syndrome. The value is not capable of being put into a phrase, as Williams seeks to do in characterizing as complex a country as the United States. "Success," "moral orientation," and "equality," can hardly be abstracted, but they are useful as items in linguistic picturization when they are seen within a dynamic whole: for example, each of Paths 1 to 7 has its own measure of "success."

The result of such analysis is the proposition that personality is not a static something capable of complete, measurable items that can be weighted, computerized, factored out; personality is a process, constantly completing itself, dynamic, beyond measurement because no snapshot view—as captured on a questionnaire—is the whole picture. The best we can do is to view the person in his various roles, as father-husband-teacher-Protestant-friend-golfer, and so forth, and from the composite construct something like Morris' vignettes. Then we can roughly assert that this life-style seems to add up to a series of actions and attitudes in his leisure that are consonant with his "total" outlook. If one is restless in his off-work hours and gets into his sports car for aimless drives on the weekends, it is not true that his restlessness begins on Friday at 5 P.M. Even as a routine welder during the week in the body shop of General Motors, he is the same person, inhibited by the limitations of his work: in his free hours he is truer to himself, as in Path 4. So pleasurable may be his anticipation and recollection of the weekends that he may change his job, coming closer to a coherence or continuity. I knew a fireman in this situation; fishing was his bag. He left his job in Illinois and drove along the west shore of Florida until he found a small motel along the Gulf. He's owned it now for many years, fishing daily only a few feet from his home and work.

There is need for considerable research along these lines: the degree to which men have modified other facets of their lives, even work itself, to satisfy their desires to play and leisure. But again, there were no identifiable values to which they were attracted, apart from the general life-style of work, family life, and friendship. It is the holistic pattern that may be seen in the kinds of bulks or groupings, whether we see these groupings as Riesman, Thomas and Znaniecki, or Charles Morris did. The labels they give to their groupings are not crucial. The general whole is the whole that we see in a Henry Littleboy on Beacon Hill. For this reason the problem of specifying values in a linguistic sense is more difficult in respect to the smallest unit—the person. It is, of course, difficult because the values and the behavior actions or patterns are completely merged. The person may lie to himself, as he often does, or he may in one role be in conflict with himself in another role: as a poker player his financial interests may contradict his interests as a father. The play role is more clearly closer to the "real" person, precisely because it is a role most freely chosen, easiest to avoid, the end toward which work-for-maintenance was the means. "By their friends shall they be judged" is a useful folk observation, ostensibly because they usually have less freedom to choose colleagues in work.

The resolution that the person makes in his leisure is therefore a more useful clue to his "real" values than in his works. The conflict of youth and their parents within the family context is also more evident—if such conflict exists—in the leisure sphere than in such matters as what the food for tonight will be. When the family lives in a small community, where its values are derived from the same value systems that dominate other families, the young feel stifled. They have nowhere to escape except among other young people who are equally stifled; but consensus about victimization, as in the case of prisoners everywhere, enhances the sense of subordination. As with the prisoner in his daydreams, youth then often converts its daydreams of deviancy and freedom into restlessness on a physical plane; it finds itself in Amsterdam, Rome, Mexico City, Fort Lauderdale, or Woodstock. It has spilled over, splashed around, splintered away and, in *being*, it has felt complete; no other values are necessary, and Vietnam, racial inequality, or the Chicago Convention of 1968 are merely sparks, reference points, vocabularies, monuments of the prison wardens and *their* wardens.

LEISURE CULTURE AND VALUES

The articulation of values as a basis for leisure is found more explicitly in such subcultures as ethnic or religious groups. For a major instrument of their solidarity is the reiteration and ceremonialization of their uniquenesses, expressed words and other symbols—the business community of America, nonworking women of the world, intellectuals, artists, professional sports players, and many others. Each of these groups has values which are sufficiently distinct from overall values of their societies.

The only simple case in which a clear-cut relationship can be drawn between leisure behavior and values are the subcultures that are *total*, that is, in which the values are so strong as to form actual groups living together voluntarily. Professors, for example, do not qualify; academic life, even though its values are strong, is only a part of their life-style. Some of their leisure, such as their voracious reading of science fiction, is a clear case of escape from the hard reality of the classroom or laboratory.

A more useful example for our purpose is the recent explosion of communes in the United States. The *New York Times* concludes that they number 2000 in 34 states. The National Institute of Health estimates the number of urban communes alone to be over 3000. Within this world there are differences in motivations and structures, so that Herbert Otto could distinguish 16 types, by their emphasis on agriculture, nature, craft, spiritual-mystical, denomination, church, politics, political action, service, arts, teaching, group marriage, homosexuality, growth-centered, mobile or gypsy, and street or neighborhood.[19]

As different as they are, there are fundamental values that all communes express.

"Certain common viewpoints, almost a *Weltanschauung*, are shared by members of the contemporary commune movement. First, there is a deep respect and reverence for nature and the ecological system ... members stress the rehabilitation of *all* lands and the conservation of *all* natural resources for the benefit of *all* people. ... Communes widely accept the idea that life is meant to be fundamentally joyous and that this is of the essence in doing, and enjoying, what you want to do —'doing your thing.' Work in this context becomes a form of joyous self-expression and self-realization. ... A strong inner search for the meaning of one's own life, an openness and willingness to communicate and encounter, coupled with a compelling desire for personal growth and development, are hallmarks of the movement."

It therefore should be of little surprise that in most communes there is a deep interest in "spiritual development." One could expect that a time-budget study of such groups would find a considerable proportion of the 24 hours—and undoubtedly in "odd" hours—devoted to relevant discussion or individualistic contemplation.

As soon as we leave these groups, the relationship to leisure behavior becomes overladen with other influences, motivations, or variables. Even orthodox groups, such as Jehovah's Witnesses, the Salvation Army, Seventh Day Adventists, and others who live among the mainstream, if not of it, must be affected by external factors. I recall the young professor from a Mennonite College who came to my classes to find out how his group might develop a rational (spiritual?) accommodation between the values of his people and the tendencies of their youth to sneak off to movie houses or indulge in other "impure" practices.

One question becomes, therefore, how can we approach the various forms of leisure in relation to some scale of values that are outside of leisure itself? Is there an objective or cosmic criterion or value that can be assigned?

LEISURE ACTIVITIES-EXPERIENCES ON A SCALE OF VALUES

As I write these words in my home, I am listening to a recording of Kempff playing the "Emperor Concerto." A little while ago, an extract from "Fiddler on the Roof" came over the radio. It is possible to say certainly that each piece of music meets a different need, either in responding to the moods of one person or in satisfying the tastes of several persons. This is safe sociology, but it avoids the issue by shifting attention to *people;* when we say that we must respect the rights and tastes of others (i.e., bingo is "as good" as Beethoven, depending on the person), we have struck an admirable tone of respect for others, or in the principle of "inviolability," as E. T. Hiller used the term.[20]

Thus the question with which the social sciences do not, and should not, deal is the quality of leisure orientations in themselves, and in their application to the desirable of the emerging society. Is it possible to delineate a qualitative evaluation of leisure?

On only one principle is this possible, I submit, and that is *the criteria of creativity, complexity, confrontation, as distinct from the criteria of acceptance, simplicity, or avoidance.* The problem is evident in the nature of mass culture. Simply put, it is the issue of active versus passive life-style, the resignation or confrontation, of the distinction that Myrdal applies to national development as modernism versus traditionalism or, of what is political terms is conservatism versus liberalism. Liberalism has within its tradition the concept of activism; it not only welcomes the need and possibility of change, it is a motivation of change, or in the language of recent social science, its logical consequence is a body of "change-agents."

Of course, in our day there are confusions in these familiar terms. Those to whom we turn—or whom we avoid—as liberals and radicals (youth, hippies, commune members) are now conservors of land; they fight big universities and big businesses. And those firm disciples of law and order and private initiative now inject an unending procession of new gadgets based (as in the case of cars and fashions) on planned obsolescence and new demands on government to save giant businesses from bankruptcy or to keep out foreign goods.

Yet in spite of this seeming reversal in roles, the old labels have a force that cannot be so easily dismissed. We can still talk of a dialectic of personalities as they face the world,[21] "the Dionysian and the Apollonian (Nietsche); the tough-minded and the tender-minded (William James); the Prometheans and the Epimetheans (Spitteler); the extroverts and the introverts (Jung); the anals and the orals (Freud); the redskins and the palefaces (Laurence); the viscerotonics, the somatolonics, the cerebrotonics (Sheldon); the towards-others, the against-others, the away-from-others (Horney); the tradition-directed, the inner-directed, the other-directed." (Riesman)

To this collection, Gerald Sykes adds another set, the contemporary men of action or of thought. The first are horizontals, moving in an earthward direction toward social adjustment; the men of thought are the verticals, moving skyward toward individual fulfillment. There is an inevitable conflict between them and between those whom he calls the Aztechs and the Toltechs, updating the Mexican tribes.

"Both the modern men of thought and the modern men of action are incomplete in themselves, and need an education they will get chiefly from their opposite numbers. The nature of the extraordinary new wealth that they share, however, makes it possible for them to avoid the humiliations of the humanizing dialogue that might save both from their characteristic vices. One of the most difficult of personal dramas, the fusion of thought and action, is being declined."[22]

The argument is advanced here that the leisure area provides the arena for such a fusion. Fusions and reorderings are rational paths to take in a time of transition; such a time as we are in is an age of uncertainty and ambivalence. It is not the time for closing out our options but, as the future is more controllable and attainable, its goals cannot be created *a priori;* there is nothing original to say about values except in the newness of a new fusion from older models.

These models come from both work and play; the fusion we seek for a leisure in the cultivated society leans on the strengths, but not necessarily the familiar structures of each. From work we obtain the elements of meaning, need, structure, application, discipline, objective achievement, and functional relationships to others. The word "work" may disappear in 50 years, as Buckminster Fuller holds, but these qualitites will not, because they address themselves to habits and states of mind that have long been vital.

What is happening is in the revival of play in its essence instead of in than its appearance. In play we find the strong elements of freedom, independence, spontaneity, and timelessness. Religion itself as celebration and play—taking off from Josef Pieper—has recently found renewed attention. *Praise of Play* by Robert Neale goes to *ludere,* the root of illusion, as *play,* which he sees as the full use of human capacities. Harvey Cox's important book, *A Feast of Fools,* begins with W. H. Auden's lines, "I know nothing, except what everyone knows—if there when Grace dances, I should dance." He, too, argues for the values of celebration and festivity.[23]

Of course, the components of work and play, considered broadly in both cases, each find completeness from the other in a dialectic of mood and emphasis; creative work has its elements of detachment and humor, as creative play may lean in part on deep commitment and tension.

The new world we are moving toward can ill afford an all-play emphasis and, motel editorials to the contrary, the era of ongoing work has seen its day. Some fusion is in order for each of us. Work, which used to be the source of rootedness, becomes in a technological society a source of alienation; art, which many had considered to be peripheral and irresponsible, now becomes the source of order for many.

But the fusion does not refer to specific types of work, or to specific types of play, such as the arts. Ralph Glasser has performed a public service in disposing of "culture" as a "good thing" *per se* in *Leisure, Penalty or Prize?*[24] I have noted early that the term leisure is not to be restricted to any activity. We begin with qualities, behavior, attitudes —not with designated lists of actions. I do not say now that *every activity,* ideally, is a fusion of work and play elements; one's leisure is not this game of chess or that glass of Scotch, this book or that trip to Yellowstone. One's leisure is the full range of his activities and experiences, which consists primarily of elements already submitted: freedom, pleasant expectation and recollection elimination of the formal work role, seriousness or frivolity, and above all, voluntariness. Chess, for example, relies heavily on concentration and skill; fishing has its long period of waiting and oneness with nature. Neither is the whole; both contribute to it.

There are forms of leisure that are neither play nor work; that is, they consist of lethargic withdrawal, alienation, formless nonactivity. Much television watching falls into this category: experience that is immediately forgotten, requires no effort, commits neither mind nor body, and creates little or no change in the viewer. The usefulness of such experience is only that it fills time; but it is time that remains empty. It serves only as an instrument of temporality, not substance. One example is sleep, when sleep is not required for the body; drugs, hard and soft, fall directly into this negative group. Any "activity" that seems to result is uncontrolled, whether physical, mental, or emotional. This is not play, but withdrawal; one is played on.

Contemplation does not fall into the negative quality I am now describing. Contemplation is active, it brings mind into the situation, confronting it, and as its origin suggests—*contemplari*—it is to *"gaze attentively." When one contemplates, he studies and considers, drawing on his experiences and not his books. There are, of course, various kinds of contemplation.*

We can contemplate from an I-centered orientation: who am I, why am I in this situation, how I feel about something at this time in my life? . . .

We can contemplate on matters outside of us, such as the state of the world, America's foreign policy, or the condition of our community.

We can contemplate about the most general matters, such as the wonders of God and nature, the meaning of life and death.

We can contemplate in the sense of looking forward to something, like a wedding, or to life after death.

We can contemplate in the sense of daydreaming, since if this does not become a preoccupation to lead us to unfeasible goals, it can create a confusion in realities.

We can contemplate creatively, letting an idea germinate for a story to write, a song to compose, a speech to make, a building to design.

We can contemplate by reliving struggles of the past, as did Viktor Frankl, preparatory to developing his theory of logotherapy.[25]

None of these is synonymous with thinking. For I would put thinking under the category of work; it has the elements of tension, system, and discipline. To contemplate is, on the other hand, to muse or meditate. I should put contemplation with play—play of the mind. It is a prescription for all ages, but especially for older persons, since it need not be followed by formal study and it feeds on one's past experiences.

But while we draw up analytical prescriptions, we face another issue that philosophically was central to Greek thought—the distinction between images and reality, or between shadows of actions and the actions themselves. This takes us to a consideration of symbols. Leisure has always been a powerful symbolic vehicle, a gesture and a disguise.

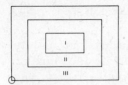

Chapter 15
The Symbolic System

WHAT ARE SYMBOLS?

The anthropologist, Sapir, spoke of symbolism as enjoying two properties. First, the symbol implies meanings "which cannot be derived directly from the content of the experience"; it is "referential," such as oral speech or the telegraph code. The second type is always a "condensation" of energy, because its importance, with the flag as a classic instance, is "out of all proportion to the apparent triviality of meaning suggested by its mere form." As the system of symbolic reference becomes more highly sophisticated, the meaning becomes more generalized and less specific—such as shaking a fist to note anger when no actual enemy is present. Sapir turns to etiquette as a classic example of both dimensions; it is, most simply, a set of rules for socialized behavior yet, in the total sense, its gestures identify or alienate one from social cliques, castes, or other exclusive groups.[1]

The problem of defining the symbol is, of course, no less than the most difficult problem of all scholarship, of philosophy especially, and of society as a whole: that is, the meaning of meaning or, as some would have it, the nature of truth. Plato's cave example of the shadows has never been excelled. For man, as far as we know, distinctive from all other animals in precisely this regard, not only perceives, he reads into his perceptions; he looks at another person not only in the physical, neurological, biological, cognitive, or pure asocial sense, but he sees a man, a woman, a pretty something, a fat one, a thin one, and so on; each of these conceptions enriches or enlarges the bare mechanistic photography and gives it social color, depth, interpretation, a sound price, and a value. These meanings are relics of both the past and present cultures. It is by these meanings, indeed, that we define "culture."

No man and no institution can escape symbolism. It is the core of all language; it is imbedded in every action. The purpose of the analysis, starting with that premise, is to pull out of the general symbolic context that we call "culture" the types of symbolic purpose and practice that are more dramatic, conscious, and observable. "I see a flag" consists of a string of words that, from a linguistic view, is all symbols, enabling a communication by prearrived social consensus. The actual flag as an object is more artificial or conscious; a revolutionary may even stamp on the flag or turn it upside down, but he will not expurge the word from his vocabulary. Similarly, even the athiest uses the word "crucifix," and the speeder uses the term "uniform" as he seeks to escape the policeman. The flag, the uniform, and the crucifix are objects, and therefore, they denote a greater "condensation" of symbolic energy. A third dimension consists of actions, such as the ritual of a church or a court trial. The Harmon list is divisible as follows.[2]

Symbols of
reference: Posture, position, Heaven and Hell, colors, numbers, legendary persons, and so forth.

Symbols of
action: Gesture, dance, washing, marriage ceremony, arts, and so forth.

Symbols of
objects: Plants, animals, buildings, food, dress, and so forth.

All social institutions are rich in all three types, suggested in a few random examples.

Institution	Reference	Action	Objects
Marital	Love, respect, duty	Kiss, eat together	Home, wedding ring
Political	Power, justice	Election, trial	Flag, city hall
Educational	Learn, research	Lecture, read	Classroom, book
Economic	Rich, poor	Work, pay bills	Dollar bill, stock exchange

Leisure as a whole is also rich in all of these symbolic dimensions. Some terms of reference include "play" and "relaxation"; some symbolic actions are the pattern of any game or the behavior of a theater audience; material objects are endless, from beach balls to cars and to TV sets.

It would be incorrect to assume that leisure is any richer in symbolism than other institutions. This is not its uniqueness. Nor, given the large variety of potential types of leisure activities and experiences, can we say that the range is larger than the variety to be found in the many forms of religion. It is a qualitative difference from other institutions. Indeed, leisure is itself a *language with its unique vocabulary.* The syntax of that language consists of social roles (as words) and of social patterns (as the movement among roles).

Society is a drama of social roles. Not all roles are of the same importance; some are equal to others, others are superior or inferior. The key role tells us, as in the case of the king, that he is generally, if not always, superior. But, for the rest of us who are more chopped up in relation to others, our equality, superiority, or inferiority depend on what role we are playing: we all have many roles—father, mother, worker, friend, member of a congregation, political party member, or player of games.[3]

Durkheim, in his *Elementary Forms of Religious Life,* develops the relations of rituals to the interaction of roles. Freud's discussion of several roles comes out of his insights into a great ritual drama, Sophocles' *Oedipus Rex.* Kenneth Burke treated all action as communication with others; his "dramatistic conception" has been carried forward by his student, Hugh L. Duncan.[4]

Without exploring any of these avenues of thought, it is evident that there exists a sufficient tradition to examine leisure as a symbolic expression. I turn to the arts and to sports as examples.

These generalizations will be illustrated in two forms of behavior that are important to leisure studies—arts and sports.

Arts and Sports: Symbolic Aspects

The symbolic aspects of art are of concern to a number of disciplines, especially aesthetics, but the symbolic use of art as a leisure pursuit deals with audiences and images among the general society and is therefore a subject area within sociology and psychology.[5] At the same time it is not an area that lends itself readily to quantitative analysis, and it must absorb historical and philosophical materials; these conditions too often ward off contemporary young scholars, who move into more dramatic and secure interests.

The sociology of sports, on the other hand, presents a more tractable area. Since Spencer wrote about the concept of "play" in 1873, this basic concept has been developed by Groos, G. Stanley Hall, Freud, Veblen, Dewey, Piaget, Simmel, George H. Mead, Huizinga, and more recently, Erving Goffman, Eric Berne, Roger Callois, and Magnane. In tracing the recent history of the sociology of sport, Loy and Kenyon note that in 1967 a committee on sport sociology was formed within the International Sociological Association. The accumulation of serious literature in this field beyond the journalistic level has been described as "astonishingly great"; its focal point is the *International Review of Sport Sociology.* Over 30 colleges and universities in the United States offer courses in sports sociology, almost always in departments of physical education.[6]

Both arts and sports can stand on their own, as ends, as humanistic experiences that need no further rationale. Art for art's sake can be matched with sport for sport's sake, both containing elements such as movement, style, climax progressive challenge, or complexity.[7]

On the other hand, the instrumental (Loy and Kenyon call this the "normative" approach in sports sociology) aspect or expectation in both refers to them as tools for character formation, national honor, and social control. One might think that a homely example of this is the assertion that sports keeps the boy "off the streets" and out of court; but I have heard the same claim made by some music educators. If a contrast has to be drawn, the general view from *within* each profession is quite opposite: in the arts one will hear the emphasis on the *paidaic* aspect, that is, as pure end, and such an orientation as the psychological or medical is allocated to the (often suspected field) of music or art therapy. Thus I associate art with fantasy as an end. In the sports and recreation profession, the weight of justification is invariably on instrumental means, especially its impact on the body from exercise and on moral values through "team play," "spirit," "honor," and so on. Identity, however, is a means and is parallel to instrumentation in leisure.

The attraction and selection of these spheres, either for participation in arts and sports or as followers, is also affected by a contrast in symbols —one with femininity, the other with masculinity. Only recently, according to one writer, has the female image entered the sports world. George H. Sage writes:[8]

"Until recent years, women have played a minor role in the history of sport. Women were virtually excluded from sports in ancient Greece (except Sparta). Indeed, women were strictly barred from even viewing the Olympic Games, and punishments were prescribed for any woman caught at the Games. The women did, however, create their own program of sports—The Heraea Games, in honor of Hera, the wife of Zeus. These were athletic events, held every four years, for women only. This might be called the beginning of women in sports. But only in the past 50 years, with the emancipation of women from home responsibilities and their securing of equal status with men in most spheres of life, have women begun to take a prominent part in the world of sport."

Compare this with a summary of women's place in only one period of musical life, the Renaissance. Henry Lang writes:[9]

"Musical organizations founded and conducted by women were numerous, especially in Italy, and the religious in almost every convent were devoted to music...While women took an active part in musical life, their chief merit and contribution to Renaissance art was their interest in the furthering of music. In their brilliant 'salons,' which antedated the famous literary drawing rooms of the French women of letters and royal mistresses, they were the centers of attention; poets, artists, and musicians owed them inspiration and encouragement."

This close association of arts and femininity has nothing to do with the overwhelming presence of male composers and performers. I am talking about the general image in the society, and the identity of arts with the feminine is one of the concerns of every high school orchestra director; this applies more to stringed instruments than to woodwinds and brass, which are in the band—and the band is far more male from its association with the military.

On the fantasy as well as the identity levels, the American boy is encouraged to see himself as the great football star instead of the pianist or painter; and in spite of changes that one can point to, even in the school, Gregory Stone's story rings true about the military psychiatrist who uses interest in sports (e.g., knowing who won the last World Series) as an index of masculinity.

With the discussion of instrumental symbolism above (sports in the formation of "character"), we had an *internal* factor; but both sports and arts share a common *external* symbolic power—identification of the performing group with social class, royal court, fraternity, college, community, or nation. Baseball, football, or basketball teams represent Boston, or Philadelphia, or Minnesota in name only; the players are engaged, season by season, in what one writer calls the "peculiar economics of professional sports which operate in their own context of 'slave labor.' " [10] It was the job of public relations offices to create the fantasy of Washington as the "home" of the Senators and, when that team "deserted" in 1972 to play in Houston, the town reacted as to treason. In something like a symphony orchestra, it is true that the individual players have generally lived there. For example, a good proportion of the Boston orchestra actually were born and trained in that city.

In both sports and arts a close symbolic tie develops that, on the national level, is akin to propaganda in its instrumental value. We compete, to all intents and purposes, with the USSR when each sends to the other its ballet companies and its athletic stars.

In his selection and use of leisure experiences, the person is affected by what Sapir (in the first page of this chapter) called the "condensation of energy" inherent in symbols. He goes to see the Mets play the Tigers not just to see two capable teams in a contest, but to root for his town to beat the other. The Olympics are based almost entirely on seeing the honor of one's country upheld. This context in leisure would be difficult to measure by quantitative scales, yet its impact on identifying the person with his community or other collectivity is unmistakable: a soccer team that represents the English village; the football team of Cleveland. In both cases, these teams even serve the new resident by providing an immediate tool of identification to help become symbolically settled. I suggest, in passing, more research on the usefulness of leisure activities in our moves from one community to another, as in finding persons of the same interests, or in finding a continuity from one library or club to similar facilities in the next place of residence.

A more systematic relationship of symbolism to the larger subject of leisure will follow the order of components mapped out in Chapter 2. Under "conditions" I will select one element, *time;* under "selection" the two aspects to be observed are *fantasy* and *identity;* under the third component, "function," the symbolic elements are *childhood, secularism, and social class;* finally, the component "meaning" will center on the symbols of *appearance* and *Heaven.* In each case the application of roles will help tie the analysis more closely to illustrations from the activities and experiences of leisure.

CONDITIONS

There are symbolic aspects of age, sex, residence, income, health, race, family, education, religion, work, and time. *Time,* it would seem, is the most objective and measurable of all these. Don't time-budget studies continue to serve as a basic tool of research in our field for this very reason? What could be simpler in conception than such data: how long did you sleep last night, how many hours did you work, eat, devote to personal care, and the like? In this tradition, we have the volume by Sorokin and Berger to guide us, the classic studies of Lundberg and his associates, the recent international studies directed by Szalai, and the current family research in Syracuse by Dr. Katherine Walker. Of all the 20 components considered in the scheme of Chapter 2, time is the only one that, objectively speaking, is precisely alike for everyone—seconds, minutes, hours, days, weeks, months, and years.

Yet, as already noted, the potential content or possible alternatives of an hour today are far more than they were before the days of rapid transportation and communications. The hour's value goes up, especially when hours of free time can be contiguous in what has been called *bulk,* as distinct from *fragmentary.* Furthermore, an evening's free time has one physical or mental connotation when it follows a heavy day on the farm or in the mine than if it relates to an office job, or if it is the day one starts retirement.

However, the selection, use, and meaning of time has direct relationships to its subjective or psychological aspects. One instance is the allocation of leisure events to the time of day, to the end of the week, or to seasons of the year. The advent of electric lighting has extended the evening and intensified that portion of the 24 hours for sociability. We are all aware of how time seems to "go faster" when we are enjoying ourselves or become committed to a task. These are elementary and familiar aspects of the subject and have been treated by Bergson, Priestly, and others. Yet a systematic and ongoing concern with the subject has not become a part of the tradition of sociology, psychology, or psychiatry. Industrial psychology has approached the topic mechanistically as part of the heritage of Taylorism, but it has not dealt on any major level with the relationships of time use and attitudes to the change from industrial to postindustrial or computerized processes. For example, it took traffic jams in large cities to remind us that there is no rational reason for tens of thousands of workers to arrive at and depart from Manhattan at the same times; daytime work, after all, was a hangover from agricultural life. Furthermore, as American businesses have become more and more involved with workers in other cultures, they have had to adjust to different time and leisure patterns; Fall 1969 witnessed some revolt of European workers against the traditional midday two hour siestas, which shortens the bulk time at the end of the day for TV watching. Kant set the stage for contemporary discussions of time as an activity of the mind and one form of men's sensibilities. "Time," wrote Kant, "is not an independent substance nor an objective determination of things. . . . Time is nothing but the form of inner sense, that is, of the perception of ourselves and our own inner state . . . what it does determine is the relation of ideas in our own inner state . . . apart from the subject, it is nothing at all. . . . From this we infer the transcendental ideality of time [which] cannot be said either to subsist by itself . . ."[11] The sociological implications of Kant's insights were provided by Durkheim, who showed that the mind obtained these categories of understanding from the collective (the society). There followed the applications of both of these pioneers, as in Granet's work on China, Mauss' on the Eskimo, and Piaget's on children. Pieron developed a behaviorist psychology of time, and Janet studied men's adaptation to time.

Our result of these studies is the consensus that a more complex activity requires more attention, is usually more interesting, and seems to go quicker than a simpler activity. Boredom, in reverse, emerges from a dearth of anything absorbing; time seems to "crawl," as in the opposite case it "flew." These expressions in the vernacular are, of course, contrary to Kant's insight that time is nothing except a relationship and a sensibility; in everyday speech, we do attribute qualities and even an anthropomorphic state to time: it is "scarce," we have "more" of it or "less," we "kill" time, "waste" it, "ignore" it—or by itself it "passes," "ceases," "expires," "drags," "crawls," "flies," or "disappears."

A second important obvious observation is that we get used to rhythms of life, such as sleeping, eating, and working. The Greek and Medieval contributions provided the boundaries: the first, by giving us the invention of hours, and the second, by the invention of clocks. But even before that, the night and day or the change of seasons were apparent to everyone. Thus, from the roots of agricultural need, the daylight and the summer became times for productive work; by contrast, the winter and the night we left for nonwork, sociability, sleep, rest, the "Devil's work," and sin.

Over a period of the year, and thence an accumulation of years that comprises a lifetime, there developed among the Greeks a circular "temporal horizon," a time perspective that included an anticipation and recollection of events such as rituals and ceremonies. Indeed, these events—then and today—were highlighted by collective celebrations such as the Christian tradition of the Resurrection, which comes with the beginning of growth. But the distinction was that the Christian "temporal horizon" is ambivalent, or contradictory: it is a linear and progressively downward horizon that starts from the Garden of Eden at the same time that its rituals and ceremonials derive their power from repetition.

Too little inquiry has been made by contemporary social sciences of the translation of temporal rhythms and discontinuities into the lives of individuals and families or the changes in traditions of subcultures, communities, and of whole cultures. On the national level, the Communists tried to do away with the sacred connotations of the week, whether the holy day on Sunday for Christians, Saturday for Jews, or Friday for Moslems. As Wilbert Moore notes,[12] in 1929 the USSR turned to a continuous workweek, with one day in five taken off for rest (but not all workers on the same day). Chaos resulted. Two years of this occurred and, in 1931, a six-day week was started, with the same day off for all. In 1940 the Russians returned to the familiar seven-day week, including Sunday as the common day of rest.

With all the variations among cultures, the divisions of day, week, and year became the core of traditions and attitudes that made symbolic sense of work and nonwork, profane and sacred, movement and rest. There were, and are differences, as among the Jews who view the setting of the sun as the beginning of a new day.

Yet the week is an artificial construct, purely a historical tradition, and lacking, as Jack Goody notes,[13] "any definite basis in the external environment"; it is entirely a "social construct." As George Sarton recalls for us in his monumental history of science,[14] among the ancient civilizations the year, month, and day had astronomical roots; but something longer than one and shorter than the others was needed for religious and civil arrangements. The Babylonians and later the Jews came to the seven-day week from the seven planets and from Genesis. Again, the seven planets were associated with seven deities, and became accepted throughout the Roman world. Sarton says it was almost a "casual" acceptance, extending from hebdomadism or the sacredness of the number seven.

"It was the extraordinary convergence of those tendencies that insured the success of our week. It was established automatically; at any rate, we have no document or monument evidencing any kind of governmental or religious sanction. . . . Humanity was spared infinite troubles by the anonymous inventors. . . ."[15]

Throughout man's history since those ancient days, there have been some exceptions to the seven-day week, such as the three-, four-, five-, or six-day periods in some parts of west Africa, southeast Asia, and Central America; the Romans had eight-day periods. Work for six days was for long the yardstick and yet, as the psychologist of today tells us and a plane trip abroad confirms, our bodies work on a cycle of 24 hours that persists for several days after it is changed. Thus the day of "rest" was too short and, indeed, a Finnish research team reports that even the weekend is gone too quickly to achieve complete "rest" from a physiological view.

With inroads of the four-day workweek, the imbalance of work and nonwork time is somewhat rectified on both the symbolic and biological levels. An extension of nonwork time to almost *half* of a man's total time even during his productive years and to *full* time in his retirement suggests that the clock and the wristwatch are declining in concrete and symbolic value. It may be that a useful and simple indicator of the "postindustrial" society will be this decline. As a student exercise on this point, we found in St. Petersburg, Florida that whereas 20 percent of persons between roughly 20 and 30 wore wristwatches, as many as 60 percent of those past their 70 wore watches. (Women, both young and old, seem to have far less capacity than men to guess the time.)

All this suggests that in the next decade, as flexible life-styles increase, and especially a new proportion of rest or leisure days to work days set in, it is in the framework of the week that most of our symbolic transformation will take place. Sunday, traditionally, will remain the day of rest —although its sacred motivation is diminishing and we are often busy playing or traveling on that day. Saturday has been, for many five-day workers, the day for doing chores such as shopping and cleaning house. Friday will begin to take the place of Saturday, giving us what the French already call "two Sundays."

All societies recognize and live by a yearly cycle, and it is within this temporal horizon that the month falls. The calendar month of 30 days came from the Egyptians and, of course, was pegged to observations of the moon. The menopause of women no doubt had an impact on sex as leisure, but otherwise the months are identified with the seasons. Here there are also symbolic undertones that are on the verge of change. Dominant in the creation of the calendar were religious factors, planning for agriculture and the organization of trade based on projections of weather. Ritualistic seasons developed—especially in the Christian world around Christmas and Easter—leading to a rising anticipation and preparation as those times approached. The "spirit" of Christmas, for example, began to permeate the days and weeks beforehand. This facet of leisure, which I have earlier referred to as "the element of pleasant anticipation," has become the mainstay of commercialization, often reducing the actual holiday to hollow gift exchanges. The holiday, often more a secular leisure than a sacred day of ritual, frequently assumes the qualities of a potlatch—to outdo the giver with a larger gift to him—thus playing directly into the commercial calendar.

Winter leisure has traditionally been geared around such events as Thanksgiving, or such activities as skiing, hayride parties (do they still exist?), ice-skating, or playing in the snow. In a more affluent society the winter is becoming a time for the second vacation; Eastern Airlines and others encourage this thought of the "pleasant expectation" and gladly ticket their share of the 30 million annual tourists to Florida in the heavy season from the end of November to early May. I have already spoken of annual religious festivals in early America that had side-effects of social life and mate selection. Our present pilgrimages go right to the point. Thus our climatalogical shrines are no more the Last Resorts of the rich, but of a wide spectrum of ages and motivations.

The symbolic aspect of time is also evident in the occasions that are geared to the life cylce, such as school graduations, confirmation by the church, birthdays, anniversaries, and weddings (even funerals to a lesser extent), all of which become focal points for family gatherings, cutting short or eliminating one's commitments to work.

The clearest designation of leisure roles on the canvas of time symbols is the division into the end of the day, the week, the year, and the working lifetime. The appropriateness of various activities or experiences is related here to the enlargement of available time represented in this continuum. In quantitative terms, we move through a continuum from several hours after the day's work to the potential of many years in retirement. These differences provide differential images toward access to spaces, images of freedom, and a choice of leisure alternatives.

The relationships are complex. The free evening's relationship to space is affected if one has a car or access to a jet plane, if he is well or ill, if he lives in Manhattan or in a desert. Similar conditions apply to other time periods. As I noted in Chapter 1, the "hour" as a unit of potential use has expanded enormously. There is no applicable single scale: how can one compare the possibility, for example, of placing a three-minute telephone call after 7:00 p.m. from Florida to California for $1 with the absence of telephones 50 years ago? A graph curve of travel would run off the page. Or, how would one set up scales of the change in access to images after the invention of radio and television?

The reason that "future shock" did not occur in the past half century among those 20 million who are now over 65 and who witnessed these changes is that none of them were Rip Van Winkles; they all grew up through these changes, and were sufficiently impressed with the differences within their own horizons of time so that change itself became a part of their expectation.

This section ends where it properly began, with Kant. Time is content and sensibility. The mind, acting in relationship to man's culture, brings meaning to time as man develops his various ways of keeping time in structures of hours, days, weeks, months, years and seasons. Leisure takes place *in* time, but the forms of leisure—outdoor activity, for example—add a symbolic level of reality *to* time. Finally, the change in other realities, such as less work, enlarges the stage on which we may play out our leisure roles. Even the mass-produced watch—"a personal time keeper that individuals consult with the obsessive regularity of the White Rabbit in *Alice in Wonderland*"—[16] is less central as absences from jobs become longer and more free of guilt.

SELECTION

The two types of symbols to be discussed here are leisure *fantasy* and *identity.*

Leisure activity, in much of its essence, is in part a matter of projected anticipation, as noted in the formulation of the construct in Chapter 2. "Pleasant anticipation and recollection" (the phrase used there) is related to visions, daydreams, imaginary prospects. Fantasy is used, therefore, in a broad sense as an opposite of reality, and even more loosely as antithetical to the regular and the routine. One not only plans his trip abroad, he opens his imagination to the prospect of adventures—meeting new people or exploring a new countryside. As a stranger in the other environment, he is unfettered in his new roles; he may be a Babbitt at home and see himself as a Don Juan on the ship.

Our observations of persons about to retire gives evidence of leisure as fantasy. The man who has golfed or fished on occasional holidays may now look forward to uninterrupted months or years of such freedom. Once he retires this feeling may last six months, and the fantasy is blunted with the dull edges of boredom. In this sense, perhaps there is some distinction from religious fantasies; symbolic activities such as prayer, material objects such as stained windows, and symbolic references or languages such as music are each supported by long tradition, controls, and special persons (priests, the Pope, etc.) to represent and remind the congregant. The golfer has a bit of this support in the form of his game partners, the golf club, some literature, and golf heroes.

We know very little about this component of leisure: the search must be an interdisciplinary effort, bringing psycholinguistics together with psychiatry, psychology, anthropology, and sociology. Such research issues will become more prominent as leisure students come closer to the interests of counseling and mental health.

The second uniqueness of leisure as symbolism refers to *identity.* The search for identity *through* leisure and *in* leisure is a far more difficult one for each of us than through work, religion, education, or even family life. In all of these contexts of institutions our roles are more unequivocally locked in than in leisure. I am generalizing, and in the section below I will note considerable distinctions between the forms: for example, one is highly "locked in" playing chess, but he can leave the game at any time and never play again; this is more difficult in his role as worker, husband, student, or member of a church.

This relative freedom puts greater burden on us in selecting the behavior of leisure, because the selection is less dictated. Riesman's "autonomous" man has more freedom and greater responsibility in the same sense. The choices, even in leisure, are often associated with influences such as social class, and this degree of obligation eases the problem. The choice of behavior is thus lightened, as well as the choice of identification in language symbolism.

On the other hand, obtaining our identity through or in leisure is easier if our fantasies or day-dreams are well oiled and exercised. What shall I do tonight is no problem if I know myself: that I enjoy a good motion picture, or walks in the park, or beer with my neighbor. There is a learning period when one does not know himself, especially in young marriage, for then "myself" has to be rediscovered *vis-a-vis* someone else.

FUNCTION

The relation of symbols to the functions of leisure will be discussed briefly under the aspects of *secularism, childhood,* and *social class control.*

As an image of the secular, the statement is almost self-evident. We can start with the antipathy of the religious and the sacred toward it. The Christian church, as an example, has always feared play, leisure, recreation—by whatever the name—as oriented toward the Devil. One reason, I suppose, is that the player, in the largest sense, is not as controllable as the prayer; play such as gambling defies the principle of just reward for the task well done (with effort, let it be added). This is why bingo is contradictory to all the church is supposed to represent. Play is also secular in its tendency to distract one from the "main" tasks. It is no accident that the *Puritan ethic*—work as just and as blessed— is a religious concept. Historically it seems to have emerged from the early organization of Christainity around the needs of poor persons; these hard workers would find, then or now, little hope in an earth-oriented philosophy of social reform. The church was neither a poliitical or social force for revolution; its orientation was Heavenward. In this important sense it broke from Judaism, which *did* emphasize the world of men instead of angels, and which, neither then and now, divided man into flesh and spirit.[17] It might not be too much of an exaggeration to suggest that in the symbolic religious war that was triggered by the Industrial Revolution, the Judaic ethic is winning over the Puritan ethic by leaps and bounds.

The second image of leisure is to serve the function of regaining childhood through *delight in play*. We know from Piaget and Huizinga that play is significant, and its influence in the development of people or of society is incalculable. But the essence of delight is total immersion, spontaneity, expression, and a freedom of spirit between its interesting participants. This need not mean that play has no rules, any more than that the playing of music is uncontrolled. The spirit of it all is delight, not growth or productivity or effort. And this is the general purpose of leisure in all of its forms. Even writing a book or a symphony, if undertaken in this spirit instead of as a professional commitment, partakes of play and delight in the resolution of self-imposed problems. When it comes to delight and its anticipation, we are therefore inclined to overestimate the amount of time we will have for such activities tomorrow, and to underestimate the time we will need for chores of keeping alive and going.

The third relation of leisure as symbol to its functions is that of control. Social class illustrated the point. Here, too, there are parallels between art and sports. There have been sports associated in the ideology of various societies with the rich, the poor, the blacks, the rural population, and the old. A social class, after all, can be based on any set of elements, since it is "any permanent division in society which is differentiated by relatively persistent dissimilarities in rank and separated from other strata by social distance."[18]

MEANING

I turn now to leisure itself as a symbolic meaning or essence, indeed, as noted earlier, *as a language with its unique vocabulary.*

Putting these together, the symbolism of leisure is one of appearances. In addition to becoming involved in the game or the song or the journey, we are telling *others* as well as ourselves, "Look, I am not busy out of necessity, now I am *myself*. It is the *real* me, what I want to be and do. See, I can quit any time, I can choose my playmates." I suspect this explains some of the restlessness mentioned in Chapter 6 as one motivation for leisure; restlessness is sometimes fulfilled by a context of nothingness, such as one TV show after another or one highway mile after another.

Indeed, industries have been built on this symbolic value of leisure appearances, providing form to the symbol by new car styles, new Miami Beach architectural (mis-)statements, or leisure clothes, second homes, and attractive dance partners. Those who need pot, in a sense, lack the imagination to conjur up visions and appearances to satisfy their needs, and use artificial means to create a different, other-world set of appearances. Leisure, as *appearance*, is a reality of its own, with values of its own, in contrast to the concept of imitation. As appearance, leisure is a reality worth paying for. It is a statement that, like statements in religion or education, can be half truths or outright lies. The usefulness of leisure as appearance is that the mood is set by appearances; as Spencer noted years ago, we may laugh first and then see the humor, just as we may want love first and then find the other person. This gives to leisure the quality of the self-fulfilling prophecy: "God, I'm going to have fun this weekend"—a more utilitarian form of contemporary magic than "well, I'll go to the beach and see what happens."

Much has been made in contemporary social science, especially since Veblen, about the symbolic force of social class initation. Whatever the imitative factor may have been in former periods, this is a dangerous premise on which to proceed in the contemporary scene. It is too simple and dated. A major factor in the change to the personalistic dimension has been television.

What is often overlooked is that the impact of the mass media, especially television, has been to break the association of the person with stereotypes of his class. The models that now come at him every evening are numerous—models of personality, home life, community, humor, art, or language. This communication has, as McCluhan points out, created a new extension of man, affecting what man thinks and does. Such elements of his environment as the printed word or the confines of his town and his class has been broken. Direct experience is now a part of his everyday relationship to the world. To speak of social class in leisure is to think in terms of the old environment. Indeed, I would go further: *leisure that may have once been a symbol of class, especially of the upper classes as a means of conspicuous consumption, is now a fundamental release or break from class limitations.* While, in the 1930s, leisure may have served as a revolutionary force, it is now more and more counterrevolutionary. Christianity, it has been said, was counterrevolutionary: things will aright themselves in Heaven.[19] But religion, weakened in its hold over the past century, in Europe as much as—some would say more than—in the United States. There were many reasons, among them several great wars, the church's failure during Hitlerism, the growth of a science ethos, urbanization, and greater literacy. The decline of the religious hold did not leave a vacuum: instead, the concept of Heaven was revolutionized. It was simply moved to earth. No more did one have to wait; installment buying was more pragmatic and effective than prayer. Even the minister obliged with installment sermons, breaking them up into sermonettes. Our vision of Heaven is fuzzy, since we lack the discernment of a George Bernard Shaw to see how dull it could be. But put in the form of a new golf set, a flight to Hawaii, a six-pack of Schlitz or Pabst, or an air-conditioned eight horsepower Cadillac, this kind of Heaven was clearly visible on the TV screen every night or in the newspaper ads every morning.

Thus leisure became a symbol of Heaven and, when fully realized, an affirmation of the fact. God did not die; He became much more alive, in the decentralized form of Theosophical teaching—not in every tree and flower—in every commercial on TV, discount house, or car sales-man.

Clearly, with Heaven already here or obtainable by credit card, what is there to revolt about? BankAmericard goes—without the asking—to every household head in every city directory. Who is there left to shoot the first bullet? Two groups.

One group that will shoot are the blacks or others who have been poor, who see the potentials and even some improvement in their economic situation; they will shoot those who stand between them and Heaven. Leasure to them is still secondary; they want the work, or failing that, the maintenance that comes from work.

The second group is the youth, who already have used their fathers' credit cards, have had a taste of Heaven even in their early years and, like some of Shaw's characters, would rather meet in Hell. Their view of Heaven as an ideal is not that of things and goods, but strangely an old-fashioned, humanistic concept that Reich summarizes as Conscious-ness III. Leisure, to youth, could be a symbol of this old-fashioned Heaven, accepting the Hellenic view of leisure as *paidia,* which they see articulated by deGrazia. But, to them, both Heaven and leisure are schizophrenic, each containing the duality of Light and Darkness—the what-could-be versus the what-is.

Yet aside from the young and the black (and I recognize the danger of generalizing both groups in respect to space here) the larger main-stream of American life shows the voracity of the new convert as he brings Heaven within reach, into his supermarket and home.

This, then, is the finale: leisure as the symbol of Heaven, God, Life itself.

PART 5
Social/Historical Orders

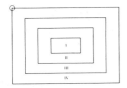

Chapter 16
The Conquest Order

Anthropologists, like their city cousins, the sociologists, have paid less attention to leisure as a total range of human behavior than we would like for our purpose. Felix M. Keesing notes this early in his essay on Recreative Behavior and Culture Change.[1]

"As compared, say, with social structure, or child rearing, or religion, behavior that is 'reactive' gets at best an unobtrusive corner in standard monographs. Except for occasional items such as Firth's analysis of 'the dart game in Tikopia' (1930), the reporting of child and adult games, entertainment, and the like, tends to be formal, with little of the rich psychological, social and cultural texture one suspects is really there, both for participants and for spectators."

Kroeber has discussed "organic play impulses" in relation to culture; Bateson develops a theory on play as one of "the great creative fields of human communication." One might, on the surface assume, for instance, that the primitive will hardly use his leisure as an instrument for change. Yet Malinowski states that in primitive civilizations the seed of progress is often found in works of leisure, since little resistance is given to developments in this dimension of life; he notes also the importance of ceremonies and games as an active force of social control.

TIME DIVISIONS AND USES AMONG PRIMITIVES

Economic specialization, as we know it, is not characteristic of primitive life. Slavery is to be found, but not in the form of a master or owner who does not work himself. There is no control over economic goods by the few as a means toward profit, with the result that some are rich and others are poor. All share in the poverty or the abundance and live economic patterns in time that depend, obviously, on the natural conditions for food and shelter, but that are not prescribed, as in a factory system. This may mean many hours of work or a few, depending on the job to be done. Melville Herskovits notes that the Siang Dyak people of Borneo worked six days of every seven; this, says Herskovits, dispels the myth of the "lazy" primitive.[2] A. I. Richards reports that among the Bema tribe in Northern Rhodesia, daily work occurs only a few times in the year. At Kampamba, in a busy season, men of all ages worked about every nine days; the average work day was 2¾ hours for men and 2 hours of gardening. Yet over a number of days the work hours varied from none to 6 hours.

Time for the primitive is reflected in what J. B. Priestley has called the *undifferentiated* state of mind; he asks, for example, about the cave paintings at Lascaux—"are they religious, are they art, are they magical devices to bring success to the hunt?"[3] Time is similarly undifferentiated. Drawing on A. P. Elkins' *The Australian Aborigines,* Priestley describes the Great Time of the life of the spirit, a time that is "all-at-once instead of one-thing-after-another." Every instant is eternal, with past, present and future emerging into one. In myths, great ancestors are not dead; the cult totem is the "door into the eternal dream time." Ritual ceremonies become reenactments of great deeds, resulting in an indifference to the passing time concept that we take for granted.

All of these examples move us toward a model of social relations and institutions that, in other ways as well, is "undifferentiated." The word I have used in Chapter 2 was "fused." This implies an interdependency that is known in anthropological literature as the functionalist approach. All of life, in such analysis flows as a single current ... all behavior is meaningful, each act performs some function, every object has its place and its usefulness.

THE FUSION OF INSTITUTIONS

With little specialization in roles, the institutions of primitive societies are clear enough for day-by-day living: the functions of a priest are obviously different from those of a ruler; yet they may be the same man. If they are not, they may work in the closest harmony, as in the Western Mono tribes of California where the shaman might cause a man to be ill who had not properly contributed to a dance ordered by the chief.

The variations among "primitives" is as great or greater than among later civilizations, so that the general argument of fusion across institutions cannot be narrowed artificially. Even in the education sphere there were formal "schools" as we know them, among some groups often related to rites by which the young were initiated into adulthood.

Junod's volumes on the Bathonga of Portuguese East Africa describe such exercises,[4] or H. A. Stayt's survey of the schools for boys among the Venda tribes.[5] In the latter, boys go from eight or nine to puberty, to study such matters as night attacks, spying, and dancing; the girls, on the other hand, get what we would call a "crash course" of six days on etiquette, dancing, and sexual matters (the training starts after menstruation). Preparation for marriage takes place in coeducation school, the *domba*.

Nevertheless, the broad pattern remains relatively simple in that among primitive societies the technological base is limited. The primitive society has no economic surplus that is sufficient to permit specialist roles, that is, persons who can be freed by the surplus so that they need do nothing but pray, or teach, or dance, or hunt. Thus the economic, political, and social realms are interrelated by the common task of confronting nature through related roles. The "law" and "government" among them may be no more than by one recognized leader acting through the traditions of his people, or extending into the complicated political system in the African Ashanti described by R. S. Rattray,[6] or the League of the Iroquois in North America. But the "political" structure among all these societies presents conceptual problems to the contemporary anthropologist who seeks to distinguish between "custom" and "law," and the same issue holds for scholars of primitive religion.

To further illustrate the general inseparability of institutions in comparison with life as we know it, I take the area of the arts, because the arts are more distant from the central core of institutions among us than other facets of life.

The ultimate basis for art as fantasy and symbol of tension resolution and of sexual life is the dance among primitives. Much has been written about the dance, and I should posit it as the chief activity and image that brings together the external themes of work, tribal organization, and the concepts of mind, body, and spirit (i.e., of the many and the one). The dance is a collective mime. Rhythm is its central impulse. In primitive life there is no difference between mind and body, or mental and physical work; the body is the agent of energy to maintain the tribe, and simultaneously the vehicle for alternate tension and resolution.[7] We will recall that later the Christian church created a sharp distinction between body and soul and prohibited the dance as an integral part of ritual because of its close relationship to sex.

The dance-drama, always highly structured, no matter how simple or complex, was not a performance; it involved everyone, even those, such as the very young, the very old, or the handicapped, who could only watch. Furthermore, these are special, not ongoing events, which meant special preparations for food and dress. In this sense there is a continuity to our own pageants. For example, the mask that was often an integral aspect among primitive traditions has lost its ritualistic value for us, but clings on for special occasions.

Harry L. Shapiro of the American Museum of Natural History was led to some observations stemming from a display of masks at the Cooper Union Museum. The mask's power comes from both the wearer and the observer. The wearer takes on the reality of what he wears, assuming its "personality" and motif; instead of losing himself, he finds release; he may, in fact, "feel an enlargement of his personality and express himself more vigorously or freely than under normal circumstances."[8] The mask was known 50,000 years ago and became closely interwoven with magic rites or tribal ceremonies in a way that can be imagined from the psychological effect it still has in release among us, as in masked balls. Throughout history, pageants and holidays such as Halloween have continued the covering of the face; in the Greek or Roman theater, they became an established practice in high art. Shapiro wonders whether the heavy make-up of some women provides a compromise with the primitive.

A primary lesson from studies of the primitive, then, is that we cannot divide functions into "work," "play," "education," because even this brief summary suggests that as man's institutions became complex and specialized, the leisure realm was left with tools and symbols of the magical and the mystical. Masks, in this case, are identified by us with "play." Astrology, especially for those who do not accept it or who do so lightly, is likewise a form of leisure, or other forms of divination such as tarot cards or the Chinese *I Ching.*

USEFULNESS OF THE PRIMITIVE MODEL FOR LEISURE STUDIES

For the hypotheses that follow, the following glossary is recalled from Chapter 2.

A = Primitive social order	}	Conquest
B = Medieval social order		
C = Industrial social order		Kilowatt
D = Transitional social order		Cogno
E = Post-industrial social order		Cultivated

HYPOTHESIS I. *Every social order above contains within it some leisure elements from every other social order.*

In tabular form, this appears:

A	B	C	D	E
b	a	a	a	c
c	d	b	b	b
e	d	d	c	c
e	e	e	e	d

For example, every society since the primitive has also entertained itself with sports and games, song, dance, pageantry, gossip, conversation, and social drinking. What was obviously missing in some was a leisure that depends on technology, especially of transportation and communications; furthermore, literacy is, by definition, absent in primitive life. A striking similarity in leisure and work structure among primitives is the tendency for a flexible time arrangement between work and leisure that appeared as a natural rhythm in "states of readiness."[9]

The reverse of these observations also seems to have some basis in fact: elements that we generally identify with later forms of society are seen in some form among the primitives. One of these is the presence of sex roles in play which, as we will see, was a characteristic emergence in medieval life. A second element that became more fully developed later was play for the sake of play; it is seen in the view held now by antropologists, but that was not always the consensus among scholars, that primitive art can be nonutilitarian.

The hypothesis does not imply that leisure is the same in the social orders A–E. The decisive aspect of A, the primitive social order, is the wholistic character of play and leisure—their integration into the unity of custom that can only by our *ex post facto* observation be neatly divided into "religious," "economic," "educational," and the like.

Hypothesis II, based on the historical scheme above, may be seen in visual form before it is verbalized.

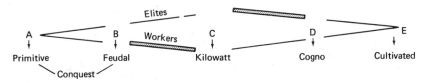

This hypothesis states that *in both the "primitive" and the "cultivated" (or "post-industrial") social orders, there is a general fusion of work and nonwork elements, and that between these two points on the continuum there is a gradual separation of the elites and the workers, reaching its climax in C (kilowatt order) and beginning a reversed trend thereafter; and that a middle-class arises with the industrial*

society, forming within the larger pattern of social order that becomes ever larger and engulfing.

In each case, a difference is drawn historically between a *higher degree* of commitment to work (━━━━) and a *lower degree* of this commitment (_____). Thus, in A, there is generally no division between classes, which I divide roughly as elites and workers. By the time we see the periods known to us as the Middle Ages, Medieval, and the Renaissance—all, in spite of their differences, *preindustrial*—these separations are clear; the feudal economic system has by now brought mankind to a full differentiation between work and leisure. The climax is reached in our own memory, preparing the way for the trend of a refusion of neoprimitivism which, in Chapter 18, I will claim is the model toward which we are moving—a model, in addition, that will stand or fall to the extent that we can develop in contemporary terms the strengths or contributions of preceding social orders.

I turn, therefore, to B, the second of our leisure models and social orders, to extend both of these hypotheses.

FEUDAL SOCIAL ORDER

In primitive society there was no division of body and mind, nor between leisure and other institutions. By the time the feudal pattern had become generally characteristic of Western Europe, dichotomies were clear in both regards. Furthermore, with the feudal system, work was physical, and the body was central for its purpose; hence the body was the attribute of the mass of illiterates, the land workers. Conversely, leisure had already become associated with nonwork, and thus with the relative minority, the more upper classes. These are the central themes and hypotheses of the second portion of this chapter.

Again, to carry through the thesis of "social orders" instead of a purely sequential or historical approach, the elements of feudal system can be seen in Egypt about 2500–1500 B.C., in Japan of the nineteenth century, and in good parts of South America today. Its climax, from an historical view, was from 1150–1250 A.D. Relying on the study of Ferdinand Lundberg, in the United States at present "*at least* 40 percent of the men, or 24 percent of all the top wealth-holders, are heirs, bringing to more than 60 percent the hereditary proportion."[10] Thus there are traces of feudalism in the United States, with such private powers as the Ghettys, Hughes, and Hunts of today or the Duponts, Deerings, and Morgans of yesterday.

The essence of the feudal system is the presence of private rule, localism in administration, and legal immunity of the lord. Personal relationships are expressed in fealty to the lord, and hence protection by him. Here we have a system of reciprocities, quite different from the collectivism of the primitive.

Poverty was the general condition of the peasant. The tools he used to till the land were largely wood, since iron was saved for the weapons of those above him in station. The swing-plough he used made it difficult or impossible to till the more fertile soils. As Charles Wood observes of life in 1000 A.D., over "90 percent of the people had to farm simply to survive, and their level of efficiency was so low that it seemed impossible to break free of the chain of limiting circumstances that threatened to bind all men perpetually to the land."[11] He suggests that the origin of jollity and feasting in late December may have originated from the lack of corn or fodder to keep their cattle going beyond that point, so that they had to slaughter and rapidly consume them at Christmas time. The children learned skills from their fathers, as in primitive societies, with no hope or even an aspiration of doing anything else. It was, for all peasants, the "only possible life."

The home, or hovel, had no comforts, no windows, and an earthen floor, many person were housed in one room, sometimes with animals sharing (and warming) the space. One bed, a table, and utensils to cook with were their possessions. Life's primary functions of producing children, of illness or death, were open to the view or hearing of everyone. One family was close to another, often engaged in common tasks on the land, and sometimes close enough to compose a village, with its advantages of friendship and gossip to provide some relaxation. Religious occasions provided periods away from work. Illiteracy was common everywhere among peasants, with the village quite isolated from news of other worlds. Time had only the sun as its indicator; one day followed another, seasons came and went, superstitions of every shape arose supported by folktales about animals and supernatural powers.

These conditions varied, of course, depending on the nation and region. Urban T. Holmes, in his *Daily Living in the Twelfth Century*,[12] speaks of the games and toys among peasant children in England—games involving balls, games imitating knights fighting, or building castles in the sand if they lived near water. Within the class system among peasants, the serf was the lowest, with payments due to the manor if he wished to move or marry. In the manor system, the peasant either held a parcel of land for cultivation or worked part time for land cultivated directly by the lord, often supervised by a steward or seneschal. In England, the top level of peasants were called freemen; they owned their land, but their style of life was not different from other peasants.

Some specialists were needed, such as the smith, the miller, the carpenter, the barber, and the tavernkeeper. They, too, like the field workers, were controlled by regulations or traditions of the lord whom they served, the laws he established, the punishments he inflicted, and his private tax system.

What we would call leisure was, in those days, largely centered at festival time—Christmas, Easter, Candlemas in February—or on the occasion of weddings. Of the dance, Morris Bishop relates:[13]

"The peasant loved to dance, often in the very churchyard before the disapproving priest but amid the approving dead. His dances, many of which survive, were performed to fiddlers' music, with chorused refrains. They had little of the sexual implications of modern dances. Monks and nuns did not always disdain to join in. There were ecclesiastical, professional, and trade dances."

In general, concludes Bishop, the average peasant knew his place in his little society; he trusted God and knew there was an afterlife. He could not judge his system and could not, therefore, become alienated. If discontented, he might escape to a larger town, and there find himself on the lowest of ranks or occupations.

The difference from all this to the life-style of the feudal aristocracy was dramatic. Its primary concern, as Wood observes, was "to squeeze the greatest revenue from the soil. The lord of the manor was little concerned with the misery of his tenants; that was their problem, and as long as rents continued to be paid and services performed, he saw little necessity for enquiring into living conditions and even less for doing anything about them."[14]

These counts appointed viscounts, or deputies, to assist in administering the counties. By the tenth century, castles had been invented as the center of defense from other counts and as the symbolic head of authority. Private wars over boundaries, personal quarrels, or the desire to acquire more land were common among the counts in a society without strong control governments. Knights, originally no more than warriors on horses were, in the tenth century, called on for administrative function of manor life. Yet fighting remained the core of life's meaning for the aristocrats and their knights, centered around concepts of manhood, honor, strength, a symbolic allegiance to women, and little regard for life. The medieval period covered perhaps 250 years, characterized many countries. The nature and effect of feudalism varied considerably from country to country.

In spite of the disparities, which incidentally apply to the primitive world as well, the juxtaposition of the primitive and the medieval have a highly significant meaning for the student of leisure. This meaning is derived from a contrast with the industrial ("kilowatt") social orders.

The feudal life-style was one of contrasts in nonwork as well as work life-styles. It is important to state that class lines—indicators of prede-termined destiny at the point of birth—were given ideological support from the church. *The surrender of this support, together with the inher-ent depersonalization of work through advanced industrialization, were the twin forces that provided the ideological foundation for con-temporary leisure.*

The feudal society enabled the aristocrats to accumulate the instru-ments for class-oriented recreation: lands to hunt on, troubadours to entertain them, excess food for feasts, and workers to provide taxes for their soldiers or their possessions of art, jewelry, gardens, boats, and—above all—of time.

If the first quarter of hypothesis II above is reproduced, we have a depiction from "conquest" to "feudal" ($<$) with, as yet, no substantial middle class. For that we must turn to what I call the kilowatt social order, where it becomes not just a new dimension but, in respect to leisure, the overwhelming economic, social, and psychological factor.

Another distinction from the successive societies derives from a choice of the term "conquest social order" to help us view as large a grouping as primitive and feudal. In the broadest sense, the former represents a conquest of man over nature or nature over man; the latter, a conquest of man over man. I see this general meaning of the constructs that provide the resting points of Hypothesis II earlier in this chapter.

Social Order	Major themes
Conquest	
Primitive	Man–nature
Feudal	Man–man
Kilowatt	Man–things
Cogno	Man–man
Cultivated	Man–nature

These themes will be amplified in the next few chapters, and provide another understanding of how leisure is closely related to its social order. They prepare us also, for the subsequent characterization of the time ahead of us as "neoprimitive." The next task moves us a little further: it is to see how the industrial or kilowatt order set in, with its meaning for leisure.

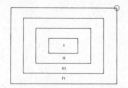

Chapter 17
The Kilowatt Order

The kilowatt, or industrial social order, is machine powered, not muscular. It is driven by batteries, generators, control boxes, and ultimately by computers. Two types of displacement take place. First, machines replace muscle; second, machines supplement and almost supplant the mind. The growth of science, as in postfeudal England, demands large cities; cities in themselves become a magnet attracting people by their excitement, their regular working hours, freedom from others, and the variety of occupation. This type of society was characterized by vast migrations of the nineteenth and twentieth centuries, inventions, mass education, revolutions in transportation and communications, the decline of religion, a loosening of family ties, political revolutions and the influence of Marx, Freud, and Darwin. This, until recently, was our own society. Its most advanced examples are the United States, Japan, and Sweden. Among the main features of such contemporary societies, in contrast to the "Conquest" model is the presence of a middle class as an economic, social, and symbolic reality.

The analysis of these developments often takes the form of tracing the growth of mass production through the machine. Yet, as Peter Drucker has well argued, it is not only the invention of the machine that was highly important, but the separation of man from the machine that brought special meaning to this era. In this latter aspect we have a social and a technological phenomenon. "In fact," notes Drucker, "the worker no longer produces even in the plant; he works. But the product is not being turned out by any one worker or any one group of workers. ... It is a *collective* plant. The individual worker ... cannot even point to a part or a process and say: this is my work."[1]

There are many questions that could be raised from this conclusion, and the most important would be, how did this come about? From the view of leisure studies the important questions start from the other end: *What was the meaning of the separation once it was achieved?* The origins of the separation are pertinent for us only as this affected the ultimate meaning. Another way of posing this question is, *If there are various kinds of free time, what are the unique qualities of time which is made available by the use of machines to do the work?* A second order of question follows: *What is the relationship of the meaning of man's disengagement from the machine to the behavior patterns that take up the new "free" time?*

First, it is apparent that there are various ways of being free from work. One can be temporarily or permanently ill; one can be too young or too old; or unemployed, even though willing to work; or rich enough to manage without it; or freed for short or longer periods by inclement weather, shortage of raw materials, broken machines, or lack of customers.

Coming to the second question above, it is a reasonable assumption that there are emotional and psychological differences between these conditions or—more directly to our point here—between all of them and the freedom from work that is unique when it springs from cybernation. This kind of "freedom," too, affects some workers more than others, to be sure, but its common characteristic is that the man who is displaced by machines must be neither "rich" nor "unemployed" by traditional standards. Another peculiarity of this situation is that this common man, this potential economic Everyman, is unprepared. There are traditions about being unemployed or being one of the idle rich. For each the society has expectations and services. The unemployed, if bodily able, should look for work; since the New Deal, they should expect to obtain their basic needs from some public agency. The rich, if they are part of a Kennedy, Rockefeller, or Buckley type of family (or nobility in other societies), should enter public service and should expect doors opened to enroll their energies. Among the nonwork roles that have an historical grounding are the ill or the handicapped.

As to the technologically displaced man, there were several reasons for the unpreparedness in such a role: the rapidity of mass production, the even more rapid approach of cybernation, the topsy-turvy emergence of a "middle-class-leisure class," and the momentum of a work ethic that did not jibe with real aspirations. Note some aspects of the first—the rapidity of the development.

RAPIDITY OF MASS PRODUCTION

There is hardly need to recount the enormous sweep of historical or social changes that took place from the midfifteenth to the midnineteenth century: geographical discoveries, colonization, worldwide trade, the origin and growth of factories, the development of large cities, the creation of middle-class merchants and professional groups, the rising universities, the surrender of feudal monarchies to national political units, the articulation and application of concepts such as freedom and democracy, the new heights of the physical sciences and the beginning of the social sciences and the Protestant movement. Localism and agricultural society gave way to expanding political and industrial units of power and production. Within all this was the discovery of America and its settlement, constituting a new force on the international scene of trade and ideology.[2]

Indeed, the relative rapidity of mass production as we know it was, by any long-range historical time scale, almost a sudden development. As late as the beginnings of the present century, the largest industries were still family owned; a factory of 500 workers was unusually large. Henry Ford's revolution is within the living memory of millions still alive. It revolved around a simple principle that one process, and not many, should be done in one place.

One index of the historical rate of these changes is the development of technical education for those who had before then been the farmers or domestic-system production workers. The English had taken an early lead in the new industrialization, with inventions by Arkwright, Watt, and Crompton. The continent, meanwhile, was busy with revolutions and wars. As Germany and other nations became aware of new industrial opportunities, adult education for skills was organized by governments and labor unions. The "mechanics institutes" came in about 1820, soon numbering over 200. Manchester alone had 1000 night school students in classes for arithmetic, algebra, geometry, drawing, and grammar. That these studies also encouraged a broader insight into potentials and aspirations is indicated by the comment of some employers, that "I would rather see my servants dead drunk than I would see them going to the Mechanics Institutes," or "*they were being educated above their station.*" A day school for boys was opened in 1835 in Liverpool, and other towns soon followed.

Eventually there were technical high schools in France, Germany, and Switzerland, becoming an integral part of the compulsary educational system. By 1880 the continental schools were catching up to the English, and the quality of their industrial products, as in the case of Belgian iron girders, was as high.

The iron and steel technology, first begun in England, was brought to a new level by such German firms as the Krupp ammunitions makers. Chemistry became a driving curriculum in the German universities.[3]

An interesting question arises from all of this: the degree to which this technical education not only had in it the implicit danger of "social unrest," as some employers felt, but also the inherent potentiality of enlarging the workers' visions on matters affecting his nonwork patterns. He learned to read; the classes depended partly on oral articulation. The union movement's turn toward political and economic power was (unlike the subsequent American scene) accompanied by a sense of cultural responsibility that is still evident in Europe today. The growth and articulation of the socialist movement was not limited to interaction in purely economic language, but also in broader social and historical symbols: in the theater, in literature, in lectures and debates, mimes, and in socializing among workers. In short, the economic transition from late feudalism to early industrialization was interwoven with the beginnings of a new democratized facility in nonwork symbols and of identity with historical and cultural forces. I will return to this theme later, when a subsequent question develops on the bridges from the industrial to a postindustrial condition.

The general theme of industrial growth and meaning will be noted now in respect to several broad propositions leading up to some characteristics of leisure as it is related to this type of social order.

The machine, in its early stages, needed men who were of a different mentality than before. And, as Descartes pointed out in his Discourse on Method, men were ready in the seventeenth and eighteenth centuries to put their knowledge into the sort of practical action not needed previously. Mumford has summarized several examples of this transition: the three-masted sailing ship, and the building of canals from the sixteenth century onward; domestic glass windows; the division of the home into specialized rooms, and the metal piping of water in the house; the application of nonhuman energy to various pottery, brick-making, transportation, and brewing. Shipping became an essential industry of the young capitalistic emergence, as did advances in mining and smithing.

The success of this new integration of machine and man won out over muscle power alone, especially as the financing and enlarging of technical processes came under the growing control of stock companies; that is, companies in which those who invested and owned the equipment were removed from workers and had no stake in what happened to them. With profits, growth, and efficiency as the primary interest of absentee owners, it was only a matter of time until the large private owners—the Krupps, for instance, and later the DuPonts—had to leave whatever paternalistic traits they had brought into large industry to confront the size, outside competition, and growing complexity of their own operations. Thus a twofold, paradoxical, proposition emerged.

The success of mechanization led to increasing dependence on the machine by man and simultaneously to increasing independence of the machine from man. Man became depersonalized, part of the machine. Literally, almost, he became a machine by becoming adept at small, isolated fragmentations of a whole product. The assembly line constituted his productive nerve center, so that each worker was indispensable to others who depended on a carefully timed synchronization that was guided, not by the rhythm of men, but by the nature of the product. Charlie Chaplin's caricature of the worker in "Modern Times" was widely recognized. It was essential, to protect the continuity of process and prevent its breakdown, that workers doing the same job became interchangeable—as replaceable, in fact, as other parts of the machine. Thus standardization of labor accompanied standardization of parts of the product, and individualism in production was doomed. The more successful mass production became, the more it demanded, and obtained, the depersonalized man. And, of course, the transition to literal automation—whose ultimate rationale is the elimination of man as even a cog in the machine—could not be considered as a radical innovation within industrial logic: it was a natural and desirable goal.

But, at the same time, man became a larger consumer of the machine's product, whether in canned foods or in cars. The machine process, through standardization, brought an array of products to the common man; the invention of purchase by installments heightened this product-narcotization, so that man found himself bound to the machine as both producer and as consumer. A whole business, advertising, was invented to seal and insure the dependence of man on new products, to accept obsolescence of the recent new, and to develop a desire for fad and fashion. Advertising became the basis for man's addiction to things, while abstract knowledge (information theory, electronics, physics) became the basis for the machine's freedom from man.

Of course, this dual, paradoxical development ran head-on into the Puritan ethic. The ethic of work left man with no source of dignity if the machine replaced man, and the ethic of perfectability—the larger theological framework even of the work ethic—required more than the consumption of things. For the basis of the work ethic was not mere *work*, but self-actualization of man *through* work. A new and a crucial segment in the society therefore developed out of this new dilemma, and only in the industrial or kilowatt social order could it have happened: a new segment of the population with a new role to play—the managers and proprietors. The next proposition turns to them.

The new industrial system, which required the full allegiance of the worker in a consumer and producer ethos, also required the full allegiance of the owner or manager. The landowner of the Medieval period had been a player and a warrior. With the beginnings of capitalism he turned more directly to the productive processes. He had little choice in the matter. For one thing, the new system, starting with "commercial capitalism," was a risky business that could not be run by overseers, as the land had been run. Second, the energy that earlier had gone into wars and games of war (like hunting) now found a natural outlet as the small private armies were replaced by the military might of newly formed nations. Third, the Calvinist ethos of work and business brought even a certain nobility, conferring a social status on the businessman that had earlier been reserved for the landowner; for a long time, as business became crucial, but before its ethical acceptance, merchandising and money lending was left to the Jews, and it shared the same low level of respect. In time a good thing was seen and taken over by respectable elements. Both the businessman and the manufacturer were becoming hard workers, less and less capable of play, and unneeded in war. The businessman became the idol and model for the worker at the very time that the worker himself was becoming enslaved by goods and freed by machines. Less work to do for the worker came at the same time as his growing desire for products, and more work for managers and owners came at a time of growing corporate power. Managers, as studies show empirically, work longer than their employees, since they, too, are enslaved by the industrial system—self-enslaved, to be sure, and that may be greater enslavement. For both levels, the technological system has produced a crisis, embodied in Hypothesis II of the last chapter, and pinpointed below in the transition from B to C.

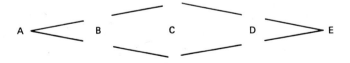

This sketch implies a historical movement in which machines need men less as they improve: men need to work less: men need products of machines more: the worker becomes alienated from work: managers and proprietors become alienated from leisure.

The full impact of this general analysis is more evident if now we turn to the United States of the last 60 years and, even more carefully, divide this two-generations of time (and change in values) exactly in half. The second period (1940–1970) is a crucial period in which the end of the kilowatt and the beginnings of the cogno social orders took shape.

The United States shares many of the general characteristics that were traced in the preceding section, but it has an economic and leisure history of its own. Some of its uniquenesses have already been suggested in Chapter 11. Most important, in respect to the present analysis, is the lack of a feudal tradition. By the time that workers migrated here they were already beyond the passivity that the theology of Heaven had helped engender. They came for positive reasons; economically, they came to better themselves. Labor unions here, too, were at first outlawed, and until the F. D. Roosevelt era suffered from decades of subordination that accompanied an expanding society with a ready supply of cheap labor.

With the beginning of World War II, labor had become a giant. Its voice was heard in the political as well as the economic sphere, although its political traditions were more internal and covert than in European tradition. Labor was able to exert serious power at contract time, with little interest in human relationships, except for a few groups such as the Ladies Garment Workers in New York. Sidney Hillman was concerned with the housing of his needle workers; John Lewis, in contrast, thundered away for wages of his miners and assumed that better housing would follow. It was a pragmatic leadership, with a logic of immediacy in no mood to open meetings with a prayer. Its platform for "3 X 8" (three hours each of sleep, labor, and living) was not devised to sacrifice income for convenience. It has never really fought further technology, but sought only to maintain or increase its income and, along the way, to take whatever side benefits that technology might bring. But in these regards, labor was only reflecting the national mood.

America's industrial development began in 1648, with an iron works in Saugus, Massachusetts that produced 300 tons per year. In little more than 300 years (1971) the gross national product reached $1 trillion and, in only two decades was more than tripled (Table 25).

This industrial giant showed an estimated growth in value of its industrial and commercial facilities from $142 per capita in 1850 to $736 in 1900 and over $1000 per capita in 1949, or a growth over seven times in a century.[4]

The study of leisure turns our primary attention from production figures to consumption. We can assume that both rose proportionately. Obviously, the total expenditure picture must be divided between con-

TABLE 25
Gross national product, 1950–1972

1950	$ 284,769 million
1955	397,960 million
1960	503,734 million
1965	684,884 million
1969	931,403 million
1970	977,080 million
1971	1,055,450 million
1972	1,155,155 million

sumer expenditures and other uses of money, as for construction, purchase of capital equipment, or government purchases of goods and services; the first, in fact, comes to about two thirds of the total and is expected to remain that high. It is further obvious that, as Chapter 8 noted, a considerable disparity exists in per capita income of various segments and social classes; to the degree that leisure can be measured by expenditures, we can expect an impact of income on accessiblity to certain kinds of leisure.

In a gross summary of relative expenditures for the entire population in about 40 years (1909–1952) the expenditures for recreation ranked third in percentage of growth (Table 26).[5]

TABLE 26
Growth of recreational expenditures, 1909–1952, in relation to other expenditures

Rank of Proportionate Growth	Percent of Increase, 1909–1952
1. Consumer transportation	1500
2. Medical care and insurance	1100
3. Recreation	1060
4. Household equipment and operation	810
5. Education (private)	750
6. Food, liquor, tobacco	695
7. Clothing, accessories, personal care	535
8. Housing and utilities	360
9. Religion	330
10. Welfare (private)	100

Again, as I suggested in Chapter 5, if transportation is, even in an estimate of 50 to 60% placed under "recreation," then the relative growth in recreation in the four decades is by far the most dramatic of the 10 items.

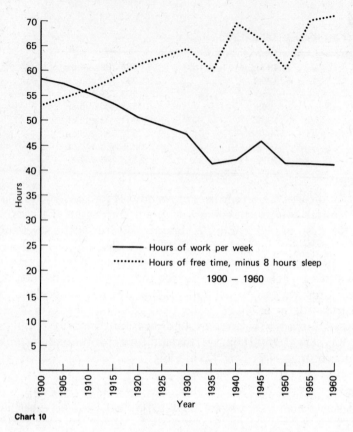

Chart 10

Hours of work and free hours per week, minus 8 hours of free time, 1900–1960

Again, the quantity of leisure is seen in the number of free hours of the first six decades of the century (Table 27).

The general directions are clear, as translated in the following visualization (Chart 10).

The solid line, representing work hours per week, goes down regularly except for an interruption in the first half of 1940, during which the war called for more work. The top line, "free time," moves in a generally upward progression and again reflects an interruption for the war years; and although 8 hours for sleep is subtracted, making a residual week of 112 hours, obviously some of that free time is used for necessary personal and family tasks such as eating.

Here, indeed, is the worker's growing freedom—*from* work and *for* time; *from* the machine and *for* leisure; *from* simplicity and confor-

TABLE 27
Number of free hours, minus eight hours for sleep, 1900–1960

Year	Free Hours	Adjusted
1900	53.5	
1905	54.8	
1910	56.4	
1915	58.6	
1920	61.4	
1925	63.0	
1930	64.9	
1935	60.3	
1940	69.5	70.1
1945	66.4	67.9
1950	60.9	71.7
1955	70.4	72.1
1960	71.0	72.9

mity *to* complexity and alienation. There are to be defects in the model, since an economic and statistical view is incomplete. We do not see in the picture the distinctions between worker and employer/manager that have been considered above; nor, applying to everyone, does the picture above show that an hour in 1960 is far larger in its actual or political work than it was in 1900. But the main view is there. It needs now to be related in a general way to the general theory of this volume, that is, to the conceptual scheme, so that finally we may extract from the kilowatt model the characteristics that are useful for a statement of goals in Chapter 19.

THE KILOWATT MODEL IN THE CONCEPTUAL SCHEME

Within Level I of our model, every element has been seriously affected. Consider some important changes of the past 100 years in reference to "conditions" that set the objective stage for leisure. Length of life in the United States has gone up from 47.3 in 1900 for males to 67 in 1969; for women the jump was from 46.3 to 74.3. The roles of women have been broadened in relation to sex. There has been an enormous movement of populations, from one country to the next, and within states of the United States. The income or purchasing potentialities of the middle and lower economic groups has shot up. Relations among races have been given both a new legal and political-social basis, with the result that on the one hand, the black and other minorities here have gained access to both the symbols and the realities of leisure experiences and, on the other, in their struggle to obtain equal rights, the black community has provided a remarkable demonstration of leisure devoted to collective goals in their communities.

Family life has changed in the past century, generally in the direction of more equality for women and participation by children. Education's expansion to cover everyone's childhood and youth is a major development. Religion, over the century, has lost its hold as a source of control and enlarged its functions in the community, thereby moving slowly toward a concern with the world, its values, and therefore, of leisure. Chapter 12 had much to say on the changing nature of work. Finally, the preceding pages have visualized the expansion in time; I have previously noted the importance of "bulk time" and the rising potential of the hour.

A natural consequence of these changes has been the enlargement of potentials in leisure selection, especially through new communications and transportation. On the matter of the functions and meanings of leisure, as they have been influenced by all of this, there can be less consensus. In these matters, social sciences move from direct observation to a greater reliance on reports by participants, as through questionnaires and, correspondingly, categories of data among the scientists necessarily give way to assumptions and theories. Thus, on questions of "happiness" from leisure of the kilowatt order, there is less certainty than on the availability of leisure alternatives. This general observation of the descriptive *vis-à-vis* the interpretative holds true for all the elements within Levels II and III of the conceptual scheme. One simple example is the matter of expenditures for leisure. Certainly, in any descriptive account, this is a crucial index of change. Owens provides the following data from 1901 to 1961 (Table 28 and Chart 11).[6]

Unfortunately, there is no formula, as yet, to indicate some measure of "constant time" that could be added to "constant dollars" for an accurate assessment of leisure in our time. As suggested in Chapter 1, social time is a potential of experience and the alternatives provided by our civilization; the use of an hour cannot be equated with eras before the communications and transportation possibilities that we take for granted.

More important, the technological variable can go only to a limited point. It shows itself up as ideologically shortsighted in the recent example of Professor Jay W. Forrester of MIT who, in his *World Dynamics*, seeks to computerize *quality of life* of a nation as a combination of material standard of life, available food supply, degree of pollution, and degree of overcrowding. These are broken down into key indicators,

TABLE 28
Per capita demand for recreation, 1901–1961—constant dollars

1901	18.1	1941	62.1
1906	21.8	1942	64.2
1913	30.3	1946	85.9
1919	30.5	1947	77.8
1923	32.9	1948	67.4
1926	39.0	1949	66.6
1929	50.1	1950	73.5
1930	50.0	1951	71.2
1931	45.5	1952	74.1
1932	37.5	1953	75.6
1933	35.7	1954	77.1
1934	41.5	1955	81.6
1935	43.9	1956	84.5
1936	50.3	1957	84.7
1937	54.3	1958	83.6
1938	50.8	1959	88.5
1939	54.3	1960	89.7
1940	56.8	1961	91.5

and 45 equations are constructed to demonstrate the interrelations of the variables for purposes of projections. Yet, as the Rumanian scholar, Silviu Brucan, notes in a summary of his recent volume, *The Dissolution of Power,* "The main difficulty in social prognoses, unlike technological or economic extrapolations, is that social or political processes cannot be conceptualized as yet by means of numerical parameters." Among the processes that still defy the quantitative indicators are the four that run as interweaving threads through the kilowatt social order.

1. An increasing dispensability of man by the machine, leading to an historical inversion: before we were afraid of machines, now we are afraid of being freed from the machine.
2. An increasing moral and philosophical issue: the moral, who should work; the philosophical, what goals are there to replace an ethic of equating work with justification for life.
3. A large *purchase* of leisure through goods and services provided by the private sector (cars, TV, tourism, etc.).
4. A large *use* of leisure through spaces and facilities provided by the public sector (highways, parks, beaches, etc.).

The combination of the last two produced the democratization of culture at its best and "mass culture" at its worst. *But the remarkable fact of our time is that none of the four would have been pertinent to*

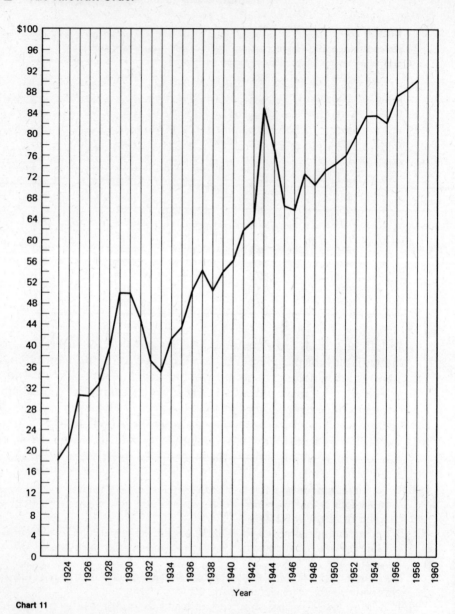

Chart 11

Per capita demand for recreation (constant dollars), 1901–1960

societies before the industrial or kilowatt. And the crucial fact of the
cogno social order, the time of dialogue and transition, is the need for
a reconciliation between each pair: that is, between (1) types of motiva-

tion represented by private and public alternatives in leisure, and (2) man's loss of work as a source of values and the need to find and structure nonwork values.

We can best approach our present situation, the cogno order, by assuming that it is a transition, that the familiar order of production is coming to a close, banged out of existence with the dropping of the first atomic bomb. A social transition is the time for considering where a society has been and where it wants to go, the strengths it has to build on, the realistic barriers it faces. From the kilowatt order, there are values that can be useful toward a philosophy in which leisure plays a major part. But, indeed, cannot the same be said for other cultures and social orders of the past? There are many roads to Heaven. Which shall we take? That is the issue of the cogno society as it seeks to know itself —its past and its future.

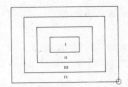

Chapter 18
The Cogno Order

One of the major concerns of historiography is generalization by types of social systems that are sufficiently distinct to be given names such as Romantic, Ancient, Medieval, Primitive, and so on. Revisions are made in familiar classifications from the advantage of passing time, ideological purposes, or applicability to specific themes.

A major problem, one among many in these historical constructions, is how to handle the in-between, transitional periods. Leisure lends itself to a consideration of transitional elements, as illustrated in Chart 12 by Professor William R. Burch, Jr., of Yale's School of Forestry.[1] He starts, as representing the preindustrial period, with an ethnographic study of the Tikopia by Firth. The Maori of New Zealand already began to accept industrial techniques. Suye Mura is a Japanese village, not quite as far along as the English village, Gosforth.

Burch's typology is purely descriptive. The theory forwarded in this volume noted that the transitional period we are now in is leading to a convergence of work and leisure; the present period is primarily one in which the mass are learning to leave the work ethic and to undertake the leisure life-style in a more natural way.

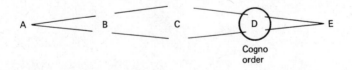

Tied to this development were several major forces, already anticipated in the past chapter: (1) a growing aspiration for secular, nonproductively overted time, based on growing experience and greater abundance. (2) the growth of machines and cybernation to free man from traditional arrangements in work; and (3) a growing criticism with technology, and a corresponding attraction of the preindustrial, humanistic ethos.

374

Chart 12

Burch: Typology of leisure patterns

ECONOMY SOCIETY	PREINDUSTRIAL		TRANSITIONAL	PRODUCTION	CONSUMPTION
	Tikopia	Maori	Suye Mura	Gosforth	United States of America
LEISURE VALUES	Celebration of work done		Refreshment to do more work: "work ethic"		New synthesis developing
	Leisure intermixed with work; labor viewed negatively		Distinction developes between work and play	Leisure and work sharply delineated; labor viewed positively	Work has aspects of play; play takes on aspects of work; leisure big business
TIME ORIENTA-TIONS	No calendar; Lunar calendar		Shift from lunar to Gregorian calendar, seasons diminishing in import-ance-market values introduced	Gregorian cal-endar tied to marked fluctua-tions more than seasonal varia-tions	Time rational; segmented; time has price; rhythms set by technological and social inventions
	Life tied to cycles of the seasons				
	Activity governed by intrinsic requirement				
EXCHANGE	Reciprocal–barter		Money introduced		Money
ORGANIZING INSTITUTION	Communal–Sacred		Sacred–State		State–Commercial
SEX	PLAY		PRODUCTION		CONSUMPTION
AMOUNT OF TIME AVAILABLE	4–6 hour work days, 150–175 holidays	8 hour work days, 150 holidays	Increasing amount of time devoted to work; less and less holidays, 60–80 hour work weeks	45–60 hour work weeks; 60–70 holi-days or vaca-tion days per year	Average 3,700 hours free time per year

A brief observation of the third development—criticism of technology—was due in part to the dramatic suddenness of events. It may be said that the cogno age began on August 6, 1945, at 8:15:17 A.M. with the dropping of the first atomic bomb. Even the birth of Christ was not as sharply defined and universally accepted in its own time as a revolutionary beginning of something destined to extend far and deep. The birth of the atom bomb, on the other hand, was electrifying to all men everywhere. It began on age of transition and confusion. Chapter 2 spoke of this period as "a period of acquiring great knowledge and also of great doubting and assessing."

The debate on technology has gone through several phases since the dropping of the bomb. At that time it became a moral debate, often turning into theological dimensions.[2] The church was not entirely successful in leading it, since its own record during World War II left much to be desired among even sympathetic segments of the Western world.

Among scientists themselves, especially in the university community, the debate turned to the "human meaning" of science or the "responsibility" of the scientist. Among the most enlightened discussants was the *Bulletin of Atomic Scientists,* published at the University of Illinois, which still remains a central forum. It was to this general theme that MIT turned as it commemorated its centenary in 1961.

A second aspect of the debate became part of the space age, which, between President Kennedy's statement of intentions and the first walk on the moon nine years later, happened to come at a time of earthly problems crying for solutions and for funds.

The third and current phase of technological critiques grew out of the environmental concerns. It became evident that pollution in all of its forms was a penalty of the ethic of bigness, comfort, overpopulation, and urbanization.

Of these, the most significant for our purposes is urbanization, because much of the attack has come from young people in the form of a positive plea for return to humanism and the simple life. Whether the word leisure was used or not, it seems to encapsulate the general critique of technology in a positive form; in the broad sense, it stresses the ends of life, and thus argues that technology should be relegated to the level of means.[3]

This general approach suggests a major hypothesis for the analysis of leisure; but now it is time to make the theme explicit. In rough form, we may state that the new phenomenon of mass leisure *is a secondary or indirect consequence* of a complex of forces, of which technology is only one. If we look again at the total conceptual scheme, the most general and far-reaching influences—the outer level—is the most important.

Obviously, *no one level of analysis can account for leisure of the person, the family, the group, or the nation.* To assume so is to oversimplify. Only an interaction of the four dimensions—the institution, the clusters, the cultures, and the constructs—can supply a full explanation. They must be viewed together for their influence; leisure, once it develops, feeds back into the totality.

The predictive value of this scheme is evident. *The further the influence is from the activity itself, the greater is its tendency to bring more expansive, wholesale changes into leisure; the more closely the force is to the activity itself, the less is its potential influence.* The problems are twofold: one, can we predict the direction of change in all of the levels and, if so, what will its effects be on leisure?

On Level IV, it is a reasonable projection that *change itself* will remain a "constant" for the next 15–25 years, since the seething influences of computerization, population mobility, international tensions, racial tensions, morality transformations, and radical departures in education will all continue. This suggests an ongoing transformation in leisure as well, supporting the tendencies toward deviancy, innovation, explorations (as in tourism), and continued reliance on the use of electronic and other equipment.

On Level III, it is a reasonable projection that crucial changes will take place in the value and symbolic systems. With added analytic tools at our disposal, the division of persons into more active or dynamic and less active or dynamic will be easier to observe. As the technological society also becomes psychiatrically oriented, its members will look at leisure in a more and more instrumental light—as a mental hygienic measure to remain more alive. Some would even hold that leisure can be more productive toward the humanistic goal for life-styles than any amount of education or intellectualizing. An example of this position is found in the work of Dr. Meyer Friedman in San Francisco. His research team draws a clear relationship between life-style and heart attacks. More important than diet or exercise in shortening life is what he calls Type-A behavior, which is ambitious, competitive, aggressive, and impatient. Time urgency is crucial to such a person who hates to be kept waiting or worries over deadlines. He has no time for hobbies; if he plays games, they must be competitive. He strives to have things, and pays little attention to human values. To restructure such life-styles Dr. Friedman recommends a new emphasis on leisure, with suggestions on how to listen, read books that require concentration, learn to enjoy food, set aside a retreat area within the home, plan some idleness for every day, and restructure trips and vacations.

On Level II and Level I we come to more specific social changes. For example, the core of change for Level II will be in the realm of communication and transportation. The former is the more important of the two, with perhaps more side effects of "consequences." It affects far more of the world's population than new possibilities in travel; its impact on change is beyond that of educational enlargement. Communications, considered not only as a fact in removing distance, but also as an instrument of symbol and image making, is a crucial element in the formation of new aspirations. The access of images, especially through television, is the chief reason for concluding that the hour now has far more potential than the hour of past decades. Finally, as Georges Friedmann does well to point out, the new communications not only brings these new images to us, it also keeps us from the reality.[4]

"...the film, as compared to the stage-play, to dramatic art, is characterized by a certain absence of man: absence of active participation on the part of the spectator, and, on the other hand, absence of the actor, of the human being in the flesh, with his direct action on those who see and hear him. .... The radio allows millions of people, sitting by their fireside with their feet in their slippers, to be present at a football match, a meeting, a music hall performance, a lecture, a symphony concert. But would it not be more true to say that the radio allows, in many cases, *a certain form of absence?* Television . . . deserves the same description."

The new communications serves as the bridge between the inner dynamic of leisure and the external elements of Level IV. A few rudimentary reminders of its growth are useful.

Table 29 indicates the growth of radio sets for Canada, the United States, and Western Europe between 1938 and 1962.[5] Each of these major areas had the following number of radio sets per 1000 inhabitants:
The contrast is seen on Chart 13.

The new "access" in the United States, which produced a noticeable upturn after 1950, was due to the surge in small transistor radios. This

TABLE 29
Radio sets per 1000 persons, 1938–1962

	1938	1950	1955	1960	1962[a]
Canada	96	370	386	449	504
United States	314	560	798	975	1006
Western Europe	117	155	201	230	246

[a] Data for 1961.

provided many Americans with the ownership of a second or even a third radio in the home for the kitchen or the bedroom. Canada and Western Europe, of course, had similar potential, but less economic surplus for such luxury.

Ownership of television sets for the same areas, but for a shorter range in time (TV did not begin its commercial career until abour 1946),[6] is shown in Table 30.

These numbers are seen in Chart 14.

TABLE 30

Television sets per 1000 inhabitants, 1950-1962

	1950	1955	1960	1962
Canada	3	121	219	235
United States	70	227	310	322
Western Europe	2	21	77	105

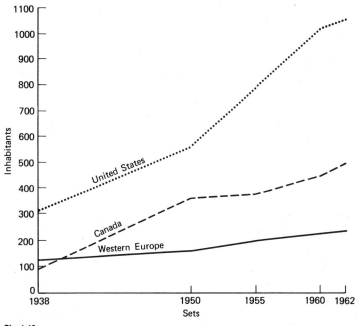

Chart 13

Number of radio sets in the United States, Canada, and Western Europe (sets per 1000 inhabitants), 1938–1962

Very shortly after television became available in 1950, 70 of every 1000 persons in the United States already had a set. In 12 years, this number multiplied only 4.6 times, whereas the Canadian number increased 75 times and the Western European number multiplied 52 times. The European economy started its remarkable post-World War II recovery in 1944, especially, as Chart 15 indicates, for Germany, in 1947.[7]

However, by January 1969, fully 95 percent of all United States families had TV sets; color sets were owned then as follows in different regions of the nation.

Northeast	29%
Northcentral	34%
South	29%
West	40%

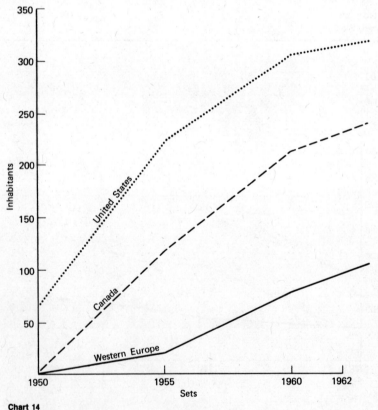

Chart 14

Television sets in use in the United States, Canada, and Western Europe (sets per 100 inhabitants), 1950–1962

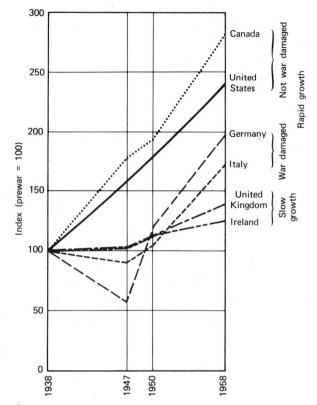

Chart 15

Growth of GNP in selected countries of Western Europe and the western hemisphere, prewar to 1947, 1950, and 1958

    Of those with color sets, 54 percent of families had two or more sets. By 1971, 98.8 percent of all American households had a black and white TV set, and 51.1 percent owned an additional set for color.[8]

    Thus, on several major scores, current technology has spurred the new interest in leisure: by actual or potential replacement of human labor by machines, by the spread of worldwide images, and by the debate on priorities and ends. In each case, these are *by-products* leading toward leisure instead of a direct assault on the problem. After the Rachel Carson book there was an observable move toward the elevation of environmentalism to *a direct* instead of an indirect concern. One would be naive to assume that leisure is at the point of national consciousness where it can attract a comparable concern. For one, the environmental issue is observable, in the ruination of nature, dramatic health hazards as in air pollution, or the plethora of billboards. Already, as a basis for the agitation and legislation, a strong conservationist movement stands. Furthermore, young people, geared mentally to causes, but often finding themselves rejected in the political process, found in environmentalism a set of issues that combines the threads of action, education, the future, a critique against special interests, and specific as well as general data. No Paul Ehrlich of the leisure movement has yet emerged to popularize the issue.

Thus, in the course of the forthcoming debate on values for the emerging social order, I anticipate that leisure will profit along the way. Its overall impact is a *composite* of the impact of such areas as the mass media, adult education, the arts, or public recreation, and this synthesis —the core of leisure research of policy—is too broad and diffuse for dramatic public interest.

Thus we come to a strange analytic impasse: leisure becomes a massive new force, psychologically and economically, yet one that comes together from the convergence of many subparts or forces such as technology, population moves, family changes, or the evolving values of youth. The analysis in such a situation is difficult enough. More difficult yet is the planning that will take place.

Should it be a planning that starts with some of the root causes, such as flexible time plans in work? How far, for example, should the leisure field concern itself with the four-day workweek? During the 1971 sessions of the White House Conference on Aging, some speakers at the "roles and activities" section made strong appeals for legislation to end poverty among older persons; when others suggested that, after all, other sections of the conference were already concerned with economic matters, their reply was that these issues were indivisible. And, to a real extent, they were right. Yet strategic lines must be drawn for policy.

A second issue of planning in times of such rapid change is the difficulty of determining anchors in point of time. As far as technology seems to have changed our living patterns in the past few decades, the statement is often heard that, really, things are just beginning. Patrick Hazard takes this stance when he says, "The trouble with the coroners of Mass Culture is that they find a morbid satisfaction in writing obituaries on a society just doffing its swaddling clothes." [9] Our time sense, historically considered, is badly distorted in the cogno society. What was a "long-time," or "long-range planning" yesteryear has lost all meaning.

Furthermore, the most reliable assumptions are under reappraisal in such an unstable time—the purpose of the family, the viability of the city as a way of life, the credibility of our government. Illich has raised serious questions about the basic usefulness of the school. Where, indeed, can we turn? Occasionally we turn to our nostalgias, as in the highly profitable motion picture "Love Story" or the public television presentation of the "Forsyte Saga." Occasionally we stage something like a walk on the moon to provide a national lift and adventure, in addition to its contribution to science. Sometimes a war provides a rootedness through familiar symbols. Georges Friedmann argues that the new dynamic is the universal groping toward *pleasure.*

Yet reducing the leisure phenomenon of our time to a single motivation—pleasure—is too simple. The position to which I have come is that the primary factor of the transition that is here called cogno, that is, the factor that must dominate the planning philosophy, is that *a neoprimitive convergence is taking place* between work and leisure. The convergence is, of course, far more complex than it is in primitive social orders. Some examples of the current convergence are seen in dualities such as the following.

1. Near-far	6. Automobile-home
2. Old-young	7. Male-female
3. Urban-rural	8. Work-leisure
4. Domestic-international	9. Indoor-outdoor
5. Black-white	10. Conscious-subconscious
	11. Child-adult

These are only elements within larger fusions of the familiar institutions: political, economic, social, religious, familial, recreation.

Many questions emerge from this broad hypothesis. It is, after all, a juxtaposition of homogeneity versus heterogeneity. Long ago, in perhaps the most fundamental of all sociological propositions, Spencer laid out this dynamic direction of social transformation "from indefinite, incoherent homogeneity to a definite, coherent heterogeneity. . . ." The matter of directions of society gave way to a variety of linear, cyclical and fluctuational theories that have been brilliantly summarized and criticized by Pitirim Sorokin. An even more complex set of problems was raised by Sorokin himself, seeking to identify the various types of integrations that characterize the society. His types—Sensate and Ideational—are already classical terms and the basis of his significant critiques of American life. He has harsh things to say about this age, and was joined by the English historian Toynbee in a gloomy set of predictions that grew out of a cyclical view of history.[10]

The theory with which this volume concludes on leisure cannot be said to fall into the "cyclical" tradition, because it is a single large pattern instead of a set of repetitions. Yet the terminology of "neoprimitivism" does fundamentally suggest a grand A-B-A historical pattern (<>). Certainly this model is contrary to the evolutionary hypothesis of a Spencer; the differences between the "fusions" of the primitive and the cultivated are too different to speak of historical repetitions. What we have is a physical, material basis in which the present move toward nature is already colored by hundreds of centuries of urbanization, crowding, progressive hurry, and *Gesellschaft*. The child has seen so much packaged foods in the supermarket that the farm has lost its productive magic—if he ever gets far enough from his father's car to see the inside of a farm.

And of all the fusions, that of work-nonwork is the most perplexing. On the surface it appears to be so simple: let the machines carry on! What more could one ask than the vision that Aristotle pictured—the economy "in which the shuttle would weave by itself, the lyre would play by itself, and loaves of bread would spring out of the oven untouched by human hand." The trouble is that by the time all this comes to pass, man becomes jaded and loses the vision and daring. Recall the head of the U.S. Patent Office who resigned in 1865 with the statement that everything had by now been invented! Or the vision of Harvard astronomer as late as 1908 who could write that:

"The popular mind often pictures gigantic flying-machines speeding across the Atlantic carrying innumerable passengers in a way analogous to our modern steamships . . . it seems safe to say that such ideas are wholly visionary, and even if a machine could get across with one or two passengers the expense would be prohibitive to any but the capitalist who could use his own yacht. Another popular fallacy is to expect enormous speeds . . . to suppose that the flying machine could be used to drop dynamite upon an enemy in time of war." [11]

So the vision of freedom in nonwork, too, has become sophisticated, educated, and removed from its childlike delight. Problems develop where celebration should prevail: fear sets in on the long week and on the prospect of retirement. Living—just living—becomes an issue, as time hangs heavy. The shuttle weaves by itself, and one hops into his car for a restless running about, paying for gadgets to lower the windows with a button and to turn on a record with stereophonic sound.

The planning for leisure that comes from this condition must indulge in a giant semantic game, to bring a new perception to an old situation —the perception of guiltlessness and relaxation in a guilt-ridden and uptight era. The transition to the heaven on earth is not smooth and happy. We must first plan the mood, the philosophy. Only then is there a place for content. The plan of answers is less difficult than the plan to address new questions, that is, to get away far enough from the "realities" of today into our inner recesses and resources. Yesterday it was at least physically simple; there were places and retreats away from the city, and time was deliberately devoted to the intercourse of what Milton called "fit conversing souls."

"To achieve this it was necessary to leave the city and all its cares—and thus the Renaissance villa came into being. . . . Here they discussed the themes of the day: the nature of beauty, honor, love, nobility, riches, the liberal arts." [12]

The suburban home of today is hardly the villa on the Mediterranean, but there are parallels: in its discussions, helped by TV interviews or late-evening talk shows; space developments may equal the former discourses on astrology; the Pentagon papers and Watergate may hold as much interest for our day as Columbus' letter in its time.

The situation of today has its plusses and minuses. It has a longer tradition to study and better access to all the paraphernalia for the task. It can build on more strengths, but the first task is to recognize them. The second is to act on them. The third is to solidify the directions, so that the cogno society of self-questioning may move toward a philosophy of some assertion and confidence—a cultivated society.

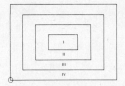

Chapter 19
The Cultivated Order

Our look at the future of leisure might begin with the "future" as seen by men of the past whose vision can be checked by the present. The examples to be used were written in 1516, 1887, and in the twentieth century.

In Sir Thomas More's *Utopia,* written in 1516, no one works more than six hours a day. Free time is not misspent; there are lectures in the mornings, and considerable other time goes toward cultivation of the mind. Other activities described by the traveler Raphael Hylhtodeny include riding horses, extensive gardening, games such as chess, travel, music, and conversation. True pleasures of the body are attained in satisfaction of the senses and in a total harmonious state; pleasure of the soul comes from the contemplation of the truth.[1]

Julian West, the reporter of Edward Bellamy's *Looking Backward,* is hypnotized in 1887, to awaken in 2000 A.D. He finds that Boston and his country are quite different. The people have by now taken over business and industry. Everyone from 21 to 45 is employed by the government. As to the implications of this early retirement:

"Your workshops were filled with children and old men, but we hold the period of youth sacred to education, and the period of maturity, when the physical forces begin to flag, equally sacred to ease and agreeable relaxation."[2]

In this society, families have private dining rooms in public buildings, "But"—as Dr. Lete tells Julian West—"it is not our labor, but the higher and larger activites which the performance of our task will leave us to enter upon, that are considered the main business of existence."[3] Then comes the major philosophy of this society.

"Of course not all, nor the majority, have those scientific, artistic, literary, or scholarly interests which make leisure the one thing valuable to their possessors. Many look upon the last half of life chiefly as a period for enjoyment of other sorts; for travel, for social relaxation in the company of their life-time friends; a time for the cultivation of all manner of personal idiosyncracies and special tastes, and the pursuit of every imaginable form of recreation; in a word, a time for the leisurely and unperturbed appreciation of the good things of the world which they have helped to create. But whatever the differences between our individual tastes as to the use we shall put our leisure to, we all agree in looking forward to the date of our discharge as the time when we shall first enter upon the full enjoyment of our birthright, the period when we shall first really attain our majority and become enfranchised from discipline and control, with the fee of our lives vested in ourselves."[4]

Brave New World, by Aldous Huxley, is often compared with Orwell's *1984* as a picture, not of an ideal Utopian world, but of the world toward which we seem to be moving.[5]

Huxley's new world is located in England. Its mottoes or values are community, identity, and stability. Five classes of people are produced in test tubes to insure these state aims. Children are carefully trained through "sleep teaching" to accept the predescribed ways of living and thinking. The drug *soma* serves to regulate moods; except in time of work, adults should react as children. There is no "leisure from pleasure." The Library, explains Dr. Gaffney, "contains only books of reference. If our young people need distraction, they can get it at the feelies. We don't encourage them to indulge in any solitary amusements." The lower classes do not find life hard. It's light, it's childishly simple. No strain on the mind or the muscles. Seven and a half hours of mild, unexhausting labour, and then the *soma* ration and games and unrestricted copulation and the feelies. What more can they ask for . . .?

Shorter hours have been tried in this society, resulting not in greater happiness, but in the use of more *soma*. Excessive leisure would be cruel. Some leisure is used to increase consumption by the use of complicated apparatus; children are encouraged in erotic play. Some vacations are spent in rocket travel to far distances. The major value that dominates everything is found in the view, "Universal happiness keeps the wheels steadily turning; truth and beauty can't."

In H. G. Wells' "Modern State," described in *The Shape of Things to Come,* there is no private ownership of property. In the history of 1929 to 2105, there is at the end "the reluctant lifting of one prohibition after another."

"We may now go naked, love as we like, eat, drink and amuse ourselves with our work or as we will, subject only to proper respect for unformed minds. Properly nourished people do not take to gluttony, properly interested people are not overwhelmed by sex."[6]

A World Council had been created in 1978; by 2000 only a twentieth of the world population comprises the ruling group. Leisure is feared in this society; new work is invented to keep the people busy. Gambling is punished; horse racing, sport, and cards are on exhibit only in museums. As any ordinary man travels to all parts of the world, he takes no luggage; everything is available everywhere, and disposable clothing eliminates laundry. Much time is spent in clubs modeled after the Baths of Rome. "Here from the start were grouped the gymnastic and sports halls, dancing-floors, conference rooms, the perpetual news cinema, libraries, reading-rooms, small studies, studios and social centres of the reviving social life."[7]

Perhaps in no detail have we yet approached either extreme of these visions and warnings, whether in control by drugs, artificial weather, paper clothing, world government, complete automation, Big Brother, or a widespread "contemplation of the truth" and a harmonious state of the body. Yet general forecasts point toward all of these and many other possibilities within the framework of either a creative welfare philosophy of Bellamy or a technological society controlled by Old Ford of Huxley's world.

A highly important collection for general predictions has been made in the volume *the year 2000 A.D.* by Herman Kahn and Anthony J. Weiner of the Hudson Institute, as an outgrowth of the "Commission on the Year 2000" established by the American Academy of Arts and Sciences.[8]

Kahn and Weiner look forward to 80 percent of the population being in magalopolitan areas, especially the 80 million in Boswash (Boston to Washington), an eighth of the population in Chipitts (Chicago to Pittsburgh, north to Canada), and a sixteenth of the United States in Sansan, from San Diego to Santa Barbara or even to San Francisco. There will be a heavy emphasis on government, professions, and nonprofit organizations. Leisure is given as one of the major areas of change in the decades ahead.

The Commission itself, headed by Dr. Daniel Bell, is pursuing its far-ranging attempt to develop techniques for prediction as well as to provide a substantive view of social change and its implications. An interim report was its Summer 1967, issue of *Daedalus,* a now indispensable addition to the futurist literature. Karl Deutsch of Yale sees the government sector growing from a third to 40 or 50 percent. Stephen Graubard, editor of this journal and a historian, wonders aloud on the diminishing lines between "public" and "private" interests. Bell sees the university, not business, as the new source of power and values in several articles. Daniel P. Moynihan foresees a "wedding-cake federation," with more state and local use of central funds.[9]

In *The Hidden Dimension,* Edward T. Hall discusses two new fields to solving problems of overcrowding.[10]

1. "Proxemics" is his term for the "interrelated observations and theories of man's use of space as a specialized elaboration of culture." The adequate space necessary for one culture may differ from another. Ethnic groups such as the Negro and the Puerto Rican derive satisfaction and security in a dense situation. Other groups need more space, but he thinks all people need outdoor areas.
2. Territoriality is the basic concept of animal behavior. From animals and birds we learn how cannibalism, mass suicide, and homosexuality can reduce population. Overstressed animals suffer from circulatory disorders, heart attacks, and lowered resistance to disease. He cites the Black Death plague as an example. A thorough study of the French family with regard to housing was made by the Chombard de Lawves, a husband and wife team who combine the skills of sociology and psychology. They made a startling discovery in the number of square meters needed for each person in each unit; they found that social and physical pathologies doubled when less than 8 to 10 square meters for each person was present.

Instant communications are expected to decentralize cities, like industries, since only a small percentage of the population will work. C. P. Snow predicts 80 percent of the population will be underemployed in a leisure-oriented society looking for a purpose in life.

What will the average income be for a man paid very possibly not to work? A brief income history helps to appreciate the answer. In New York in 1967, $4000 a year was required for a "modest but adequate living standard" as noted in Herman Miller's *Rich Man, Poor Man.*[11] In 1971, $5200 was required, a 28 percent increase. He predicts a $7000 requirement by 1975 (in 1961 dollars). However, a recent study showed the necessity for $9500 for today's family of four. The predicted income for 2000 A.D. is $35,000 in 1966 dollars. Kahn foresees work during two to three months of the year and the pursuit of avocations during the rest of the year.

Businessmen are not oblivious to the future trends. Recently, businessmen, educators, and government officials gathered to dedicate the new $1 million Manager Learning Center of the American Foundation for Management Research in Hamilton, New York and to discuss the state of management in 2000 A.D. They had three educated guesses about the future.

1. Labor unions will be weakened or phased out, with the government assuming more labor benefit programs.
2. Corporation officials will spend time with government in "residences," therefore playing a bigger role in running government.
3. Businessmen will work less and study more.

They all agreed with one aspect of management that will not change. ". . . the manager's decisions will be made in the pit of his stomach," just as he does today, said Norman J. Rean, Special Assistant to the Secretary of the Navy.[12]

As businessmen of the future tap the rich resources of the university of the future, they will be relinquishing their authority as the primary institution of society to the university. Knowledge will be the source of meaning, purpose, and happiness in life.

Bell predicts that what is crucial in the postindustrial society is not merely a shift from property or political position to knowledge as the new base of power, but a change in the character of knowledge itself. Education in 2000 A.D. will be unrecognizable to today's educator. The present school structure will disappear. Buildings will be round, hexagonal, or made up of clusters of units, with movable walls and furniture. There will be an instructional materials complex containing a library of books, tapes, slides, films, carrels for individual television or computer instruction, and possibly a central computer console through which students will be able to obtain research information in minutes from an "information retriever," which could be miles away, by code dialing.[13]

Future educational devices will include computer keyboards and screens for individual use and talking typewriters designed especially for teaching preschoolers and retarded children to read and compose sentences. They will also be used by older students and adults for remedial work.

Some students of the future may never go to school but will have dial access to programmed materials in school, library, or media center, and packaged instructional programs to put on home television sets for a color-learning adventure. Other students will have individualized study at school or at a learning center. This may occur as early as the 1980s.

William T. Knox, a scientific advisor to President Johnson, stated, "By 1980 perhaps half of the public school districts and all of the colleges and universities in the U.S. will be employing remote terminal, direct-access computers."

Again, the details of such forecasts are unimportant; the general rapidity of change cannot be ignored, whether in respect to physical conditions or to attitudes, values, and behavior patterns. Leisure is at the forefront of these probes and changes. If planning in general has more relevence now than in previous, more traditional societies, then planning for leisure is especially necessary. The fundamental issue is the balance between the provision of alternatives and the fundamental element of personal freedom.

PLANNING FOR THE FUTURE OF LEISURE

The purposes of planning for leisure are (1) to arrive at goals that are desirable and (2) to prevent the development of conditions that are undesirable.

Comprehensive planning can realistically establish what we want to see happen in the short- and long-term goals.

1. In the short run (by 1985 A.D.) we desire the widest use of present and emerging possibilities during a period that can be described as one of enormous technical and social change.
2. In the long run (2000 A.D.) the wisest use of leisure in a period that has achieved some stability, maturity, and a direction in the values that will dominate the early twenty-first century.

Comprehensive planning can realistically establish what we do not want to see happen in either the short- or the long-term periods.

1. For the short run we want to avoid a *laissez-faire* drifting of present forces that affects the leisure concerns of our society and that minimizes our potential controls over the situation.
2. For the longer run we want to avoid a *fait accompli* of values or of behavior patterns that will have maximized the most undesirable fruition of present tendencies to the end of the century.

AREAS OF PLANNING

Two kinds of areas are pertinent: (1) a sequence of analytic steps and (2) a series of substantive contents. As to the first, five major sequential steps emerge from the many types of discussions in the volume: *research, philosophy, policy, implementation,* and *evaluation;* this quintet of areas is not limited to the field of leisure alone, but applies to all matters of public policy, such as education, tax structure, military activity, regulation of the mass media, and so on.

1. *Research* includes the full range of studies in all parts of the world, already illustrated throughout this volume; it deals with the determination of issues and the gathering and interpretation of relevant data.
2. *Philosophy* includes a general position of values within which the data can make some sense toward its use. To quote Myrdal once more: "A 'purely factual' study—observation of a segment of social reality with no preconcep-

tions—is not possible; it could only lead to a chaotic accumulation of meaningless impressions."

3. *Policy* consists of actual decision making, whether by public, commercial,
nonprofit corporation, group, or person, and hopefully based on data about
an issue and a philosophy or point of view.

4. *Implementation* includes all the steps needed to carry out policies illustrated
by governmental agencies, school curricula, private vacations, or any form
of action.

5. *Evaluation* is the judgment of results during or after the behavior or as the
process takes place; it can be a formal and conscious act, but may also go on
intuitively and informally.

In actual life, as in a description of how the government passes a law
or a company launches a product, these five steps overlap. The most
common and crucial overlapping occurs between steps 1 and 2; since
the facts *do not* speak for themselves, the personal, group, or governmental philosophy helps determine whether data or issues are perceived. Examples of the perception of issues are seen in the federal
branch of the American government, which seems, just in the past few
years, to recognize officially that hunger really exists; according to some
black leaders, President Nixon did not really perceive the present issues
involved in the race problem; Senator Fullbright has written of America's inability to see the "arrogance" of our power *vis à vis* other nations.

Each of these points is briefly discussed now with special reference
to our topic.

Research in leisure planning has as some of its purposes:

1. *To contribute to a constant awareness of relevant questions or issues.* The
major issues have been classified in Chapter 1 as economic-political, moral,
and time-use or substance. All three will intensify with the decades, with the
economic-political as probably the most crucial; in the next 15 years the
labor unions will have come to some firm positions on negotiating for higher
computer use, and industry will have moved far in multiplying its number
of computers. Since leisure cannot be discussed intelligently without following work and related economic matters, leisure studies will move increasingly beyond time-budget counts or inventories of play-content to the
relation of leisure to serious commitments, that is, to studies of nonwork
content in respect to values and motivation. With the possibility of a smaller
proportion of the population working (in the old sense) and a larger number
in "volunteer" services in their own communities or elsewhere, there is
likely to develop a new "class" structure as a basis for conflict—those, like
professional persons and social planners who "work" and those whose status
(as in the WPA work roles) are somewhat ambiguous. The major contention,
when we have a guaranteed annual income and the need to choose or assign
the directions of freed energy, will be the selection of those who are paid for
going to some form of continuing education.

This suggests only some of the issues in which social scientists who presently specialize in studying work and those who study nonwork (leisure, family life, religion, etc.) will find themselves dealing in a context of social change.

2. *To develop interdisciplinary states of mind and techniques.* This tendency, slow as it is presently within the traditional university structure, will be forwarded immensely when nonacademic institutions such as large industry move more explicitly into recognized advanced educational programs. Already, in 1969, the announcement came that federal funds would be given to such private and industrially sponsored education. Scholarship in the field of leisure will profit immensely from the break with traditions of college departments and entrenched disciplines.

3. *To develop sophisticated models or "scenarios" of leisure for the future.* Kahn and Wiener's volume provides one set of examples. Utopias—some of which this chapter summarized—provide other types of models. The "ideal construct" technique developed by Max Weber is in the same direction. To my mind, the most important set of models that need immediate attention are those built on the theme of *simultaneity* or *flexibility* in life patterns.

4. *To continue and enlarge the techniques of international studies.* Several major factors enter this need: (a) the momentum from already successful international effort, headed by Szalai and Dumazedier; (b) the increasing rate of tourism; and (c) the impact of TV and motion pictures as international phenomena.

5. *To create a social science of leisure that is more and more oriented toward public policy.* This desirable tendency does not negate the ideal of objectivity, but enhances its influence in the nonacademic community.

6. *To isolate indicators of the postindustrial society.* Daniel Bell's analysis (largely, the move to theoretical forms of knowledge and the increase of service, rather than production, workers) is "too technocratic" to Dumazedier. In his opinion, what we need in research is:

   a. To reanalyze the fundamental quantitative process of industrial society in which there is an increase in production and a decrease in the amount of work.

   b. To make a new type of analysis of the qualitative changes, which are the consequence of this quantitative process of economic, social, cultural, and individual life, whereby industrial life becomes postindustrial.

The word "indicators" in relation to the changing society is currently being employed additionally by those who are pushing for annual reports on the condition or quality of our national life. One report urging the adoption of such indicators as part of an annual report was *The Behavioral and Social Sciences: Outlook and Needs,* issued by the National Academy of Sciences and the Social Science Research Council. We would presume that leisure would become an integral element among such indicators. From the summary of the report we note:

"We have data on educational opportunites, adequacy of housing, infant mortality, and other statistics bearing on health, highway accidents, and deaths from violent crimes, civil disorders, reflections of cultural interests, (library use, museum and theatre attendance, and recreational activities).[14]

Many observers, both the suspicious and the applauders, are carefully following the so-called Club of Rome, an international association of 50 specialists from many fields; this group is sponsoring the Project on the Predicament of Mankind, which feeds data into an MIT computer on the factors that supposedly govern the destiny of mankind; presumably the machines will arrive at some solutions.

Philosophy in leisure planning may be based on several principles.

1. Leisure, as a totality, should be concerned and utilized *as both ends and means.* Its philosophy of function is not static, but varies in its moods, uses, meanings, and contents. Any monochromatic ideology for leisure is to be rejected as overly simple. Its functions, and therefore any policy that follows, are dynamic and flexible.
2. *Commitment is a basic need for the new leisure rather than nonwork.* The nature of commitment in both leisure and work may, indeed, be alike, such as self-growth, serving others, or being needed.
3. *Leisure experience should utilize the benefits of technology, but its implicit values should be humanistic.* In meeting the threat of scientists as a base for values, leisure can best serve a changing society by adopting the general position of the Judaic-Hellenic concept of happiness, growth, and service to man. This is not incompatible with taking advantage of such technologies as the mass media, but hopefully within the context of sensitive taste and discriminating judgment.
4. *The models for leisure activities-experiences should profit from man's historical and world experience as well as his present and future orientation.* Many cultures, medieval, preindustrial, East and West, ancient, rural and urban, hold elements for study and even adaptation.

The issue goes much further. What the seemingly simple statement above really says is that leisure is the most potentially revolutionary force of the postindustrial times. What it says is that leisure, largely the product of technological revolution, can be the best assurance that the problems caused by technology are not solved by more technology. If in any real sense it can be a source of values, the values that it can generate are humanistic. Joseph Schumpeter, the conservative Harvard economist, wrote that the very success of capitalism contains the seeds of its own destruction; humanism cannot destroy science, but scientism can. Of the three major issues noted in Chapter 1, the first is most revolutionary in our time: the use of machines to free masses of workers while raising the output of energy. The moral issues relating to values and the matter of the uses of time are familiar in one way or another to many societies.

5. *Mass culture provides certain strengths that must be recognized and built on for the future of leisure.* The current state of "mass culture" is not to be taken as a demonstrated inevitable victory of control by industry over individuality, but of a transitional period in which a generation has been subjected to a barrage of mass media signals—which are easy to absorb—without the requisite experience with and exposure to high levels of taste—which requires effort. Indeed, the old cliché that the "masses" easily surrender, or that artists dilute their levels in the face of democratic publics, has always misstated the criteria to be applied and it has twisted history. The criteria should never be the conversion or the commitment of masses to high levels —this has not been the case in the past—but that the accessibility of the mass to high levels has produced a new base and a hope to anyone who cares to leave mediocrity. Building a new culture depends on this accessibility. That the democratic possibility often comes to fruition is seen in the highly active creative life that, contrary to the American reality of 50 years ago, now is to be found in educational, community, and professional arts in all parts of the country; or in the enormous segment (about 20 million) of adults who participate in weekly systematic liberal arts education.

6. *A philosophy for leisure must be grounded in purposes instead of in the establishment of priorities in content.* Categories of leisure are useful, even essential, in analysis of behavior; they can be arrogant when used as devices for judging others by the yardstick of one's own values. The test of a democratic leisure is not only the exposure of every man to the widest range of possibilities and levels, but the right to his own selections. Since every behavior pattern emanates from purpose, it is to that purpose that efforts of modification must go. Indeed, one purpose can often be expressed in several forms of leisure. Purposes to be encouraged in leisure are not qualitatively distinct from values that have been advocated by other systems of experience such as religious or humanistic traditions. We cannot expect a consensus in leisure purposes to any greater extent than we find it in other realms of experience; but we can expect that public leaders in the area of leisure should become sensitive to the ethical or personal values that they represent, to make them explicit, and to develop categories of activities on the basis of values instead of convenience, status, or popularity.

7. *Yet, and in no way contradictory to the view above, leaders in leisure fields should be persons who possess a commitment to their own tastes.* Of all the questions that will develop on the matter of leadership to meet the conditions of the decades ahead, the most important is that of attitudes and values instead of that of specialized skills. The attitudes should be those of generalists who can help determine policies for all age groups and all backgrounds, who can work easily with public and private agencies, who know much of

the United States and are not strange to other parts of the world. There will always be a need for organizers of community centers, park systems, and similar special agencies, or of specific activities within them. The new need is for leaders who can develop policies that follow from a philosophy to suit the new conditions; it will hopefully be a philosophy that can contribute a sense of excellence.

These principles could be enlarged, but there is a danger of elaborating on a vapid level; there needs to be an interplay of philosophy, policy, implementation and evaluation in more concrete or circumscribed situations.

Policy and implementation in leisure planning might move in several directions.

There can be no one "policy for leisure" in the United States, or even for a state or local community. There can be policies—plural—with responsibility that belongs naturally to such agencies as the government, labor unions, private business, the church, education, the home, the public recreation commission, the private person, and so on.

However, it is possible to divide all policy and implementation into two broad categories: those that concern *organization* and those that relate directly to *content.* Among the first, organization, fall such matters as equipment, access, communications, cost, preparation, safety, standards, and leadership. This is primarily a function of local, state, or national units. In view of the perennial attempt to balance centralist and decentralist forces, the 1970 Rotterdam meeting of a section from the Council of Europe was especially interesting. Dealing with the theme, "Facilities for Cultural Democracy," representatives from the 19 Western nations emphasized the need to "democratize culture." Indeed, even the local neighborhood was stressed as a planning unit, as in the resolution.

"The Council of Europe should recommend to all member countries that the planning of the public authorities take full account of socio-cultural needs, desires, and initiatives expressed at the level of local neighborhoods, and that all socio-cultural planning should have a reserve margin in its budgeting to respond to unprogrammed demands coming from the resident population."[15]

In the United States, the commercial and public structures of recreation exist side by side, sometimes in competition with each other; sometimes, as in the case of public roads built to facilitate transport to commercial sport events, one reinforces the other.

In the more socialistic countries, the organization of leisure is often in the hands of labor unions, communities, or ministries of culture.

There the organization of leisure has in the past followed, or it has responded to, changes in political-economic ideology. A change in the next few decades may be expected, because issues such as tourism will become more and more fundamental sources of relatively cheap income and will therefore influence political decisions.

The leisure theme, on a federal level, is dispersed among many agencies—the Park Services, the Office of Education, the Department of Commerce, and so on. This is as it should be, because the subject matter cuts across our concerns for national parks, adult education, the regulation of mass media, labor-management contractual trends, and hundreds of other themes. In some ways this is like the arts which, as August Hecksher noted in his special report to President Kennedy, were represented on a federal level by about 25 agencies. The establishment in 1965 of the National Endowment of the Arts and Humanities did not eliminate those agencies, but provided a single, official spokesman with funds to initiate programs and to serve the states directly.

As to leisure, it has almost no aspect that is not touched directly or indirectly by some level of federal government. The following list is only partial.

1. The increasing critical matter of environmental pollution, whether of air or water or time. The examples of the tragedy of Lake Erie or the oil episode at Santa Barbara only follow and do not exceed the pollution of the airways.
2. The acquisition and care of public lands for recreation, such as national park areas, and the protection of these lands from pressures for outright sale, concessions to lumber interests, or even the dam-building policies of the Army Corps of Engineers. Struggles involving the Grand Canyon, Mineral King,[16] and the Everglades Park versus an airport construction come to mind.
3. Government programs involving special leisure-time areas such as adult education, recreational programs within OEO, the Office of Aging, library services, and the Endowment for the Arts.
4. Participation by government in labor-capital relationships, including studies and programs connected with the impact of automation.
5. Tax policies that affect our use of discretionary income.
6. Desegregation of play spaces, as decreed by the Supreme Court in 1954.
7. Research, such as the studies of the Outdoor Recreation Resources Commission.
8. Recreation programs of the military establishment.
9. Federal regulation of radio and television; postal policies on pornographic reading materials; controls over tourism.
10. Federal funding of the Public Broadcasting Corporation.

I will comment on only a few of these.

Environmental Control

Senator Jackson, addressing his Congressional colleagues on October 8, 1969, noted that in the past decade such words as "conservation," "preservation," and "multiple use" have given way to the larger concepts of "ecology," "environment," and the "inner-relatedness" of every aspect of the physical environment. But this physical environment is unlimited in its impact on man's total life—biological, social, aesthetic, and recreational. New knowledge is required of these interrelationships, since the environmental tragedy that we confront "threatens, it degrades and destroys the quality of life which all men seek."[17] He lists this catalog of the inadequacy of present knowledge about:

". . . Haphazard urban and suburban growth; crowding, congestion, and conditions within our central cities which result in civil unrest and detract from man's social and psychological well-being; the loss of valuable open spaces; inconsistent and, often, incoherent rural and urban land-use policies; critical air and water pollution problems; diminishing recreational opportunity; continuing soil erosion; the degradation of unique ecosystems; needless deforestation; the decline and extinction of fish and wildlife species; faltering the poorly designed transportation systems; poor architectural design and ugliness in public and private structures; rising levels of noise; the continued proliferation of pesticides and chemicals without adequate consideration of the consequences; radiation hazards; thermal pollution; an increasingly ugly landscape cluttered with billboards, powerlines, and junkyards; growing scarcity of essential resources; and many, many other environmental quality problems."

One can only agree with the Senator. However, this dramatic list summarizes the penalty of an industrial technology and a profit ideology in which the broad public—the victim of this list of crippling, growing tragedy—unwittingly joins hands with the polluting agents that have profited enormously from the public. The Environmental Policy Act of 1969 was introduced in the House and the Senate, relying partly on a report developed for the Senate Interior Committee.[18] That report, developed under the leadership of Dr. L. K. Caldwell of Indiana University, notes that there does not presently exist an "environmental intelligence system" within the divisional, specialized structure of the American university. Specialists have contributed: geographers, physiologists, epidemiologists, evolutionists, ecologists, social and behavioral scientists, historians and others. "But," notes the report, "the knowledge that exists has not been marshalled . . . to the formulation of a national policy for the environment."[19]

One of the proposals to fill this need for synthesis has been the formation of a National Institute of Ecology. This Institute would, independently but with public funds, carry on interdisciplinary field research
for the field that ecologists describe as "the scientific study of life-in-
environment." The report that Caldwell developed points out that
however the field of ecology or any fusion of academic disciplines
should be strengthened, the need still exists for a high-level agency in
the executive branch for "reviewing and reporting on the state of the
environment."[20]

"Leisurology," it would seem, should join with ecology in pressing the
government for alternative policies in these reviews and reports. The
Caldwell report calls for a unified approach involving the executive,
legislative, and judicial branches instead of a myriad of committees that
now regulate or relate to recreation, land reclamation, atmosphere,
research, oceanography, and other facets of the problem. Coordination
and information gathering would be two basic functions of such a body.

Those of us concerned with leisure, by supporting this general concern and inquiry toward federal action, are saying something that has
hardly been said before among professionals in the field of leisure; that
is, leisure behavior, attitudes, and the availability of spaces are bound
up more and more with the *total* behavior, attitudes, and space-use of
our society—on a worldwide basis. Recreationists, conservationists,
ecologists, regional planners, and others who now find a common front
have for too long gone in their own directions.

Furthermore, I have come to believe that a concept of "total environment" for a unified approach must attempt a rethinking of the concepts
"indoors" and "outdoors." Students of leisure, particularly, have
become the prisoners of these concepts.

Measuring Public Costs and Values of Outdoor Recreation

Government is continually faced with its own evaluation of public expenditures. One traditional "measure" has been the reaction from the
citizenry, expressed through its election of officials who are for or
against governmental involvement; another is in the formation of pressure groups that, between election periods, make their position known
to the government and to the public itself; a third measure of satisfaction with public policy is in the use of polling techniques, familiar for
over 25 years; and then there are the normal expressions of critiques
in letters to editors, articles in newspapers and journals, and all the
innumerable evidences of public opinion.

The government itself, however, more often and more actively, pur-
sues its own attempts to measure and evaluate its services. For instance,
various agencies pursue their own polls. Most agencies, such as the

Departments of Commerce, Agriculture, and Justice, are in close touch with businessmen, farmers, local police departments, and other segments whom they serve. Yet there is need for independent evaluation. In some services, such as the postal function, evaluation is relatively easy, as in measuring the time factor in delivery. Other services are more elusive. The Brookings Institution, an independent organization devoted to research in economics, government, and foreign policy, held a conference on this theme, with outdoor recreation as one of the areas for discussion.[21] As Professor Robert Dorfman of Harvard University notes in his role as chairman of the conference, "Evaluation of project worth—particularly expenditures for services—is exceedingly difficult, partly because it is difficult to foresee the consequences of such projects and partly because it it hard to appraise their social values."[22]

Ruth P. Mack, of the Institute of Public Administration, and Sumner Myers, of the National Planning Association, tackle the problem of measuring the benefits of outdoor recreation. They conclude, first, that money measures, or market prices, are unsatisfactory; empirical work on this level can, however, be done, especially about what different people "are willing to pay for various sorts of recreation."[23] Second, they conclude that recreational benefits along a scale of utility and social welfare can be demonstrated by a weighting system through which varying conditions of supply are converted to merit-weighted user-days. Obviously, the formulation of criteria for determining these weights is crucial. Three levels of criteria are seen: immediate enjoyment, long-term benefits for the person, and benefits to the nation as a whole. The first can be ascertained by direct studies of persons, as through interviews or questionnaires. The long-range benefit rests more on general assumptions about participation in a natural environment and has been studied by the University of Michigan in terms of the continuity of outdoor experience by those who assess its value for themselves; the conservation movement represents another expression of the same assumption. Benefits to the nation are not spelled out by the authors in their preliminary formulation.

The government, according to Mack and Myers, makes three major decisions: (1) how many dollars to spend in comparison to the private economy; (2) how much to spend on outdoor recreation in relation to other public purposes; and (3) how to obtain maximum benefit from each dollar spent.[24] They do not treat the first. The second can be somewhat measured. In the latter case, for example, real comparisons are constantly being made between the "wilderness and Coney Island;

recreation for different age-income groups (young and rich vs. old and poor); recreation provided free to the users vs. that at market or other prices."[25]

How, then, can this comparison proceed in view of the dollar measure of the "relative merit of different sorts of recreation for different sorts of people"? The number of dollars they are willing to spend is not a satisfactory measure, partly because the potential merit of an activity often is not known by its possible users. With frankly halfhearted belief, Mack and Myers suggest three sources of relevant data for evaluation measurement: average expenditure per hour for all private and public recreation (they arrive at almost $75 per year per person); average expenditure for "away from home" recreation ($188 per family); and the average expenditure for pleasure driving (36¢ per hour per person). The authors conclude this part of their discussion by suggesting some hypothetical comparisons in the "cost" of using a public facility, such as an oceanfront park (but with a somewhat higher "price—about 12 percent for the latter to allow for its exclusion of "undesirable elements"). Altogether, these students are aware of the very limited usefulness of this approach, but with some value for "establishing user-fees for publicly owned parks or even for facilities within them."[26]

The authors then turn to "merit-weighted user days" as the second major approach to the measurement of government expenditures for outdoor recreation. The crudeness of assessing "merit" on a comparison of days is recognized by the writers: "A day spent by a child at a day camp in the country has long-term value . . . an adult's day of picnicking in a crowded park has, on the average, few of these sorts of values.[27] The "criteria" are therefore discussed in a tentative way by the authors, as suggestions to be pondered by "considered judgment and the political process." These are 14 in number and include items such as governmental responsibility in setting standards for private provision, the "development of recreational facilities and programs as a method of expanding and deepening use," provisions for well-conceived and well-balanced variety to meet different tastes, a just distribution of facilities in respect to different ages, incomes, and background of people as well as geographical spread, and "meeting the requirements of the future. . . ."[28]

Relative weights are illustrated by comparing three hypothetical parks, showing that Park I is preferable because it would, on the basis of projections, attract more poor families and more persons from greater distances. Such comparisons, say the authors, would make it possible for the government to conclude, for example, that "a million dollars spent on outdoor recreation would add most efficiently, say, 300,000 of the most beneficial user-days that can be presently designed."[29]

I suppose that two economists, assigned the challenging task of "measuring" the benefits of government "investments" by the distinguished Brooking's Institution, could hardly come up with an analysis that negates the science of economics. In a review of an effort by two economists to evaluate the "cultural boom," I noted that their conclusions exceeded the evidence of their data.[30] In the present case, I am inclined to say that Mack and Myers, instead of going beyond, chose to hide in the first part of the study behind the safe limits of their discipline. In both their introduction and conclusion, they almost dismiss money measures: "market prices . . . do not serve the purpose; nor can other satisfactory dollar measures of merit be continued(p. 72)"; and "the dollar-value approach seems seriously limited as a method for intra-program analysis (p. 100)." On the 28 pages in-between they nevertheless go so far as to create a dollar and cents comparison of private and public recreational areas providing similar services. In his commentary on the Mack-Myers efforts, Howard E. Bell, of the Department of Outdoor Recreation, almost can be heard to sigh in envy of the "energy economists, farm economists, water economists, and transportation economists" who, he says, "are far ahead of us, in concepts and methodology and in application of the present state of the benefit evaluation art."[31] To illustrate further Bell's concern with the possibility of applying economics yardsticks to all human activities, we have his very interesting paragraph:[32]

"Another deep-seated myth is that there are unique or special intangible qualities associated with the outdoor recreation experience which stand forever as insurmountable barriers to quantitative analysis. There are, of course, normative and value judgments associated with the aesthetic and sociological facets of most outdoor recreation activities but this is also the case with practically every other concern of human beings. Cosmetics, painting, music, drama, much of our food and drink, most of our clothing, certain features of our cars and our houses—all have wrapped up in them aesthetic components of deep values and significance, or prestige and status and power components. Collectively, they represent a veritable spaghetti bowl of value-judgment factors—intangibles that no man in his right mind would attempt to submit to measurement by conventional quantitative techniques. Does this present their being dealt with intelligently and objectively from an economic point of view? Does this exempt them from the rationalities and irrationalities of market analysis, from pricing, from regulation, or from the more or less whimsical fluctuations in supply and demand? It does not. Even Ladies Aid Societies and Cub Scout dens have budgets."

Bell's own spaghetti-bowl of analogy is revealing. Yes, the value judgments inherent in music, drama, and other arts *have, indeed, prevented* any intelligent or objective application of economic theory to them. That is one reason that the arts are in such financial straits in the United States: because the business-world mentality of profit and loss in red and black ledger pages are *not applicable* to any determination of their utility or value to the society. Prices of a symphony concert can be determined on such elementary criteria as what the interested public will pay but, since this is never enough to carry the arts, the necessity has arisen for subsidies from public funds, as is the case in all of Europe. I suggest, regretfully, that there is no economic formula comparable to the Mack-Myers ingenious formula for choosing between Parks I, II, and III, which will rationally denote an allocation of $10, 20, or 50 million to the Endowment for the Arts next to the Bureau of the Interior. There are budgets for the Ladies Aid Societies and the Cub Scouts, but there is no cosmic or federal budget that can measure the relative value to human beings of collecting clothes for needy families and learning to untie rope knots. Behind the economists' formulations, whether they like to admit it or not, are assumptions or reflections of relative worth. The government economists of the USSR proceed with different meanings about governmental functions and, for this reason, their government sees fit to allocate about $2 *billion* per year (in American dollar value) to send their arts abroad, and the United States something less than $1 *million* per year.

Similarly, the use-weighting advocated by Mack and Meyers is based on a typical American business assumption that the government should measure the value of a service (such as a park) by what people want, as evidenced by its use. To some large degree this approach is justified, since the government is an extension or intention of the people; they must see themselves reflected in the services of their own democratic government.

Yet, in part, it is also true that the people delegate authority to officials or agencies that will open new doors through educational leadership, experimentation and research. The primary example of this is education in the large sense, and desegregation rulings in particular. Government is by no means, like business, exclusively a mechanism for *response.* Even the world of business has moved away from the traditional position of creating and selling what the public wants; it now *creates* consumer "wants" in every commercial on TV; it plans for change in attitudes at the same time that it plans new products.

If leisure is to be still considered as it traditionally has been—a filler-in between work periods—the old business response pattern is valid for government services; if new business assumptions and educational responsibilities for government as well are granted, the "user-weighted" techniques are too narrow as a basis for allocation of funds.

Admittedly, the setting of possibilities and goals by government—in leisure or any other area—and implementation by funding raises enormous questions: what goals, whose goals, how long-range, and so on. Recent presidents, including Nixon, have established goal-making agencies, because planning for tomorrow is more than merely projecting that tomorrow by indicators, however well established; planning deals with changing *values* and choices among alternative possibilities, and a monetary commitment to some alternatives over others.

Thus the government on all levels becomes a partner in the new task of synthesizing (1) a realistic picture, based on solid research, on what people want to use, (2) a systematic attempt to study trends of leisure patterns, (3) a serious concern with the quality of life, and (4) relevant allocations of funds.

As to economists or others who are properly given some responsibility of evaluating the many claims on the tax dollar, this responsibility does not rest on applying one special technique as a holistic approach. Neither the economic, sociological, nor psychological approaches to issues can subsume all that counts in life. The old maxim still prevails, even with the increasing accuracy of our social and natural sciences: policy decisions for government should be in the hands of intelligent, humanistic generalists. They are not "amateurs" or "laymen"; an intelligent senator of integrity and experience is a professional at tapping many special skills. As difficult as this is in such specific matters as judging missile systems or aid to foreign countries, it is more difficult in the qualitative issues of the quality of life and excellence that we want for ourselves and our posterity. Among the difficulties of the latter—and I go back here to Chapter 1—is the issue of *observable relevance*. Everyone knows that the cities are in trouble and that crime is high, although we disagree on solutions. Fewer even recognize, as late as 1975, the decadence of the environment and the necessity for legal or other solutions. Only a handful, even in academic circles, not to speak of government, have yet seen leisure in the total sense of changing life and values as they pertain to leisure opportunities, uses, meanings, and public policies. More can hardly be expected without a growing concern from among many interested groups within the nation. It may be too much to expect that from a democratically oriented government there can emerge a philosophy for leisure when religious, educational, social welfare, business, union, and other relevant groupings have not dealt seriously with the issue.

General Functions of Government on Leisure

Reference to the conceptual chart presented in Chapter 2 will point out the complexity of governmental relationships to our total subject. Each of the four levels is integral to policymaking.

On Level I, the amount of *time* available for leisure is not alone a matter of personal choice, or even of employer-employee agreements. The consequences of developments such as computerization more and more will bring in various decisions by lawmakers affecting guaranteed income plans, provisions for job retraining, and retirement policies. The matter of *choices* in leisure centers mostly on the alternatives made available to the public, as in the provision of public spaces.

Level II denotes the major locations of communications and, in the process that draws the person ever closer to the world either through or omitting the intermediary points of family, group, subculture, community, region, and nation. Government has a direct hand in matters such as regulation over airways, provisions for public highways and, ultimately, for guarding the conditions of peace as a basic context.

On Level III, the *energy system* is no more and never has been all privately owned. Our economic development is a long history of subsidies, as everyone knows, but the "military-industrial complex" against which President Eisenhower warned the country upon leaving office has sharply accentuated to the point where, in 1968, the largest defense contractors were using over $13 billion of federally owned plant and equipment, and John Galbraith openly wrote that these are "really public firms and should be nationalized."[33] By 1975, oil-producing nations affect energy decisions here. (Iran has already begun studies of leisure *vis à vis* social modernization).

The historical points of Level IV touch government most directly in the plans that it makes for the future, especially in the philosophies that come with successive national administrations.

Given this real situation, we have the right to ask whether the federal government is now equipped to deal with issues of leisure in the comprehensive way that is now often referred to as a "system." The answer is clearly no. Nowhere is there an agency in which a total view can be obtained or in which holistic or integrated action can be taken. Bits of the picture are handled, in typical governmental structure, by innumerable agencies, such as offices of aging, education, commerce, or interior. On almost any issue, of course, there is some unavoidable, occasionally even advisable, overlapping; we would expect, for example, that the agencies concerned with parks will carry on special studies on travel patterns to national areas even though the Department of Commerce is simultaneously studying broad transportation and travel patterns. Yet, at a point in American history, each central interest has been given a centralized agency for purposes of providing the main thrust for active functioning—labor, agriculture, business, education, and the like.

The position is here taken that already, with 15 percent of our consuming expenditure devoted to "recreation," we are about ready for a central federal vehicle devoted to this interest; and this aspect of American life will inevitably grow more central. Such an agency could and, in the shuffling of bureaucracies, probably would be placed within an ongoing agency, such as HEW. My view is that this would be a mistake, assuring it less attention than the times warrant. It is conceivable, but hardly probable, that the Department of Labor could be extended in name and purpose: "The Department of Labor and Leisure."

More germane and effective would be a new commission comparable to the Atomic Energy Commission or the Civil Aeronautics Board in its independence to incorporate the general concern with future directions, but with dramatic pinpointing of new work issues of the postindustrial era, perhaps called the Commission on Leisure and the Quality of Living. Its functions could follow those of any competent agency, covering the major areas already suggested in this chapter. The following general comments are provided as addendum to the points made earlier.

DATA. A primary responsibility should be to serve as the central agency for secondary and primary research on the actual situation on the extent of leisure time, expenditures, and activities, leadership training programs, retirement programs in recreation, and the like. Not only is there no such single source—neither in university, private, or governmental circles—but the data issued by such groups as the Department of Commerce is misleading, or at least incomplete, for our purposes. For example, any category of expenditures that lumps into one item the purchase of "radio and television receivers, records and musical instruments" indicates a basic unawareness of the subject from the view of uses and meanings.

More, important international studies such as that conducted recently by Szalai and his colleagues should be able to call on an official agency—with trained personnel in leisure studies—for consultation and cooperation. This does not forego the continued cooperation of groups such as the University of Michigan Survey Research Center.

Finally, this aspect of the Commission's function would provide an integrating factor for the initiation of data that cuts across present fragmentations such as the aged, the arts, education, and the outdoors. Indeed, relevant studies by all agencies or legislative and executive bodies, such as hearings on the impact of technology would, in the proposed Commission, be sifted for public dissemination and discussion in the context of issues on leisure raised in the present volume or in writings by others.

PHILOSOPHY. There is a natural aversion to the thought of government, under any guise, developing or propounding a "philosophy" of leisure.[34] Aversion or not, the simple fact is that governmental agencies —and any administration as a whole—is articulating a philosophy all the time. And, to pull out an old cliché, even the self-judgment that it has no philosophy *is* a philosophy. Priorities in federal expenditure are the more direct articulation of positions and values such as subsidy to literacy through favoring of educational material in the mails, the position (at least, on paper) that private TV has obligations to the public in return for use of the airwaves, the conservation policies of the Department of the Interior, and so on. The President's State of the Union message is another form of value statement.

In operation, an agency on leisure on high governmental levels need not abdicate its right to make explicit its own philosophy. In addition, its leaders should participate in the discussion with private and public bodies here and abroad which, in growing numbers, are seeking to explore issues and evolve positions.[35] The thrust of association with them should be, first, to lend credence to an official interest by government in the dialogue, second, to serve as an input agent from such events to various government agencies and to the executive and legislative branches, and third, to serve the proposed Commission itself as a foundation for its own policies and implementative programs.

POLICIES and IMPLEMENTATIONS. There would, no doubt, be large segments of policymaking and implementation that could be allocated directly by the proposed Commission, partly as new programs, partly as a natural place for programs in recreation that are presently located within the poverty program, the Older Americans Act, and others. Equally important could be its role as consultant and research arm; these services are available to all other agencies of government.

However, my own view is that the major emphasis of the Commission should be research and philosophy instead of policy and implementation. Its contribution largely should be to provide a sensitivity to these issues and an understanding. There are presently a large number of services within government; it is their fragmentation that cries for some unifying force. It may seem that ideally, the home for such an enterprise is on the university level, but several factors argue for an arm of government: (1) the need for an official office that is open for consultation and serves the integrative function as an internal office of government with daily contacts and official relationships, and (2) the posibility of use of authorized funds for concrete projects. No private or campus group has these advantages, although it may have others.

EVALUATIONS. I have already said something in this chapter about economic —monetary evaluations of recreational activity. Everyone is aware of the current penchant for empirical assessments of expenditure impact; bright young scholars in government everywhere are trying to "define" and "measure" everything from poverty to education. There are a few hard-core areas, such as the Council for the Arts and Humanities, that appear to hold their own (but their appropriation is miniscule) on the basis of judgments and impressions of programs by mature juries. Within a commission on leisure we would expect the usual tensions between the "closed" and the "open" system advocates: the first are those who require tight definitions and place weight on items such as attendance figures, costs, polling techniques, and statistical tables; the second are those to whom *access* is a virtue, even though immeasurable, who find that human perceptions and meanings are often noncomputerizable, and who secretly hope the situation will always remain that amorphous.

Is it too much to expect that there is room for a group of philosophers *within* government, men and women capable of coherent articulation and thought, able and willing to mingle with social scientists and bureaucrats, but able and willing to stand on their own? There is room for a group of such persons who might serve the *entire* federal service as wandering nuisances, sitting in freely and unexpectedly on any committee hearing, addressing Congress, and even serving the President. One thinks of such men as Lewis Mumford, Buckminster Fuller, or Robert Hutchins. The purposeful development of such a free-floating group of honorary civil servants had been considered during the short Kennedy regime. But if it is revised, and a more concrete home base is required, I suggest the Commission on Leisure and Quality of Living. Here they immediately find the theme that, concrete enough, relates them on an imaginative level to many other governmental services and agencies. As an alternative, they might be assigned to the Select Committee on Technology, Human Values and Democratic Institutions, which was proposed to the House on November 19, 1969, by Representative C. E. Gallagher of New Jersey.[36] Indeed, a combination of the two proposals is not impractical. These are the directions of thought toward which government must move in meeting new social issues.

INTERNATIONAL PROGRAM

A constructive program on the international level can be conceived and executed. Indeed, tourism and television function on this level, and their impact will increase in the next decades. A basic principle of such a plan is that it must be *nongovernmental* to reduce the chances of ideological friction. However, this does not exclude the participation of such international groups as UNESCO, the Council of Europe, W.H.O. or the I.L.O. The plan must reach all ages and tastes and offer possibilities of interrelating its major thrusts or elements. The following proposals and current developments are offered as only tentative steps in this broad direction. The several steps are discussed under articulation, education, and organization.

Articulation

The first step is to make large numbers throughout the world aware of issues arising from the new society. One major technique is the motion picture, supplemented with new cassette systems that are rapidly developing. Toward this end, the Leisure Studies Program, in 1971, issued a memorandum to leisure specialists and to some national officials related to the production of films. The project was discussed favorably in several eastern countries (Romania, Yugoslavia, and Czechoslovakia) and several Western nations visited in May 1971. In 1972 the project was adopted by two Italian groups, the Italian Society for Authors and Publishers and MIFED (Milan International Films and Documentaries), which is an integral part of the Milan Trade Fair. An executive committee has been established, with the heads of the two Italian groups, the director Roberto Rossellini, and myself. Following a working conference in October 1972, consisting of many film producers, leisure authorities, and representatives of several world agencies, plans are being laid for a permanent organization devoted entirely to reaching a worldwide audience; the primary objective will be to develop knowledge of social and technological changes and the new issues they raise for man.[37]

Education

Education for leisure properly extends through all ages. The first segment for an international plan is the elderly, because the adult education is less well developed and tradition-bound than education for young people. The elderly, even in less developed societies, are on their own more and more, and are most in need of guidance about themselves. It is, furthermore, a group that falls well into international planning. One useful structure already exists in the International Center for Social Gerontology of Paris. Its third set of "lessons" for gerontologists of Eastern and Western countries, held in Dubrovnik in May 1972, was entirely given to the need for education in leisure. The new restructuring of UNESCO provides an even larger sponsorship.

As to education for children and youth, there is one major issue above all others: how can schools develop a changeover from institutions of preparation for work to one of preparation for living in the total sense? Positive action toward this concern is already underway in a major European futuristic research, sponsored by the European Cultural Foundation.[38] Educators from the United States have been more capable of revising certain areas such as physics and mathematics than social science, which might serve as an umbrella; nor has the profession as a whole yet grasped the enormity of social changes to be confronted by their present students in adult life. England has gone further in its total reappraisal, partly because of class changes following the war, the subsequent Open University, and debates on the "comprehensive" school.

Organization

There are examples of grass-roots movements among segments of mass publics whose purpose is to improve themselves and their knowledge of possibilities. One is the cooperative TV listening group in Japan. Another is the familiar folk high school tradition in Scandinavia. Dumazedier, whose reputation in the leisure field rests on his research, also began a movement known as People and Culture 25 years ago. There is a national agency to serve as consultant and coordinator, but the movement consists of hundreds of groups of various size that, based on their own needs and tastes and the resources of their communities, are democratic units for common leisure activity; one major purpose is growth in taste and experience instead of mere activity repeated. The German *vereins* are another case of cooperative effort in leisure.

In the United States we have numerous clubs, sports associations, and so forth, but what might be attempted is a series of groups, consisting of mixed generations, that begin with discussions of the use of time and then try experimental experiences until patterns emerge. A world conference of the groups mentioned above might be useful, to begin a needed world inventory of such democratic efforts.

THE PERSON

No matter how affective and comprehensive the plans and service of local, national, or international bodies may be, some share of responsibility in coming to the cultivated society rests with the individual. Ultimately, he accepts, modifies, or rejects all the communications signals that come his way and the facilities that are available to him.[39]

Much that has been discussed in this volume has dealt, directly or indirectly, with the person. Only slight translation is needed to convert some of this into policies that can be adopted by the individual, or that could become the basis of a counseling program. For example, Chapter 4 discusses various "conditions" (health, income, etc.) that affect leisure. The ways in which each person assesses and takes advantage of each objective factor may be rational or nonsensical by your criteria or mine, but such decisions are made constantly: can I afford this type of vacation; shall I accept the job offer in London partly because I enjoy its theater; shall I attend this important football game so soon after my illness?

On the matter of selection, Chapter 5 notes the interplay of objective, subjective, and intermediary factors. Counseling can help the person to know himself, but only he can finally balance one's self-determination of his craving for a hard drug, his intellectual awareness of its possible harm, and his response to pressures of a peer group.

In this sense, counseling for leisure has the same function of counseling in the area of education, work, family life, or emotional illness: to help the person to understand himself or to know the world and lead him toward a resolution of the two; his perceptions on both levels (his qualifications for various types of jobs, his roles as a husband, etc.) are clarified. The guidance we can provide the person for his leisure fall within this tradition of counseling. If any major marks in leisure counseling can be isolated, they are first, the inexperience we possess in this field and second, the greater difficulty of evaluating results. In counseling for work careers, there are some clear criteria, such as use of skills, income, the job market; the marriage remains or it clearly dissolves; the patient returns to society or he does not; the pupil improves his learning skills.

In leisure counseling, the inevitable issues are those ties up with goals; and who, looking at the sets of dichotomies spelled out in Chapter 6, can draw up measurable evaluations of the advantages of rest or restlessness, freedom or restraint, sociability or withdrawal? Who will tell another from behind his own desk, even with academic degrees on the wall to awe the client, that the prescription for leisure will, in this case, be five points for traditional, assumptive, safe activities, next to two points for new, creative, transformative experiences?

Again the burden is on the person for mastering himself within the set of objective conditions that surround him, in part changeable, in part immovable and set for life.

One's leisure, in the end, is his choice of life. More and more we can choose—at the age of 20, 40, or 60—to be as "young" or as "old" as we wish in our life-styles; similarly, we now, by the decade, have greater choice of the philosophy of life we care to accept and live out. It is a new freedom in the realms of family, work, friendships, religious beliefs, and the degree of education we want.

Somehow, a strange paradox sets in. The scholars and critics—even the social scientists, who should know better—stress the negative, pointing to the strains of rapid social change. And, indeed, factors such as alienation and crime are properly identified as offshoots of old work and community patterns in process of radical alteration. Yet the search for "happiness" (as Georges Friedmann terms it) or leisure in its total spirit has been a positive accomplishment and suggests an attainment and a new hope of monumental dimensions in the decades ahead. It may be suspected that one reason for the pessimism is that science fiction writers are reading too much social science, with its frequent negativism toward mass culture.

Fortunately, the ordinary person has little problem in accepting a free Saturday, or a three-week vacation. In spite of the proper identification by gerontologists of problems that beset the elderly (problems largely related to economic maintenance, health, or the transitionary stages to retirement), the bulk of older persons seem to adapt themselves well enough to bulk free time. The image we get of mass alienation or boredom may reflect the world of the campus, where most of the critical writing comes from, a world in which there is little communication between the creative and the analytic elements. Those absent from concerts are not only business and engineering faculty (and students), but frequently social scientists as well. Yet it is there—wherever creative elements of the society can be observed—that we obtain our clues to change as well as on a level of validity as basic as in the psychiatric wards or prison cells.

Our final overview of the person as he confronts the new world of free time is that he has somehow been ahead of the cultural critics. In the mass, he will not constitute the cultivated society; but from that mass, he will attain the level and set the direction in greater measure than was possible a half century ago on the basis of his own desires and abilities.

What this book has been about, therefore, is the convergence of many new factors and new opportunities, among them leisure. Its importance stems from the difficulty we have in isolating and in conceptualizing it, so integral and related is it to work, human values, class divisions, family life, and the "quality of life," about which more will be heard in the years ahead.

Leisure, ultimately, is an opportunity to master time—and ourselves.

Footnotes

CHAPTER 1

[1]William J. Baumol and William G. Bowen, *Performing Arts—The Economic Dilemma, A Study of Problems Common To Theatre, Opera, Music and Dance,* The Twentieth Century Fund, New York, 1966.

[2]Dennis Gabor, *Inventing the Future,* Penguin Books, 1963.

[3]Robert Theobald, *The Economics of Abundance,* Pitman, New York, 1970.

[4]Juanita Kreps and J. J. Spengler, "The Leisure Component of Economic Growth," *The Employment Impact of Technological Change,* Appendix, Vol. II, National Commission on Technology, Automation, and Economic Progress, U.S. Government Printing Office, Washington, D.C., 1966, pp. 353–397.

[5]Merrill, Lynch, Pierce, Fenner and Smith, Inc., *Investment Opportunities in a $150-Billion Market,* 1968, 48 pp; *A Look at the Leisure-Time Industry,* May 1970, 13 pp., and *Changing Leisure Markets,* March 7, 1972, 19 pp.

[6]A relatively short history of recreation in general, including the United States, is found in M. H. Neumeyer and E. S. Neumeyer, *Leisure and Recreation,* A. S. Barnes and Co., New York, 1949. A more intensive and interpretative history is Sebastian de Grazia's *Of Time, Work and Leisure,* The Twentieth Century Fund, New York, 1961. For some suggestions in the summary of this section, I am indebted to Dr. Dennis K. Orthner, prepared at Florida State University, M.A. thesis under Professor William Tait.

[7]James Leyburn, *Frontier Folkways,* Yale University Press, New Haven, 1933, p. 1.

[8]Foreward, p. 11, *Civilization at the Crossroads,* Radovan Richta, editor, Prague, 1969.

[9]P. Tillich, "The Person in a Technical Society," in *Varieties of Modern Social Theory,* H. M. Ruitenbeek, editor, E. P. Dutton, New York, 1963, p. 287.

[10]Preface, Vintage Books, 1962, p. vii.

[11]Bantam Books, 1970, p. 44.

[12]In a lecture to the Institute of Philosophy and Sociology, Polish Academy of Science, November 1974, I proposed the use of leisure data and trends as indicators of the movements and national decisions related to technology. The Socialist societies, by virtue of their present degree of industrialization and interest in leisure issues, may be in a position—together with the "under-

developed" areas of the world—to make basic decisions on leisure and environment. For reports on leisure in those countries, see a special issue of *Society and Culture*, European Centre for Leisure and Education, Prague, No. 3, 1972.

CHAPTER 2

[1]Sebastian de Grazia, *Of Time, Work and Leisure*, The Twentieth Century Fund, New York, 1962; Joseph Pieper, *Leisure, the Basis of Culture*, tr. Alexander Dru, Faber, London, 1962. For a short summary of various conceptions of leisure, including play theories, see John Neulinger, *The Psychology of Leisure*, Charles C. Thomas, Springfield, Ill., 1974; James F. Murphy, *Concepts of Leisure*, Philosophical Implications, Prentice-Hall, Englewood Cliffs, N.J., 1974; M. J. Ellis, *Why People Play*, Prentice-Hall, Englewood Cliffs, N.J., 1973; James O'Leary, "Skole and Plato's work ethic," *Journal of Leisure* Research, Vol. 5, No. 2, Spring 1973, pp. 49–55.

[2]For Max Weber's construct, see Talcott Parsons, *The Structure of Social Action*, The Free Press, Glencoe, Ill., 1949, pp. 601–610. For other conceptualizations of leisure and critiques, the following is suggested as a beginning: Geoffrey C. Godbey, *An Analysis of the Methods for the Quantitative Measurements of Leisure*, doctoral thesis, Pennsylvania State University, June 1968; Sonia Gold, in *Values and the Future*, K. Baier and N. Rescher (editors), The Free Press, New York, 1969, pp. 282–288; Jacques Coenen, *Leisure Culture and Cultural Policy*, Ministry of Cultural Affairs, the Netherlands, prepared for Council of Europe, Symposium on Socio-cultural equipment of towns, Rotterdam, 1970, manuscript, 66 pp.; Erwin K. Scheuch and Rolf Meyersohn, *Soziologie der Freizeit*, Krepenheuer and Witsch, 1972; Marie-Francoise Lanfant, *Les Theories du Loisir*, Presses Universitaires de France, 1972; Joffre Dumazedier, *Toward A society of Leisure*, The Free Press, New York, 1967; his article, "Leisure" in *International Encyclopedia of the Social Sciences*, No. 2; and his most recent volume, *The Sociology of Leisure*, Elsevier, Amsterdam, 1974.

[3]Bennett M. Berger, "The Sociology of Leisure: Some Suggestions," *Industrial Relations*, February 1, 1962, pp. 31–35. For critical comments on research methods, see two essays in *Society and Leisure*, European Centre for Leisure and Education, Prague, No. 2, 1972: A. W. Bacon, "Leisure and Research: A Critical Review of the Main Concepts Employed in Contemporary Research," pp. 83–92 and C. Neil Bull, Comparative Methods in Leisure Research, pp. 93–104.

[4]De Grazia, op. cit., p. 15. The European Centre for Leisure and Education previously issued annotated bibliographies on Czechoslovakia (1968 and 1970), German Democratic Republic (1961–1971), Poland (1971), Great Britain (1972), and an *International Selective Bibliography on Leisure*, 1969–1971 (1971, front draft). See also the bibliography in *Journal of Leisure Research*, National Recreational and Park Association, Arlington, Va., Vol. 1, No. 1, Winter 1969, pp. 58–68; *Indreations Bibliographiques, sur Les Loisirs*, Marie-Christine Choquet, International Center of Social Gerontology, Paris, 1972; *Workers' Leisure, an*

416

Annotated Bibliography, International Labour Office, Geneva, 1967; *Bibliography of Leisure, 1965–1970, Indexed and Annotated,* Fred W. Martin, Program in Leisure Education, Recreation and Related Community Service, Teachers College, Columbia University, New York; *A Directory of Scholars Who Identify with the Areas: The Sociology of Leisure, the Arts, and Sport,* Alan G. Ingham et al, Department of Sociology, University of Massachusetts, Amherst, Mass. Frauke Hobermann, *Kritische Freizeit-bibliographie* (Bucher und Sammelbarde), Department of Sociology, University of Hamburg, Germany, 1971.

[5]Lin Yutang, *The Importance of Living,* John Day Co., New York, 1937, pp. 150–151.

[6]A. R. Martin, Bulletin of the New York Academy of Medicine, quoted and summarized by Brooks Atkinson, *New York Times,* April 24, 1964.

[7]H. G. Manz, "The Socialist Mode of Living and the Time-Budget of the Population," 7th World Congress of Sociology, Varna, Bulgaria, September, 14–19, 1970.

[8]W. Ulbricht, quoted by Manz, ibid.

[9]B. Grushin, *Problems of Free Time in the USSR,* publisher unspecified, undated, probably 1968 or 1969.

[10]Albert Salomon, in *Conflicts of Power in Modern Culture,* p. 542.

[11]De Grazia, op. cit., p. 351.

[12]Jacques Ellul, *The Technological Society,* Vintage Books, New York, 1964.

[13]Fairchild, *Dictionary of Sociology,* Philosophical Library, New York, 1944.

[14]H. L. May and D. Petgen, *Leisure and its Use,* A. S. Barnes, New York, 1928.

[15]Paul Weiss, "A Philosophical Definition of Leisure," *Quest,* V, December 1965, p. 1, quoted in G. C. Godbey, *An Analysis of the Method for the Quantitative Measurement of Leisure,* doctoral thesis, Pennsylvania State University, June 1968.

[16]A. Szalai, "Trends in Comparative Time-Budget Research," *American Behavioral Scientist,* IX, May 1966.

[17]G. A. Lundberg, M. Komarovsky, and N. A. McIllnery, *Leisure—a Suburban Study,* Columbia University Press, New York, 1934.

[18]De Grazia, Op. Cit., pp. 7–8.

[19]Bernard S. Phillips, *Social Research, Strategy and Tactics.* Macmillan, New York, 1966, p. 59.

[20]Abraham Kaplan, *The Conduct of Inquiry,* Chandler Publishing Company, San Francisco, 1964, p. 271.

[21]John C. McKinney, in *Modern Sociological Theory in Continuity and Change,* H. Becker and A. Boskoff (editors), Dryden Press, New York, 1957, p. 190. Critics of radical empiricism include Znaniecki, Sorokin, Mills, Myrdal, Gouldner, and Friedrich. On the other side will be found Lundberg, Dodd, Lazarsfeld, Guttman, and others. Any recent history or summary of social science can be consulted.

[22]See especially Znaniecki's books, *The Method of Sociology,* Farrar and Rinehart, New York, 1934; *Cultural Sciences, Their Origin and Development,* University of Illinois, 1952; *On Humanistic Sociology,* University of Chicago Press (selections by Robert Bierstedt), 1969.

[23]Johann Huizinga, *Homo Ludens,* Beacon Press, Boston, 1950.
[24]B. Groethysen, "Renaissance," *Encyclopedia of the Social Sciences,* Vol. 7, 1934 ed., pp. 278–285.
[25]David Riesman, "Abundance of What?" *Bulletin of the Atomic Scientists,* Vol. 14, No. 4, April 1958, p. 130. See also August Hecksher, "The Quality of American Culture," *Goals for Americans in the Report of the President's Commission on National Goals,* Prentice-Hall, Englewood Cliffs, N.J., 1960, pp. 127–146.
[26]Kenneth E. Boulding, "After Civilization, What?," *Bulletin of the Atomic Scientists,* Vol. 18, No. 8, October 1972, p. 4.
[27]J. Dumazedier, *Toward A Society of Leisure,* The Free Press, New York, 1967, pp. 16–17.
[28]Volume 9, pp. 248–253.
[29]Op. cit., pp. 3–4.
[30]Paul A. Weiss, MASA (Martian Academic Space Agency), "Life on Earth," *The Graduate Journal,* University of Texas, Austin, Vol. VII, No. 1, Winter 1965–1966.

CHAPTER 3

[1]Werfel Franz, "The Calendar of Sleep," *Poems,* Princeton University Press, 1945.
[2]Sebastian de Grazia, ibid, p. 365.
[3]Howard S. Becker, "Becoming a Marihuana User," in *Mental Health and Mental Disorder,* Arnold Rose, editor, W. W. Norton, New York, 1955, pp. 420–433.
[4]L. C. Payne, *Not by Affluence Alone* . . . International Publishing Corporation, London (private volume) pp. 18–19.
[5]Oscar Lewis, *La Vida,* Introduction. Vintage Books, 1968.

CHAPTER 4

[1]Unpublished paper, Herald Swedner, "Regulated Time and Free-Time," University of Lund, Sweden. For studies of activities among older persons, see M. Kaplan and Claudine Attias-Donfut (editors) *Educational and Leisure-Time Activities of the Elderly,* special edition, *Society and Leisure,* European Centre for Leisure and Education, Prague, Vol. V, No. 4, 1973.
[2]Herman P. Miller, *Rich Man, Poor Man,* Crowell Co., New York, revised ed., 1971.
[3]Max Kaplan, *Leisure in America: A Social Inquiry,* John Wiley, New York, 1960, p. 31.
[4]Harold L. Wilensky, "Emerging of Life Styles: A Microscopic Prediction About the Fate of the Organization Man," read to a session of the Research Committee on Leisure and Popular Culture, 7th World Congress of Sociology, Varna, Bulgaria, September 1970.
[5]Sally Hacker, "Dimensions of Work and Leisure," submitted to Research Com-

mittee on Leisure and Popular Culture, 7th World Congress of Sociology, Varna, Bulgaria, 1970. Some of her research indicated that aside from such pursuits as golf, there is generally little correlation between occupation and choice of leisure. On this, see "Active Leisure Activities as Related to Occupation," D. A. Cunningham, H. J. Montoye, H. L. Metzner, and J. B. Keller, *Journal of Leisure Research,* Vol. II, No. 2, Spring 1970, pp. 104–111.

[6]Ted K. Bradshaw, "Culture Through Education: The Effect of Educational Experiences on Cultural Leisure Patterns," paper read at 1971 meetings of Pacific Sociological Association, Honolulu.

[7]Helena Strzeminska, "Education Status and Time Budgets," in *Use of Time,* Szalai ed. Mouton, The Hague, 1972, p. 390.

[8]E. Mesthene, "How Technology Will Shake the Future," Harvard University Program on Technology and Society, Reprint no. 5 from *Science,* Vol. 161, No. 3837, July 12, 1968.

[9]Juanita Kreps, "The Allocation of Leisure to Retirement," Appendix in *Technology, Human Values and Leisure,* M. Kaplan and P. Bosserman, editors, Abingdon Press, 1971.

[10]Max Kaplan, op. cit., Chapter 18.

CHAPTER 5

[1]William R. Burch, "The Social Circles of Leisure; Competing Explanations," *Journal of Leisure Research,* Vol. 1, No. 2, Spring 1969.

[2]R. J. Havighurst and K. Feigenbaum, "Leisure and Life-style," *American Journal of Sociology,* Vol. LXIV, No. 4, January 1959, pp. 396–404.

[3]David Riesman, op. cit., *The Lonely Crowd,* with Reuel Denney and Nathan Glazer, Yale University Press, New Haven, 1950; Culture and Social Character, *The Work of David Riesman Reviewed,* Seymour M. Lipset and Leo Lowenthal, editors, The Free Press, Glencoe, Ill., 1961. See also John Neulinger, *The Psychology of Leisure,* Charles C Thomas, Springfield, Ill., 1974, especially pp. 109–113, and J. Neulinger and Albert J. Brok, Reflections on the 1973 American Psychological Association leisure symposium in *Journal of Leisure Research,* Vol. 6, No. 2, Spring 1974, pp. 168–171.

[4]David Riesman, "Some Observations on the Study of American Character," *Psychiatry: Journal for the Study of Interpersonal Processes,* Vol. 15, No. 3, August 1952, p. 333.

[5]Riesman, *The Lonely Crowd,* p. 334.

[6]Riesman, ibid., pp. 120–127.

[7]Riesman, ibid., pp. 5–6.

[8]Riesman, ibid., pp. 356–363.

[9]Riesman, ibid., pp. 363–367.

[10]Emanuel Kant, *The Critique of Pure Reason,* Section I—Space, Section II—Time, in Errol E. Harris, *Fundamentals of Philosophy,* Holt, Rinehart and Winston, New York, 1969, pp. 467–472.

[11]*The U.S. Book of Facts, Statistics and Information, Statistical Abstract of the U.S.,* 1971.

[12]Ibid., plus data for 1969, 1970, and 1971 from 1974.

[13]S. de Grazia, in R. Kleemeier, *Aging and Leisure,* op. cit., p. 118.
[14]*The American Almanac: The U.S. Book of Facts, Statistics, and Information,* Grosset and Dunlap, New York, 1970, Table #476.
[15]*Profiles of Children,* 1970, White House Conference on Children, Superintendent of Documents, U.S. Government Printing Office, Chart 12, Table 123, p. 17.
[16]Ibid., Chart 13, Table 124, p. 17.
[17]*The American Almanac,* op. cit., Table 123.
[18]*The American Almanac,* op. cit., Table 1199.
[19]Bernard Mueller, *A Statistical Handbook of the North Atlantic Area,* Twentieth Century Fund, New York, 1965, Table IV-1 and IV-2.
[20]*The Use of Time: Daily Activities of Urban and Suburban Populations in Twelve Countries,* Alexander Szalai, editor-in-chief, Mouton, The Hague, 1972.
[21]Ibid., The use of free-time in Torun, Maribor, and Jackson, by Zygmunt Skorzynski, Part II, Chapter 5, pp. 265–289.
[22]Ibid., p. 284.

CHAPTER 6

[1]Harvey Cox, *Feast of Fools,* Harvard University Press, 1969.
[2]Kenneth Roberts, *Leisure,* Longmen, London, 1970, p. 89.
[3]S. R. Parker, *The Future of Work and Leisure,* MacGibbon and Kee, London, 1971, p. 56.
[4]J. Dumazedier, *Toward a Society of Leisure,* Free Press, New York, translation 1967, original, 1962, pp. 13–17.
[5]Ibid., p. 16.
[6]*The Recreation Program,* Athletic Institute, Chicago, 1954, pp. 2–3.
[7]Charles K. Brightbill, *Man and Leisure, a Philosophy of Recreation,* Prentice-Hall, Englewood Cliffs, N.J., 1961, p. 18.
[8]Op. cit., p. 28–29.
[9]E. A. Jordan, *The Good Life,* University of Chicago Press, pp. 92–94.
[10]There are current uses of this technique in other fields. For example, a similar technique is used in a study by the General Electric report called "Our Future Business Environment: A re-evaluation." This report is summarized by Mr. Ian H. Wilson in *The Futurist* for February 1970, pp. 5–9. The continua that were adopted for their purpose set up contrasting values such as: war-peace, nationalism-internationalism, uniformity-pluralism, etc. With modification, their description could apply to the following sets of functions: "enhancement of one value implies a diminution of the other ... Each society and generation has tended to seek its own new balance between these contrasting pairs, with the weight shifting from one side to the other as conditions and attitudes change." The major proponent of the dialectical method in sociology was Georges Gurvitch, *Dialectique et Sociologie,* Paris, 1962. See P. Bosserman, *Dialectical Sociology,* Porter Sargent, Boston, 1968.
[11]Charles Johnson, quoted in Gunnar Myrdal, *An American Dilemma,* p. 1435, footnote 39.

[12]Johann Huizinga, *Homo Ludens: A Study of the Play Element in Culture,* Beacon, Boston, 1950, ch. 1.

[13]A. Hauser, *The Social History of Art,* Knopf, New York, 1952, Vol. 2, p. 949.

[14]H. P. Fairchild, *Dictionary of Sociology,* Philosophical Library, New York, 1944, p. 275.

[15]For example, see Gordon Dahl, *Work, Play, and Worship in a Leisure-Oriented Society,* Augsburg Publishing House, Minneapolis, 1972.

[16]Quoted by Jean-Paul Clebert in *The Gypsies,* Penguin Books, Middlesex, 1963, p. 40.

[17]Pitirim Sorokin, *Studies in Altruism,* Beacon, Boston, 1950.

[18]Stanley Parker, op. cit.

CHAPTER 7

[1]George Braziller, Inc. From *Subverse: Rhymes for Our Times* by Marya Mannes; reprinted by permission of the publisher, Copyright © 1959 by Marya Mannes and Copyright © 1959 by Robert Osborn.

[2]From *Chinese Love Poems,* 1959. Reprinted by permission of Doubleday and Company, Inc.

[3]From *The Three Sisters* by Anton Chekhov, translated by R. Hingley. Reprinted by permission of Oxford University Press.

[4]R. Mukerjee, *The Social Function of Art,* Philosophical Library, New York, 1954, p. 86.

[5]John Dewey, *Art as Experience,* Capricorn Books, New York, 1934, p. 344.

[6]James A. Michener, *Iberia, Spanish Travels and Reflections,* Random House, New York, 1968.

[7]Joseph Pieper, *Leisure: The Basis of Culture,* Pantheon, 1952.

[8]Pieper, Ibid., p. 26.

[9]Pieper, Ibid., p. 40.

[10]Pieper, Ibid., p. 44.

[11]Pieper, Ibid., p. 47.

[12]Pieper, Ibid., p. 55.

[13]Pieper, Ibid., p. 73.

[14]Thorstein Veblen, *The Theory of the Leisure Class,* Mentor Books, 1953, p. 48.

[15]Veblen, ibid., p. XII.

[16]David Riesman, *Individualism Reconsidered,* Free Press, Glencoe, Ill., 1954, pp. 271–304; see also Riesman, *Thorstein Veblen,* Scribner, New York, 1953.

[17]A. B. Wolfe, *Conservatism, Radicalism, and Scientific Method,* Macmillan, New York, 1923, p. 207.

[18]Morris R. Cohen and Ernest Nagel, *An Introduction to Logic and Scientific Method,* Harcourt, Brace, and Co., New York, 1934, Chapter 20.

[19]John C. McKinney, "Methodology, Procedures and Techniques in Sociology," in *Modern Sociological Theory,* Becker and Boskoff, editors, the Dryden Press, New York, 1957, p. 190.

[20]Ivan Gadourek, "Drinking and Smoking Habit and the Feeling of Well-Being," *Sociologia,* Neerlandica: see also Vol. III, No. 1, Winter 1965–1966, pp. 28–40, Netherlands Sociological Society; Douglas K. Hawes, A Survey of Leisure

Time Utilization and the Satisfactions Derived Therefrom," June 1970, prepared for seminar of Dr. Alfred Clarke, University of Ohio, Columbus.
[21]Robert Havighurst, "Life Styles and Leisure Patterns: Their Evolution
Through the Life Cycle," *Leisure and the Third Age,* Third International
Course of Social Gerontology, International Center of Social Gerontology, Dubrovnik, May 15–19, 1972, pp. 35–48.
[22]Stanley Parker, *The Future of Work and Leisure,* MacGibbon and Kee, London, 1971, p. 83.
[23]Parker, ibid., p. 84.
[24]Parker, ibid., p. 109–110.
[25]Parker, ibid., p. 62.
[26]M. Kaplan, *Foundations and Frontiers of Music Education,* Holt, Rinehart
and Winston, New York, 1966, pp. 19–20.
[27]Otto Rank, *Art and Artist,* Tudor, New York, 1932. See especially Chapters
1, 2, 12, and 13.
[28]Wolfe, ibid., p. 12.
[29]Wolfe, ibid., p. 216.
[30]Ralph Glasser, *Leisure, Penalty or Prize?,* MacMillan, London, 1940, p. 62.
[31]Glasser, op. cit., p. 65.
[32]Glasser, op. cit., p. 66.
[33]Glasser, op. cit., p. 58.

CHAPTER 8

[1]M. Zelditch, "Family, Marriage and Kinship," Chapter 18, *Handbook of Modern Sociologies,* Robert E. Faris, editor, Rand McNally, Chicago, 1964, p. 680.
[2]Zelditch, op. cit., p. 681.
[3]Kenneth Roberts, *Leisure,* Longmen Group Ltd., London, 1970, p. 41. For an
empirical study of relationships between age groups, see S. B. R. Yoesting and
D. L. Burckhead, "Significance of Childhood Recreation Experience on Adult
Leisure Behavior: An Exploratory Analysis," *Journal of Leisure Research,* Vol.
5, No. 1, Winter 1973, pp. 25–36.
[4]Katherine Walker, "Homemaking Still Takes Time," *Journal of Home Economics,* Vol. 61, No. 8, October 1969.
[5]Tom Wicker, *The New York Review of Books,* February 11, 1971.
[6]Cf. p. 65, this volume.
[7]Cf. p. 53, this volume.
[8]Dr. P. Maydl, public statement, International Conference on Leisure and
Gerontology, Tampa, Florida, and Kingston, Rhode Island, January 21–27,
1971.
[9]See Bruno Bettelheim, *The Children of the Dream,* MacMillan, 1969.
[10]Herald Swedner, "An Internordic Research Project: Theatre as a Social Institution," *Society and Leisure,* Prague, 1969, pp. 112–117.
[11]Some observers, including this one, felt that the focus on youth, with even the
possibility of demonstration, was more than the planners—designated by the
White House—were willing to risk. Not only were they separated, but the youth

part of the conference was originally scheduled for Estes Park, Colorado. *Profiles of Children*, 1970, White House Conference on Children, U.S. Government Printing Office, Washington, D.C.

[12]Ibid., Chart 22, Table 87.

[13]Margaret Mead, *Culture and Commitment*, Doubleday, Garden City, 1970. For special articles on the leisure of children and youth, see *Society and Leisure*, European Center for Leisure and Education, Prague, No. 1, 1970.

[14]France Govaerts, *Loisers des Femmes et Temps Libre*, editions de L'Institut de Sociologie, Universite Libre de Bruxelles, 1969.

[15]Charles M. Gaitz and Chad Gordon, "Leisure and Mental Health Late in the Life Cycle," *Geriatrics Annals*, Vol. 2, No. 11, November 1972. M. Kaplan, "Older people and the Leisured Society," Institute of Gerontology, University of Michigan, September 12, 1972. M. Kaplan, "Implications for Gerontology from a General Theory of Leisure," International Center for Social Gerontology, Paris (Dubrovnik Conference, May 15–18, 1972). For excellent discussions on several specific areas of activity among the elderly, see Jacqueline T. Sunderland, "Older Americans and the Arts," National Council on Aging, Washington, D. C., 1972; Claudine Donfut, *Vacances: Loisir du 3ᵉ Age?* Caisse Nationale de Retraite des Ouvriers du Batiment, Paris, 1972.

[16]1971 White House Conference on Aging, *Toward a National Policy on Aging*, Final report, Vol. II, pp. 49–56. For condition on the elderly and the policies of other countries see, M. Kaplan and C. Attias-Donfut, *Educational and Leisure-Time Activities of the Elderly*, special issue of *Society and Leisure*, European Centre for Leisure and Education, Prague, Vol. 5, No. 4, 1973.

[17]Michelin Green Guides, *Chateaux of the Loire*, Dickens Press, London, 4th edition, p. 15.

CHAPTER 9

[1]E. T. Hiller, *Social Relations and Structures*, Harper and Brothers, New York, 1947, p. 247.

[2]F. Znaniecki, *Social Relations and Social Roles*, Chandler, San Francisco, 1965, p. 229.

[3]Znaniecki, ibid., p. 202.

[4]This paragraph and the rest are taken from my 1960 volume, pp. 171–172.

[5]See Chapter 2.

[6]George H. Mead, *Movements of Thought in the Nineteenth Century*, University of Chicago Press, 1936, p. 378.

[7]Mead, ibid., p. 376.

[8]Simmel, quoted in M. Kaplan, 1960, p. 174.

[9]The next five paragraphs are taken verbatim from my 1960 volume, pp. 175–175.

[10]This paragraph to the end of this section are taken verbatim from my 1960 volume, pp. 180–182.

[11]Donald Bell, The Theory of Mass Society, *Commentary*, Vol. 22, No. 1, July 1956, p. 80.

[12]Arnold Rose, Professional and voluntary organizations and aging, *A Handbook of Social Gerontology*, Clark Tibbitts, editor, University of Chicago Press, 1960.

[13]Arthur Jacoby, "Members of Instrumental and Expressive Associations: a Comparison," unpublished, sent to the writer in April 1962, and quoted with permission of Professor Jacoby.

[14]M. Kaplan, *Foundations and Frontiers of Music Education*, Holt, Rinehart and Winston, New York, 1966, p. 65.

[15]M. Kaplan, 1960, Chapter 7.

[16]David Gottlieb, *Journal of Social Issues*, Spring 1969, Vol. XXV, No. 2, p. 97.

[17]Charles Reich, *The Greening of America*, Random House, New York, 1970, Chapter IV.

[18]*Developments in Aging—1970*, a Report of the Special Committee on Aging, U.S. Senate, March 1971, report 92–46.

[19]G. Kolko, quoted in Ferdinand Lundberg, *The Rich and the Super-Rich*, Bantam Books, New York, 1969, p. 19. For an example of leisure in an economically poor region of another country, see Antonio Ciampi, *Il Tempo Libero in Calabria Dal 1958 Al 1968*, SIAE, Viale della Letteratura, Roma, Italy.

[20]M. Kaplan, 1960, p. 98.

[21]St. Clair Drake, "The Social and Economic Status of the Negro in the United States," *Daedalus*, Fall 1965, pp. 777–778.

[22]Herbert Kohl quoted in *A Seminar on the Role of the Arts in Meeting the Social and Educational Needs of the Disadvantaged*, H.E.W., Washington, D.C., Office of Education, Project 7–0254, 1967, p. 112.

[23]From Ferdinand Lundberg, *The Rich and the Super-Rich*. Published by arrangement with Lyle Stuart. Copyright © 1968, Ferdinand Lundberg.

[24]Jacob Burckhardt, *The Civilization of the Renaissance in Italy*, Modern Library, New York, 1954, p. 303.

[25]Ibid., p. 305.

[26]S. de Grazia, op. cit., p. 322. Bengt R. Hoffman, "Theological Annotations on the Leisure-Work-Poverty Complex, with an Ethical Postcript," *Lutheran Quarterly*, Vol. 22, No. 3, August 1970.

[27]Betty van der Smissen, "Effects of Recreation on Individuals and Society," *Recreation Research*, National Recreation and Park Association, Washington, 1966, p. 32.

CHAPTER 10

[1]M. Kaplan, 1960, pp. 113–115.

[2]T. Lynn Smith, "Some Major Current Social Trends in the United States of America," *International Social Science Journal*, reproduced in Congressional Record, November 7, 1969, p. 513.

[3]Gordeon Sjoberg, "Rural-Urban Dimensions in Preindustrial, Transitional, Industrial Societies," in *Handbook of Modern Sociology,* Robert E. L. Faris, editor, Rand McNally, 1964, p. 149.

[4]Vincent Smith quoted in F. J. Teggart, *Theory and Processes of History,* University of California Press, 1941, p. 290.

[5]Alois Svoboda, *Prague,* Olympia, Prague, 1968; Sanche de Gramont, *The French, Portrait of a People,* Bantam Edition, New York, 1970; John Gunther, *Twelve Cities.*

[6]Cf. M. Kaplan, The Urban Framework for New York and Leisure, in *Leisure: Issues and Trends* (forthcoming).

[7]Jean Gottman, *Megalopolis,* Twentieth Century Fund, New York, 1961.

[8]S. E. Morison, *The Maritime History of Massachusetts, 1783–1860,* Houghton-Mifflin, Boston, p. 244, quoted in Jean Gottman, op. cit., p. 211.

[9]Jean Gottman, op. cit., p. 213.

[10]Gottman, op. cit., p. 3.

[11]Gottman, op. cit., p. 369.

[12]Gottman, op. cit., p. 378.

[13]Gottman, op. cit., p. 382.

[14]Jack Rosenthal, "The Outer City: U.S. in Suburban Turmoil," *New Yorker,* May 30, 1971.

[15]Lewis Mumford, *The City in History,* Harcourt, Brace and World, New York, 1961, p. 483.

[16]George Sarton, *A History of Science,* W. W. Norton, New York, Vol. 1, p. 386.

[17]Mumford, op. cit., p. 484.

[18]Mumford, op. cit., p. 485.

[19]Mumford, op. cit., p. 495.

[20]R. S. Lynd and H. M. Lynd, *Middletown, a Study in American Culture,* Harcourt, Brace, 1929, and *Middletown in Transition,* 1937.

[21]Regional Planning Council, Table 14.

[22]We have found the best one-volume historical and travel guide to Yugoslavia to be J. A. Cuddon, *The Companion Guide to Yugoslavia,* Harper and Row, New York, 1968.

[23]Philip Hauser, Presidential Address, 63rd Annual Meeting, American Sociological Association, "The Chaotic Society: Product of the Social Morphological Revolution," *American Sociological Review,* Vol. 34, No. 1, February 1969.

[24]Sjoberg, op. cit., p. 147.

[25]These tourist studies along the Dalmatian Coast have been aided considerably by the important leisure studies program being carried on in the University of Zagreb by Professor Miro Mihovilovich and his colleagues.

CHAPTER 11

[1]W. J. Cash, *The Mind of the South,* Doubleday Anchor, New York, 1954.

[2]Gunnar Myrdal, *An American Dilemma,* Harper & Brothers, New York, 2 Vols. 1944.

[3]Hasan Ozbekhan, "The Triumph of Technology: 'Can Implies 'Ought,' '" System Development Corporation, June 1967, SF-2830.

[4]M. Knowles, *Handbook of Adult Education in the United States,* Adult Education Association of the U.S.A., Chicago, 1960, p. 25.

[5]Jesse Bernard, *American Community Behavior,* Dryden Press, 1948, p. 586.

[6]For an unusual statement of a business philosophy at its idealistic best, see Curt Davis in *Documentary Report of the Tanglewood Symposium,* Robert A. Choate, editor, MENC., Washington, 1968.

[7]See Alvin Toffler, *The Culture Consumers,* Pelican Books, New York, 1965.

[8]Pitirim Sorokin, *Contemporary Sociological Theories,* Harper & Brothers, New York, 1928, pp. 529–30.

[9]Source, Table 1278, *The American Almanac,* U.S. Book of Statistics and Information, Grosset and Dunlap, New York, 1972.

[10]Taken from Table II-9, p. 46, B. Mueller, *Statistical Handbook of the North Atlantic Area,* Twentieth Century Fund, New York, 1965.

[11]Dumazedier, op. cit.

[12]Boekman Stichting, Keizersgracht 609, Amsterdam.

[13]Hugo de Jager, "Listening to the Audience," Publications of the Sociological Institute, Utrecht, 1962, No. 4; *Culture Transmission and Concert Attendance,* Leiden, 1962.

[14]Dumazedier, op. cit.

[15]Szalai, ed., op. cit. For comments and further illustrations of the time-budget approach, see essays by P. Feldheim, G. Manz, G. Lippold, Z. Staikov, Z. Strzeminska, I. G. Cullen, and Z. Skorzinski in *Society and Leisure,* European Centre for Leisure and Education, Prague, Vol. V, No. 1, 1973.

[16]Reference to differing amounts of free time between the sexes is to be found in many parts of *The Uses of Time.*

[17]Szalai, ibid.

[18]Szalai, op. cit. For the best single source on leisure studies in Eastern Europe, see quarterly issues of *Society and Leisure,* European Centre for Leisure and Education, Jilska 3, Prague, Czechoslovakia; *Leisure in Czechoslovakia,* L. Hrdy, Czech Academy of Sciences, Sociological Institute, 1969; *Annotated Bibliography on Leisure,* Poland, 1968–1970.

[19]See *Society and Leisure,* European Centre for Leisure and Education, Prague, 1971, articles: A. E. Bejan, D. Buruiana, and P. Datculescv, *Le Rapport Entre Statique et Dynamique Dans La Structure Du Loisir Chez Certaines Categorics De Jeunes,* Centre De Reserches Sur La Jeunesse, Bucurest 1, Rue Onessi, 9–11, Roumanie, presented to 7th World Congress on Sociology, Varna, September 1970; and U. A. Artiomov, B. P. Kutyriov, and V. D. Pajrushev, "From Time: Problems and Perspectives," USSR Academy of Sciences, Siberian Department, Dept. of Sociological Problems and Social Planning of Labour Resources, Novosibirsk, paper submitted to 7th World Congress of Sociology, Varna, September 1970. See also Alen Simirenko, editor, *Social Thought in the Soviet Union,* Quadrangle Books, 1969, Chapter 12 by Simirenko; Boris Grushin, "Problems of Free Time in the USSR."

[20]Govaerts, op. cit.

[21]M. Mihovilovich, *Women's Position in the Family and Society of Croatian,* Institute for Social Research, University of Zagreb, Zagreb, Yugoslavia, 1971.

[22]Kazimierz Zygulski, *Le Role de la Culture dans L'Utchsation des Loisirs,*

Varsovie, 1968. In this connection, the world of leisure studies is especially interested in the Leisure Development Center established in 1972 in Japan with funds from the Ministry of International Trade and Industry, The Economic Planning Agency, and various private organizations, with Dr. Shigeru Sahashi as director. *Toward a Leisure Society, (The Prospects for a Leisure Society in Japan by 1980)* outlines several important research studies already completed or under way. Address: Toranomon Mitsui Bldg., Kasvmigaseki 3-Chome, 8-1, Chiyoda-Ku, Tokyo. For an American's interpretation of that culture, see David W. Plath, *The After Hours: Modern Japan and the Search for Enjoyment,* University of California Press, 1969. Other national studies that provide considerable data that is inherently important, but additionally useful on the part of national "character" or "ideology" are: C. Kirsh, B. Dixon, and M. Bond, *A Leisure Study—Canada, 1972,* Arts and Culture Branch, Department of the Secretary of State Government of Canada; and K. K. Sillitoe, *Planning for Leisure,* Government Social Survey, Her Majesty's Stationary Office, London, 1969. See also Chapters 1–15 in M. Kaplan, *Leisure: Issues and Trends,* forthcoming, containing discussions of leisure studies in 14 nations. Indispensable to national research development in recent years are the Bibliographic Series titled "Annotated Bibliography on Leisure," European Centre for Leisure and Education, Prague: for example, on Czechoslovakia (1960–1969), Great Britain (1962–1972), United States (1969–1971), USSR (1961–1973).

CHAPTER 12

[1] K. Davis, "Social and Demographic Aspects of Economic Development in India," W. E. Moore and J. J. Spengler, editors, *Economic Growth: Brazil, India, Japan,* Duke University Press, 1955, quoted in W. E. Moore, "Social Aspects of Economic Development," *Handbook of Modern Sociology,* Rand McNally, Chicago, 1964, p. 892.
[2] Gunnar Myrdal, *Asian Drama, An Inquiry into the Poverty of Nations,* Pantheon, New York, 1968, Preface, Vol. 1, p. IX.
[3] Robert Theobald, op. cit.
[4] Ariano Tilgher, "Work: What It Has Meant to Men Through the Ages," Harcourt, Brace, New York, 1930, selection in *An Introduction to Social Science,* Don Calhoun, et al., editors, J. B. Lippincott, Chicago, 1957, book 2, p. 104.
[5] De Grazia, op. cit., p. 41.
[6] Harold L. Wilensky, "The Uneven Distribution of Leisure; The Impact of Economic Growth on 'Free Time,'" *Work and Leisure,* E. O. Smigel, editor, College and University Press, New Haven, 1963, p. 109.
[7] Harold L. Wilensky and Charles N. Lebeaux, *Industrial Society and Social Welfare,* Free Press, New York, 1965, pp. 50–54.
[8] S. Pollard, "Factory Discipline in the Industrial Revolution," *Economic History Review,* Vol. 16, 1963–1964, pp. 245–259, quoted in J. B. Schneewind, *Values and the Future,* Baier and Rescher, editors, Free Press, New York, 1969, p. 129.

[9]Interview of Ford by Samuel Crowthers, *World's Week*, quoted by William Francois, *Automation: Industrialization Comes of Age*, Collier Books, New York, 1964, p. 36.

[10]Riva Poor, *4 Days, 40 Hours: Reporting a Revolution in Work and Leisure;* on the U.S. Steel situation, Bruce Alexander has prepared an unpublished report, *Survey of Extended Vacations*, undated, education office, U.S. Steel Workers, Pittsburgh.

[11]Data for Table 19 provided by the Belgian Centre D'Analyse et de Programmation.

[12]Robert Theobald, editor, *Social Policies for America in the Seventies: Nine Divergent Views*, Anchor Books, 1969, footnote, p. 152. Also see his *Free Men and Free Markets*, Doubleday Anchor, New York, 1963, and *The Guaranteed Income*, Doubleday, 1966.

[13]*Resources of American Future*, John Hopkins University Press, Baltimore, 1963; see also Geoffrey Moore and Janice N. Hedges, "Trends in Labor and Leisure," *Monthly Labor Review*, February 1971; for the argument that the workweek is becoming longer, see Peter Heale, "Leisure and the Long Weekend," *The Monthly Labor Review*, July 1966. See Fred Best, editor, *The Future of Work*, Prentice-Hall, Englewood Cliffs, N.J., 1973.

[14]J. B. Priestley, *Men and Time*, Aldus Books Limited, London, 1964.

[15]Donald N. Michael, *Cybernation: The Silent Consumer*, Center for the Study of Democratic Institutions, Santa Barbara, 1962.

[16]Michael, ibid.

[17]Michael, ibid.

[18]Juanita Kreps, *Technology, Human Values and Leisure*, M. Kaplan and P. Bosserman, editors, Abingdon, 1972, Appendix: see also Dennis F. Johnston, "The Future of Work: Three Possible Alternatives," *Monthly Labor Review*, May 1972.

[19]Kreps, op. cit.

[20]Jacques Ellul, *The Technological Society*, Vintage Books, New York, 1964.

[21]Robert A. Nisbet, "The Grand Illusion: Appreciation of Jacques Ellul," *Commentary*, Vol. 50, No. 2, August 1970, p. 43.

[22]Ellul, op. cit., p. 402.

[23]Judson Gooding, "Blue Collar Blues on the Assembly Line," *Fortune*, August 1970.

[24]*New Society*, November 2, 1972. For two excellent studies of flexitime proposals and successes, see Archibald A. Evans, *Flexibility in Working Life*, OECD, Paris, 1973; A. S. Glickman and Zenia Brown, *Changing Schedules of Work*, American Institute for Research, Washington, 1973.

CHAPTER 13

[1]Stephan Potter, *The Theory and Practice of Gamesmanship*, subtitled, *The Art of Winning Games Without Actually Cheating*, Bantam Books, New York, 1965, pp. 17–18. For a recent collection of scholarly papers on sports, see *Sport*

in the Modern World—Changes and Problems, Scientific Congress, Munich, 1972, Springer, Verlag, Berlin-Heidelberg-New York, 1973.

[2] *The American Almanac,* Grosset and Dunlop, New York, 1971.

[3] *New York Times,* report by Lesley Oelsner, August 9, 1971.

[4] Lujo Basserman, *The Oldest Profession,* Stein & Day, New York, 1968, p. 252.

[5] Ibid., p. 254.

[6] M. Kaplan, *Leisure in America,* pp. 216–217.

[7] G. Simmel, *Soziologie,* Leipzig, 1908, p. 685, translated in R. E. Park and E. W. Burgess, *Introduction to the Science of Sociology,* University of Chicago Press, 1921, p. 322.

[8] Ibid., p. 325.

[9] Jindra Kulich, "The Czechoslovak Standard System of Training of Adult Educators," *Convergence,* Toronto, p. 66, Vol. 1, No. 1, March 1968. See also UNESCO, A Retrospective International Survey of Adult Education (Montreal, 1960 to Tokyo, 1972), Tokyo, July 5–August 7, 1972, UNESCO, Paris, 1972.

[10] A. M. Ivanova, "Survey of the Literary Campaign in the USSR," *Convergence,* Toronto, Vol. 1, September 3, 196i, p. 23. For a general summary of issues on adult education and leisure as seen by Eastern European scholars, see special volume of *Society and Leisure,* European Centre for Leisure and Education, Prague, *Adult Education and Changes in the Way of Life,* Vol. VI, No. 2, 1974, also No. 2, 1971. Additional commentary and data will be found in *Leisure and Education,* Bela Falussey, editor, Society for the Dissemination of Sciences, Budapest VIII, Brody Sandor, 1974.

[11] Richard W. Cortright, "American Literary—a Mini-Analysis," *Convergence,* I. 3., September 1968, pp. 63–64.

[12] Eric Hoffer, *The True Believer,* Mentor Books, 1951.

[13] De Grazia, op. cit., pp. 435–436.

[14] Alvin Toffler, "The Culture Consumers," in *The Sociology of Art and Literature—a Reader,* M. C. Albrecht, J. H. Barnett, and M. Griff, editors, Praeger, New York, 1970, p. 485.

[15] Table 339, p. 211, *American Almanac, Statistical Abstract of the U.S.,* 1974. For the most comprehensive data on the economics of the arts in the United States see the Ford Foundation study, *The Economics of Art,* New York, 1974.

[16] M. Kaplan and Carol Pierson, "Creative Arts in Adult Education," *Handbook of Adult Education in the United States,* Malcolm Knowles, editor, Chicago, 1960.

[17] *Encyclopedia of World Art,* article, "Museum and collections," McGraw-Hill, New York, 1965, Vol. X, Columns 377–417.

CHAPTER 14

[1] Robin Williams, *American Society: A Sociological Interpretation,* Alfred A. Knopf, New York, 1951, p. 375.

[2] Robert Lynd and Helen M. Lynd, *Middletown,* Harcourt, Brace and Co., New York, 1929; *Middletown in Transition,* Harcourt, Brace and Co., New York, 1937.

[3]James Leyburn, *Frontier Folkways*, Yale University Press, New Haven, 1933, p. 1.

[4]R. & H. Lynd, op. cit., Vol. 1, p. 225.

[5]R. & H. Lynd, ibid., Vol. 2, pp. 411–412.

[6]R. Williams, op. cit., Chapter 11.

[7]Max Lerner, op. cit.

[8]Max Weber, *The Protestant Ethic and the Spirit of Capitalism*, Allen and Unwin, London, 1930.

[9]F. J. Teggart, *Theory and Processes of History*, University of California Press, Berkeley, 1941, p. 300.

[10]F. S. C. Northrop, *The Meeting of East & West*, The Macmillan Co., New York, 1946.

[11]Talcott Parsons, *The Structure of Social Actions*, passim, The Free Press, Glencoe, Ill., 1949.

[12]W. I. Thomas, *The Unadjusted Girl*, New York, 1923.

[13]H. Stein and R. A. Cloward, *Social Perspectives on Behavior*, Free Press, Glenco, Ill., 1958, p. 263, quoted in Judith Blake and Kingsley Davis, "Norms, Values and Sanctions," in *Handbook of Modern Sociology*, Robert E. Faris, editor, Rand McNally, p. 462.

[14]Quoted in Sylvia Porter's column, "Your Money's Worth," May 17, 1971.

[15]Charles Reich, *The Greening of America*, op. cit., Random House, 1970.

[16]J. Ellul, *The Technological Society*, Vintage, New York, 1964, p. 401.

[17]Thomas and Znaniecki, op. cit.

[18]Charles Morris, "Individual Differences and Cultural Patterns," *Conflicts of Power in Modern Culture*, Harper, New York, 1947, pp. 82–84.

[19]Herbert Otto, "Communes: The Alternative Lifestyle," *Saturday Review*, April 24, 1971.

[20]E. T. Hiller, *Social Relations and Structures*, Harper, 1948, pp. 192–193.

[21]Gerald Sykes, *The Cool Millenium*, Prentice-Hall, Englewood Cliffs, N.J., 1967, p. 24.

[22]Sykes, *Ibid.*, p. 25.

[23]Harvey Cox, op. cit. See also Gabriel Vahanian, "Ethic of Leisure," *Humanitas*, Vol. 8, No. 3, November 1972.

[24]Ralph Glasser, *Leisure, Penalty or Prize?*, Macmillan, 1970, especially Chapter 6.

[25]Viktor Frankl, *Man's Search for Meaning*, Beacon, Boston, 1963.

CHAPTER 15

[1]Edward Sapir, "Symbolism," in *Encyclopedia of the Social Sciences*, MacMillan, New York, 1968, and the Free Press, pp. 493–495.

[2]*Dictionary of Folklore, Mythology and Legend*, Funk and Wagnalls, New York, 1950, pp. 1094–1097.

[3]Florian Znaniecki, *The Social Role of the Man of Knowledge*, Columbia University Press, New York, 1940.

430

[4]Burke, quoted in Hugh D. Duncan, *Communication and Social Order,* Oxford University Press, 1968, p. 147.

[5] *The Sociology of Art and Literature: a Reader,* edited by Milton C. Albrecht, James H. Barnett, and Mason Griff, Praeger Publishers, New York, 1970.

[6]J. W. Loy, Jr. and G. S. Kenyon, *Sport, Culture and Society,* Macmillan Co., 1969.

[7]M. Kaplan, "The Arts and Recreation: Cooperation and Integrity," prepared in January 1973 as a working paper for a series of conferences and arts and recreation, sponsored jointly by National Recreation and Park Association, U.S. Park Service, and Endowment for the Arts.

[8]George H. Sage, *Sport and American Societies: Selected Readings,* Addison Wesley Co., Reading, Mass., 1970, p. 288.

[9]Paul Henry Lang, *Music in Western Civilization,* W. W. Norton, New York, 1941, p. 302.

[10]Walter C. Neale, "The peculiar economics of professional sports," Loy and Kenyon, editors, op. cit. This issue was the basis of a football players strike in 1974. See B. G. Gunter and Nelson Butler, "Strike One: A Survey of Public Attitudes Toward Baseball Strikes," Sociology Department, University of South Florida, Tampa.

[11]Emanuel Kant, Transcendental Aesthetic, Section II, in Chapter 29, *Fundamentals of Philosophy,* E. E. Harris, editor, Holt, Rinehart and Winston, New York, 1969.

[12]Wilbert Moore, *Man, Time and Society,* Wiley, New York, p. 122.

[13]Jack Goody, "Time: Social Organization," *International Encyclopedia of Social Science,* p. 34.

[14]George Sarton, *A History of Science,* Vol. 2, Norton Library, 1959, pp. 326–331.

[15]Sarton, ibid., p. 329.

[16]Jack Goody, op. cit., p. 38.

[17]M. Kaplan, *Leisure in America,* pp. 101–103.

[18]E. T. Hiller, *Social Relations and Structures, a Study in Principles of Sociology,* Harper and Brothers, New York, 1947.

[19]The material from here to the end of the chapter constituted part of an article, "Communications in a Heavenly Context," in *Arts in Society,* University of Wisconsin, Vol. 9, No. 2, Summer-Fall 1972.

CHAPTER 16

[1]F. M. Keesing, in *Men and Cultures,* Selected papers of the 5th International Congress of Anthropological and Ethnological Sciences, 1956, University of Pennsylvania Press, p. 130.

[2]Melville Herskovits, *Man and His Works,* Knopf, New York, 1956, p. 269.

[3]J. P. Priestly, op. cit., p. 138.

[4]Henri Q. Junod, *The Life of a South African Tribe,* London, 1927, Vol. pp. 71–94.

[5]H. A. Stayt, *The Bavenda,* London, 1931, p. 101 ff.

[6]R. S. Rattray, *Ashanti,* London, 1923 and *Ashanti Laws Constitution,* Oxford, 1929.

[7]Jack Lindsay, *A Short History of Culture,* Fawcett Premier Book, 1962, p. 127; G. P. Kurath, "Dance-Folk and Primitive," in *Standard Dictionary of Folklore, Mythology and Legend,* Funk and Wagnalls, New York, Vol. 1, pp. 276–296.

[8]Harry L. Shapiro, *New York Times,* Cf articles on masks in *Standard Dictionary of Folklore, Mythology and Legend,* Funk and Wagnalls, New York, Vol. 2, pp. 684–687; Franz Boas, *Primitive Art,* Dover Publications, New York, 1955, p. 9.

[9]E. R. Lean, "Primitive Time-reckoning", in *A History of Technology,* C. Singer, E. J. Holmyard, and A. R. Hall, editors, Oxford University Press, New York and London, 1954, pp. 116–117.

[10]Ferdinand Lundberg, *The Rich and the Super-Rich,* Bantam Books, Canada, 1968, p. 25.

[11]Charles T. Wood, *The Age of Chivalry,* Universe Books, New York, 1970, p. 35.

[12]U. T. Holmes, *Daily Living in the Twelfth Century,* University of Wisconsin Press, 1964.

[13]Morris Bishop, *The Middle Ages,* American Heritage Press, New York, p. 246.

[14]Charles Wood, op cit., p. 44.

CHAPTER 17

[1]Peter F. Drucker, "The New Society: The Anatomy of the Industrial Order," in *An Introduction to Social Science,* Calhoun, Naftalin, et al., editors, J. B. Lippincott, New York, 1957, book two, p. 29.

[2]J. K. Wright, *The Geographical Expansion of European History,* Holt, New York, 1928; J. H. Robinson and C. A. Beard, *The Development of Modern Europe,* 2 vols., Boston.

[3]For more details on these and other educational policies related to the industrial revolution, see pp. 788–793, *Europe's Needs and Resources,* J. F. Dewhurst and associates, editors, Twentieth Century Fund, New York, 1961.

[4]Source, Department of Commerce (Alaska and Hawaii beginning in 1960); data abstracted from *1974 World Almanac,* p. 85.

[5]*America's Needs and Resources,* op. cit., p. 104.

[6]John D. Owen, *Price of Leisure: an Economic Analysis of the Demand for Leisure Time,* McGill-Queens University Press, 1970, p. 86.

CHAPTER 18

[1]Presented in a special lecture to the Department of Recreation and Parks, Texas A & M University, 1967, reprinted here with the kind permission of Professor Burch.

432

[2]Following the dropping of the Hiroshima bomb, I attended a secret meeting called by government offices with selected clergy and educators. The former argued this point; the rest of us noted the momentum of creative ideas, and that fundamental science had unforseen applications.

[3]*Technology, Human Values and Leisure*, M. Kaplan and P. Bosserman, editors, Abingdon Press, 1971, pp. 117–118. For a good summary of this subject as of several years ago, see Norman Kaplan, *Sociology of Science*, pp. 852–881, sp. pp. 871–875 in *Handbook of Modern Sociology*, Robert E. L. Faris, editor, Rand McNally, Chicago, 1964.

[4]Georges Friedmann, "Techological Changes and Human Relations," *British Journal of Sociology*, 1952, reprinted in *The Substance of Sociology*, Ephrian H. Mizrachi, editor, Appleton-Century-Crofts, New York, 1967, pp. 460.

[5]From *A Statistical Handbook of the North Atlantic Area*, Bernard Mueller, Twentieth Century Fund, New York, Table IV-12, p. 103. Countries within Western Europe included for this purpose were Austria, Belgium, Denmark, Finland, France, Germany, F.P., Greece, Iceland, Ireland, Italy, Luxembourg, Netherlands, Norway, Portugal, Spain, Sweden, Switzerland, and the United Kingdom.

[6]From ibid. IV-12, p. 103.

[7]From Table 1–2; and OEEC, Statistics of National Products and Expenditure, No. 2, Paris, 1957 and General Statistics, Paris, July 1959. Taken from *Europe's Needs and Resources*, J. F. Dewhurst et al., Twentieth Century Fund, New York, 1961, p. 4.

[8]From *American Almanac*, 1972, *U. S. Book of Statistics and Information*, Table 788.

[9]Patrick Hazard, *Arts in Society*, University of Wisconsin, Vol. III, No. 3, p. 312.

[10]P. Sorokin, "Social and Cultural Dynamics," selection in *The Making of Society*, Robert Bierstedt, editor, The Modern Library, New York, pp. 474–475; Arnold J. Toynbee, *A Study of History*, Abridgment of volumes I–IV, by D. C. Somervell, Oxford University Press, 1947, New York, p. 259.

[11]*Harpers*, No. 1177, June 1948.

[12]Iris Origo, "The Pursuit of Happiness in a Villa," *Horizons*, Spring 1969, & 1, 2, p. 15.

CHAPTER 19

[1]Thomas More, *Utopia*, Van Nostrand, New York, 1947, p. 118.

[2]Edward Bellamy, *Looking Backward 2000–1887*, Houghton Mifflin, Boston, 1931, p. 63.

[3]Ibid., p. 63.

[4]Ibid., p. 196–197.

[5]A. Huxley, *Brave New World*, Garden City, New York, 1932, p. 86.

[6]H. G. Wells, *The Shape of Things to Come*, Hutchinson & Co., London, 1933, p. 404.

[7]Ibid., p. 410.

[8]Herman Kahn and Anthony J. Wiener, *The Year 2000: A Framework for Speculation in the Next Thirty-three Years,* MacMillan, New York; Within the enlarging literature of "futurology," there are to be found frequent references to leisure: for example, *Some Prospects for Social Change by 1985 and Their Impact on Time/Money Budgets,* S. Enzer, D. Little, F. D. Lazar, Institute for the Future, Middletown, Conn., 1972; For an introduction to the work in this development, see issues of *The Futurist,* Washington, D.C. For a summary of organizations throughout the world engaged in future research, see Irades, Istituto Ricerche Applicate Documentazioni e Studi, *Social Forecasting: Documentation, 1971,* Ideas, Men, Activities.

[9]*Daedalus,* Summer 1967, Journal of the American Academy of Arts and Sciences, 280 Newton St., Brookline, Mass.

[10]Edward T. Hall, Jr. "A Microculture Analysis of Time," in *Men and Cultures,* A.F.C. Wallace, editor, University of Pennsylvania Press, 1956, p. 119.

[11]Herman Miller, *Rich Man, Poor Man,* Signet Book, New York 1964.

[12]*American Foundation for Management Research;* all businessmen should read Peter Drucker, *The Age of Discontinuity,* Harper and Row, 1970; also, *The Environment of Change,* Aaron W. Warner, editor, Columbia University, Dean Morse and T. E. Cooney, 1970.

[13]Daniel Bell, "The Study of the Future," *The Public Interest,* No. 1, Fall 1965; also, cf. The Futurists, *Time,* February 25, 1966, no author given.

[14]*The Behavioral and Social Sciences' Outlook and Needs,* National Academy of Sciences and Social Science Research Council, Washington.

[15]*Facilities for Culture Democracy,* Council of Europe, Rotterdam Symposium, October 5–9 1970, p. 28.

[16]See "Protectionists vs. Recreationists; The Battle of Mineral King," *New York Times* Magazine Section, August 17, 1969.

[17]Senator Henry Jackson, *Congressional Record,* October 8, 1969, S 2125.

[18]Indiana University. The full report appears in the *Congressional Record,* October 8, 1969. S 12127-S 12132. Its appendices provide a highly valuable documentation of technical reports, conferences, and symposiums, journals, relevant legislation; and all the pertinent federal agencies. It is followed on pages S 12136 to S 12140 by the Congressional White Paper on a National Policy for the Environment. Its Parts 1 deals with "aspects of environmental management," Part II with "alternatives for Congressional action." This is followed by the full National Environment Policy Act of 1969 as passed by the Senate, with differences between S 1075 and the House Resolution 12549; these differences, as of October 1969, had not yet been worked out in conference.

[19]*Congressional Record,* op cit. S 12129.

[20]Op cit., S 12130.

[21]Robert Dorfman, editor, *Measuring Benefits of Government Investments,* The Brookings Institution, Washington, D.C., papers presented on November 7–9 1963. Other areas discussed were government research and development, high school drop-outs, civil aviation, urban highways, urban renewal and syphilis control.

[22]Ibid., p. VII.

[23]Ibid., p. 72.

[24]Ibid., p. 76.

[25]Ibid., p. 77.

[26]Ibid., p. 88.

[27]Ibid., p. 89.

[28]Ibid., pp. 90–93.

[29]Ibid., p. 104.

[30]Cf. M. Kaplan review of Baumol and Bowen's *The Performing Arts: an Economic Dilemma* in *College Music Symposium,* Rutgers University, Vol. 7, Fall 1967, pp. 135–140.

[31]Op. cit., p. 102.

[32]Ibid., p. 106.

[33]J. Galbraith, *New York Times* Magazine Section, November 16, 1969.

[34]See Arthur Schlesinger in *Technology, Human Values and Leisure,* op cit., pp. 68–91.

[35]See H. Douglas Sessoms, Leisure Society Value Systems, in *Concepts of Leisure: Philosophical Implications,* James F. Murphy editor, Prentice-Hall, Englewood Cliffs, N.J., 1974, p. 22.

[36]See *Congressional Record,* November 19, 1969, H 11134.

[37]See the full conference proceedings, *International Meeting for the Production of Documentaries and TV Films on Leisure,* Convegno Internazionale per la Produzione di Documentari E Telefilm sull Impiego del Tempo Libero, Italian Society of Authors and Editors, Rome, 1973. (Available from University of South Florida Bookstore, Tampa, Florida, 33620); M. Kaplan, International Program for Films on Leisure, *Lo Spettacolo,* Anno 23, n. 3, July–September 1973.

[38]European Cultural Foundation, 5 Jan Van Goeyenkade, Amsterdam The Netherlands, *Europe 2000: Education,* September 1971.

[39]For an earlier approach by representatives of the recreation profession on these matters, see Charles K. Brightbill, *Man and Leisure,* Prentice-Hall, Englewood Cliffs, N.J., 1961; H. D. Corbin and W. J. Tait, *Education for Leisure,* Prentice-Hall, Englewood Cliffs, N.J., 1972; For a more universal and excellent contemporary discussion see Nels Anderson, *Man's Work and Leisure,* F. J. Brill, Leiden, 1974, especially his last three chapters. Finally, for a brilliant exposition of all these matters—indeed, of the major issues of the present volume, the reader is referred to *The Leisure Riots* subtitled A Comic Novel, by Eric Koch (Tundra Books, Plattsburgh, N.Y., 1973). The book depicts what happens in 1980 when a bored segment of the population, living on $40,000 pensions, begins to sabotage various symbols of leisure, and the President creates a research group to develop solutions. Koch is an official of the Canadian National Radio Broadcasting Corporation.

Author Index

Subject Index